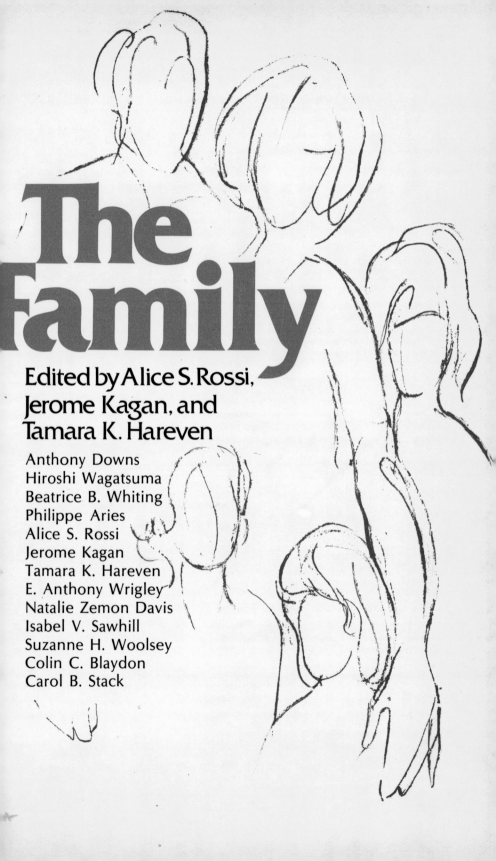

The Family

Edited by Alice S. Rossi,
Jerome Kagan, and
Tamara K. Hareven

Anthony Downs
Hiroshi Wagatsuma
Beatrice B. Whiting
Philippe Aries
Alice S. Rossi
Jerome Kagan
Tamara K. Hareven
E. Anthony Wrigley
Natalie Zemon Davis
Isabel V. Sawhill
Suzanne H. Woolsey
Colin C. Blaydon
Carol B. Stack

The Family

Essays by

Alice S. Rossi

Jerome Kagan

Tamara K. Hareven

E. Anthony Wrigley

Natalie Zemon Davis

Isabel V. Sawhill

Suzanne H. Woolsey

Colin C. Blaydon

Carol B. Stack

Anthony Downs

Hiroshi Wagatsuma

Beatrice B. Whiting

Philippe Aries

T.M

The Family

Edited by ALICE S. ROSSI
JEROME KAGAN
TAMARA K. HAREVEN

W · W · NORTON & COMPANY · INC · *New York*

Copyright © 1978, 1977 by the American Academy of Arts and Sciences
Published simultaneously in Canada by George J. McLeod Limited,
Toronto. Printed in the United States of America.

First Edition

Library of Congress Cataloging in Publication Data
Main entry under title:
The Family.
  Bibliography: p.
  Includes index.
  1. Family—Addresses, essays, lectures.   I. Rossi, Alice S., 1922–
II. Kagan, Jerome.   III. Hareven, Tamara K.
HQ728.F29   1978   301.42   77–16798
ISBN 0–393–01167–4
ISBN 0–393–09064–7 pbk.

1 2 3 4 5 6 7 8 9 0

Contents

Preface to the Issue, "The Family"

ON BOTH SIDES OF THE ATLANTIC, in the United States and Europe, the family is today the subject of almost unremitting scrutiny, giving credence to the belief that an institution so persistently watched over must indeed be in jeopardy. While reports of imminent disaster—indeed, the possibility of the final demise of the family—circulate widely, books are written to show how exaggerated are all such claims, and how tailored they are to the needs of the news media, searching always for the sensational and the novel. So long as the explosion of interest in the family is seen principally as the expression of concern for an "endangered" institution, there is no possibility of correctly interpreting the events of recent decades, nor of estimating how major developments have affected perceptions, mores, and beliefs, not only as they have touched the family but also as they have affected other institutions related to it.

There are at least two major errors, commonly believed, that this volume is intended to refute: first, that the family is a weak organism, constantly under attack, largely inert, and incapable of warding off great and powerful bullies, whether they appear as world-shaking events, such as, for example, the industrial revolution, or as more parochial forces, such as the expansion of the power and authority of the federal government in the United States; second, that objectivity about the family is easily achieved, that those who recommend changes are interested only in the general welfare, that their facts are incontrovertible, and that their passions are under close and deliberate control—in short, that they are "objective" scholars or public servants, without political or other partisan interests. These are serious mistakes; they ought not to be indulged in. Nor, for that matter, ought we to proceed in the naive belief that we know all (or much) of what we need to know about the family—that the time for theorizing is over—and that only action, to alleviate admitted injustice, will now suffice. This volume, while explicit in many of its recommendations for change, starts with the premise that serious and substantial inquiry into the family is of relatively recent origin, that it now involves numerous academic disciplines and professions, and that we are only now beginning to profit from certain of the research that is going on.

The demythologizing process is only in its earliest stages. We still accept a largely fictitious view of family organization in the past, recalling a stability and order that never existed, but that is intended to put into bold relief the massive untidiness of contemporary family life. Many treat the modern family as a fragile and delicate object—the "Victorian lady" of yesterday—buffeted on every side and scarcely able to cope with the threats to its authority. We refuse to see why the family is at the very center of many of our contemporary political debates, and why it is impossible to talk about equality (or liberty) without talking also about the family, or why "family policy," even in its patchwork American forms, has larger social purposes, related to the education, health, and welfare of all citizens. Despite the pretense of uniformity in family life throughout the industrial world, the differences are in fact conspicuous, not only between individual nations, but also between various classes and regions. Uniformities exist, obviously, but not always of the kind that are looked for.

The new expanded interest in the family is generating new data of every sort; it is also stimulating the development of hypotheses about society never previously entertained. This is a good time to be studying the family.

Alice Rossi, in presenting a biosocial perspective on parenting, realizes that she is taking issue, explicitly and implicitly, with many who argue for sex equality, and who will be uncomfortable with much of what she says about the unique role of the mother. In 1964, in *Daedalus*, she wrote a highly controversial paper on "Equality Between the Sexes," which she subtitled "An Immodest Proposal." Her article here must be seen as "an immodest interpretation," intended to generate debate. She expects this to happen; indeed, she welcomes it. As she says:

> This paper brings up many important questions for future investigation, debate, and policy formation. It may also rankle those who hold ideological positions concerning sex equality that accept the present structure of work in industrial societies and urge an identical, equal participation of women and men in the workplace, in home maintenance, and in child-rearing that is modeled on the male pattern of great emphasis on work and little emphasis on family and home. It may be more acceptable to those who question the desirability of a work-dominated life and to those who see both strength and meaning in the family support, community-building, and institutional innovation in which women have been so long engaged. There will be those who see in this analysis a conservative justification for the status quo, for traditional family and work roles for men and women, but that is a risk one takes to reach those who will see a more radical vision in the analysis: a society more attuned to the natural environment, in touch with, and respectful of, the rhythm of our own body processes, that asks how we can have a balanced life with commitment both to achievement in work and intimate involvement with other human beings. In my judgment, by far the wiser course to such a future is to plan and build from the most fundamental root of society in human parenting, and not from the shaky superstructure created by men in that fraction of time in which industrial societies have existed.

If Alice Rossi's paper treats the family from the perspective of the parent, particularly the mother, Jerome Kagan is interested in exploring the institution from the perspective of the child. He sees how early in school the American child comes to appreciate the values prized by society, and how quickly this translates into a judgment on parents and on self. Kagan explores the relations between the child and the mother, trying to explain what is indeed "special" in this relationship. The family, as both a source of protection and a target of attachment, serves also as a principal means of communicating information. The child's sense of virtue (or value), including his own value, is substantially influenced by what he experiences in the family. Because it is generally assumed that the lack of parental affection in childhood will predispose a child to future psychic illness, Kagan asks whether that proposition is valid. The complexities of that issue are fully explored. So, also, are the influences of social class, which Kagan shows to be extremely important. As he explains: "The lower-class child during the years prior to adolescence gradually comes to realize that he possesses little of what the culture values. That insight, which is a component of his class identification, carries with it a sense of impotence. . . . Not surprisingly, there is a readiness to hide or deny that impotence. The desire to conceal the psychological weakness he imputes to lower-class membership leads to readiness to take risks, an easier disposition for aggression, and a tendency to assign responsibility for failure to external events." Kagan pays attention also to the significance of ordinal position in the family, reflecting particularly on the problem of the first born. In his conclusion, he considers the plight of the modern Western family. His studies of families in other cultures have suggested that the "identity" problems so characteristic of our own society are by no means universal.

If both Rossi and Kagan have emphasized the importance of the family for children, Tamara Hareven's contribution is to lay to rest the canard that the family "broke down" under the impact of urbanization and industrialization. On the contrary, the resilience of the institution was so great, Professor Hareven says, that it actually ended up by contributing to both processes. Families, she writes, acted as "agents of change, socializing and preparing their members for new ways of life, facilitating their adaptation to industrial work and to living in large complex urban communities." Also, families did not simply abandon all their traditional traits as they adjusted to industrial demands; ethnic and cultural differences survived. Hareven's chief concern is to explain the significance of the concept of "family time," which governs the major decisions taken within the family. Granted that the nuclear family has not changed greatly in the last two centuries, she wants to show how the timing of important family events—home-leaving, marriage, childbearing, etc.—have changed, and how all this relates to larger events in the society. "Family time" will differ between various ethnic groups; it will also show changes in different historical periods. The idea that families knew greater stability, indeed, greater conformity, in the past is precisely the opposite of the truth, Hareven says. Because of increased longevity, there may be more three-generational families extant today than there ever were in the past. A whole notion of family disintegration in today's world is implicitly denied by Hareven's evidence. Compulsory school attendance, child-labor laws, mandatory retirement have imposed certain rigid patterns of timing in the society, and these, in turn, have created greater uniformity in family behavior. Also, there is increased isolation of individuals in contemporary society. The yearning for privacy—the adoption by all classes of middle-class standards—has tended to exclude strangers and kin from the household. The nuclear family, with its role segregation along age and sex lines, is different from what existed in America a century or longer ago. This, however, ought not to induce nostalgia for that earlier order, elements of which are largely mythical. "The family," Hareven writes, "has never been a utopian retreat from the world, except in the imagination of social reformers and social scientists. Some of the major problems besetting family life today emanate from the heavy demands placed upon it by individuals in society who require that it be a haven of nurture and a retreat from the outside world. The modern family's growing discomfort suggests the need for expansion and diversity in what we expect from it and in its adaptation to new social conditions with diverse timing schedules and a multiplicity of roles for its members, rather than for seeking refuge in a non-existent past."

In his "Reflections on the History of the Family," E. Anthony Wrigley is concerned with what the researches of the last fifteen years have taught us about the west European family, particularly in the pre-industrial and early industrial periods. That the family in pre-industrial Europe "discharged a far wider range of functions" than it does today is as significant as the fact that in the earlier period a substantial number of young men and women spent some years in service or apprenticeship with families other than their own. Recent findings, Wrigley explains, suggest that the west European pattern, even before industrialization, was not at all like that of other traditional societies. With late marriage among women, and many women of childbearing age remaining unmarried, a separate household at marriage, and small houses comprising only a single conjugal couple being common, Wrigley asks whether this unique complex of marriage and co-residential patterns may not have helped produce the changes generally associated with the industrial revolution. For him, the Poor Law legislation of Elizabethan England may have had a greater impact on the "decline in the relative importance of personal and family ties outside the conjugal family" than anything that happened 200 years later. The "modern" family, Wrigley implies, was in place before the industrial revolution, and may, indeed, have helped make that revolution possible.

In looking at family life in France in the sixteenth and seventeenth centuries, Natalie Zemon Davis emphasizes the overwhelming concern with making certain that the family's future would be secure, well beyond the lives of all who were then living. As Davis explains, "What is being planned for here is not merely lands, cattle, houses, barns, pensions, rents, offices, workshops, looms, masterships, partnerships, and shares, but also the occupations or careers and the marriages of children. These, too, must be designed so as to maintain, and perhaps increase, the family's store and reputation." Except for the rural and urban poor, such family planning in early modern France was commonplace. It had immense consequences, Davis explains, for the ways in which that society perceived the relations between the living and the dead; it also made the family a "privileged" institution, with its very special identity, gratifications, and rewards; it established a hierarchy within the family, with sovereignty clearly residing in the father. The consequences for the society were enormous. Such family planning influenced attitudes toward time, toward kin, toward youth, toward marriage. In the eighteenth century, family planning extended itself, despite strong clerical condemnation, into the area of contraception. Davis writes: "The extension of family planning into contraception . . . is another example of men and women in small groups deciding how they are going to conduct themselves." There had always been tension between "privatistic family values" and the more corporate values embodied in Church teaching, and Davis chooses to see this tension as possibly "creative," indicating "how and why religion or any cultural system can sometimes carry along contradictory values and keep little-used options open for centuries."

If recent historical investigations into the family have opened up wholly new vistas, providing new data, and generating new hypotheses on population, the position of women, the institution of service, illegitimacy, orphanage, childhood, adolescence, the elderly—all mentioned by Wrigley—and if it has given us a better sense of ghosts, kin, and progeny—as explained by Davis—its larger purpose has been to transform our concept of social history, making that a very different discipline from what it was a mere two or three decades ago. The implications of this "new" social history for intellectual history, political history, and economic history are only beginning to be realized now.

History, however, has not been the only discipline transformed by a new interest in the family. As Isabel V. Sawhill explains, there is now a "new home economics," and it has nothing to do, as she explains, with the making of bread or even the "raising of dough." The new discipline is concerned with marriage and fertility and the decisions taken about how goods and time may be most efficiently used in the household and the family. Again, the discipline has a very recent birth date; its origins go back only to the early 1960s, and owe much to the development of human capital theory and the theory of the allocation of time. Because the rearing of children involves an investment in human capital, and because it depends on the availability of a scarce commodity, parental time, the economist feels no reluctance in appropriating this area to others that he has already taken. The cost-benefit analysis that the economist has used in market transactions may be used also for non-market phenomena; decisions about marriage, childbearing, and labor-force participation (particularly by wives) have economic implications that merit study. Sawhill discusses some of the principal findings of this new discipline, suggesting how important is the new preoccupation with the concept of time. If T. W. Schultz is correct that the ultimate scarcity in the future will not be resources but human time, there is reason also to accept his conclusion that human fertility in the future must fall and standards of living improve. Sawhill, however, is not entirely persuaded by his argument. She says: "The process will come to a halt when there is no time left to consume the products of an affluent society and thus no reason to seek further increases in per-capita income. There will, in short, be a sufficiency of goods, given the time people will have to enjoy them. It is an interesting, if not entirely credible, view." As for her own views, she writes: "In the past, marriage was too often an economic necessity for women, and childbearing either the unintended outcome of sex or an insurance policy against the insecurities of old age. In the future, economics and technology are likely to ensure that the act of having a child and the decision to share life with another adult are more freely and consciously chosen for the personal satisfactions they entail rather than as a means to some other end. Personal values and psychological needs met by marriage, children, and family life will be the final arbiters of choice."

In family studies, the line between theory and practice—between the theoretical and the applied—is not nearly so fixed as it is in certain other areas. If "home economics" is theoretical, it also has immediate implications for practice; the same may be said for much of the work that is proceeding in disciplines as various as psychology, history, anthropology, and sociology. The federal government's support of research in many of these areas suggests an expectation of research results that may be quickly put to use. Because the federal government has no "family policy"—there is no single department committed specifically to the elaboration of such, though H.E.W. is perhaps more involved than any other—and because other agencies of government, state and local, are also involved, it is difficult to do for the United States what it is possible to do in other countries, consider "family policy" as a whole. In the United States, the problem has to be divided. We have chosen to dwell on three separate issues: day care, income maintenance, and housing. Each is suffused with deep feeling; the illusion that the facts can be made to speak for themselves needs to be quickly dispelled.

Suzanne H. Woolsey opens her article on day care with the statement: "Public discussion of federal policy toward day care for children has been carried on at high volume for at least a decade with remarkably little progress in either defining the issues or analyzing the evidence." One of the few points of agreement among supporters of day care, an unusually diverse coalition which includes, among others, " 'workfare' conservatives, unemployed teachers, the women's movement, professionals in child development and social welfare, and entrepreneurs looking for a new growth industry," Woolsey says, is their belief that "expanded federal support for day care outside the family is a *Good Thing.*" Proponents of day care argue as if their scheme will provide new jobs for women, that the day-care centers themselves will employ welfare recipients, thereby getting them off the welfare roles, and that the centers themselves, if they are good, will enhance children's development. The available data do not clearly support the notion that such broad social goals can in fact be achieved through day care. Indeed, if parental preferences are consulted, it is clear that the idea of a single federally financed system of day-care centers does not command great support. Most parents, Woolsey argues, prefer forms of care that involve family members, with parents staggering their working hours, or other relatives serving for occasional or regular full-time care. Because the argument can be made that national policy ought not to rest on parental desires only, but ought to advance larger social objectives, Woolsey stops to consider the evidence that exists that might support the claims frequently made. She is unable to see how federally funded day care will increase the labor-force participation of women; nor does she see it as a long-range solution for AFDC mothers. As for the idea that day-care centers will help in the development of children, there is no evidence to suggest that one form of care is markedly superior to another. The poor and the lower middle class generally have access to members of their own family for child care; they prefer that solution; these preferences ought not to be ignored. As Woolsey says:

> The data seem to show that there is far more interest in informal care in the home or the extended family than anyone would gather from the public debate. Federal policies to help make this sort of care more affordable are lost in the cacophony of contesting arguments over one method of care—formal centers—and one way of funding it—federal support to those centers. What we need is closer concentration on what people need and want to help them cope with their child-care problems. Instead, policy makers are importuned by ideological and interest group pied pipers, promising to rid us of various forms of pestilence: oppression of women, a thoroughly unworkable welfare system, emotional disturbance, and school failure.

Colin C. Blaydon and Carol B. Stack, in considering how welfare legislation has affected the family, show sympathy for the views of Sar Levitan and Robert Taggart, who suggest that the conventional arguments used to explain "family deterioration," linking it to welfare schemes, are in fact greatly exaggerated. If the effects have not been deleterious in the ways suggested—and if there have been cooperative and collective efforts, particularly by blacks in urban areas, to withstand the ravages of their environment—this does not change the fact that the welfare system treats many low-income families and individuals unfairly. Blaydon and Stack believe that the "modern welfare policy, as it was designed, misreads not only the nature of the American economy, but also the social structure of poor families." Their own proposals for reform are intended to take cognizance of both. Looking at the AFDC program, they see the country "supporting a major cash assistance program designed to preserve a family setting for children, but in fact offering encouragement to divorce, separation, and desertion." Since the AFDC benefit is reduced if the mother goes to work, there is no incentive for her to do so. As criticism has developed of this and other aspects of the welfare system, new proposals have been put forward. None, however, seeks to establish a general family policy. Blaydon and Stack see no possibility of such a system evolving until there is a better understanding of how poor families function. The self-help domestic networks, so common among poor blacks, have been largely ignored. So, also, have been the occasional payments made by absent fathers. The pursuit of low-income fathers to force them to reimburse the state for its payments has generally been counterproductive. Blaydon and Stack do not recommend that fathers should be freed of their obligation to support their children; they ask that it be done "in a uniform and equitable way, with incentives as well as requirements for compliance." The recipients of welfare need to be given greater freedom of choice; Blaydon and Stack write:

> Welfare recipients should have as much freedom to choose where and with whom they live as do other adults. Families should be able to choose how they will function. The tradition of sharing that the poor have developed should not be undermined. Future policy should rely more heavily on cash as opposed to in-kind benefits. Programs offer in-kind benefits (surplus commodities, food stamps, social services) at least in part because policy makers distrust the poor. They think that recipients squander cash, and they want to influence the behavior of the poor by limiting their freedom of choice. There is no evidence, however, that the poor are less thrifty than the rest of us, and they are entitled to the freedom the rest of us have, which would be provided by cash benefits.

If cash benefits offer the greatest hope, and Blaydon and Stack have no doubt that they do, these must be tied to a tax structure that does not penalize the family that stays together. Blaydon and Stack propose tax reforms calculated to keep the family from dissolving.

Anthony Downs, in considering how housing policies have influenced American family life, starts at the end of World War II and reflects on what he believes to be the two major successes of the period. Construction on a massive scale ended the wartime housing shortage, making available improved housing to a vast segment of the population, and, in the process, suburbanizing the majority of the metropolitan-area populations. That major social and economic problems persist in the largest and oldest of America's cities does not, according to Downs, justify the view, commonly held, that all urban social policies sponsored by the federal government have "failed." The improved conditions under which many now live should not be ignored because of a proper concern with deteriorated conditions that prevail for many others. Downs knows that the poor are not solely to blame for their plight; indeed, he shows how the urban development process, in benefiting the non-poor majority, has imposed heavy burdens on the less advantaged. These conditions, he says, will not be remedied by a single comprehensive "national urban strategy"; the phrase, however beguiling, ignores the fact that decision-making with regard to housing is decentralized and fragmented, and that it does not easily submit to central direction. Also, because it is influenced by so much else—transportation policy, national fiscal and monetary policy, local criminal-law systems, racial integration policy, levels of unemployment and real income—one cannot hope to control all the necessary elements. The idea of dealing with major social problems through carefully planned "social strategies" is not one that commends itself to Downs; instead, he argues for a policy that some will see as simply "muddling through." Downs, in reflecting on how conditions have improved in the last twenty-five years for middle-income and upper-income families while deteriorating for millions of low- and moderate-income families living in concentrated-poverty areas within large cities, sees the two developments as linked, resulting from the same urban development process. Government policy, whether involving provisions for FHA insurance and mortgage terms, highway construction, or tax incentives, has frequently operated to give advantages to the first group and to deny them to the second. Public housing projects have proved to be catastrophic. Welfare policy, urban renewal, and highway construction have all contributed to the deterioration of vast parts of the city, and to the flight of those able to get away. Neighborhood school policies, which linked schools to the population of the areas immediately surrounding them, led to further concentration of minority-group households in vast sections of the city abandoned by those who did not wish to live beside them. Downs offers specific remedies for coping with these deteriorating conditions, but space precludes his doing more than giving them in very broad outline.

If the historical essays in the volume provide a certain perspective on how families have fared in conditions other than those that obtain today in the West, the articles by Hiroshi Wagatsuma on the contemporary Japanese family and by Beatrice B. Whiting on family life in Kenya provide yet another set of reflections on how industrialization and urbanization are affecting traditional values and norms. Wagatsuma describes a pre-World War II Japanese family lifestyle reminiscent in many ways of what Natalie Davis described for early modern France, though Confucian belief necessarily emphasized certain qualities less common in the Christian West. Among the many changes since the Second World War, Wagatsuma writes, none is more important than the loss of respect for the father and the gradual atrophying of his superior role within the family. While this change is generally attributed to "changes in values, the increased number of nuclear families, crowded housing conditions, the influence of the media as a source of information, and the father's relatively weakened financial position," Wagatsuma emphasizes also the change produced by a new constitution, by which the household ceased to be a legal entity, with all its rights and duties being taken from it. Using data from many sources, Wagatsuma shows how the role models have changed, but he asks whether these changes have not been exaggerated. The prewar father may never have been as "strong" or as "authoritarian" as he has generally been made to appear. Because the prewar data are so scanty it is difficult to know what conditions prevailed then. Wagatsuma writes: "Social norms certainly expected fathers (and not only househeads) to be responsible disciplinarians with unquestioned authority." He goes on to say: "Research seems to suggest that these norms were, and to some degree at least still are, being observed by older people, especially in rural areas." While many insist on the reality of "fatherlessness" in contemporary Japanese society, Wagatsuma is not absolutely persuaded that the situation is always accurately represented. Without denying the change that has taken place, from a Confucian role model to one patently more democratic and egalitarian, Wagatsuma asks whether the cultural norms have not changed more than the psychological preferences. "In their personalities," Wagatsuma says of Japanese fathers, "I am inclined to see more continuity than change." In any case, the unanswered questions have to do largely with how the behavior of Japanese father is affecting the socialization of his children. We have almost no information on that subject.

Beatrice B. Whiting, in writing about Kenya, suggests that "it is difficult to be anything but an economic determinist when reviewing the changes that have occurred and are in progress in Kenyan family life." She goes on to say: "The new cash economy is associated with the demarcation of traditional lineage lands into individually owned farms. It is associated with a demand for a Western type of education which is valued as a key to economic success. Changes in the division of labor have been dramatic as the child-labor force disappears into schools and men leave the farms for wage-earning jobs." The occupation of the husband, she says, is all-important in determining the character of family life. So, also, are the effects of the introduction of schooling. School expenses and a shrinking acreage are among the chief deterrents to polygyny, a marriage system that is rapidly disintegrating. Monogamous marriage has created a wholly new class of women in the country, many of whom appear to be "driving themselves beyond belief." Traditional values—generosity, good-heartedness, respectfulness, obedience, and responsibility—appear to be giving way, or at least making room for, two new values, cleverness and curiosity, thought to be essential for success. The nuclear family, if it is becoming increasingly common, does not necessarily mean the giving up of extended-family and lineage connections. Some maintain two households, one in the extended family compound, the other in Nairobi. Within the city, life is frequently difficult. Housing is scarce and expensive. Most women living permanently in the city are required to work long hours. There is no institutional care for children, and the few preschools that exist are expensive. Whiting asks whether Kenyan family life will be able to maintain its sociable tradition in these new circumstances, or whether it will become increasingly preoccupied with success and personal achievement. Her own preferences are clear; she writes: "It is hoped that they can enter the international industrial world without severing their ties with kin and neighborhood and adopt a pace of life that does not preclude traditional African sociability."

If there is a "crisis of the family," and Philippe Ariès is disinclined to believe that there is, he insists that the family's problems have been greatly magnified by the "decline" of the city and the urban forms of social intercourse that the city once provided. The family, he explains, compelled to assume the task of satisfying all the social and emotional needs of its members, is necessarily burdened. It is not surprising that the family has found such an assignment to be a difficult one. After the eighteenth century, Ariès writes, the state became increasingly intrusive, seeking to extend its sphere of control and influence. Also, as work became more specialized, the place of work was separated from the home; workers came to be supervised. Finally, an important "emotional revolution" took place; in an earlier age, many objects, natural and supernatural, received both love and attention; in the new age, these feelings focused almost entirely on the immediate family. Ariès says: "The couple and their children became the objects of a passionate and exclusive love that transcended even death." The family, he argues, became *the* private domain, almost the only safe refuge from an inquisitive society. In the nineteenth century, before the advent of the automobile, the family was a private reserve, from which males might periodically escape into the refuge provided by the city. Women and children were not equally fortunate; for them, the family and the school were everything. No other important outlet existed for them. The urban civilization, centered in the cafe and restaurant, gave men a public meeting place where they might eat, drink, and talk. A new type of social intercourse developed in the cities, largely free of society's control. In the twentieth century, this urban civilization began to break down. The automobile and television helped make possible a surburban life filled with pleasure and amenities. But the disintegration of the "social" city preceded even these inventions. Middle-class men, wishing to escape from the bustle of the city, pined for the privacy of the family in more natural, even rural settings. For a while, a precarious balance existed between the city and home. By the middle of the twentieth century, however, the family and home had clearly emerged victorious. Inevitably, the family was asked to do more, to provide what once had been given by other institutions. In many instances, the demands exceeded the capacities of the family. Ariès refuses to speak of a "crisis" in the family, but he knows that the family is incapable of fulfilling many of the functions asked of it. In his view, the "real roots of the domestic crisis lie not in our families, but in our cities."

This volume suggests what happens when a subject becomes a matter of lively curiosity and controversy for scholars in a wide variety of disciplines. The subject is made only more important when it also engages the interest of many concerned with the making of public policy. Studies of the family have never been more illuminating than they are at this moment; there has never been a more imaginative use of new documents and data; there has rarely been a more systematic questioning of established opinions. The field is flourishing as it never has before. Would that one could say the same for the study of other institutions, scarcely less important!

Thanks are due to the Andrew W. Mellon Foundation for providing funds that made this book possible. A particular debt is owed to the former president of the foundation, Dr. Nathan M. Pusey, who understood why this was a propitious time to undertake such an inquiry.

Stephen R. Graubard

The Family

ALICE S. ROSSI

A Biosocial Perspective on Parenting

Introduction

A REMARKABLE SHIFT HAS OCCURRED during the past decade in society's opinion of the family, from a general endorsement of it as a worthwhile and stable institution to a general censure of it as an oppressive and bankrupt one whose demise is both imminent and welcome. What was defined a decade ago as "deviant" is today labeled "variant," in order to suggest that there is a healthy, experimental quality to current social explorations into the future "beyond monogamy," or "beyond the nuclear family." Not so long ago many sociologists were claiming that the nuclear family was neither as fragile nor as isolated as had been claimed, but was in fact embedded in a viable, if modified, extended kin network.[1] Today, one is more apt to read that the nuclear family will oppress its members unless couples swap spouses and swing, and young adults are urged to rear their children communally, or to reject marriage and parenthood altogether.

Age and sex are fundamental building blocks of any family system. In part, the contrasting views of the family sketched above simply reflect a shift in our emphasis from age to sex. When functional theory dominated family sociology, the key was age: the treatment of generational continuity and parent-child relationships received central attention, while the treatment of sex was based on the belief inherited from the nineteenth century that accepted as innate attributes and constant features of all family systems a particular division of labor between men and women. More recently, the emphasis in family analysis has been on sex, with a heavy reliance on an egalitarian ideology that denies any innate sex differences and assumes that a "unisex" socialization will produce men and women that are free of the traditional culturally induced sex differences. This egalitarian ethos urges several programmatic changes in family organization: a reduction of maternal investment in children to permit greater psychic investment in work outside the family, an increased investment by men in their fathering roles, and the supplementation of parental care by institutional care. Frequently associated with this emphasis on equal commitment to work and family for both men and women is a corollary emphasis on the autonomy and the "rights" of the child.

The variables of age and sex are similar in being ascriptive characteristics, but they differ in one respect that is crucial to the way social scientists deal with them. Age is a basic fact of life, progressing from year to year as we traverse the life course from birth to death. We know in our flesh the changes that maturation and aging entail. Hence there has been little resistance to incorporating physiological variables with social and psychological variables in the field of human development.

By contrast, sex is an invariant ascription from birth to death, and while we can try to imagine what it is like to be the opposite sex, we can not know what it is like with any certainty. That all manner of intentional and unintentional distortion in the understanding of sex differences can flow from this fact is being shown in new studies on the role of women both in our history and in other cultures. On the other hand, many of these studies are at least in part being used to advocate political, economic, and social change in the status of women and in the relations between the sexes. One of the characteristics an active egalitarian movement has in common with social-science thinking is an extreme emphasis on cultural determinism. The activists, after all, base their political efforts on the belief that adults have the ability to change their values and goals. The social scientist—burnt by an earlier history in which biological theories were misused to justify conservatism and racism and persuaded that to admit the relevance of any innate factor reduces the explanatory power and hence the prestige of social-science theories—has been equally strongly committed to cultural determinism. Activists who are also social scientists are under a double social pressure to argue from a strong cultural-determinist perspective. The result is a tendency in much contemporary thinking to confuse equality with identity and diversity with inequality. But where age and sex are concerned, diversity is a biological fact, while equality is a political, ethical, and social precept.[2] Marxist theory notwithstanding, there is no rule of nature or of social organization that says men and women have to be the same or do the same things in order to be socially, economically, and politically equal.

It is the position of this paper that the older sociological view of the family distorted, and that the new one neglects, the central biological fact that the core function of any family system is human continuity through reproduction and child-rearing. More specifically, the paper will argue that the particular version of egalitarianism underlying current sociological research on, and advocacy of, "variant" marriage and family forms is inadequate and misleading because it neglects some fundamental human characteristics rooted in our biological heritage. Unless these biosocial factors are confronted, allowed for, and, if desired, compensated for, the current press toward sexual equality in marriage and the workplace and shared child-rearing may show the same episodic history that so many social experiments have demonstrated in the past.

These are serious charges, and they are not lightly made. In fact, they were arrived at only after a long period of personal and intellectual concern that involved confronting my own previous analysis of sexual equality in the pages of *Daedalus* and finding it wanting.[3] But it is imperative to return periodically to the most basic facts of a family system and to one's own political ideology, and to examine both against the grain of our usual presuppositions. This paper will attempt such an examination with a biosocial perspective on the sexual and parenting scripts implicit in both the older and contemporary sociological theories about family structure and sex roles. The concept of a "sexual script" is a sociological one, pertaining to the social rules and norms governing the behavior of men and women in their sexual, mating relationship to each other, while the concept of a "parenting script" refers to the social rules and norms governing the birth and rearing of children. We wish to press beneath these social concepts and the social behavior to which they refer, in order to link them to innate physiological factors in the male and female and to the mammalian heritage we share with other primates.

The paper will first sketch an evolutionary framework within which contemporary family systems can be located, juxtapose this biosocial perspective with a brief historical sketch of past hostility in the social sciences toward biology, describe the changes during the past few decades in scientific theories in endocrinology which have opened up new possibilities for closer collaboration between the biological and social sciences, and, finally, review some of the recent sociological literature on variant marriage and family forms from the perspective of how mating is articulated with parenting. Throughout, our concern will be to explore what is known and what ought to be researched in order better to assess whether proposals that affect sex roles, parenting, and parent-child relations are consistent with, or at odds with, the biology of our species. To keep this agenda within a manageable scope, the emphasis will be limited to pregnancy, birth, and the offspring's pre-school years.

Bio-Evolutionary Framework

Sociologists frequently apply a comparative perspective to the American family by using the extensive available anthropological literature on kinship systems. In doing so, they are motivated by a desire to dispel the ethnocentric bias with which affectively charged areas of life tend to be viewed, and to communicate the diversity and ingenuity of human cultures. By contrast, historical perspective on the family has tended to be limited to Western civilization. It is instructive to broaden that historical framework to a larger evolutionary one, because it underlines both the brevity and the cultural uniqueness of Western history itself, and it pinpoints the growing discrepancy between the demands imposed on us by a complex technological society and the physiological equipment we have inherited from our long mammalian past.

We are part of a mammalian primate heritage that has existed for more than 65 million years. Homo sapiens evolved only 40,000 years ago from our immediate ancestors, the primitive hominids, which themselves evolved only two to three million years ago. Washburn estimates that over 90 per cent of human history was spent in hunting and gathering societies.[4] Against this background, the two hundred years in which industrial societies have existed is a short time indeed, to say nothing of the mere twenty years in which a few of the most advanced industrial societies have been undergoing the painful transition to a post-industrial societal stage. Our most recent genes derive from that longest segment of human history during which men and women lived in hunting and gathering societies; in other words, *Westernized human beings now living in a technological world are still genetically equipped only with an ancient mammalian primate heritage that evolved largely through adaptations appropriate to much earlier times.*[5]

During this very long early period of human history, adaptation and selection processes contributed to sexual dimorphism and a sexual division of labor. That division of labor did not mean that women were restricted to childbearing and -rearing and men to productive labor for food and group defense. We are indebted to recent anthropological research for dispelling that notion, since current research has revealed that women in hunting and gathering societies almost everywhere contributed through their productive labor half or more of the basic food staples consumed in their society.[6] What it did mean was that reproductive success went to those females capable of two conjoint activities: the bearing and rearing of their young and the hunting of small game and gathering of food within a restricted geographic range compatible with infant and child care. Both these activities involved manual dexterity, physical and emotional endurance, and persistence. The counterpart selective adaptations in males were the body stature, shoulder strength, and visual acuity required for skill in big-game hunting with spears and for group defense.[7]

The residues of these selective processes can be seen among contemporary men and women, for in general men are taller and have greater shoulder strength and more precise spatial perception than women, while women generally show greater manual dexterity and emotional stamina. This is not an invariant pattern; it can obviously be modified through concentrated training that compensates for sex differences. *A biosocial perspective does not argue that there is a genetic determination of what men can do compared to women; rather, it suggests that the biological contributions shape what is learned, and that there are differences in the ease with which the sexes can learn certain things.*[8] Clearly American men predominate in some specialties, such as neurosurgery, that involve very delicate manual dexterity. Were there no strong cultural pressures in our history against the entry of women into medicine, it might be that women would predominate in that field. Indeed, in any specialty that draws upon an extremely small number of people, there are apt to be a sufficient number of men and women with the necessary skills even if the skills are differentially distributed in the total population of men and women. In less highly specialized sectors of the occupational system requiring less intensive training, one would expect a greater degree of sex-linked distribution in the work force. Thus, women workers predominate in electronic-equipment firms and men in construction work and military combat; these draw on their respective advantages in manual dexterity and shoulder strength. Functional job differentiation by sex occurs even in national armies in which women serve along with men, such as those of Israel and the Soviet Union.

Women in all cultures are likely to care for the newborn and to prepare food for household consumption. Men can learn such skills, but as a group they are less apt to show ease in infant handling and food preparation than women are. We know from the Soviet experience in training women cosmonauts and the Israeli experience in training women soldiers that specialized training of women is necessary to compensate for the male advantage in large musculature. A similar compensatory training may become necessary if more men are to care for young infants. This is an important point to realize in an era when egalitarian ideology argues against innate sex differences and assumes that a unisex education will suffice to remove whatever sex differences currently exist.

It is unrealistic to expect that we will achieve within a few generations a 50-50 distribution by sex in most human activities and occupations. It is doubtful that a unisex socialization alone can have that effect; it will require compensatory training of girls in some areas, boys in others. Since evolutionary changes take place at an infinitely slow pace through long stretches of time, each generation of males and females would require compensatory training. For many generations to come, any slackening of institutional effort directed to compensatory training of the sexes will quickly be followed by a return to sex differentiation as a consequence of the ease with which certain skills are learned by one sex and not by the other.

An evolutionary perspective also suggests a criterion for predicting what aspects of human life are most apt to entail innate, unlearned components in behavior. The more critical the behavior is to species survival through reproduction, the more apt these innate features are to be present. Hence one would expect innate factors to play a particularly important role in the mother-infant relationship for two major reasons: First of all, the female is more closely involved in the reproductive process than the male. Biologically males have only one innate orientation, a sexual one that draws them to women, while women have two such orientations, a sexual one toward men and a reproductive one toward the young. By comparison to the female attachment to an infant, the male attachment is a socially learned role. Fathering is often non-existent among other primates, and, among humans, it is more learned from women or required by the norms of kinship systems than it is innately predisposed in the male himself.[9]

Second, there is even greater need for close bonding of the human infant to its mother than there is in other species. The timing of human birth is partly a function of the evolutionary shift to an upright, bipedal posture and increased cortical size without an accompanying increase in the pelvic capacity and birth-canal flexibility of the human female. The result is that the infant is far more immature at birth in the human than in other species. Like monkeys and apes, we are what Blurton-Jones calls a "carrying" and "continuous feeding" species rather than a "caching" species.[10] As a consequence, it is more critical to the survival of humans than to any other mammalian species to provide for prolonged infant care through intense attachment of the mother and the infant. Human societies vary in the size and composition of the social group within which the mother and infant are embedded, as they do in the degree to which other adults supplement maternal care, but no known society replaces the mother as the primary infant-tender except in cases of small and special categories of women.[11]

For most of human history, any mother-infant separation was precluded simply on the grounds of prolonged breastfeeding. Work by Konner, Draper, and Howell suggest that the relationship between mother and infant in hunter-gatherer societies is characterized by close physical contact and virtually continuous nursing and long-term lactation for up to four or five years.[12] Viewed against the long period of our bio-evolutionary framework, American society has undergone an extraordinary change in a very short time in the nursing of its young: a decline in breast-feeding from roughly 80 per cent of firstborn babies in the late nineteen-twenties to 25 per cent in the early nineteen-sixties.[13] For most of human history, infants had extremely close physical contact with their mothers, with an early high of 70 per cent of the day in infancy, tapering off to 30 per cent by the middle of the second year.[14] Today, infants have body contact with other human beings less than 25 per cent of the day during the weeks following birth, and even this soon rapidly falls off to 5 per cent.[15] We shall return at a later point to other implications for child-spacing and mother-child attachment of this trend away from breast-feeding.

Mother-infant interaction carries a cluster of characteristics that suggest the presence of unlearned responses. On a strictly physiological level, infant crying stimulates the secretion of oxytocin in the mother which triggers uterine contractions and nipple erection preparatory to nursing.[16] Without even being aware of it, the overwhelming majority of women cradle their infants in their left arm, regardless of their particular handedness, where the infant can hear and be soothed by the maternal heartbeat familiar from uterine life. Close-up films of women after childbirth show a common sequence of approaches when their nude babies are placed at their side. They touch its fingers and toes with their own fingertips, put the palm of their hand on the baby's trunk, then enclose the infant with their arms, all the while rotating their heads to an *en face* position to achieve full, parallel eye contact, with increasing tension in the mother until her baby's eyes are open and the eye contact is made.[17] Even mothers of premature infants peering into incubators at their babies engage in an awkward head rotation to achieve *en face* eye contact.

Observations of mothers talking to their babies also reveal a common set of behaviors: wide-open eyes, raised eyebrows, facial expressions held for a long period of time, and a vowel elongation in speech, a composite of behavior that would strike us as bizarre if directed toward anyone but an infant, and which women find trouble repeating unless they are looking directly at their baby's face. It is also a scenario babies can turn off by dropping eye contact or averting their heads.[18] The importance of early contact for maternal responsiveness to the baby has been shown by Leifer, who found that, among mothers of premature infants, those who were allowed to handle their babies in the hospital, even briefly, showed more maternal interest months later than mothers who were not allowed to touch their newborn infants at all.[19]

It is well to confront the theoretical and political implications of a biosocial perspective on mating and parenting directly. Where age is concerned, no one would deny the relevance of maturational, physiological factors; it is commonly accepted that age differences are the result of both physiological and social factors. Where sex and gender are concerned, however, this has not been the case. Here, the nature-nurture debate has continued with, if anything, a hardening polarization in recent years. Activist scholars of the new school currently investigating sex, marriage, and parenthood are implicitly allied with the "nurture" camp, while others, such as Goldberg, Gilder, Fox, and Tiger, either argue strongly from a "nature" perspective, or hold a composite view that is strongly determined by biological factors.[20] Common to many social scientists who draw heavily on biology is a belief in biologically rooted hormonal differentiation between the sexes as being a basic determinant of sex-linked psychological characteristics and sex-differentiated social organizations. All too often, however, the biology underpining these views is itself outdated, for it is an older biology that assumed a unidirectional causation between physiological and social factors. In fact, researchers in the biological sciences have gone further in incorporating social variables into their research than the social sciences have gone in incorporating physiological variables into theirs, with the ironic consequence that there is more evidence to support the importance of social variables in the biological literature than there is evidence to reject the importance of physiological variables in the sociological literature.

To gain some perspective on this debate, it may be helpful to look back to an earlier period of intellectual history and examine how biology was utilized by social scientists, for this early usage set the stage for a hostility that still persists among social scientists toward the incorporation of biological factors in social science theory and research. We shall then examine what has transpired within endocrinology, the most relevant biological science for the issue of sex and gender differences, for developments there will suggest how many social scientists who utilize or who reject biological factors do so by drawing on an outmoded model of the relationship between hormones and behavior.

Social Science Hostility to Biology in the Past

The reluctance among social scientists to look toward the biological sciences for illumination of social behavior and social organization has a long and complex history. The founders of sociology were enamored of Darwinian ideas, and they consequently modeled their theories of social behavior and social organization on analogies to physical science, organic-equilibrium concepts, and theories of animal-species selection in a manner that makes understandable the resistance to biology of the social sciences in the early twentieth century. At its peak, from around 1880 to around 1910, Social Darwinists based their principles of social organization on biological models. Comte and Spencer were the most frequently quoted sources for the major ideas guiding applications to history, eugenics, immigration policy, etc. Protestant historians such as Henry Adams and Henry Cabot Lodge traced the origins of American democratic institutions to the early Teutonic community and political organization, paving the way for, and collaborating with, those who wished to change American immigration policy as the tide shifted from northern to southern and eastern Europe. Immigrants, blacks, south Europeans, and women were seen as biologically inferior when viewed through a conservative political filter justified by pretentious "scientific" theories.

Unfortunately, the sciences that were most relevant to these social theories and policies had not yet emerged: modern genetics and endocrinology were decades away, so the primary model was largely based on the physical sciences and biological evolutionary principles. Spencer argued that sex differences rested on the "somewhat earlier arrest of individual evolution in women than in men; necessitated by the reservation of vital power to meet the cost of reproduction."[21] The view prevailed that women's energy was drained by reproduction, leaving little for intellectual and personal growth—a deduction from the commonly accepted physical law of conservation and transformation of energy which had caught the fancy of late-nineteenth-century social scientists. Geddes went so far as to argue that sex differences arose from basic differences in cell metabolism, so that male and female sex roles were decided in the lowest forms of life, and that "neither political nor technological change could alter the temperamental tendency for males to be active and aggressive and females to be quiescent and passive."[22]

Other theorists built directly on the earlier Darwinian theory of sexual selection which assumed a superiority that evolved in the male line alone. Hence, the argument went, biology itself ordained male social and political superiority, and there was thus no point in encouraging intellectual and political development in women—indeed, many argued, it could be positively harmful. Antoinette Blackwell was alone in her time in being critical of the Darwinian theories, and ahead of genetic knowledge by twenty years, when, in 1875, she argued that Spencer "scientifically" *subtracted* from the female and Darwin "scientifically" *added* to the male, but that both were in error because characteristics are transmitted equally to descendants of both sexes: between any two moments, the males and females of the same species had evolved to exactly the same degree.[23]

By the nineteen-twenties, the pendulum had swung away from the Social Darwinist justification of the status quo. Social scientists rejected the view that Western culture, the white race, and the male sex represented the pinnacle of human evolutionary progress. Instead of correcting these views and substituting them with more appropriate interpretations of evolution and adaptation, the social sciences adopted a firm position against any relevance of biology to social behavior. Biology was split off from social anthropology with consequences that are still apparent in the hostility between physical and cultural anthropologists. Behavioral psychologists taught that habit, conditioning, and family relations early in life could account for almost all human behavior, inherited characteristics for very little. Sociological and economic theorists substituted the earlier biological models with new historical ones stressing trends toward rationality and the purposive design and control of social systems.

The only area that remained significantly unaffected by this shift from a biological to a sociological orientation was the interpretation of sex-linked characteristics, for early developments in the field of endocrinology were interpreted as supporting previously unfounded speculations about sex temperament and characteristics rooted in reproductive physiology. Although both sexes have endocrine systems, little stress was placed on the influence of hormones on male behavior—no theories emerged to suggest that male hormones stood in the way of men reaching the full peak of rational control demanded by modern societies. Female hormones, on the other hand, were thought clearly to explain women's behavior and the nature of the social structures centering on female activities. Thus, biological explanations of sex and gender survived the pendulum swing from social theories of a biologically determinist nature to social theories stressing cultural relativity and environmental determinism, and they have continued to have their place in the interpretations—if not the direct empirical measurement—of family and sex roles in the decades since the thirties.

Against this historical background, it is not surprising that recent reassessments of social-science theories have been extremely skeptical of biological explanations of sex behavior and gender roles; they are continuing the efforts begun by behavioral scientists in the nineteen-twenties in opposition to the Social Darwinists. Unfortunately, two factors have limited the cogency of these reassessments. First, in flushing out the unsubstantiated assumptions of physiologically rooted sex differences, what was substituted has not been more accurately based knowledge from the biological sciences, but a denial of any critical physiological differences that could not be explained in terms of differential socialization. Second, since not all differences could be denied, the claim has been made that the "only" difference between males and females is simply that females bear young and lactate. The use of this "only" qualifier implies that childbearing and lactation are really not significant, since few women lactate nowadays, nor is childbearing any longer the choice of all of them; even women who do have children spend a smaller and smaller portion of their lives dealing with maternal responsibilities. The more extreme feminists have gone on to argue that technological savvy now permits us, or soon will permit us, to wipe out biological differences between the sexes through menstrual extraction, test-tube conception, and laboratory breeding in place of human pregnancy.[24]

But the reproductive and endocrine systems that underlie childbearing and lactation are functioning systems within the female throughout her life cycle,[25] and to deny their significance to female psychology or to the organization of family systems is to devalue a central fact in human-species survival for which the human female plays the most critical role, to reveal the profound degree to which many women accept masculine technocratic thinking, and to by-pass the significant findings of science pertaining to reproductive and endocrine functioning.

Theoretical Paradigms in Endocrinology

Because developments in endocrinology in the past two decades are important to a biosocial perspective on parenting and are not readily accessible to social scientists and humanists, a brief sketch of the shift in the theories of endocrinology will be useful at this juncture. Neuroendocrinology, an offshoot specialty from endocrinology, emerged in the nineteen-sixties as a consequence of other developments in the field. From the nineteen-twenties to the -fifties, the primary model of endocrine functioning was of a closed internal system involving the pituitary, the adrenals, and the gonads (testes and ovaries), which were related to one another as hormone-to-hormone transducers.[26] (Hormones are chemical messengers produced by glands in one part of the body that act upon target cells in other tissues of the organism.) In the female reproductive system, the early paradigm centered on the pituitary and the ovaries and on the hormones that circulated between them through the bloodstream. Thus the pituitary secreted a follicle-stimulating hormone (FSH) that led to follicle growth in the ovaries, which in turn secreted increasing amounts of estrogen. As the estrogen circulating through the body reached a critical level, it cued the pituitary to reduce the FSH and to secrete a luteinizing hormone (LH), which then triggered the rupture of the ovum and the beginning of progesterone secretion from the follicle shell or corpus luteum. In the absence of a fertilized ovum, the estrogen and progesterone secretion levels then drop, menstruation carries off the unneeded enriched uterine epithelium, and the cycle begins over again.[27] For our purposes, the most important characteristic of this early view was that it was a closed system, functioning independently from the external environment; the glands were linked together by the flow of hormones through the bloodstream, and the system only minimally involved the nervous system.

Since the fifties, a number of research developments have led to major revisions in this theory of endocrine functioning. Central to them was the discovery that the hypothalamus was intricately involved in endocrine functioning, and, because the hypothalamus is part of the old cortex surrounding the brain stem, this also implicated the nervous system in endocrine functioning. Green and Harris[28] then established that blood flowed *from* the hypothalamus *to* the pituitary, and this set the stage for the discovery of releasing factors from the hypothalamus to the pituitary, which added a new and important link to the chain of endocrine events. Neurons producing these releasing factors in the hypothalamus receive electrical signals from the rest of the brain and are subject to "behavioral" influences and to the modulating influences of the gonadal hormones on neural circuits underlying behavior. The classic theory of hormone-to-hormone transduction yielded under the impact of these discoveries.[29] Unlike the "classic" gland which receives information from hormonal signals in the bloodstream, neuroendocrine transducers receive information from nerve impulses: they convert a neural input into an endocrine output. Social stimuli may thus impinge upon hormonal secretion through the nervous system.

Until the fifties, then, cases demonstrating that the nervous system participated in reproductive events were regarded as curious exceptions, while from the mid-fifties on, the endocrine system was demoted to the status of coequal partner with the nervous system in the control of hormonal events in the body. The broader significance of this shift is that it allows us less and less reason to expect a one-way causation between hormones and behavior; the only appropriate model then becomes an interactive-influence model.

This new theory has not yet become well enough known in the social sciences, which persist in the mistaken belief that any hormonal characteristic necessarily serves as a "causal" variable influencing behavior. In fact, contemporary endocrinologists and primatologists are just as likely to study the influence of social and psychological factors upon hormonal secretion as they are to trace the influence of hormones upon behavior. Indeed, an emphasis in current primatological research has been the manipulation of the social environment and observation of its impact on hormonal-secretion levels in the animal. For example, research has demonstrated that male rhesus monkeys who suffer defeat and diminished status in their group show a drop in testosterone secretion, which can be reversed through exposure to a female rhesus. So, too, one explanation for human homosexuality in the past had been that low testosterone levels were responsible for attraction to individuals of the same sex. Now it is just as reasonable to argue that attraction to the same sex may affect the level of hormonal secretion.[30] If there are olfactory pheromonal signals[31] in cross-sex intimate association that affect hormonal levels, then the reaction of rhesus monkey males and human homosexual males are identical in these examples, the one showing an increase in testosterone through close association with females, the other a decrease in testosterone in the absence of close association with females.

Since the discovery of the role of the hypothalamus in the passage of releasing factors to the pituitary, much neuroendocrinological research has centered on the connections between nerve cells in the cortex and the hypothalamus, to try to locate the specific populations of cells that are hormone-sensitive and find out what happens to the biochemistry within these cells, and how the neurons fit into neural pathways that regulate behavior and the hormone-producing glands. It is already known that some nerve cells in the brain are sensitive to gonadal estradiol and testosterone, while others are sensitive to the hormonal products of the adrenal glands. By injecting radio-active estradiol, for example, researchers can trace the destination of the hormone in specific clusters of brain cells and study what happens internally in such cells.

For a social scientist interested in the role of endocrine functioning for gender differences, this is a fascinating but complex area of research. It is probably fair to say that, at this juncture, research findings in neuroendocrinology put in question the interpretations some social scientists have drawn from endocrinological research in the sixties, but this new field has not yet provided definitive evidence of all that is involved in the intricate relationship between brain chemistry, hormone-producing glands, and behavior. To a social scientist reading the new research literature, it seems increasingly questionable that it is useful to call androgens the "male" hormone and estrogens the "female" hormone. Both hormones are present in both sexes, although in different balances. Androgens are important in both male and female, in humans as in rats and monkeys, for the motivational aspects of sexual behavior, that is, they are the "erotic" hormones in both sexes.

While males have higher levels of androgens than females, recent work suggests that it takes less androgen to produce an effect in the female than in the male. Androgen therapy has an effect upon sexual tonus in men only if the androgen secretion level was below normal prior to treatment; additional hormones do not increase male sexual-response thresholds. In contrast, women who undergo androgen therapy report a surge in sexual desire.[32] So, too, androgen withdrawal has more impact upon the sexual-desire level of females than of males. As long as puberty has been attained, castration (and hence the removal of the major androgen source) of a male animal does not lead to marked immediate change in sexual desire and behavior; the animals continue to perform sexually with apparent interest. The drop in sexual desire is more dramatic when the natural body source of androgen is removed from females. The ovaries and the adrenals are the major suppliers of androgen in the female; women who have had both organs surgically removed report a sharp drop in clitoral sensitivity and orgasmic response.[33] Restoration of sexual vigor by replacement therapy requires weeks in the male and only hours or days in the female.[34] There is growing evidence for rejecting the view that androgen is the "aggressive" hormone, responsible for sex differences in combativeness, a thesis some social scientists have used to explain the differential distribution of status and power between men and women in human societies. At least at the moment, it would seem more reasonable to view the androgens as "erotic" hormones than as "aggressive" hormones.

One area of research of potential significance for understanding sex differences is that centering on the organizational impact of gonadal hormones during fetal development.[35] The rat is the preferred subject for this research because gonadal-hormone impact on the rat brain takes place during the first week *after* birth and hence is readily explored in the research laboratory, while in the human it takes place early in pregnancy. During this short, sensitive phase of early brain development, the testes of the male secretes testosterone, which initiates the events that lead to sexual differentiation of the brain. One aspect of current neuroendocrinology involves tracing the impact of experimental intervention into this "critical" phase of gonadal secretion in the rat in order to understand where, how, and why brain organization is affected;[36] another involves the medical and psychological investigation among humans of discrepanices between genetic and gonadal sex and social gender assignment.

Central to this area of research is the work of Money and Ehrhardt and their associates.[37] The conclusions most sociologists have drawn from Money and Ehrhardt's research are: (1) that gender identity is fixed at a very tender age; and (2) that the sex to which an individual is assigned at birth is of far greater importance for gender identity than either genetic or gonadal sex. The researchers themselves have drawn a third conclusion: that the hormonal drama played out during fetal development has long-lasting effects which heighten the brain's capacity to comply with the demands of the sex to which individuals are assigned and in terms of which they are reared. For example, in the testicular feminizing syndrome, a genetic male with male internal gonads has external female genitalia as a consequence of a failure of androgen secretion from the testes during the critical phase of fetal development. If the infant is defined at birth as, and reared as, a female, the individual shows a relative ease of gender identification as a female. This has heretofore been interpreted by sociologists as evidence that culture overrides physiology, but that view neglects the point that these genetic males never had prenatal testosterone flowing through their brains. Their ease of gender identification as girls does not prove that a purely social influence is at work. Ehrhardt and Money pose the more complicated question of whether the failure of androgen secretion in such genetic male fetuses heightens the brain's capacity to comply with the demands of female sex assignment and rearing.[38]

Just as the intricate DNA genetic code includes a whole set of propensities for particular social behavior which goes with a given physiology, so fetal exposure to hormones may lay down propensities for male, as opposed to female, behavior after birth. It is, of course, the case that an overlay of powerful cultural pressures may drown out these constitutional propensities, though perhaps at some price to the individuals involved. *A biosocial perspective argues that such propensities shape the parameters within which learning takes place and affect the ease with which males and females learn (or unlearn) socially defined appropriate gender behavior.*

In sociology—suffering as do all the social sciences from artificial disciplinary boundaries—it is easy to forget that the basic facts of family life consist in the coming together of people with physical bodies to mate, to reproduce, and to rear the young. In its tendency to define sociological variables in terms of role script, status, and system, a further barrier is erected to any easy linkage of body process and personality to social relations and social systems. In common with the values implicit in American culture generally, the pressure here is strong narrowly to define identity and social roles in behavioral terms so that hardly any room remains for the inclinations or the genetic characteristics of our bodies.[39] What a biosocial perspective on parenting suggests is that the traditional sociological approach to the family ought to be supplemented by a direct examination of mating and parenting as behavior systems, an examination that draws freely upon whatever biological, clinical, or behavioral sciences there are that can help to shed light on human family behavior.

Having sketched a bio-evolutionary framework for viewing mating and parenting, looked backward to the hostility of the social sciences toward the biological sciences, and outlined the current theories that are guiding research in the field of endocrinology that most closely involve sex and gender differences, let us turn now to an examination of the current sociological literature on the family and analyze it in biosocial terms, organizing the discussion around the question of how mating is articulated with parenting.

Contemporary Research on Variant Marriage and Family Forms

A very diverse set of groups now shares the common view that the nuclear family and monogamous marriage are oppressive, sexist, "bourgeois," and sick. Exponents of sexual liberation, self-actualization, socialism, humanism, gay liberation, existentialism, and certain segments of feminism have joined hands in a general denunciation of the stereotyped "traditional nuclear family," although rarely defining what they mean. One infers, however, that they usually refer to a legal marriage between a man and a woman who share a household with their legitimate offspring, with the male as the breadwinner and the female as a homemaker.[40] "Variant" or "experimental" families and marriages would then include a wide array of forms, from cohabitant heterosexual couples, multilateral marriages, single-parent households, dual-career couples with or without children to families traditional in everything except consensual participation in co-marital, swinging, or swapping sexual relationships outside the marriage. This is a wide assortment indeed, and interestingly the "traditional" category has been counted at something less than a third of the actual families in the United States simply by regarding the criterion of an employed wife as being sufficient to classify a family as a variant form.[41] By doing this, of course, the researcher also artificially exaggerates the degree to which genuinely variant marriage and family forms are prevalent in our society.

But there is a further interesting characteristic of this literature. Although the titles of publications on alternate-family forms almost always refer to "families," in fact the works themselves focus almost exclusively on the adult relationship between men and women, in and out of, or in addition to, marriage. They rarely concern themselves with children, parenting, or parent-child relations. For example, the special 1972 issue of *The Family Coordinator* consists of fifteen articles published under the title "Variant Marriage Styles and Family Forms." A simple line-count content analysis, however, reveals the following (converting the line count to estimated pages): *only 5 per cent of the total 123 full-text pages in this issue deal with any aspect of parenting, child care, or the parent-child relationship.* Marriage and the male-female relationship are receiving the central attention in this new genre of family sociology, not family systems or the birth and rearing of children.

The implicit premise in much of this literature is the right of the individual to an expanded freedom in the pursuit of private sexual pleasure: I want what I want when I want it. Thus Smith and Smith variously refer to monogamous marriage as "sexual monopoly," "a form of emotional and sexual malnutrition," and a "condition of sexual deprivation."[42] Variant families, Cogswell summarizes, are entered into not with an expectation of permanence, as traditional nuclear families are, but with "the expectation that relationships will continue only so long as they serve the mutual benefit of the members."[43] A similar note is struck in Lorber's claim that "a feminist goal is total freedom of choice in sex partners throughout one's life."[44]

There are several problems posed by these views of family relations that are often revealed in the actual experiences of men and women who are currently experimenting with new forms of marriage and family relations. The sexual liberationist clearly rejects the traditional double standard; what is not clear is whether the new single standard will be modeled after what has been the male pattern, the female pattern, or some amalgam of the two. A close reading of the literature on contemporary sexual practices and on the attitudes of the young suggests the model is a male pattern: early initiation, sexual diversity, physical play through casual sex. In studies of adolescent attitudes toward sexuality, it has been found that adolescents are coming to regard sex as a "good way to get acquainted," a means to *develop* rather than to *express* couple intimacy. At the same time, extremely large gender differences still exist among the holders of such attitudes, with men two to three times more apt than women their own age to endorse the more casual attitude to sexuality.[45] The literature on co-marital sex shows that, in three out of four cases, it is the husband who initiates the seeking of other sex partners, participation tends to last about six months, the wives tend to be homemakers with neither jobs nor community involvements, and the couples are very careful to keep their sexual activities a secret from their children.[46] Sexual liberation, then, seems to mean that increasing numbers of women are now following male initiatives in a more elaborate, multi-partner sexual script.

A second issue concerns the pressure toward widening the circle of sexual partners that is implicit in the notion of expanded freedom of private sexual pleasure. If no sex is to take place under the new ideological "cult of mutual desire," there necessarily must be either a considerable decline in the frequency of sex or access to more than one partner, since any marital relationship that includes two busy people with busy lives will be frequently out of phase in sexual desire. It is but a short step to the view that spouse swapping or co-marital sex is precisely what contemporary marriages need to remain intact, healthy, and self-actualizing for both partners. For a married woman not to enjoy sex with men other than her husband, or, in some quarters, not to be bisexual is to be out of step with the times—an old-fashioned spouse or a poor feminist. The message seems to be that to be faithful, possessive, exclusively heterosexual, and able to postpone gratification are signs of immaturity and oppression. Smith and Smith argue that the ". . . conquest of sexual jealousy

... could be the greatest advance in human relations since the advent of common law or the initiation of democratic processes. The increased frequency and incidence of swinging and swapping . . . could then be viewed . . . as [presaging] a new era in sexual and interpersonal relationships."[47]

A third issue concerns the implications of ego indulgence and immediate gratification for parenthood. What is the analogue of sexual liberation here? Can women or men be parents only when they want to be or only when their children want to be parented? One would assume that any awareness of the developmental needs of children, or of the emotional attachment of parents to them, would require an answer of "no." But this is not the case in the new family sociology. The following quotation advocating communal families illustrates explicitly what is implicit in much of this literature: "By always having some children in our unit, we will be able to assume parental roles when and for as long as we want. . . . Our children will have an advantage [in that] from the adults they can select their own parents, brothers, sister, friends. . . . Our social ties will not be forced nor strained by the mandates of kinship and marital obligation."[48] Here the image is clear: in the post-nuclear-family era, the adult can turn parenthood on and off and exchange children as well as sexual partners.

In more serious studies by observers, there are hints of difficulties and strains arising when such an ideology is put into practice. In Kanter's studies of urban middle-class communes,[49] she points to a tendency to view children as miniature adults, free to establish relationships with adults other than their parents in the communal household. But since notions of discipline and tolerance of children vary among adults, Kanter reports a considerable amount of confusion among the four-to-twelve-year-old children she interviewed, as a consequence of what she calls the "Cinderella effect" (rapid demands or corrections by a number of unrelated adults to the same child at the same time). There is also evidence that the sharing of children creates emotional difficulties for many parents, particularly the mothers of the children, until eventually parents tend to reserve for themselves the right to protect and punish their children. The researchers note that very rarely did a mother allow a male communal member to invoke sanctions with her children, and even when he did, it was clear that he was acting for the mother through some form of delegated authority.[50]

Berger's work on communal families[51] also reveals stress in child-rearing. Communal ideology is extended to children through the notion of equality defined as identity, so that the children are viewed as "autonomous human beings, equal to adults."[52] Berger cites one mother who aptly caught the dilemma of this ideology in action: "What I wanted was a baby; but a kid, that's something else." Having a baby, particularly by a natural birth in a communal household, is a great occasion of collective celebration: it is organic, earthy, beautiful. Besides, babies represent human potential unspoiled by the corrupting influence of repressive institutions. But rearing a child involves obligations for which commune members are not prepared, since it means future orientation, planning, and some status distinctions between adults, who have knowledge, and children, who do not. This cuts across the communal view that tends to "regard themselves as kids, their lives as unsettled, their futures uncertain."[53] Despite the ideology, Berger notes that infants and knee babies are almost universally in the charge of their mothers, and that whatever sharing takes

place of children from two to four is largely confined to the group of mothers
with young children; only children over five are supervised by other adults, and
then with some of the difficulties Kanter noted.

The power of ideology is well illustrated in Rothchild and Wolf's recent
book on children of counterculture parents.[54] The report provides an overall
portrait of children almost uniformly neglected, deprived, and tormented;
many are uneducated, disorganized, and disturbed; a pervasive boredom and
lack of joy and serious problems of mal- or undernourishment were prevalent.
After such a sad portrait, it comes as a shock to find the authors concluding that
the communes are a success in child-rearing because they have done away with
materialism and competitiveness. In reality, the counterculture parents are
obviously trying to rear children without having to be bothered by them, a
profile strikingly similar to the earlier one by Berger.

Just as the sexual script, so the parenting script in the new family sociology
seems to be modeled on what has been a male pattern of relating to children, in
which men turn their fathering on and off to suit themselves or their appointments for business or sexual pleasure. The authors and dramatists of both the
mating and parenting scripts in the new perspectives on the family are just as
heavily male as the older schools of thought about the modern family, if not in
the generic sense, then in the sense that parenting is viewed from a distance, as
an appendage to, or consequence of, mating, rather than the focus of family
systems and individual lives. It is not at all clear what the gains will be for either
women or children in this version of human liberation.[55]

The Articulation of Mating and Parenting in a Biosocial Perspective

Western societies have long had a split image of woman—the temptress Eve
and the saintly Mary—that symbolized the polarity between sex (bad) and
maternity (good) in Christian theology. Until the twentieth century, Eve for the
most part remained outside the family as the loose woman, mistress, prostitute.
More recently, she has come indoors to reign as the sensuous wife Eve bonded
tenuously to the nurturant mother Mary. In the nineteen-seventies, the variant-
marriage literature extols a good Eve who makes it both at home and away from
home, while Mary recedes into an anti-natalist shadow, a reverse split-image, but
still a split-image: what was good is now bad, what was bad is now good. In
sociological terms, recreative sex has contemporary ascendance over procreative
sex and parenting.

Beneath this cultural scenario, however, are intimate connections between
sexuality and maternalism in the female of the species that Western society has
not reckoned with. Indeed, it could be argued that the full weight of Western
history has inserted a wedge between sex and maternalism so successfully that
women themselves and the scientists who have studied their bodies and social
roles have seldom seen the intimate connections between them. Yet the
evidence is there in female reproductive physiology, thinly covered by a
masculine lens that projects male fantasy onto female functions.

A good starting place to observe such fantasy is the initial coming together of
sperm and ovum. Ever since Leewenhoek first saw sperm under the micro-
scope, great significance has been attached to the fact that sperm are equipped

with motile flagella, and it was assumed that the locomotive ability of the sperm fully explained their journey from the vagina through the cervix and uterus to the oviduct for the encounter with the ovum. This notion persists even today in scientific publications, to say nothing of more literary examples.[56] Rorvik describes the seven-inch journey through the birth canal and womb to the waiting egg as equivalent to a 500-mile upstream swim for a salmon, and comments with admiration that they often make the hazardous journey in under an hour, "more than earning their title as the most powerful and rapid living creatures on earth."[57] The image is clear: powerful active sperm and a passive ovum awaiting its arrival and penetration, male sexual imagery structuring the very act of conception. In fact, the transport through the female system is much too rapid to be accounted for purely by the locomotive ability of the sperm. Furthermore, completely inert substances such as dead sperm and even particles of India ink reach the oviducts as rapidly as live sperm do.[58]

What, then, does transport the sperm? The stimulus comes from the impact of sexual stimulation upon the female, which by neural impulses to the hypothalamus stimulates the posterior pituitary to release oxytocin, which in turn produces uterine contractions that propel the sperm on their way.[59] Nor can the sperm immediately penetrate the ovum, for, once in the oviduct, it takes several hours of what physiologists call "capacitation" before the sperm acquires the ability to penetrate the ovum,[60] so there is not even much point to the notion of a competitive race to be the first to reach the ovum—another male fantasy.

Interestingly, oxytocin is a hormone that is a clear link between sexuality and maternalism: it stimulates the uterine contractions that help the sperm on their way to the oviduct; at high levels it produces the stronger contractions of childbirth; and it causes nipple erection during either nursing or loveplay. Whether the sucking is by an infant or a lover, oxytocin acts upon the basket cells around the alveoli, causing them to constrict, and in the case of nursing, to squeeze out the milk in the phenomenon known as "milk let-down."[61]

The interconnection between sexuality and maternalism makes good evolutionary sense. By providing some erotogenic pleasure to the mother of a newborn baby, there is greater assurance that the child will be nursed and the uterus restored to pre-pregnancy status. The fact that the clitoris is not in the birth canal contributes to sensual pleasure in the immediate post-birth period of greatest infant fragility. Pregnancy and childbirth in turn improve the gratification women derive from coital orgasm, since orgasmic intensity is directly related to the degree of pelvic vasocongestion, and vasocongestion increases with each subsequent pregnancy.[62] On either score, then, human female physiology both contributes to the personal sexual gratification of women and assures their continued cooperation in species survival.[63]

There is some evidence from both physiological and anthropological research of the connection between sexual attitudes and childbirth experiences. Grimm[64] and Newton[65] report a coherent syndrome of good sexual adjustment and low incidence of nausea during pregnancy, easier and shorter labor, desire for and success at nursing, and preference for natural childbirth. Mead and Newton[66] report that childbirth is remarkably short and painless in a society with relaxed sexual attitudes, such as that of the South American Siriono, where birth is an easy, public event controlled by the mother herself, but that it is a prolonged painful process among the Cuna in Panama who prevent young girls from learning about either coitus or childbirth until the final stages of the marriage ceremony. Western societies have historically approximated the Cuna to a greater extent than the Siriono.

Contemporary writers reveal more than they intend when they distinguish between recreative and procreative sex. In the "beyond monogamy" literature, this distinction is typically the starting point in discussions of the advantages of an "open" marriage, swinging, or spouse swapping, which are premised on fully effective contraceptives: sexual freedom is possible because no pregnancy will follow from the multiple sex encounters a woman may have in a given month, and, should one occur, there is always the back-up of an abortion. By the same token, however, pregnancies which are wanted or permitted to come to term are assumed to be legitimate ones in the context of a "primary" relationship. Even when birth is a joyful public event in a communal household or in an Israeli kibbutz, where the child will be reared largely in the children's houses, there is apparently as strong a mother-infant bond as in the American nuclear family. Thus proponents of experimental family forms continue to link parenting to either marriage or a stable "primary" relationship. It is questionable whether the single mothers who head the households that include eight million children under eighteen retain responsibility for their children because they are "stuck with the kids" simply as a result of cultural pressure, as some current family critics claim. It is more likely that the emotional ties to the children are more important to the mothers than to the fathers. It is probably still the case that the vast majority of women can have ex-spouses but not ex-children.[67]

As pregnancies become increasingly intentional and freely chosen, and less often the unintended consequences of the pursuit of sexual pleasure, this fundamental salience of the mother-child relationship may become stronger, not weaker, than it has been in the past. Infants may respond to anyone who provides stable loving caretaking, but the predisposition to respond to the child may be much greater on the part of the mother than the father, a reflection of the underlying dual orientation of the female to both mate and child, a heritage that links mating and parenting more closely for females than males, and one rooted in both mammalian physiology and human culture. If a society wishes to create shared parental roles, it must either accept the high probability that the mother-infant relationship will continue to have greater emotional depth than the father-infant relationship, or institutionalize the means for providing men with compensatory exposure and training in infant and child care in order to close the gap produced by the physiological experience of pregnancy, birth, and nursing. Without such compensatory training of males, females will show added dimensions of intensity to their bonds with children.

Obstetric Management of Childbirth

Since the biological sciences, medicine, and clinical psychiatry have been more closely associated with one another than sociology and psychology have been to any of them, one might think that obstetric management of childbirth would reflect an awareness of female physiology in the psychological experience it provides for the woman during pregnancy and birth and the impact it may have upon the bonding of mother and newborn. There is no evidence that this has been the case. In fact, there is hardly an instance in human life in industrial societies that has shown so great a degree of technological interference with a natural process than American obstetric management of pregnancy and birth. In the past fifty years, spontaneous birth in a familiar setting has been replaced by medically managed deliveries, and, as noted earlier, breast feeding has been largely replaced by bottle feeding.

Until very recently, obstetric practice received very little criticism in the United States, despite the fact that many aspects of obstetric management have warranted it—to name just some of them: heavy reliance on anesthetics which produces drugged babies prone to respiratory distress and apathetic response at birth, the use of instruments which risk brain damage and newborn trauma, obstetric insistence on horizontal delivery tables which prolong second-stage labor because the body is not working with but against gravity, foot stirrups which stretch the perineal tissue so that physicians feel justified in performing routine episiotomies that would otherwise be unnecessary in most cases, premature cutting of the umbilical cord which robs the newborn of up to a quarter of its blood supply and prolongs the third stage of labor because the placenta remains engorged, and, perhaps most important from a psychological perspective, the use of general anesthesia which cheats the mother of consciousness at the moment of birth, at precisely the point when hormonal levels and the euphoria of accomplishment could contribute to a positive experience for the woman and a deep attachment between mother and child.[68] A search of the literature yields no studies which contrast the early attachment of the mother and infant when the mother was fully conscious at the birth with that when the mother was anesthetized, but, in several well-designed studies, Klaus and his associates have found that the earlier the contact of a mother with her newborn and the longer that contact, the greater the mother-child attachment at the end of the first month.[69] Kennell reports the persistence of such early-contact effects at the end of the first year of the child's life.[70] In this critical area, the medical field may have grossly exaggerated the degree of difference between human mothers and other primate mothers, for numerous studies have found that separation of the mother and infant at birth produces impairment in their relationship and in the development of the young.[71] From the point of view of the health and well-being of the newborn, American babies are cheated of a good start in life: the Apgar scores[72] of infants born in home settings with midwife attendants in poor sections of Appalachia show healthier babies than those born in private obstetric practice in many hospitals in wealthy suburbs. In the Netherlands where birth is managed in as natural a way as possible, babies show markedly better Apgar scores of physical well-being at birth than American babies do.[73]

It is surprising that so little research has been done on the impact of pregnancy upon women from the point of view of the impact of medical management of pregnancy and birth.[74] A flood of literature can be found on the relation between hormones and behavior,[75] but little has been done to extend our understanding of the impact of the sharply elevated hormonal levels during pregnancy and what their contribution may be to attachment behavior, particularly when women have, or do not have, first contact with their babies during the post-birth hours when hormonal levels are still high. We already know of fluctuations in estrogen and progesterone levels during the female menstrual cycle and the mood and behavioral correlates of those fluctuations,[76] yet the fact that estrogen levels show a tenfold increase and progesterone a hundredfold increase during pregnancy has not stimulated comparable research.[77]

Studies of this sort are important also, of course, for their implications regarding the often unanticipated impact of pregnancy and birth upon young women. A more sociological perspective is also needed, one that deals with the distortion of the natural process involved in the medical management of birth. In medical literature, the model of pregnancy is apt to be couched in terms of intrapsychic forces within the woman—e.g., that pregnancy involves a "regression" to childhood as the mother identifies with the fetus (and hence provides a rationale for patient infantilization by obstetricians?). But pregnancy and birth take place in a social context, and they clearly demonstrate the impact of technocratic management to the detriment of women and their babies. Most recently, the use of fetal-monitoring equipment during the early stages of labor has provided an unprecedented amount of information on the course of labor. Physicians were so ill-prepared for it that a steady increase in Caesarian deliveries has resulted in hospitals using such equipment, suggesting yet another new pressure in the direction of technological takeover of a natural process.

Parlee[78] and Rossi[79] have suggested that one reason for post-partum distress among women may be the isolation in which women find themselves when they return with their babies from the hospital. This, too, is a radical departure from the experience of the species in our long history. In earlier stages of human history, mothers moved in a world crowded with supportive kin who supplemented their care of infants, a situation in sharp contrast to the experience of most American women today. Not only is the natural process interfered with through medical distortion of spontaneous birth, the mother separated from the baby for most of the critical first days of life, the infant fed on a rigid hospital schedule, and kept in a brightly lit and noisy nursery, but then the mother is sent home with her infant to cope as well as she can totally on her own. If she breaks down under this strange regimen, she is regarded as incompetent to handle "normal" female responsibilities.

Social scientists who have been concerned with the transition to parenthood in American families have been puzzled by the fact that post-partum depression increases with the parity of the birth. Sociological expectations had been that a first birth would represent more of a "crisis" than later births, since it is a "new" experience and an important transition in family structure. In fact, it is multiparous women who show greater emotional stress,[80] perhaps because of the shorter intervals between births that have become common in Western societies only in relatively recent human history. In the larger framework of human evolution, breast-feeding imposed its own control on the spacing of births, for lactation together with physical activity and a low sugar and carbohydrate diet kept body fat low enough to prevent ovulation and hence to assure a child spacing of three or more years, the number depending on the cultural norms that governed the duration of breast-feeding.[81] With our enriched diets, lactation no longer serves as a good ovulatory inhibitor.[82] Jane

Lancaster[83] has pointed out that the modern practice of deliberately timing births close together may be an aberration from desirable practice and a key factor in the stress many women experience in coping with their young.

By neglecting the biosocial dimension of human life, American society may set the stage for unprecedented stress in the lives of young mothers and an impoverishment of the quality of their relationship with their children. A second child who is born when the first child is under two years of age is not only taxing on the mother's physical and emotional stamina, but whatever support system of kin and friends the mother has is more apt to consider her "experienced" in mothering by the second birth and consequently to give her less, rather than more, assistance. In the absence of any adequate empirical investigation of the effects of family size,[84] birth spacing, and the presence or absence of supplementary aid in the care of the child, no scientific guidelines exist by which women who wish to make informed decisions can space their pregnancies. The ability to plan pregnancies by contraceptives is a partial achievement at best, if it is not coupled with some notion of what optimal spacing is. The anticipated drop in family size implied by the current low-fertility plans of young women does not settle the issue, because the spacing between two births may be as brief in a two-child as in a four-child family.

One final aspect of the pregnancy issue may be of even greater significance in the future, as more women work through the months of pregnancy. In light of the Supreme Court ruling in November, 1975,[85] that mandatory laying-off by the employer of women during the last three months of pregnancy and the first six weeks following childbirth is in violation of the Fourteenth Amendment, the practice of working throughout pregnancy may increase in future years. This is not purely a legal or women's-rights issue, for a correct assessment of its implications calls for knowledge we do not yet possess. We need to know two things: what the effects of stress during pregnancy are for the healthy development of the fetus, and what the effects of working environments are upon the health of the pregnant woman and the fetus. The latter issue is of growing concern in light of Hunt's estimate that more fetuses are in the American workplace now than there were children in our mines and factories in the whole history of American child labor.[86] Yet no large-scale investigations have been undertaken of the potential influence on the fetus of the vast array of chemicals and synthetics among which many women now work.

Second, some evidence has been found that psychological stress in the mother may be transmitted to the fetus prenatally. Ferreira[87] found that the infants of high-stress mothers show more irritability, crying, irregular bowel movements, etc., than infants of low-stress mothers, behavior that is as clear on the first day after birth as it is on the fifth—a significant point because, in the hospital involved, mothers have no contact with their infants for the first twenty-four hours after birth, and consequently observations of the baby on the first day clearly took place before any mother-infant contact. The study suggests, therefore, that prenatal environment includes more than simply food intake from the mother; it embraces the mother's attitudes and expectations concerning the child, in a process that probably involves the emotional state of the mother and its effects upon maternal body chemistry and, from there, on the nervous system of the fetus. Some women may find that withdrawal from their customary activities during pregnancy is conducive to anxiety, while others may find continuing their customary activities has that effect. Here again, we need to know more about the social circumstances and the personal character-istics that affect anxiety levels in women during pregnancy, so that guidelines might be developed to assist them in deciding whether to continue full-time employment, adopt a part-time schedule, or withdraw altogether, according to their susceptibilities to stress.

Children and Work

In the long evolution of the human species, women have always engaged in productive labor along with childbearing and -rearing. Hence women in indus-trial societies are not departing radically from the past when they combine child-rearing and employment. All women work, and they always have—sometimes as producers of goods and services on the land and in the household, sometimes for wages in the marketplace. The questions now are where women work during pregnancy, how adequate the support system is that provides assistance to mothers of very young children, and what the best conditions are for the healthy development of the preschool child. In this last section, attention will focus on these aspects of early child development.

That it is a critical subject is suggested by the sharp increase in the past decade in the employment of mothers with at least one child under three years of age, for such women show a labor-force participation rate that has more than quadrupled in the past decade. It is widely expected that the trend toward employment among mothers of very young children will accelerate in future years, so that urgent questions of child care will continue to be with us.[88] Unfortunately, the rationale for child-care programs in the past has been the needs of the economy or the needs of the mother, not the needs of children. Public programs have been developed to encourage women to enter the labor force in wartime or to attract women to industries in regions with an inadequate labor supply.[89] Recent efforts to fund day care have been similarly motivated: to permit, or coerce, welfare mothers to support themselves, or to compensate for inadequate care of the child in impoverished homes. Feminist efforts have been similarly focused on the needs of women, with child care justified as a necessary means to permit participation by women in the labor force at a rate and a level of job commitment equal to that of men.

As a consequence, little has yet been done to disturb the idea that under the best of all circumstances, the best place for young children is in the home under the mother's care. Even as innovative and dedicated a child-care researcher as Bettye Caldwell reports[90] the difficulty with which she struggled to rid herself of the concept of child "care" as a substitute or supplement to maternal care, and to use instead the concept of a "supportive environment" for optimal growth in the child. It was a big step for Caldwell to move from the idea of caring for a child in a custodial sense or as compensation for an impoverished home to the idea of a growth center as a kind of third parent that could contribute creatively to the child's development in ways the best home could not provide. American attitudes toward child care have a long way to go before they reach the level of Swedish appreciation of the pre-school years as a developmental stage when contact both with peers and with trained personnel can make vital contributions to healthy child development.

Once this shift in perspective does take place, it becomes possible to compare the family home with a growth center in a new light. Much has been made of the isolation of the young mother with preschool children in the suburban home, cut off from her former life, isolated from adult stimulation. By the same token, such a household is an isolating hothouse for young children, too, cutting them off from easy access to other children of their own age. Birth-order effects may be attributed to the pecking order that is built into the structure of the sibling set in the small-family household, a hierarchy of an invidious sort: at the top, the oldest child—bigger, smarter, stronger, bossier, an aristocrat with the ego-blustering that sometimes goes with that status; at the bottom, the youngest child—smaller, weaker, less knowledgeable—incompetent compared to the older siblings and turning to cuteness and attention-seeking as a result. In the past, when larger groups of adults and children provided the context within which children were reared, this pecking order did not occur. We have already noted that close child-spacing is a phenomenon of quite recent development. Close spacing between children may also have stimulated far more sibling rivalry than existed in the past: the birth of a sibling may be felt far more keenly as displacement when a child is between one and four years of age than it is when the child is older. Indeed, precisely because women have little support from other women, care of the newborn can in fact so preoccupy a mother that neither her time nor her energy is sufficient for the slightly older child. In other words, there may be a social reality behind the subjective sense of displacement in the three-year-old following the birth of a younger sibling. By contrast, when five years intervene between births, the older children have already reached an age at which peers from neighborhood and kindergarten reduce their dependence on their mothers. They are also old enough to help the mother, serving as assistant in home and baby care that makes the mother/older-child relationship an alliance. The result can well be less emotional and physical fatigue for the mother, a forward step in the growth of skills and independence in the older child, and warmth, rather than rivalry, in the sibling relationship.

In the modern circumstance, growth centers in which young children regularly spend part of each day may help to teach humility to the oldest child and self-confidence to the youngest. It can also be viewed as a means of shifting back toward a more natural way of life for both women and children.[91] Multi-family households, in which the sexual and parenting lines of the nuclear families remain intact but which include overlapping and shared living space, would similarly provide children with access to peers and parents with built-in support systems for alternating child care, coping more easily with family emergencies, and easing the combination of work and family responsibilities carried by both male and female household members.

Conclusion

This paper has utilized a biosocial perspective in two ways, one drawing on endocrinology and focused on internal physiological functions, the other drawing on bio-evolutionary theory and concerned with parenting in the course of our history as homo sapiens. We have tried to show that current theories in endocrinology emphasize the interaction between body hormones and social behavior or psychological state, an approach with great promise for joint research by social and biological scientists that would enrich our understanding of both physiological and social processes.

We also analyzed human parenting in a bio-evolutionary framework and argued that species survival has been facilitated by physiological factors in the bonding of the mother and the newborn. Innate factors in the infant, such as sucking, grasping, and crying, have been appreciated for a long time, but no comparable recognition has been given to the reciprocal innate predisposition in the mother to relate intensely to the infant. In particular, the implications of this attachment have not found their way into sociological thinking about family systems and sex roles. Because more than 90 per cent of human history has been lived in hunting and gathering societies, human evolution has pressed toward sexual dimorphism along lines appropriate to such societies. This means that reproductive success favored females skillful in bearing and rearing their young, in small-game hunting, and in food gathering, and males skillful in large-game hunting and defense. The physiological equipment we bring to our present complex societies is adapted to quite different circumstances.

While family systems vary enormously in the relationship of the adult male to his offspring and in the extensiveness of the social support system in which the mother and infant live, little or no cultural variation can be found in the physical proximity and emotional closeness of the mother and the infant in the early months following birth. Indeed, until relatively recent times, breast feeding assured close physical and emotional ties between women and their offspring for several years after birth. Modern obstetrical management of pregnancy and birth was examined as a technological intervention in that natural process, an aberration in human history which may be impairing the most important relationship in human society.

A biosocial perspective on parenting stresses the influence of physiological factors on women as a consequence of hormonal cyclicity, pregnancy, and birth. It cautions against the view that equity of affect between mothers and fathers in their relationship to the very young infant and toddler is easily attainable. Family life and parent education in youth, even when available to both boys and girls, may not be sufficient to override the contribution of pregnancy and birth. Consequently, there may be a biologically based potential for heightened maternal investment in the child, at least through the first months of life, that exceeds the potential for investment by men in fatherhood. Significant residues of greater maternal than paternal attachment may then persist into later stages of the parent-child relationship. We would hazard the prediction that the mother will continue to be emotionally the most important parent figure even for those who grow up in self-consciously androgynous households.

The application of a biosocial perspective to current explorations of marriage and parenthood puts serious questions to the cultural determinism to which the social sciences have long adhered. The sexual and parenting scripts underlying much contemporary literature on the family is one-sided in its stress on the male-female relationship and its virtual ignoring of the birth and rearing of children. An egalitarian ideology in fact involves profound difficulties when applied to child-rearing. Communally reared children, far from being liberated, are often neglected, joyless creatures. Beneath ideologically prescribed sharing of child care among all adult members is often found a delegation of authority by each mother only to other mothers of young children. Men are rarely involved in the care of the very young; as in more conventional families, the male is more apt to deal only with older children.

A final theme in the paper concerned the social deprivation of both women and children in the isolated contemporary household: women are deprived of the social support system of other women, which in the past helped to lighten the burdens associated with rearing very young children, and children are deprived of easy access to peers and adults other than their parents during the important early years of growth and development. It is likely that child-growth centers can become a means of compensating for the isolation of children that results from the residential and work patterns typical of urban industrial society. At the same time, in recent years, we have seen too many social programs end up crippled by inadequate funding, bureaucratic red tape, and corruption to advocate putting all our energies into child-care institutions. Smaller groups of cooperating couples or women heading their own households may in the end provide more suitable social-support groups for both parents and children.

This paper brings up many important questions for future investigation, debate, and policy formation. It may also rankle those who hold ideological positions concerning sex equality that accept the present structure of work in industrial societies and urge an identical, equal participation of women and men in the workplace, in home maintenance, and in child-rearing that is modeled on the male pattern of great emphasis on work and little emphasis on family and home. It may be more acceptable to those who question the desirability of a work-dominated life and to those who see both strength and meaning in the family support, community-building, and institutional innovation in which women have been for so long engaged. There will be those who see in this analysis a conservative justification for the status quo, for traditional family and work roles for men and women, but that is a risk one takes to reach those who will see a more radical vision in the analysis: a society more attuned to the natural environment, in touch with, and respectful of, the rhythm of our own body processes, that asks how we can have a balanced life with commitment both to achievement in work and intimate involvement with other human beings. In my judgment, by far the wiser course to such a future is to plan and build from the most fundamental root of society in human parenting, and not from the shaky superstructure created by men in that fraction of time in which industrial societies have existed.*

*The author wishes to express gratitude to the Ford Foundation for a Faculty Research Fellowship (1976) and to the University of Massachusetts for a Biomedical Sciences Support Grant (RR07048 [1975]), which supported part of the work associated with this paper. The author is particularly indebted to Charles Doering, Anke A. Ehrhardt, and Bruce McEwen for their extremely helpful comments on an earlier draft of the endocrinology section. Parts of the paper draw upon my unpublished presidential address to the Eastern Sociological Society, "The Missing Body in Sociology," Philadelphia, April, 1974.

REFERENCES

[1] See, for example, M. B. Sussman and L. Burchinal, "Kin Family Network: Unheralded Structure in Current Conceptualizations of Family Functioning," *Marriage and Family Living*, 24 (1962), pp. 231-40.

[2] T. Dobzhansky, "The Pattern of Human Evolution," in J. Rolansky, ed., *The Uniqueness of Man* (Amsterdam, 1969), p. 45.

[3] A. S. Rossi, "Equality between the Sexes: An Immodest Proposal," *Daedalus*, 93:2 (Spring, 1964), pp. 607-52.

[4] S. L. Washburn and E. R. McCown, "Evolution of Human Behavior," *Social Biology*, 19 (1972), pp. 163-70; and S. L. Washburn and P. Dolhinow, eds., *Perspectives on Human Evolution*, 3 (New York, 1976).

[5] B. A. Hamburg, "The Psychobiology of Sex Differences: An Evolutionary Perspective," in R. C. Friedman, R. M. Richart, and R. L. Vande Wiele, eds., *Sex Differences in Behavior* (New York, 1974), pp. 373-92; and B. A. Hamburg, "The Biosocial Bases of Sex Differences," in S. L. Washburn and P. Dolhinow (cited above, note 4).

[6] R. B. Lee, "Subsistence Ecology of !Kung Bushmen," (Ph.D. dissertation, University of California, 1965); R. B. Lee and I. DeVore, eds., *Man the Hunter* (Chicago, 1968), pp. 30-48; and R. B. Lee and I. DeVore, eds., *Kalahari Hunter-Gatherers* (Cambridge, Mass., 1976).

[7] See A. Ros and G. G. Simpson, eds., *Behavior and Evolution* (New Haven, 1958). For an interesting and important analysis of sex-linked differences in adaptation during the transition of ape populations from dense forest to open savanna and their implications for early hominid sex differences, see N. Tanner and A. Zihlman, "Women in Evolution. Part I: Innovation and Selection in Human Origins," *Signs: Journal of Women in Culture and Society*, 1:3, part 1 (Spring, 1976), pp. 585-608.

[8] D. Hamburg, "Emotions in the Perspective of Human Evolution," in P. H. Knapp, ed., *Expression of Emotion in Man* (New York, 1963), pp. 300-17; and B. A. Hamburg (cited above, note 5).

[9] See E. W. Count, *Being and Becoming Human: Essays on the Biogram* (New York, 1973). In recent years, more men are participating with their wives in prenatal training for natural childbirth and, with a lowering of the birth rate, more obstetricians and hospital administrators are willing to cooperate in their desire to participate at the birth. The critical comparison that we need in order to trace the physiological advantage women have over men in parental attachment is that of child attachment between the sexes among couples with such prenatal preparation and birth sharing compared to couples with more conventional, obstetrically managed, pregnancies and births.

[10] N. Blurton-Jones, ed., *Ethological Studies of Child Behavior* (Cambridge, 1972).

[11] From this perspective, the eighteenth- and nineteenth-century pattern in the English upper class of sending infants to be wet-nursed by rural women was an extreme aberration in human history. More common exceptions would be feeding by other women as a result of illness, death, or nursing inadequacy of the biological mother.

[12] R. B. Lee and I. DeVore (cited above, note 6).

[13] This is an overestimate for two reasons: first, first-borns are more apt to be breast-fed than later-borns, and second, the figures include "any" effort at breast-feeding, which means the low 25 per cent includes women who nursed their babies for only a few days or weeks, or supplemented nursing with bottle-feeding from birth on. See C. Hirschman and J. A. Sweet, "Social Background and Breastfeeding among American Mothers," *Social Biology*, 21 (1974), pp. 39-57. Personal observations and informal discussion with pediatricians suggest some increase in breast-feeding among well-educated women in the nineteen-seventies, but it is not yet known how extensive this is on a national level.

[14] This is obviously subject to cultural and climatic conditions: it takes a warm climate and positive views toward skin contact before high physical contact between mothers and infants will take place. A Bushman mother in Africa clearly has greater opportunity for body contact with her infant than an Eskimo mother has. On the other hand, a society that defines human perspiration as unpleasant may minimize skin contact between mothers and infants even when climatic conditions favor it. We suspect American mothers have very little more body contact with infants in summer than winter, or in southern Florida than in northern Maine.

[15] See R. B. Lee and I. DeVore (cited above, note 6). The high frequency of thumb-sucking among American babies and toddlers and the continued high level of orality among adults may be linked not only to the lower levels of sucking gratification implicit in bottle-feeding compared to breast-feeding, but to a more general deprivation of sensual physical contact. Contemporary infants experience situations unprecedented in the evolution of the species, including separate sleeping quarters, being left in the care of comparative strangers, being fed by bottle, and being limited to a low level of skin contact with their mothers. The author is indebted to Jane Lancaster (Delta Regional Primate Center, New Orleans, Louisiana) for these latter observations (personal communication, 1976). There has been little attention paid to the importance of skin contact; a notable exception is A. Montagu, *Touching: The Human Significance of Skin* (New York, 1971).

[16]See A. V. Nalbandov, *Reproductive Physiology* (San Francisco, 1964), and N. Newton, "Psychologic Aspects of Lactation," *New England Journal of Medicine*, 277 (1967), pp. 4-12.

[17]M. H. Klaus, J. H. Kennell, N. Plumb, and S. Zuehike, "Human Maternal Behavior at First Contact with her Young," *Pediatrics*, 46:2 (1970), pp. 187-92; and M. H. Klaus, R. Jerauld, N. Kreger *et al.*, "Maternal Attachment," *New England Journal of Medicine*, 286:9 (1972), pp. 460-63.

[18]D. Stern, "Mother and Infant at Play: The Dyadic Interaction Involving Facial, Vocal, and Gaze Behavior," in H. Lewis and L. Rosenblum, eds., *The Effect of the Infant on Its Caregiver* (New York, 1974), pp. 187-213.

[19]A. D. Leifer, "Effects of Early, Temporary Mother-Infant Separation on Later Maternal Behavior in Humans" (Ph.D. dissertation, Stanford University, 1970). This is not to argue that there is no learned component in these examples, for clearly there is. Early physical contact in the Leifer study, for example, can be viewed as one aspect of learning how to relate to the infant. The intent is only to suggest that there are innate factors in the total blend of maternal and infant behavior as a corrective to the exclusive environmentalism that too often characterizes social-science thinking and the literature on child development. Not only have they focused exclusively on the influence of the mother on the child to the neglect of the influence of the child on the mother, but the characteristics they single out have tended to be exclusively social and psychological. The first research, that by M. Lewis and L. Rosenblum on the influence of personality characteristics in the infant and young child upon the mother, was not published until 1974. So too, child abuse was thought to be caused purely by parental frustration and personality disturbance until recently it was realized that typically only one child in a family is abused, and that some children removed from their families continued to be abused in successive foster homes where no children had ever been abused before them. See D. G. Gil, *Violence Against Children* (Cambridge, 1970). Gil's review found excessive fussing, strange and irritating crying, and other exasperating behaviors were often reported for such children, and that they elicited negative reactions not only in the parents, but also in foster parents, social workers, and, in one study, the researchers themselves. In other words, the child's characteristics, including constitutional factors, can elicit abuse quite independently from the parents' psychological characteristics or their treatment of the child. In a more normal range, Robson and Moss found that attachment of mothers to their babies weakened by the end of the third month if the baby's crying and fussing did not decrease according to the pattern of most infants by that age. See K. S. Robson and H. A. Moss, "Patterns and Determinants of Maternal Attachment," *Journal of Pediatrics*, 77 (1970), pp. 976-85.

[20]S. Goldberg, *The Inevitability of Patriarchy* (New York, 1973); G. F. Gilder, *Sexual Suicide* (New York, 1973), and R. Fox and L. Tiger, *The Imperial Animal* (New York, 1971).

[21]J. Conway, "Stereotypes of Femininity in a Theory of Sexual Evolution," in M. Vicinus, ed., *Suffer and Be Still: Women in the Victorian Age* (Bloomington, 1973), pp. 140-54.

[22]*Ibid.*, p. 144.

[23]A. Blackwell, "Sex and Evolution," in A. S. Rossi, ed., *The Feminist Papers: From Adams to DeBeauvoir* (New York, 1973), pp. 356-77.

[24]S. Firestone, *The Dialectic of Sex: The Case for Feminist Revolution* (New York, 1970).

[25]An excellent recent review of this literature is by H. Persky, "Reproductive Hormones, Moods, and the Menstrual Cycle," in R. C. Friedman *et al.* (cited above, note 5).

[26]In fact, for many years endocrinologists held to the definition of a gland as an organ that transformed an input hormonal stimulus into an output hormonal response. In keeping with this, they demanded three types of experimental data to prove that an organ functioned as a gland: (1) an *ablation* experiment, in which the removal of the organ led to characteristic changes in the activity of other organs; (2) a *substitution* experiment, in which an extract of the missing organ returned the body to normal functioning; and (3) a *transplantation* experiment, in which the organ continued to play its role in the feedback system after transplant from its original site in the body to another (this was not universally true; it applies to the ovaries, less so for the testes, since the production of testosterone is sensitive to temperature, but not to the pituitary which has to remain somewhere in the *cella tursica*). Thus, if the testes of a cat were removed, cutting off the major source of testosterone, predictable changes would develop in the animal's appearance and behavior; if testosterone was injected into the castrated cat, the animal would resume normal male behavior; and if the testes were transplanted to the chest, so long as good access was present to the bloodstream, normal functioning would resume. See R. J. Wurtman, J. Axelrod, and D. E. Kelley, *The Pineal* (New York, 1968).

[27]Seen against the female menstrual cycle, this internal system involves a gradual rise of estrogen secretion during the first half or follicular phase of the cycle, a temporary drop as ovulation takes place, a secondary surge of estrogen secretion together with a sharp rise in progesterone secretion in the luteal phase, and a final decline of both hormones in the premenstrual phase preceding the onset of the menstrual flow. See A. V. Nalbandov (cited above, note 16); and R. C. Friedman *et al.* (cited above, note 5).

[28]G. W. Harris, *Neural Control of the Pituitary Gland* (London, 1955).

[29]Thus when a pituitary from a male animal was transplanted to a female animal, there was a

remarkable adaptation in which the male pituitary (which is not cyclic) changed its pace and released gonadotropins in a way that supported the normal ovulatory cycles of the female host. This suggested that the pituitary received signals from the hypothalamus which indicated whether it should function as a male or female pituitary, hence determining what hormones it would secrete in what amounts and when.

[30]How or why or even whether this is a firm finding is not yet established, but the direction of causal interpretation has been challenged by new theories in endocrinology. In this, as in many other areas of research, the relationship between hormones and behavior is now assumed to be interactive.

[31]There has been a recent upsurge of interest in the role of pheromones as attractants between individuals of a species, typically involving cues of scent. Although olfaction is clearly of greater importance in cross-sex attraction among monkeys than it is among men, it may find its reflection in our cultural tendency to deny, cover up, and deodorize body scent that restricts our awareness of the role of odor in human attraction and repulsion, both within and across sex lines.

[32]A. H. Sopchak and A. M. Sutherland, "Psychological Impact of Cancer and Its Treatment, VII: Exogenous Sex Hormones and their Relation to Life-Long Adaptations in Women with Metastatic Cancer of the Breast," *Cancer*, 5 (1960), pp. 857-72.

[33]S. E. Waxenberg, "Psychotherapeutic and Dynamic Implications of Recent Research on Female Sexual Functioning," in G. D. Goldman and D. S. Milman, eds., *Modern Woman: Her Psychology and Sexuality* (Springfield, Illinois, 1969), pp. 3-24.

[34]See C. Young, R. W. Goy, and C. H. Phoenix, "Hormones and Sex Behavior," *Science*, January 17, 1964, pp. 212-18. Some researchers have suggested that because males in utero are exposed to high levels of maternal estrogens, while females in utero have no exposure to androgens, this may account for the greater sensitivity of females than males to androgens. The important point here is that some caution must be exercised before any easy extrapolation is made from sex-linked hormonal-secretion levels to the complex social behaviors that interest social scientists.

[35]J. M. Reinisch, "Fetal Hormones, the Brain, and Human Sex Differences: A Heuristic, Integrative Review of the Recent Literature," *Archives of Sexual Behavior*, 3:1 (1974), pp. 51-90.

[36]It has been shown, for example, that if the testes of a newborn male rat are removed, his brain retains a female pattern of differentiation. Even if treated in adulthood with testosterone, he shows poor male sex behavior (mounting), while if given estradiol, he will show strong female sex behavior (lordosis, arching of the head and rump with genital presentation). What happens in the critical phase of development is permanent, suggesting that testosterone influences neuron development and synaptic contact with other neurons. Bruce McEwen reports current research on the effects of estradial on sexual differentiation in the rat brain, e.g., that newborn rat brains have enzymes which convert testosterone to estradial. Research is now pursuing the possibility that estrogen receptors in the brain actually mediate sexual differentiation. The author is grateful for the opportunity to read McEwen's review of this research in manuscript.

[37]J. Money and A. A. Ehrhardt, *Man and Woman, Boy and Girl* (Baltimore, 1972).

[38]A counterpart syndrome among genetic females with internal female organs but masculinized external genitalia is the result of their mothers having taken diethylstilbestrol, which has an androgenic effect, to prevent miscarriage during early pregnancy. This syndrome poses the same problem: clearly these individuals, if defined as male at birth, develop a male gender identity, or, if surgically corrected to appear female, they develop female gender identities. But in the latter case, Ehrhardt suggests some departures from "typical" profiles of females, including much less interest in "girlish" activities, less responsiveness to young infants, and a greater preference for older children. See A. A. Ehrhardt, R. Epstein and J. Money, "Fetal Androgens and Female Gender Identity in the Early-Treated Adrenogenital Syndrome," *Johns Hopkins Medical Journal*, 122 (1968), pp. 160-67.

[39]J. Money, ed., *Sex Research: New Developments* (New York, 1965), p. 139.

[40]B. E. Cogswell and M. B. Sussman, "Changing Family and Marriage Forms: Complications for Human Service Systems," *The Family Coordinator*, 21:4 (1972), pp. 505-16.

[41]*Ibid.*, p. 507.

[42]J. R. Smith and L. G. Smith, eds., *Beyond Monogamy: Recent Studies in Sexual Alternatives in Marriage* (Baltimore, 1974).

[43]B. E. Cogswell, "Variant Family Forms and Life Styles: Rejection of the Traditional Nuclear Family," *The Family Coordinator*, 24:4 (1975), p. 401.

[44]J. Lorber, "Beyond Equality of the Sexes: The Question of the Children," *The Family Coordinator*, 24:4 (1975), p. 465.

[45]A recent example of this large gender difference was found in the attitudes of freshmen entering college in the fall of 1975: two-thirds of the male, but only one-third of the female, freshmen in this national sample agreed with the view that sex was all right even if the couple have known each other only a very short time. See American Council on Education, *The American Freshman: National Norms for Fall 1975* (Washington, D.C., 1976). In a study by Sorensen of 13- to 19-year-old adolescents, two-thirds of the males but only one-fifth of the females thought sex was "all right with some-

one known only for a few hours." See P. Sorensen, *Adolescent Sexuality in Contemporary America* (New York, 1973).

[46]J. R. Smith and L. G. Smith (cited above, note 42).

[47]*Ibid.*, p. 38.

[48]R. Thamm, *Beyond Marriage and the Nuclear Family* (San Francisco, 1975), p. 124.

[49]R. M. Kanter, D. Jaffe, and D. K. Weisberg, "Coupling, Parenting and the Presence of Others: Intimate Relationships in Communal Households," *The Family Coordinator*, 24:4 (1975), pp. 433-52.

[50]*Ibid.*, p. 447.

[51]B. Berger, B. Hackett, and R. M. Millar, "The Communal Family," *The Family Coordinator*, 21:4 (1972), pp. 419-28.

[52]*Ibid.*, p. 422.

[53]*Ibid.*, p. 427.

[54]J. Rothchild and S. B. Wolf, *The Children of the Counterculture* (New York, 1976).

[55]Rather than a variant family form to replace the nuclear family in the future, it may be that the phenomenon of communal households will eventually develop into a form of half-way house between leave-taking from the parental home in late adolescence and the final establishment of a family with the birth of a child. Marciano sees communes as analogous to monastic retreat houses—places for renewal, self-integration, and new experiences during a phase of life—rather than as a permanent pattern for most adults. See T. D. Marciano, "Variant Family Forms in a World Perspective," *The Family Coordinator*, 24:4 (1975), pp. 407-20. The emergence of the pattern itself may be a function not simply of the "alternate culture" of the nineteen-sixties but also of changes in the role-set sequence of late adolescence. Prolonged education and residential segregation on campuses mean a long period of exposure exclusively to peers and the encouragement of egocentrism in the absence of adult responsibilities. This pattern may have contributed to the development of the communal residence as an intermediary between the completion of school and the assumption of adult responsibilities. It may also reflect the demographic composition of young people in college in the sixties and seventies, since these cohorts were born in the late forties and fifties, when the number of children in American families was relatively high, and these cohorts therefore contain a much larger proportion of middle- and later-born children than did previous cohorts. The more social, gregarious characteristics associated with middle- and last-born birth-order positions may have contributed to the attractions of communal living. This possibility could be checked by ascertaining the birth-order distribution of communal residents compared to non-communal control samples of comparable age-sex groups in the population.

[56]For example, Norman Mailer has a fantasy of sperm slung across a "few inches of eternity—his measure, his meaning, his vision of a future male." See N. Mailer, *The Prisoner of Sex* (Boston, 1971), pp. 197-98.

[57]D. M. Rorvik, *Brave New Baby: Promise and Peril of the Biological Revolution* (New York, 1971).

[58]A. V. Nalbandov (cited above, note 16), pp. 106-7; 225-26.

[59]It is interesting to note that the amount of oxytocin released increases with the increased sexual excitation in the female and is greater still if female orgasm is attained. It is also the case that uterine contractility is greater during the follicular and ovulatory phases than it is during the luteal phase of the menstrual cycle. See R. Berde, *Recent Progress in Oxytocin Research* (Springfield, Illinois, 1959).

[60]This makes very dubious the theory that the smaller-headed, long-tailed Y sperm is apt to reach and penetrate the ovum before the heavier X female sperm, as Shettles and McCary have argued in suggesting procedures for determining the sex of the child or accounting for the very high sex ratio at conception. See D. M. Rorvik (cited above, note 57); and J. L. McCary, *Human Sexuality* (New York, 1967). A period of capacitation prior to penetration makes less important the speed with which sperm reaches the oviducts.

[61]R. Berde (cited above, note 59).

[62]M. M. Sherfey, "The Evolution and Nature of Female Sexuality in Relation to Psychoanalytic Theory," *Journal of the American Psychoanalytic Association*, 14:1 (1966), pp. 28-128.

[63]Provide a woman with a rocking chair, and the far-away look of pleasure one often sees among nursing mothers is much closer to the sensual Eve than to the saintly Mary. Many American women never experience this fusion, however: persuaded by their culture to share men's dissociation of sexuality from maternalism, they may react negatively to the sensual component of nursing and give it up very early on. Yet a culturally permissible association between sexuality and lactation stimulates maternal milk supply, as shown by Campbell and Petersen's finding of a positive correlation between the amount of milk ejected and the degree of sexual arousal. B. Campbell and W. E. Petersen, "Milk Let-Down and Orgasm in the Human Female," *Human Biology*, 25 (1953), pp. 165-68.

[64]E. E. Grimm, "Women's Attitudes and Reactions to Childbearing," in G. D. Goldman and D. S. Milman (cited above, note 33), pp. 129-51.

[65]N. Newton, "Interrelationships between Sexual Responsiveness, Birth and Breast Feeding," in J. Zubin and J. Money, eds., *Contemporary Sexual Behavior* (Baltimore, 1973), pp. 77-98.

[66]M. Mead and N. Newton, "Cultural Patterning of Perinatal Behavior," in S. A. Richardson and A. F. Guttmacher, eds., *Childbearing: Its Social and Psychological Aspects* (Baltimore, 1967); and N. Newton, (cited above, note 65).

[67]By contrast, the relations of divorced men to their children suggests much less close emotional bonds. Hetherington reports an initial post-divorce increase in contact between fathers and their children, but by a year or so later, the contact declines and the father-child relationship is about what it was before the divorce. E. M. Hetherington, M. Cox, and R. Cox, "Beyond Father Absence: Conceptualization of Effects of Divorce" (unpublished paper, 1975). This does not mean, however, that change is not taking place. Under the influence both of desire and of pressure from their wives, many young men are attempting to establish closer emotional and social ties to their young children. Should these marriages fail, the fathers may continue to show closer ties with their children than previous cohorts of divorced men. Indeed, there are growing numbers of divorces in which child custody is granted to the fathers. How extensive this pattern will become in the future and whether paternal investment and attachment to children will approximate that of maternal attachment are open questions at this point. The author's prediction is that the gap may narrow, but not close, unless males receive compensatory training for parenthood far in excess of anything now envisaged.

[68]See S. Arms, *Immaculate Deception: A New Look at Women and Childbirth in America* (Boston, 1975); D. Haire, "The Cultural Warping of Childbirth," *I.C.E.A. News* (Milwaukee, 1972); and N. Newton, "Emotions of Pregnancy," *Clinical Obstetrics and Gynecology*, 6:3 (1963), pp. 639-68.

[69]M. H. Klaus *et al.* (cited above, note 17).

[70]J. H. Kennell in a discussion of early human interaction at the Third Annual Conference on Psychosomatic Obstetrics and Gynecology, Philadelphia, 1975, cited in M. A. Parlee, "Psychological Aspects of Menstruation, Childbirth, and Menopause: An Overview with Suggestions for Further Research," paper given at a conference on New Directions for Research on Women, Madison, Wisconsin, May 31-June 2, 1975 (mimeographed).

[71]C. Kaufman and L. A. Rosenblum, "The Reaction to Separation in Infant Monkeys: Anaclitic Depression and Conservation-Withdrawal," *Psychosomatic Medicine*, 29:6 (1967), pp. 648-75.

[72]Apgar scores are 10-point scores based on the skin color, breathing/crying, activity, and pulse of the infant at birth.

[73]D. Haire (cited above, note 73).

[74]V. Larsen, "Stresses of the Childbearing Years," *American Journal of Public Health*, 56 (1966), pp. 32-36. Unique for its time, Larsen asked women directly about the stresses they experienced in connection with pregnancy and birth. She reports that a large percentage of the stress and difficulty women remember in connection with birth had to do with hospital routines, the delivery itself, and the restrictions imposed on them during their hospital stay.

[75]M. Ferin, F. Halberg, M. Richart, and R. L. Vande Wiele, *Biorhythms and Human Reproduction* (New York, 1974).

[76]H. Persky, in Friedman (cited above, note 5).

[77]There is some evidence from animal research that this is a fruitful area to explore. See J. Terkel and J. S. Rosenblatt, "Maternal Behavior Induced by Maternal Blood Plasma Injected into Virgin Rats," *Journal of Comparative and Physiological Psychology*, 65 (1968), pp. 479-82. Terkel and Rosenblatt found a factor in the blood of rats within forty-eight hours after birth which, when given to virgin rats, quickly stimulated maternal behavior. Animals treated with estradiol, progesterone, and prolactin become responsive to pups by the second day after receiving the hormones. See H. Moltz, M. Lubin, M. Leon, and M. Numan, "Hormonal Induction of Maternal Behavior in the Ovariectomized Rat," *Physiology and Behavior*, 5 (1970), pp. 1373-77. The capacity for maternal-response behavior may well be present without these added boosts of hormones, but the endocrines do seem to activate, or speed up the activation of, maternal behavior. Since the extraordinarily high levels of hormonal secretion during pregnancy drop very quickly after birth, they may play a role in intensely activating maternal behavior only if the infant is seen, held, and nursed very shortly after birth, something typical obstetric practice in American hospital settings rarely permits, even in natural-childbirth cases.

[78]M. A. Parlee (cited above, note 70).

[79]A. S. Rossi, "Transition to Parenthood," *Journal of Marriage and Family*, 30:1 (1968), pp. 26-39.

[80]M. B. Cohen, "Personal Identity and Sexual Identity," *Psychiatry*, 29:1 (1966), pp. 1-14.

[81]In their research among the !Kung Bushmen in Africa, Lee and Devore (cited above, note 15) have shown the critical role played by diet and breast-feeding patterns for change in fertility rates. Among nomadic Bushmen, an average birth spacing of 3.8 years is a consequence of unusually active lives among women, coupled with a low sugar and carbohydrate diet; together with breast-feeding, this profile does not permit the critical volume of fat to be regained for about three years after a baby is born. Such lactation-related infertility does not work very well among sedentary Bushmen because their enriched diets lead to faster fat gain, with the result that birth spacing drops to every two years, i.e., very like settled agriculturalists in peasant societies. In innumerable African so-

cieties today, the real threat of both population excess and impoverishment of health among babies is the adaptation of the Western pattern of bottle-feeding babies and the changed content of maternal diets. See D. Dumont, "The Limitations of Human Population: A Natural History," *Science*, 187 (February 28, 1975), pp. 713-21.

[82]Perez and his associates investigated the relationship between breast-feeding and first ovulation after childbirth. They found some postponement of ovulation when women nursed their infants with no supplementary feeding for the first nine postpartum weeks, but thereafter the chances of ovulation increased despite the continuation of full nursing. See A. Perez, P. Vela, G. S. Masnick and R. G. Potter, "First Ovulation after Childbirth: The Effect of Breastfeeding," *American Journal of Obstetrics and Gynecology*, 144:8 (1972), pp. 1041-47. Masnick has warned that adequate research on the relationship between nursing and the resumption of ovulation is yet to be done. G. S. Masnick, "Biosocial Aspects of Breastfeeding," A.A.A.S. Symposium, Boston, February 18-24, 1976 (mimeographed).

[83]J. Lancaster, personal communication.

[84]Although there has been a great deal of research on family size, there has been little on the effect of child spacing on maternal psychological health, the quality of parent-child relations, or the impact on the parental marriage, particularly with adequate controls to exclude the impact of choice and accident in closely timed births, long-term goals of the parents, etc. For examples of research and thinking about the impact of close child-spacing, see J. D. Wray, "Population Pressure on Families: Family Size and Child Spacing," in National Academy of Sciences, *Rapid Population Growth* (Baltimore, 1971), pp. 403-61; and H. T. Christensen, "Children in the Family: The Relationship of Number and Spacing to Marital Success," *Journal of Marriage and Family*, 30 (1968), pp. 283-89. Clausen reports that in the longitudinal data at the Institute of Human Development in California, mothers with three or more children closely spaced recalled the early years of their motherhood as a period of extreme exhaustion and discouragement. See J. A. Clausen and S. R. Clausen, "The Effects of Family Size on Parents and Children," in J. T. Fawcett, ed., *Psychological Perspectives on Population* (New York, 1972).

[85]American Civil Liberties Union, *Civil Liberties*, 310 (January, 1976), p. 1.

[86]V. Hunt, "Reproduction and Work," *Signs: Journal of Women in Culture and Society*, 1:2 (1975), pp. 543-52.

[87]A. J. Ferreira, "The Pregnant Woman's Emotional Attitude and Its Reflection on the Newborn," *Journal of Orthopsychiatry*, 30 (1960), pp. 553-61.

[88]Most children of employed women continue to be cared for in private homes, either their own or someone else's, and by relatives more often than by non-relatives. Among the relatives the husband tops the list, followed by the child's grandmother, older sibling, or aunt. A survey of day-care facilities in 1970 found that only 1.3 million children of working women are supervised in either licensed or unlicensed facilities. See Westinghouse Learning Corporation-Westat Research Inc., *Day Care Survey, 1970: Summary Report and Basic Analysis* (Washington, D.C., 1971). This is a small number of children provided for, but it is in fact a doubling of the total licensed day-care facilities by 1973 compared with a comprehensive child-care survey in 1965. See Women's Bureau, *Child Care Arrangements of Working Mothers in the United States*, U.S. Department of Labor, Children's Bureau Publication No. 461 (Washington, D.C., United States Printing Office, 1968).

[89]V. Kerr, "One Step Forward—Two Steps Back: Child Care's Long American History," in P. Roby, ed., *Child Care—Who Cares: Foreign and Domestic Infant and Early Childhood Development Policies* (New York, 1973), pp. 151-71.

[90]B. Caldwell, "Infant Day Care—The Outcast Gains Respectability," *ibid.*, pp. 20-36.

[91]It should be noted that, in recent years, there has been a drift in East European countries away from day-care centers for children less than three years old. Not only is such care extremely expensive—the younger the child is, the more costly its care—but there have been rumblings that all is not well in terms of the very young child's welfare in such group-care institutions. Some Czechoslovak researchers have suggested that the under-three child's nervous system can not take the noise and bustle of being with others his own age all day. After a lively national debate on this issue, the Czechs have moved away from group care for the youngest age group toward foster care in private homes and long-leave policies for employed mothers. See H. Scott, *Does Socialism Liberate Women? Experiences from Eastern Europe* (Boston, 1974). In Tiger and Shepher's recent book on the kibbutz, it is difficult to get behind the authors' gleeful pouncing on any shred that can be taken as evidence of renewed familism among kibbutz women in order to tell if they have any evidence that the youngest children in the kibbutz fare less well in children's houses than do older children. The authors merely report the mothers' desires for more contact with their children, without specifying the age of the children to which they are referring. See L. Tiger and J. Shepher, *Women in the Kibbutz* (New York, 1975).

JEROME KAGAN

The Child in the Family

SCHOLARS HAVE A FETISH for positing hypothetical entities, assuming their reality, and spending too long a time debating their definition. Social scientists today debate the meaning of "morality," "emotion," "intelligence," and "family," just as physical scientists in the past quarreled over the nature of aether and phlogiston. The physical sciences find it a little easier to relinquish devotion to specific essences because they are able to gather empirical data that are sufficiently persuasive to reveal the inaccuracies of their original conceptions. The less potent social sciences are burdened with too many crusty words that over time have come to have a life of their own—floating free of reality in hallowed halls that seem inviolate. Social scientists spend too much time arguing over the preferred definition of an entity and too little time seeking the functional relations among the relevant events, for the entity is merely an abstraction that holds the realities in a coherent relation to one another.

Since social scientists probe dynamic processes, they are disposed to orient toward the future and to find the hidden functions of their intellectual inventions. Unfortunately, they frequently assume that there is one "best" function to be discovered, rather than acknowledge that "purpose" depends upon the perspective of the target. In *The Eternal Smile*, Lagerquist has God reply to an interrogator, who asks "What purpose did you have in mind when you created man?," with "I only intended that man would never be satisfied with nothing."

These problems of definition and inferred function plague any discussion that deals with the family. Inquiring into the purposes of the family is not unlike asking about the purposes of a poem. The answer depends on the position of the respondent, whether poet, professor, publisher, or critic. In both modern and less modern communities, the functions of the family depend upon the perspective taken—that of the state, husband, wife, or child.

The Functions of the Family

The state's perspective: Most government officials in America—elected or appointed—believe that the family, not the state, is the preferable unit for nurturing and socializing the child because they assume that most families try to do the best they can for their children and because it is more economical for the state if the family has this responsibility. The state will be both less efficient and less benevolent. A second purpose of the family is thought to be that it keeps employment steady. Husbands and wives will retain their jobs with the same

33

employers for long periods of time because they feel responsible for the family's economic welfare. If they do not have that responsibility, they might be more prone to occupational mobility and erratic patterns of employment.

The parents' perspective: From the perspective of the parents, the family offers a different set of resources. It can be a locus of solace and psychic relief—a space where anger, depression, and despair are permitted more open expression than they are outside the walls of the home. In what is seen to be an increasingly impersonal and mutually suspicious environment, the family provides each adult with an opportunity to feel needed and useful. The family provides conditions that invite its adult members to serve and to minister to a mission that transcends the self—the opportunity to beget and raise a child. Adults, like children, are naturally disposed to exploit their basic abilities. The child walks when he has the necessary physical coordination, talks when his temporal lobe has sufficiently matured. Nature has awarded the adult, especially the mother, a unique capability: although not all women are curious to exploit that talent, most are eager to test their effectiveness as a sculptor of new life.

Raising children has another psychological benefit: It offers parents an opportunity to validate the value system they brought to adulthood. Sometimes it is similar to the one they took from their families two decades earlier, sometimes it is a radical transformation, struck from intense childhood pain and carried to adulthood in a vow not to visit upon the next generation the destructive practices and philosophies that scarred their lives. Each parent has a chance to promote a hard-won set of ethics and to test the utility of standards that took many years to create. In a sense, each parent is a scientist testing a personal theory of human development with each child.

The child's perspective: The intent of this essay is to examine the family from the child's perspective; there the family participates directly in at least three basic processes. It provides the first targets for identification and attachment, and it disseminates information regarding the profile of actions, appearances, and thoughts that the child must command if he is to attain a sense of virtue and competence. These are intrafamilial processes, the effects of which are mediated by direct psychological contact between the child and other family members. But each family is not just a continuing set of human interactions; it is also a structure, defined in part by the number and functions of its members and embedded in a larger network. In societies stratified by class, as ours is, the family's socioeconomic position exerts a profound influence on many aspects of the child's development.

The text of this paper follows a simple plan. We shall first consider the intrafamilial mechanisms of identification and attachment, and then the ways in which the child extracts information regarding his value and talent. Next we shall summarize some of the developmental correlates of class membership, and, finally, deal with the intriguing consequences of one aspect of family structure—namely, the child's ordinal position.

The Family as a Model for Identification

During the first half of their second year, children acquire a sense of the symbolic. An indication of this new competence is usually seen in their play with toys. Now, but not six months earlier, a little girl will treat a piece of clay as if it were a cookie and pour imaginary tea from a small teapot into an even smaller cup. This new capacity, which is soon amplified by language, leads the child to apply symbolic labels, many of which have a strong evaluative connotation, to herself and others. Children learn the language categories for age and sex, come to appreciate that they have the same last name as the rest of the family, and realize that they share anatomical and psychological qualities with their parents, especially with the parent of the same sex. It is as natural for the child as it is for the adult to group objects or events that are similar into a common category. Indeed, as early as twelve months of age some American children will treat dolls, toy animals, and foods of different kinds, sizes, shapes, and colors as members of discrete conceptual categories, suggesting that the one-year-old has the capacity to extract invariant attributes from an array of events and create a symbolic home for them.[1]

The process of noting shared qualities among objects is applied to the self and members of the family, and by age 3 or 4 children are likely to believe they are more similar to their parents than to any other adult they know. Young children also believe they share more attributes with the same-sex than with the opposite-sex parent, an understanding that is articulated at the level of metaphor. When they are shown pairs of designs differing in size, hue, or angularity and are asked to select the one that typifies each parent, most boys and girls agree that the father is larger, darker, and more angular than the mother. And young boys regard themselves as larger, darker, and more angular than girls.[2]

Although the belief that one is similar to another is the most important component of identification, the child's evaluation of the parents' desirable and undesirable attributes is a dimension of particular importance. For most young children, the parent is perceived to be physically stronger and psychologically more competent, powerful, and nurturant than the child—regardless of the parents' actual strength or competence vis-à-vis other adults in the community. These attributes are also regarded as desirable by the child. The third ingredient in the process of identification is the child's assumption that if he were to become even more similar to his parents he would be able to share vicariously in the affective consequences of their desirable resources and experiences with greater intensity. He would feel stronger, more competent, and more powerful. The child's belief that he shares basic qualities with a parental model, together with the vicarious sharing of the model's inferred affective states, comprise the formal definition of identification.

During the early school years, the child comes to appreciate—often for the first time—the attributes the wider society values or derogates. The American child realizes that material wealth, a certain pattern of cognitive abilities, and particular vocations are valued; excessive drinking, an unskilled job, a home in disrepair, and an inability to read or write are undesirable, and therefore potential sources of shame and humiliation. That knowledge produces a sharp change in the child's conception both of his parents and of himself, for the insight regarding society's evaluation of his parents is taken as a diagnosis of the self. Hence the family's social class position and the specific psychological characteristics of parents and siblings influence the degree to which the child's conceptualization of himself is positive or negative.

The Family as a Source of Protection and Target of Attachment

The family provides alleviation of distress from the moment of birth, but, as infants approach the second half of the first year, they begin to seek out parents and others who care for them when they are apprehensive or uncomfortable. This disposition to seek proximity to particular people in times of distress has acquired the name "attachment." The major implication of this phenomenon is that only a limited number of people possess the power to allay the infant's distress quickly. Those who hold this power are precisely the ones the infant looks to or moves toward when it is uncomfortable.

A child can be attached to more than one caretaker, and most children have a stable hierarchy of preferences that is tied to the quality of the interaction rather than to its duration. The results of two recent studies support the assertion that the biological parent in the Western nuclear family has a mysterious ability to remain the preferred target of attachment, even for young children who spend a considerable amount of time with substitute caretakers outside the home.

The first of these studies was an investigation of the effect of group care on Chinese and Caucasian children during the first two and a half years of life.[3] One group attended a day-care center in Boston five days a week from age 3½ months through age 30 months. Each child attending the center was matched by ethnicity, social class, and sex with a child being reared at home. When the children were 20 months old, they were placed in an unfamiliar setting with the mother, an unfamiliar woman, and, for the day-care children, the primary day-care teacher, but, for the children raised at home, a friend of the family. During the 45 minutes of observation, the child was deliberately made uncertain on two occasions by having the three adults suddenly exchange seats. All the children—those raised only at home as well as those attending the day-care center—went to their mother for comfort when they were tired, bored, or apprehensive because of the unexpected provocation. There were no important differences between the behavior of the children raised at home and those attending the center. If the child approached anyone at all, it was typically the mother. This does not mean that the day-care children were not attached to their caretakers, for if the mother was absent, as she was when the child was at the center, they sought the primary caretaker.

In a related investigation,[4] Nathan Fox observed children living in infant houses on Israeli kibbutzim. The infants visited the parents' homes for only a few hours each day around the dinner hour, spending the rest of their time in the infant house with a *metapelet*. These children were observed individually in an unfamiliar room on the kibbutz with the mother, an unfamiliar woman, and their *metapelet*. The children were more secure when they were left with the mother and a stranger than they were with the *metapelet* and stranger—as evidenced by the greater amount of time they spent playing, and less time spent hovering near the familiar adult caretaker. Both of these studies imply that the number of hours a child is cared for by an adult is not the critical dimension that produces a strong attachment. There is something special about the mother-infant relationship. The parent appears to be more salient than substitute caretakers to the child. It is not clear why this is so.

One possibility is that the parent is both more affective and more unpredictable with the young child and, hence, is a greater source of uncertainty. A conscientious and sympathetic caretaker of a group of children outside the home is aware both of the psychological diversity among the children under her care and of the differences in values between each parent and herself. As a result, she is unlikely to hold rigid standards for such things as talkativeness, cooperativeness, cleanliness, aggression, quality of play, or the age at which particular developmental milestones should appear. Because she is less profoundly involved with the children than are the parents, she will be more relaxed than they are about these standards. It is neither a source of pleasure if one child is precocious in learning to drink from a cup, nor a source of apprehension if another spills his milk. This tolerance for diversity leads the caretaker to allow each child considerably more latitude than the parent would to behave in accordance with his temperament and relative level of maturity, especially in Western countries. With the exception of extremely destructive or regressed children, the caretaker does not ordinarily impose constraints when the child seems occupied and happy. As a result, the caretaker does not become a source of uncertainty for the child. Finally, group-care settings are typically more routinized than the home, and the actions of caretakers therefore are apt to be more predictable.

By contrast, the typical mother is emotionally involved with her infant, and more likely to display strong affection and to convey emotionally charged messages. In addition, she holds standards by which she judges the child's development, and she watches for deviations from them. One mother may believe that any defiance of her authority is a sign of future rebelliousness, and she quickly reacts to it with disapproval or punishment. Most American mothers hold standards for cleanliness and against destruction of property, physically dangerous acts, and aggression toward others, as well as notions of the proper ages for walking and talking. The mother diagnoses the deviations of the child's developing profile from her idealized standards; when they become too large, she intrudes and attempts to shape behavior so that it conforms more closely to her understanding of what is appropriate. Each intrusion, whether punishment, praise, or command, punctuates the child's behavior and consciousness and creates a temporary state of uncertainty that alerts the child to the mother and to the action the child has just issued. The next time the child is in a similar situation or entertains the possibility of initiating an action associated with prior intrusions, he remembers that intrusion and again experiences uncertainty. Only after parental response to a particular class of actions has been consistently repeated will the child establish a firm expectation, and only then will his uncertainty subside. This line of speculation suggests that the typical mother is a more frequent and distinctive source of uncertainty for her child than the usual surrogate caretaker. The parent is less predictable, more difficult to understand, and a more frequent source of joy and excitement. Psychoanalytic theorists would say that the mother was more highly "cathected" than the caretaker; in the more modern language of cognitive psychology, the mother would be described as more "salient."

The Communication of Information to the Child

The salience of the mother, as revealed in studies of attachment phenomena, raises the more general question of what constitutes psychological information for the child. There is no doubting that parental practices and attitudes, whether viewed as rewards and punishments or simply as communications, influence the child's development. Therefore, we need to determine the relation between what the family members do and say, on the one hand, and the child's representations of what they do and say, on the other. The form of that relation is at present enigmatic.

Conceptualization of the relation between physical energy and psychological sensation was absolute during the latter part of the nineteenth century, when it was assumed that visual sensation was a function of the absolute amount of light energy impinging on the retina. We now know that homogeneous stimulation of the retina results only in a constant experience of illumination that is independent of the wave length and intensity of the physical stimulus.[5] Similarly, if one immerses a finger in a jar of mercury which produces a constant pressure against the skin, there is no perception of pressure on the finger. The recognition of pressure is felt only at the surface, where there is a transition from mercury to air. It is at the transition—at the point of contrast—that one processes information about the physical sensations coming from the two parts of the finger.

The perception of information thus depends on change and contrast. Hence, it is not surprising that a young infant's attention is drawn to visual events that move or have contour contrast and to auditory events that are rhythmic and rich in transitions. Indeed, it is believed that we perceive hunger when blood-sugar level changes rather than at any absolute blood-sugar level. It might be productive to assume that the conceptualization of self and others is monitored by a similar principle. The child may most easily draw psychological conclusions about the quality of self and others when he detects nodes of contrast between himself and someone else, or among others, in either objective or symbolic attributes. This hypothesis assumes that the most effective influences on the child are contained in perceived contrasts.

Consider an example: For a child who is rarely chastised, a sharp rebuke for a new misdemeanor is an important piece of information which should lead to future inhibition of that action. For the child who is continually chastised, rebuke for the same misbehavior would, we suggest, have a minimal effect because the rebuke is not in sufficient contrast to normal parental action and therefore not sufficiently different from the child's adaptation level. The rebuke does not attract much of his attention and hence elicits little or no reflective interpretation.

The attentiveness of a 2-year-old, who is just beginning to impose categories on experience, will be drawn to nodes of contrast between himself and others. He will notice differences in physical size, capacity to coerce, and instrumental competence between himself and his parents. The parents will become salient objects, and the qualities of contrast (size, power, competence) will invite categorization. Since the degree of contrast between self and other children of the same age in these dimensions is minimal, one would expect another child to be a much less salient event, and there is some indirect evidence that this is in fact the case.

The infants attending the day-care center described earlier were in the company of a dozen or so other children their own age five days a week from the age of 3½ months through their second year. Signs of apprehension to an unfamiliar adult typically emerged at about 7 to 8 months of age and peaked at 12 to 13 months. Signs of apprehension to an unfamiliar peer did not emerge until a few months later and did not peak until about 15 to 20 months of age.[6] We regard the apprehension to a stranger at 7 months to be the result of uncertainty over the stranger's actions toward the child and the child's proper reactions toward the stranger. The temporary inability to resolve those sources of uncertainty produces apprehension. We think that apprehension when faced with unfamiliar adults appears a few months earlier than apprehension toward other children, even among infants who are exposed daily to many peers, because attention is not often directed toward children of the same age during the first year of life, and knowledge of peers is less firm during early infancy. This is, in part, because the peer is not a source of strong contrast in size, power, and competence. After the first year, when social interactions with other children become more frequent and seizing property and parallel play emerge, peers generate more contrasts and consequently become important sources of information. Now the child becomes vulnerable to apprehension in the presence of unfamiliar peers.

The effects of the actions of parents on the child may also be better understood if one pauses to ask: What are the background experiences of the child and what will be treated as a signal against that background? The potential utility of this conceptual stance toward social experience is best seen when one contrasts an American family with one from a different culture. We shall take as an example the Utku of Hudson Bay. When a child is 2 or 3, Utku parents begin to inhibit his aggression and anger with a form of silent treatment: they consistently ignore him when he displays these actions. The child thus learns to expect this response to aggression. Since all children are treated this way, the 5-year-old does not witness much aggression in other children, nor, for that matter, among adults. This experience combined with the adult shaming of aggressive behavior is effective, and one rarely sees aggression among children over 4 or 5 years of age.[7] A Western adult may have the impression that such a society is repressing its anger and hostility. Yet none of the theoretically expected symptoms of repression occur. We interpret this to mean that there is no fixed effect of prohibitions on aggression and anger in children. Since the American child is exposed to peers and adults who are occasionally aggressive, he is uncertain about social reactions to, and permissiveness toward, aggression. An American parent who continually punished anger and aggression would probably create symptoms in the child, but only because the punishment was interpreted in a particular context. The American child is in conflict; the Utku child is not.

These special cases lead us to conclude that it may be impossible to state the principles underlying functional relations between specific parental practices and particular behavior in the child, except, perhaps, in the extreme, where consistently harsh physical abuse creates serious physical distress. Although there may be few functional relations between concrete experiences and the child's growth, it is possible that lawful relations exist between the child's conceptualization of experience and his subsequent psychological structures. But those conceptualizations are not tied in a simple way to experience. The categorizations depend on nodes of contrast, ratios, and relations between background experience and the figural present.

The Child's Sense of Virtue

In addition to being a source of identification, a target of attachment, and a haven in times of distress, the family communicates to the child its value or virtue, which in our culture depends to a great extent on the child's belief that he is competent and capable of attracting parental love. Children, like adults, cannot avoid evaluating the self on a dimension of virtue, and their always uncertain decisions are functions of different classes of experience.

One source of information comes from the child's evaluation of how good or bad he believes his actions, thoughts, and motives to be, a judgment based on the congruence between behavior and standards, as well as the evaluative reactions of others toward him. Every child learns standards of actions and thought which the local culture regards as morally proper. Although items on the list will vary with the society, a universal list is likely to contain obedience to parents and the absence of aggression, excessive selfishness, dishonesty, and irresponsibility within the family.

A second component of virtue rests on the child's perception of his value in the eyes of his parents. The young child awards extraordinary wisdom to his parents. If they behave as if he were valuable he takes these actions as evidence of his essential goodness. If they behave as if he were without worth, he begins to question his capacity to be valued by another. Initially, the child does not question his parents' ability to value him, but assumes instead that something about him prevents a positive reaction. It must be noted, of course, that there is no absolute set of parental practices that will inform the child of his value; the child imposes that meaning on his parents' actions.

Some American psychologists have assumed that one specific set of parental behaviors always signifies acceptance or rejection, for there is remarkable agreement among investigators about the maternal behaviors designated as indicative of these parental attitudes.[8] Inflicting harsh physical punishment and lack of social play and affection were typical signs of maternal rejection in these studies, and consequently it would be almost impossible for an American psychologist to categorize a mother as being both aloof and loving at the same time. Alfred Baldwin has reported that in rural areas of northern Norway where farms are separated by many miles, one sees varieties of maternal behavior that an American observer would regard as symptomatic of rejection in an American mother. The Norwegian mother sees her 4-year-old sitting in a doorway blocking the passage to the next room. She does not ask him to move but bends down, picks him up, and silently sets him aside so she can pass through. A middle-class observer would be tempted to view this apparent indifference as indicative of dislike. However, most mothers in this Arctic outpost act that way, and the children do not behave the way rejected children should according to our theoretical propositions.

An uneducated black mother from North Carolina slaps her 4-year-old across the face when he does not come to the table on time. The intensity of the act tempts our observer to conclude that the mother resents her child. However, during a half-hour conversation, the mother indicates her warm feelings for the boy. She hit him because she does not want him to become a "bad boy," and she believes physical punishment is the most effective socialization procedure. Now her behavior seems to be issued in the service of affection rather than hostility.

In the seventeenth century, European and American colonial parents were advised to beat their children in order to tame the evil inherent within them. Otherwise respectable and well-educated parents inflicted severe punishment upon their dependents—punishments that would be classified as extreme abuse today. Samuel Byrd of Virginia, for example, made a dependent of his drink "a pint of piss" because he wet his bed.[9] Then, as now, many children of upper-class English families rarely remained at home with their parents. After birth they were sent to a wet-nurse in a nearby village until weaning, perhaps at two years of age: then they returned home, but briefly, before again being sent out, this time to boarding school. Plumb[10] notes that Sir Robert Walpole (born in 1676) rarely spent more than a few weeks each year in his home between the ages of 6 and 22. But since this pattern was common, it is unlikely that parents regarded themselves as cruel or children as being rejected. Evaluating a parent as rejecting or accepting cannot be based solely on the parent's behavior, for rejection, like pleasure, pain, or beauty, is not a fixed quality; it is in the mind of the rejectee. It is a belief held by the child, not an act performed by the parent.

After the age of two, an important discontinuity arises in the child's interpretation of parental behavior, for he begins to evaluate the actions of others in symbolic terms. The 5-year-old is conceptually mature enough to recognize that certain resources parents possess are often difficult to obtain. The child views these resources as sacrifices, and interprets their receipt as signs that the parents value him. The child constructs a tote board of the differential value of parental gifts, whether psychological or material. The value of the gift depends on its scarcity. A ten-dollar toy from a wealthy father is not a highly valued resource; the same toy from a father out of work is prized. The value depends on the child's personal weighting. This position would lead to solipsism, were it not that most parents are sufficiently narcissistic not to want to give the child long periods of uninterrupted companionship. Consequently most children place a high premium on parental company. Parents are also reluctant to provide unusually expensive gifts, so that they, too, acquire value for many youngsters. Finally, the American child learns that physical affection means positive evaluation, and is persuaded to assign premium worth to that experience as well. Therefore, some uniformity among children in our culture can be found with respect to the evaluation of parental acts that indicate acceptance or rejection. But the anchor point still lies within the child.

It is possible that the child's perception of value in the eyes of his parents assumes a prominence in our culture that it may not have had in earlier periods, or may not have in other contemporary societies. Many American children are uncertain over whether they are valued by their families, and many parents are eager to communicate to their children that they love them. Unhappiness, failure, and psychological symptoms in adolescence and adulthood are often explained as being the result of the absence or withdrawal of parental love during early childhood. But prior to the mid seventeenth century, Europeans rarely referred to the importance of the love relationship between parent and child when they speculated on the conditions that promoted optimal development.[11] The child's future was more dependent on Divine than parental love. The child needed a good education and faith in God; parents provided physical care, consistent discipline, and a model for proper behavior.

By the end of the seventeenth century, however, explicit recognition of the significance of the love relation between parent and child, while not unknown earlier, had become more commonly recognized. Locke advised parents to love their children, noting: "He that would have his son have a respect for him and his orders must himself have a great reverence for his son."[12] Rousseau warned that, if parents—and he meant both mothers and fathers—did not establish affectionate ties with their children, vice was inevitable. Anticipating Bowlby's emphasis on the infant's attachment to a single caretaker, Rousseau advised against the mother having a wet-nurse or substitute caretaker. But if that decision had been made, then "the foster child should have no other guardian, just as he should have no teacher but his tutor. . . . A child who passes through many hands in turn can never be well brought up."[13]

This increased emphasis on the love relation between socializing adults and children was paralleled by an emerging self-consciousness about the child's independence, individualism, and personal motives. The child was being differentiated as an entity separate from the family. Unquestioned loyalty and acquiescence to God and family were losing their moral force to autonomy and narcissism. Rousseau and Pestallozzi both anticipated the mood of the twentieth century: Rousseau wrote that "the only natural passion to man is the love of himself"; Pestallozzi that "consciousness of your own personality is the first object of Nature." From the beginning of the eighteenth century until the present, the emphasis on the importance of the child developing an articulated, differentiated, autonomous ego has continued to grow. The spread of that idea is correlated with the attribution of formative power to parental love. Is this correlation causal, the joint product of more fundamental factors, or an accident? We favor the second of these positions and shall try to support that view.

As the urban middle class grew in size, children became less obvious economic advantages. Since fewer youth were needed to help with agricultural work or to care for infants and young children, the role of many children gradually changed from an object of utility to one of sentiment. Although children contributed less to the family's economic position, they could enhance the family's status by mastering academic skills and attaining prestige in the larger community. As a result, more parents began to identify with their children because of the latter's potential for accomplishment.[14]

This change in the child's function in the family could have produced an enhancement of the attitude we call parental love. If a farmer needs his horse for plowing he worries about the animal's health and takes precautions to prevent injury or escape. But it is unlikely he will identify with the animal, for the horse is only an instrument to be used by the competent adult to attain a goal. The farmer who enters his thoroughbred in a show in order to gain status is more likely to identify with the animal, for it possesses qualities the owner lacks. The emotional state that follows a successful plowing is one of satisfaction and perhaps reduction of apprehension, but the state that follows public accolade is one of self-enhancement. The object responsible for that good feeling can generate the emotion we typically label "love." As middle-class families began to regard their children as emerging objects of art who would enhance a parent's sense of self, feelings of love were amplified.

An additional basis for an increased consciousness regarding affectionate relations between parent and child rests on the assumption that seventeenth-century parents began to recognize that an aloof, authoritarian attitude, which seemed to be effective in producing obedience and conformity in children, was not conducive to autonomous achievement. The latter profile requires a different set of parental attitudes. Fear of authority is a potent incentive for inhibition, but it is far less effective as a goad for continued striving toward goals which require the invention of ideas and actions. The desire to maintain the positive regard of parents is a more appropriate incentive for the latter, and it is possible that the seventeenth-century middle-class family recognized that principle, or at least became more conscious of it, as the stereotype of the ideal child changed from passive conformity to active, autonomous mastery.

It is also possible that when families moved from rural areas to the city the child was more often outside the supervisory influence of a family member for some part of the day. Hence it became necessary to use the threat of withdrawal of favor as a source of disciplinary control. When the child is continually surrounded by adults or older siblings, each of whom is within several hundred yards of his action, mischievousness is constrained. When the child is alone or more distant from the home, the policeman must be symbolic, and the society may have discovered that parental love and its potential withdrawal can play the supervisory role at a distance.

We recently collected extensive observations on the location and activity of Indian children growing up in two small neighboring villages on Lake Atitlan in the Guatemalan highlands. During the first five years of life, the children were within 100 yards of their home over 80 per cent of the time and under direct or indirect surveillance by a family member on at least two-thirds of the occasions when our observers appeared on the scene. Under these conditions it is not only difficult for a child to misbehave, but it is also clear to all members of the community that there is no reason for any child to be uncertain about the availability of human resources to provide care or control when it is needed.

The economic and social changes that led to new parental attitudes may have also created new nodes of uncertainty in children. The pre-adolescent in a fifteenth-century farming village had an opportunity, each day, to realize that he was an object of value, since his work made a material contribution to the family's welfare. His virtue was evident in the results of his work. It was more difficult for the 13-year-old son of a middle-class official in eighteenth-century London to enjoy that advantage. His sense of virtue was based less on the products of his labor and more on his psychological qualities. He could not point to a plowed field or a full woodpile as a sign of his utility. As a result, this child may have been more uncertain about his value, more dependent on parental communications assuring him of his worthiness, and more preoccupied with parental attitudes toward him.

Thus the correlation between the emphasis on the child's independence and autonomous achievement (and the decreasing concern with conformity and the child's economic contribution to the family) and the awarding of formative power to attitudes of parental affection may have theoretical substance. It reflects, in part, the growth of a folk theory implying that confidence, independence, and the desire for accomplishment require a belief in one's value and potency and a reluctance to lose parental love. We do not know whether the folk theory is valid empirically or merely believed to be correct by the community.

The power that modern Western society attributes to parental love—or its absence—has an analogue in the theories of illness held by some non-Western communities. (By illness, we mean consciousness of a source of physical disability or psychological discomfort, not the physical locus or material cause of dysfunction.) The possible causes of illness include spirits, loss of soul, sorcery, sin, accident, God, witchcraft, or failure to live a meritorious life. Rarely are the actions or attitudes of one's family considered to be a possible source of illness in most of these non-Western societies. By contrast, twentieth-century Western society assumes the family can be a primary cause of a small set of illnesses that we normally call psychiatric—depression, phobias, obsessions, autisms, schizophrenia, criminality, and, in the infant, failure to thrive. Since phobias, depression, and madness are also present in non-Western societies, why does the modern West believe that the family's practices toward the child—excessive rejection, restriction, or aloof authoritarianism—can produce psychiatric illness during childhood, adolescence, or adulthood? We are not talking about the strong emotion a parent feels toward a young child, but rather the belief that a child's perception of the favor in which he is held can exert a profound influence on his present and future state. Modern parents are convinced that if the child believes he is loved, he will be free of a major source of distress—to be out of favor is to be vulnerable to anxiety.

Adolescents learn of scientific theories that articulate unformed premises about parental rejection and psychic illness. They learn that a person must feel loved in order to be psychically healthy. Occasions for anguish in adulthood are interpreted as delayed reactions to lack of parental love during childhood, rather than the results of the wrong zodiacal sign, being born on the wrong day, or invasion by evil spirits. Our books, magazines, and television dramas all announce the healing and prophylactic power of parental love and the toxicity that follows closely on its absence.

American adults seek out psychiatrists, new love objects, or peers who they hope will love them and dissolve their anguish. This faith in love is not unlike the faith in the curative power of the potion or incantations of a shaman. If the person believes in the curative power of the ritual—be it love or potion—he will feel less anguish after participating in the ritual. As no one would quarrel with the real power of prayer or potion to alleviate disquiet, we do not quarrel with the healing power of love. Both are real and not metaphysical events. But the potency of both depends on a prior belief in their effectiveness.

Recent inquiry into the dynamics of the relation between native healer and patient in Taiwan provides a model for the healing functions of the family.[15] The patient holds a set of hypotheses regarding the possible causes and cures of his particular state of distress. He then seeks a healer who he thinks shares his beliefs about etiology and treatment. That state of mind makes the patient receptive to the healer's diagnosis and prescription and increases the likelihood that he will leave the healer feeling better.

Kleinman notes that a well-educated Taiwanese would not visit a native healer, and, even if he did, he would not be helped because he would have no faith in the shaman's powers or in his theory of illness. Similar results have been found for modern forms of psychotherapy in the West. The patient who believes in psychoanalytic theory is not likely to be helped by a behavior therapist; the patient committed to Reich's ideas will be resistant to the counsel of a nondirective Rogerian. Thus, the necessary conditions for being helped psychologically include not only a state of distress which the person feels he cannot alleviate, but a concomitant conviction that the healer possesses psychological power and shares the patient's beliefs regarding the causes and cures of distress.

Let us assess the child-parent relationship in these terms. The child begins to construct simple theories of the reason for his psychic anguish sometime after 4 or 5 years of age. The child's sources of distress include uncertainty about possible harm, task failure, and parental disfavor, as well as guilt and shame over violations of societal standards. The child's theory of cause is partly a product of the parents' communications. Hence, the child automatically shares some of their beliefs about etiology, and views the parents as having a special power that derives to some extent from their greater size, competence, and prior success in alleviating his distress. Before the age of 2, parental actions of comforting, feeding, and attention have become goals to seek when in distress: in most parts of the world, young children who are frightened or in pain approach their caretaker to be touched, fed, or reassured. Even among chimpanzees, a subordinate chimp will approach and hold out a hand to a dominant member, who will touch the subordinate as if to indicate reassurance. (Recall, also, that before the Enlightenment, the touch of a king was believed by some to have potent healing powers.)

A special power to persuade and heal is awarded to the person who has attained to an extraordinary degree a valued quality or competence. During the child's early years, parents have this power. During pre-adolescence, older siblings and peers can earn a similar respect, if they possess the desired qualities. During adulthood, this power is held by the members of the community who have attained whatever qualities are prized. The child has been told by his family what qualities are admired, and he recognizes that his parents possess them in greater abundance than he. Consider a 6-year-old middle-class American child who is afraid to play with other children in the neighborhood. His parents provide an explanation for his feelings and offer some advice. In a middle-class suburb, the mother tells the child that the boys outside are basically friendly and that he must fight his anxieties; it is his responsibility to initiate contact with them. But if we shift the location to an inner-city ghetto, where a particular family views most of the children on the block as a polluting and dangerous influence, the mother may give the opposite advice. In each situation, each set of suggestions is viewed as wise, and each can reduce the child's apprehension.

When the American child in a nuclear family experiences distress, the parents remind him that they will take care of him—he need not worry because the family is present. Both child and parent share the belief that attentive nurture from a sympathetic adult has healing power and that its absence is a major source of anxiety. In many small subsistence-farming villages where the child is cared for continuously by the mother, older siblings, aunts, or grandparents, the psychically alleviating experiences are not parental presence, but obedience and hard work. Indeed the capacity for work holds as central a position among the Mayan Indians of Guatemala as the capacity to give and receive love does in the West. An investigation of the Indian view of valued human qualities revealed that wealth and hard work were the most valued adult characteristics. Adjectives describing the capacity to love children were not among the qualities named as being characteristic of adults, suggesting that this attribute is not viewed as important in the Mayan's construction of reality.[16]

Now we must ask whether lack of parental affection in childhood does indeed make a serious contribution to future psychic illness. Is that proposition valid?

It is not easy to answer that question for reasons that are not strictly empirical. When we ask whether temperature contributes to the probability of snowfall we need only gather easily obtainable objective data to answer the query. But in the case of the contribution of parental rejection to psychic illness, we are in difficulty because we are asking whether a mental state in the child (the belief that one is not favored) makes a contribution to a future mental state (fearfulness or hostility) in the adult. That question has two quite different forms.

The first form is phenomenological and concerned only with the adult's belief in the validity of the functional relation. If a person believes that an early set of experiences (or mental states) is influencing his present state, he will act as if it were so. The second form of the question is public—or scientific; it asks if there is an empirical relation between the child's perception of favor or disfavor and later adult sequellae. At present, the second question has not been answered satisfactorily because, as indicated earlier, parental rejection is not a specific set of actions by parents but a belief held by the child. The only way to avoid this frustrating position is to determine whether there is a lawful relation, in a given culture, between certain parental actions and communications and the child's belief that he is, or is not, favored. There are no data to our knowledge that have demonstrated unequivocally that there is a relation between specific parental actions and the child's belief. Working-class American parents punish and restrict the child much more than middle-class parents do, yet there is no evidence to indicate a class difference in perception of parental favor. When we look at other cultures, we find that Kipsigis mothers, for example, have older siblings care for their young children, while Israeli mothers on kibbutzim use *metaplot*. Again, there is no evidence to indicate that one group of children feels more in parental favor than the other. We are tempted, therefore, to suggest that each child constructs a theory regarding those actions that he thinks imply parental favor or disfavor. The content of the theory is based on local conditions and will not necessarily generalize to other communities in any detail.

The possibility that one might *not* be valued by one's family is common in Western society. Historical events may have been responsible for making this possibility a major source of anxiety and, therefore, of illness, just as they have been responsible for anxieties about nuclear waste, racial violence, and municipal defaults. Mayan villagers worry about hunger, slanderous gossip, and the iction of the gods. A society can create a source of distress by introducing a new belief, just as it can create new hazards to lungs by inventing cars and factories, or hazards to viscera by adding carcinogens to food and water.

The Child's Sense of Competence

The child also needs information on his profile of talents. Naturally a child focuses on the instrumental competences that the local society values, whether they be physical endurance, ability to fight, eloquence, or mathematical skills. Each community promotes a valued set of skills, a preferred vocabulary, a style of problem solving, and a standard of adequate performance. Initially the child has no absolute definition of what constitutes skilled behavior and is forced to look to other children—peers and siblings—for standards by which to judge his abilities. Only much later, perhaps by late adolescence, will he have incorporated some standard sufficiently firmly to allow him to judge his competence by performance alone.

The families who have power and feel they are an integral part of the society are more effective in promoting the socially valued skills with their children than are those who feel disenfranchised. They communicate to the child their optimism about his eventual mastery. Hence the family's social class exerts a major influence on the child's sense of competence, not only because the lower classes use and encourage a slightly different style of language and strategy for solving problems, but also because they treat the children differently and communicate more tenuous expectations of success regarding those skills promoted by the dominant class. Lower-class parents may communicate their sense of helplessness and inadequacy to the child, leading him to a more pessimistic view of his chances for success in the larger environment.

The Influence of Social Class

The power of class can be observed as early as the first birthday. About a decade ago, we initiated a longitudinal study of 180 Caucasian first-born children living in the Boston area whom we followed from 4 to 27 months of age.[17] During the four assessments—at 4, 8, 13, and 27 months—we quantified the child's attentiveness to a set of interesting, meaningful, visual events. The 4- and 8-month-olds varied dramatically in their attentiveness, but no relation could be found during the first year between the child's attentiveness and the family's social class. However, at 13 and 27 months of age, level of attentiveness to representations of faces and human forms was correlated with the social class of the child's family, but it was unrelated to the degree of attentiveness displayed at 4 months. If we assume both that temperamental factors exert an influence on attentiveness among the 4- and 8-month-olds and that these factors remain somewhat stable, then it appears that their influence had been subdued through experiences in the home by the time the child was 2 years old. We recently evaluated the intelligence and reading ability of 68 of these children when they were 10 years old. Their qualities as infants were unrelated to either their IQ or their reading scores, while the social class of their families had the expected positive relation to both attributes.[18]

We have also completed a study of lower- and middle-class Chinese and Caucasian children, half of them attending a day-care center regularly, the other half raised only at home from 3½ to 29 months of age. The infants differed markedly in their attentiveness, vocalization, and smiling to interesting visual and auditory events during the first year. These differences did not vary with social class. But by 20 and 29 months of age, the class of the child's family had become a major predictor of attentiveness, vocalization, and smiling. Thus, in two independent studies with different families, the effects of social class emerged clearly by the second year and appeared to subdue the inherent dispositions displayed during early infancy.[19]

Observations of working- and middle-class American families consistently reveal that lower-middle-class Caucasian mothers talk less to their infants, are less likely to encourage cognitive development, especially of language, and are more intrusive and autocratic in their discipline. This is not a recent trend. Thirty years ago, Alfred Baldwin and colleagues[20] observed working- and middle-class Caucasian mothers and their young children in rural Ohio and reported that working-class mothers were more autocratic and restrictive in their practices with their children. They intruded more often into the activities of the child and were less disposed to explain punishments or give reasons for their prohibitions. Several years ago, we observed 90 first-born Caucasian children at home over a 5- to 6-hour-period on several occasions and quantified the encounters that involved maternal commands, prohibitions, and children's requests. There was an inverse relation between the educational level—and, by inference, social class—of the mother and the number of prohibitions she issued: a rate of 1 every 5 minutes for lower-middle-class parents versus 1 every 10 minutes for middle-class parents, a finding in complete accord with Baldwin's data gathered thirty years earlier.[21]

We can only speculate about the psychological consequences of this kind of upbringing, but it is not unreasonable to suggest that the greater autonomy awarded the middle-class 2- and 3-year-old accustoms him to a freedom from psychological restraint and leads him to expect that he will play the role of initiator. This belief, when wedded to the middle-class tendency to remind the child that victories and defeats are the result of his efforts or deficiencies, rather than the vicissitudes of fortune, creates a mental set toward problems in which the self is supposed to generate plans and fulfill ambitions. Obstacles can be met in one of three ways—an attempt to cope, a retreat or denial, or an expectation that someone or something will intrude. Although both the child and the adult often wish to shift the responsibility of decision or action to another entity—be it person, group, or transcendental force—the middle-class child's socialization, at least in America, appears to make it more difficult for him to do so. Questionnaire studies of middle- and lower-class children reveal that the former are a little more likely to believe that effort leads to success and lack of effort to failure, while the lower-class child is somewhat more prone to explain success and defeat in terms either of chance or of benevolent and malevolent social forces.[22]

The power of social-class experience is seen in dramatic form in the results of an extensive study of over 27,000 children who were followed from birth to age 4 in an investigation of the effects of maternal health and pre- and perinatal rauma on the intelligence-test scores of 4-year-olds. Despite the fact that the nvestigators had quantified many biological variables, including birth weight, maternal illness during pregnancy, and difficulties in delivery, the major predictor of the child's IQ at age 4 was the mother's social class. After the variance associated with class had been accounted for, the remaining biological variables added very little predictive power—only a few points—to the multiple correlation.[23] Indeed, over 25 per cent of the variation in the verbal ability of 11-year-olds can be accounted for by the father's occupation and the number of children in the family.[24]

A family's social class is associated with degree of risk for biological and psychological deficits at birth, specific practices toward the child, projection of parental views of self onto the child, and, finally, the child's identification with his class. These factors lead the typical 10-year-old lower-class child to question his ability to possess the talents and instrumental competences that the middle-class child commands. One of the firmest facts in psychology, a discipline with few replicable pieces of knowledge, is the positive relation between a child's social class and a variety of indexes of cognitive functioning, including IQ or achievement-test scores, grades in school, richness of vocabulary and memory, and inferential ability. Additionally, the middle-class American child typically has a greater expectation of success in intellectual situations, is more reflective, and is less likely to take extreme risks when given a variety of alternatives. Some of these differences are very similar to the differences noted between later- and first-born children within the same family.

This relation between social class and cognitive performance in America and Western Europe can also occur in small, isolated subsistence-farming villages in Latin America, where the difference in wealth and education among the very poor and the less poor is minimal. In many of these villages, the poorest do not own the land upon which their thatched hut rests, while the less poor do. But from the perspective of an American, all the villagers live in abject poverty. Nonetheless, village parents who perceive themselves to be somewhat better off than their neighbors have children who perform better on tests of memory, perceptual analysis, and reasoning. The correlation between the amount of land held and the size of the house—a good index of class in these villages—and test performance is often of the same magnitude as it is in the United States,[25] implying that the families of the very poor are implementing practices and communicating values to their children that are different from the actions and values of the less poor. It is also likely that these children are identifying with their families' social position in the community, as middle-class children do in America.

We do not believe that the relation between class and cognitive ability in these small villages can be attributed solely to the poorer health and nutrition among the impoverished. A recent study of a modernizing Mayan Indian village of 5,000 people located in the highlands of Guatemala showed that the most traditional Catholic families, whose practices are highly restrictive of the child, have more land and are wealthier than the less traditional Catholic families, and their children therefore better fed and healthier. Yet the performance of these children on difficult memory tests were the lowest in the village, resembling those of children living in a much more isolated and impoverished setting several kilometers away. We interpret this to mean that psychological experiences within the family are responsible for lower expectations of success or cognitive problems, less motivation to perform well, and a more suspicious attitude toward the examiner—all of which lead to poorer performance.

The child's identification with the class of his family is difficult to change, for it is not simply an opinion imposed by another or a habit produced by specific experiences in the home—although these are important—it is the product of a profound inference which is continually supported by evidence that strengthens the original belief. Many human qualities can only be known by reference to another person. We usually say a man is tall and heavy, not six-foot-three or 250 pounds. "Tall" and "heavy" derive their meaning from reference to others. A child can not know how smart, brave, handsome, or frightened he is unless he has a set of peers available to define his position on the scale. The lower-class child during the years prior to adolescence gradually comes to realize that he possesses little of what the culture values. That insight, which is a component of his class identification, carries with it a sense of impotence—not unlike the mood of the soldier in Stravinsky's *L'Histoire du soldat* after the Devil persuades him to trade his violin for a book that will give him wealth. Not surprisingly, there is a readiness to hide or deny that impotence.[26] The desire to conceal the psychological weakness he imputes to lower-class membership leads to a readiness to take risks, an easier disposition for aggression, and a tendency to assign responsibility for failure to external events.

The Effect of Ordinal Position

The differences between middle- and lower-class children, on the one hand, and first- and later-born children, on the other, show some striking similarities. It is possible that some similar mechanisms mediate these differences because members of a social class or ordinal position use the other class or position to define the self. The influence of an older or younger sibling on the child is probably felt most keenly when the child is between 2 and 10 years of age.[27] The arrival of the second child represents a threat to the first-born's relationship with the parents. For the later-born, those same years are the time when the oldest is perceived as an omnipotent and invulnerable competitor with special privileges and enviable talents. Since each sibling position has its own set of advantages and disadvantages, let us try to specify some of the psychological consequences associated with each particular ordinal position.

Research suggests that the first-born has a stronger tendency than the later-born to turn to the parents for his values and to use them, rather than his peers, as models.[28] Parents award the first-born a position of privilege because of his greater competence and age. But the first-born experiences anxiety over loss or dilution of parental care when the next infant arrives. The first-born has become accustomed to the exclusive affection of the parents. Since he is not required to share that resource before the next child appears, he comes to expect a certain amount of "attentive care." The disruption or attenuation of that care is a contrast to the past adaptation level and is thus treated as a salient event. Marjorie Konner reports that among the Bushmen, who are excessively protective of their children and who nurse them into the third and fourth years, the most terrifying nightmares of adult women refer to the anger and uncertainty that had surrounded the arrival of the next infant and their subsequent displacement.

The first-born experiences guilt over his hostility to the later-born child, for he is naturally jealous of the infant's special status, but has no way to rationalize that resentment. Since he knows—and is reminded—that babies are entitled to extra attention, the anger cannot be justified, a condition that predisposes the first-born to guilt. The later-born, on the other hand, can more easily justify his resentment toward older siblings because they are in fact aggressive and domineering toward him and enjoy privileges he does not.

The combination of identification with parental models, perception of "privileged" status which the child wants to maintain, and apprehension over ejection by adult authority leads the first-born to adopt higher standards surrounding the competences and attributes that are valued by the parents. First-born children of middle-class American parents who value school success adopt and practice that value with greater vigor than do later-born children, as indicated by the disproportionately high percentage of eminent men who are either first-born or only children. First-borns are predominant among Rhodes scholars and those listed in *Who's Who Among Distinguished Scientists*.[29] A disproportionate number of first-borns also attain very high scores on intelligence and aptitude tests and matriculate at colleges with high admissions standards.[30]

An examination of the scores of almost 800,000 participants in the National Merit Scholarship Program during the period 1962-65 revealed that first-borns had higher verbal scores than later-borns and that these differences could not be attributed to the education or income of the families of the two groups. The advantage of being the oldest was restricted to verbal talents, for no comparable difference occurred in the case of mathematical skills.[31] A similar study of a random sample of 2,523 high-school students who were administered a reading-comprehension test revealed that the higher scores of only- and first-born youths were restricted to students whose fathers had at least graduated from high school. Among adolescents from less well-educated families, the ordinal difference disappeared.[32] This fact suggests that the first-borns are likely to excel in those characteristics valued by the family.

If the parental standards stress obedience, the first-born will be more obedient. If parents promote academic excellence, the first-born will obtain better grades; if parents value a religious attitude, the first-born will be more committed to the family's religion.[33] Among Episcopalians, first-borns were more likely to be committed to the church and to be members of the ordained ministry than were later-borns.[34]

The arrival of the later-born is an incentive to the first-born to differentiate himself from the younger child. The first-born cannot ignore the new sibling's presence, and he is pushed to differentiate himself from the younger and associate himself with the values of the parents in order to retain his favored position. The first-born is propelled to adulthood by the presence of the younger sibling.

Since the later-born is exposed to the less competent talents of the first-born, along with those of the parents, he has more realistic and pragmatic standards.

The combination of a firm commitment to the standards of adults and an affinity for coherence, consistency, and order among standards leads first-borns to adopt more idealistic philosophical positions and to prefer single, unifying principles in both morality and science, in preference to ones that are pluralistic or expedient.[35]

One disadvantage of the later-born position is the sense of inadequacy in comparison with the older sibling, especially if the age difference between the two is not large, say 2 to 4 years. The later-born is apt to regard himself as less competent in those qualities prized by the family and actualized by the first-born. He does not excuse these inadequacies by acknowledging the differences in age, but concludes that he is less adequate. As with the lower-class child, this decision can lead, especially in middle-class children, to attempts to deny that conclusion. Later-born children are less cautious; they tend to get involved in physically more dangerous activities. Later-born adults are more likely than first-borns to participate in dangerous sports, such as football, soccer, or rugby, but no more likely to participate in less dangerous sports, such as crew or tennis.[36] In November, 1965, during a major East-Coast power blackout, one hundred adult men and women in a New York hotel were asked the question, "How nervous or uneasy did you feel during this experience?" The first-borns admitted to greater distress and anxiety than the later-borns.[37] Teachers were asked to nominate the two physically most cautious and the two most incautious children in their classrooms. The relation to ordinal position was striking. Children with older siblings were more likely to be classified as motorically impulsive; those with no older siblings were physically more cautious and inhibited.[38] The data imply a more conservative and cautious attitude among first-borns: they are reluctant to provoke rejection by authority or its abstract surrogates, and they seem less ready to alter established attitudes.

If this rather speculative generalization is applied to scientists, one would expect ordinal position to be associated, at least among active, eminent scientists, with the likelihood of promoting or opposing a theory that seriously questioned a dominant paradigm. This possibility was first put forward by Irving Harris in a book entitled *The Promised Seed* (1964). Recently, Frank Sulloway[39] has discovered a remarkable relation between ordinal position and attitude toward new scientific ideas. He argues that among eminent scientists, later-borns would more likely be ideologically rebellious, while first-borns would be more reluctant to disagree with a dominant theoretical position. It has already been demonstrated that there are more eminent first-born than later-born scientists than one would expect from chance, given the normal distribution of first- and later-borns in the population. Sulloway suggests that, since evolutionary theory opposed the strong nineteenth-century belief in the Creation, that theory should more likely have been discovered and amplified by a later-born than a first-born, and in fact both Darwin and Wallace were later-borns. Of 98 scientists who publicly opposed Darwin or the earlier evolutionists from 1750 to 1870 (and for whom birth-order information is available), only 35 were later-borns. Among 30 pre-Darwinian evolutionists, including Darwin himself and Wallace, only two were first-borns and one of these, Isidore Geoffroy St.-Hilaire, was also the son of an earlier (and himself later-born) evolutionist, Étienne Geoffroy St.-Hilaire. The other first-born exception,

Henry Bates, turns out to have been a close friend and scientific colleague of Wallace, who was himself largely responsible for Bates's pre-1859 conversion to the evolutionary point of view. Of the total of 69 who were either pro-evolution prior to 1859 or converted after 1859, 56 were later-born and only 13 were first-born.

Sulloway also examined the three revolutions promoted by Copernicus, Bacon, and Freud. Of 20 major opponents to the three new hypotheses, 80 per cent were either first-born or eldest sons, 20 per cent were later-born (and, more specifically, younger sons). Of the 43 early proponents, 84 per cent were younger sons and 16 per cent first-born or eldest sons. Sulloway's findings, therefore, point to the special importance for later-borns of having an older *male* sibling within the family constellation.

Finally, Sulloway examined three other modern revolutions—Lavoisier's hypothesis regarding the role of oxygen in combustion, relativity theory, and continental drift. For these three, the scientists were divided into those under age 40 and those over age 40 when the theories appeared. Of 51 opponents to these theories over age 40, 84 per cent were either first-born or eldest sons, 16 per cent younger sons. Of 28 proponents over age 40, 93 per cent were younger sons and only 7 per cent were first-born. Scientists under the age of 40 can be presumed to have had less of a personal or professional commitment to the older, established paradigms that were then under attack; hence the relation to ordinal position was not present. In fact, as Sulloway also points out, those major revolutions in science that do not simultaneously challenge deep-seated religious or social beliefs are often first promulgated by *young* first-borns (e.g., Newton, Einstein, and Lavoisier), even though an ordinal-position effect separates their older scientific peers in a highly divisive manner.[40] These results imply that the degree to which a scientist is ready to promote or oppose a major ideological system is related—and remarkably so—to his ordinal position in his family.

These theoretically consistent correlates of sibling position remind us that, despite the importance of parental behavior, the mere existence of a younger or older sibling in the family is a salient force in the psychological development of the child. The mechanisms that account for these differences do not rest only with the practices and communications of the parents, and, therefore, they are not solely a function of what is normally meant by "direct family experience." Rather, the catalyst of change is simply the introduction of "another," like the introduction of a crystal into a cloud to precipitate rain. The "other" is the catalyst that creates uncertainty in the child. In response to that uncertainty, the child alters his beliefs, behaviors, and roles.

Like later-borns, the lower-class 6-year-old comes to conclusions about his qualities after recognizing the existence of the middle-class child. The middle-class child, like the first-born, is pushed to differentiate himself from the lower-class youngster once he recognizes his presence, probably during the early school years. Thus, although direct practices issued by parents can shape the child's behavior, we will not completely understand the child's development unless we also take into account his cognitive classification of others. Each individual lives in a social structure and is aware of his position in that structure. That knowledge molds his attitudes toward himself and others, his vulnerability to anxiety and ambition, and his interpretation of the degree to which he is responsible for the outcome of his efforts.

The Modern Western Family

Although the family is a haven and a source of identification and information for all children, there are important differences between the modern Western nuclear family and the less modern, subsistence-farming-village family. Let me use for comparison a village I know best, a small isolated Indian community in northwest Guatemala. The major difference between nuclear families in this community and those in modern America is the more central role played by the Guatemalan family in the life of the child, in part, because the child makes an instrumental contribution to its survival. There is no strong peer group available to promote a set of values that competes with those of the family; the child does not have to choose between two value systems. The sex typing is more rigid, and the child's future is inextricably tied to the resources of his family. It is not possible for the adult to have an identity in the village independent from that of the family that reared him.

One of the most important consequences of the increasing geographical and psychological mobility of modern Western youth away from their families is that the identification with family has become weakened and, in some cases, nonexistent. Since there are no other institutions—college, employer, religion—to replace the family, he has no choice but to regard his beliefs and products as the primary locus of the sense of self or, in Eriksonian terms, "Identity." He is psychologically alone. He has no other group or entity to rely on—a position that seems to have the advantage of freedom from coercion and minimal constraints on autonomy of action, but which exacts the prices of loneliness and the unavailability of any person or group in which to invest strong emotion. It is for this reason that marriage and the creation of a new family are likely to experience a recrudescence in the West. We take as an axiom that the self resists depersonalization. As modern environments make a sense of potency and individual effectiveness more difficult to attain, freedom from all affective involvements becomes more and more intolerable. Involvement with a family is the only viable mechanism available to satisfy that hunger. The forces that initially weakened the family—urbanization and industrialization—have produced conditions a century later that are now likely to strengthen it. The situation is not unlike the cycle of growth in a cell: the forces that temporarily distort the cell boundaries and chromosomal material eventually produce two new healthy units.*

*This paper was prepared while the author was a Belding Scholar of the Foundation for Child Development. The research reported in it was supported by grants from NICHD, Office of Child Development, the Carnegie Corporation of New York, and the Spencer Foundation.

REFERENCES

[1] G. Ross, "Conceptual Functioning in the Infant" (unpublished).

[2] J. Kagan, B. Hosken, and S. Watson, "The Child's Symbolic Conceptualization of the Parents," *Child Development*, 32 (1961), pp. 625-36.

[3] J. Kagan, R. B. Kearsley, P. R. Zelazo, and C. Minton, "The Course of Early Development" (unpublished, 1976).

⁴N. A. Fox, "Developmental and Birth-Order Determinants of Separation Protest: A Cross-Cultural Study of Infants on the Israeli Kibbutz" (Ph.D. dissertation, Harvard Graduate School of Education, November, 1975).

⁵T. G. R. Bower, "The Evolution of Sensory Systems," in R. B. MacLeod and H. L. Pick, eds., *Perception: Essays in Honor of James J. Gibson* (Ithaca, 1974), pp. 141-52.

⁶J. Kagan, R. B. Kearsley, and P. R. Zelazo, "The Emergence of Initial Apprehension to Unfamiliar Peers," in M. A. Lewis and L. A. Rosenblum, eds., *Friendship and Peer Relations* (New York, 1975), pp. 187-206.

⁷J. L. Briggs, *Never in Anger* (Cambridge, Mass., 1970).

⁸A. L. Baldwin, J. M. Kalhorn, and F. H. Breese, "Patterns of Parent Behavior," *Psychological Monographs*, 58:3 (1945); W. C. Becker and R. S. Krug, "The Parent Attitude Research Instrument: A Research Review," *Child Development*, 36 (1965), pp. 329-69; J. Kagan and H. A. Moss, *Birth to Maturity* (New York, 1962); E. S. Schaefer, "A Circumplex Model for Maternal Behavior," *Journal of Abnormal and Social Psychology*, 59 (1959), pp. 226-35; E. S. Schaefer and N. Bayley, "Consistency of Maternal Behavior from Infancy to Preadolescence," *Journal of Abnormal and Social Psychology*, 61 (1960), pp. 1-6; R. R. Sears, E. E. Maccoby, and H. Levin, *Patterns of Child Rearing* (Evanston, 1957).

⁹J. H. Plumb, "The New World of Children in Eighteenth-Century England," *Past and Present*, 67 (1975), pp. 64-95.

¹⁰*Ibid.*

¹¹A. Ryerson, "Medical Advice on Child Rearing 1550-1900" (Ph.D. dissertation, Harvard Graduate School of Education, 1959).

¹²John Locke, *Some Thoughts Concerning Education* (Cambridge, 1913).

¹³Jean-Jacques Rousseau, *Emile*, trans. B. Foxley (New York, 1911).

¹⁴Plumb (cited above, note 9).

¹⁵A. Kleinman, "The Cultural Construction of Clinical Reality: Comparisons of Practitioner-Patient Interaction in Taiwan" (unpublished, 1975).

¹⁶M. Kieffer and A. K. Romney, "The Semantic Structure of Tzutujil Maya Personal Attribute Concepts" (unpublished, 1973).

¹⁷J. Kagan and H. A. Moss, *Birth to Maturity* (New York, 1962).

¹⁸D. Lapidus, "A Longitudinal Study of Development" (Ph.D. dissertation, Harvard University, 1976).

¹⁹Kagan, Kearsley, Zelazo, Minton (cited above, note 3).

²⁰A. L. Baldwin, J. M. Kalhorn, F. H. Breese, "Patterns of Parent Behavior," *Psychological Monographs*, 58 (1945), no. 3; idem, "The Appraisal of Parent Behavior," *Psychological Monographs*, 63 (1949), no. 299.

²¹C. Minton, J. Kagan, J. A. Levine, "Maternal Control and Obedience in the Two-Year-Old," *Child Development*, 42 (1971), pp. 1873-74.

²²J. Trotta, "Open Versus Traditional Education: Some Effects on Elementary School Children," *Journal of the New York School Board Association*, April, 1974, pp. 24-30.

²³S. H. Broman, P. L. Nichols, W. A. Kennedy, *Preschool IQ: Prenatal and Early Developmental Correlates* (New York, 1975).

²⁴K. Marjoribanks, H. J. Walberg, and M. Borgen, "Mental Abilities: Sibling Constellation and Social Class Correlates," *British Journal of Social and Clinical Psychology*, 14 (1975), pp. 109-16.

²⁵R. E. Klein, *Division of Human Development, INCAP Progress Report, 1974-75*, Guatemala City, Guatemala.

²⁶The typical reaction to the sense of impotence will vary with the culture. In the ante-bellum South, it led the slaves to assume a posture of deference and passivity, as it still does among the untouchables in India. But in modern Western societies, where caste and race are being discarded as explanations of differential wealth and power and the vicissitudes of economic and psychological forces are awarded explanatory force, the lower-class adult feels more resentful of his status. Moreover, the egalitarian ethic that "all are equal" is taken to mean "all should feel equal." If one does not feel as potent as one's neighbor, that fact is to be concealed, a state of affairs that leads to a counter-phobic reaction to deny disenfranchised status.

²⁷H. L. Koch, "Attitudes of Children Toward Their Peers as Related to Certain Characteristics of Their Siblings," *Psychological Monographs*, 70 (1965), no. 426; idem, "The Relation of Certain Formal Attributes of Siblings to Attitudes Held Toward Each Other and Toward Their Parents," *Monographs of the Society for Research in Child Development*, 25 (1960), no. 78.

²⁸S. Schachter, *The Psychology of Affiliation* (Stanford University, 1959).

²⁹F. L. Apperly, "A Study of America's Rhodes Scholars," *Journal of Heredity*, 30 (1939), pp. 494-95; H. E. Jones, "The Environment and Mental Development," in L. Carmichael, ed., *Manual of Child Psychology* (New York, 1954), pp. 631-96; A. Roe, "A Psychological Study of Eminent Psychologists and Anthropologists in a Comparison with Biological and Physical Scientists," *Psychological Monographs*, 67 (1953).

[30]W. D. Altus, "Birth Order and Its Sequellae," *Science*, 151 (1966), pp. 44-49.

[31]H. M. Breland, "Birth Order, Family Configuration, and Verbal Achievement," *Child Development*, 45 (1974), pp. 1011-19.

[32]D. C. Glass, J. Neulinger, and O. G. Brim, "Birth Order, Verbal Intelligence, and Educational Aspiration," *Child Development*, 45 (1974), pp. 807-11.

[33]A. P. MacDonald, "Birth Order in Religious Affiliation," *Developmental Psychology*, 1 (1969), p. 628.

[34]A. F. King, "Ordinal Position of the Episcopal Clergy" (unpublished senior honors thesis, Harvard University, 1967).

[35]R. Stein, "The Effects of Ordinal Position on Identification on Philosophy of Life, Occupational Choice, and Reflectiveness-Impulsivity" (unpublished senior honors thesis, Harvard University, 1966).

[36]R. L. Helmreich and B. E. Collins, "Situational Determinants of Affiliative Preference Under Stress," *Journal of Personality and Social Psychology*, 6 (1967), pp. 79-85.

[37]R. A. Zuckerman, M. Manosevitz, and R. I. Lanyon, "Birth Order, Anxiety, and Affiliation During a Crisis," *Journal of Personality and Social Psychology*, 8 (1968), pp. 354-59.

[38]L. E. Longstreth, G. V. Longstreth, C. Ramirez, and G. Fernandez, "The Ubiquity of Big Brother," *Child Development*, 46 (1975), pp. 769-72.

[39]F. Sulloway, "Family Constellations, Sibling Rivalry, and Scientific Revolutions: A Study of the Relationship Between Birth Order and Scientific Temperament" (unpublished manuscript, 1972); *idem*, "The Role of Cognitive Flexibility in Science: Toward a Comparative Anatomy of Scientific Revolutions" (unpublished manuscript, 1972).

[40]Sulloway has also found that individual exceptions to his general findings are themselves usually quite exceptional in terms of having grown up within an atypical family constellation (e.g., one in which there was an early death of a parent or a close sibling). For additional information on these and others findings, together with the criteria and historical documentation upon which they are based, see Sulloway's forthcoming book, *Family Constellations, Sibling Rivalry, and Scientific Revolutions: A Study of the Effect of Birth Order on Revolutionary Temperament in Science*.

TAMARA K. HAREVEN

Family Time and Historical Time

HISTORY IS OFTEN INVOKED TO SHOW "how we got where we are." While historical research can perform that function, it can also perform two others: it can offer a comparative perspective on the present, and it can suggest models for future change. The first of these functions is a new task more frequently performed by cross-cultural studies of "primitive" societies—that is, to compare current conditions, modes of behavior, and values with those in past societies. Such a comparative perspective does not necessarily carry built-in explanations of development and change, but it provides a vantage point from which to see both the unique and the common features of current behavior and problems, illuminating such questions as whether the family is "in trouble" or "going out of existence," and whether the crises currently experienced in American society are really "unprecedented." Through this comparison of present and past, historical analysis can point to major continuities and discontinuities in family development. A relatively new field, the history of the family has tantalized historians and scholars in other disciplines precisely because the data it addresses can illuminate issues such as these. The questions asked by family historians have much in common with those raised by sociologists, psychologists, anthropologists, and economists. The contribution of historians lies in the change-over-time perspective which informs their questioning and in the social and cultural context specific to the different time periods under investigation.[1]

Historical studies about the family share with the "new social history" an interest in studying whole populations rather than simply the "great" individuals or elites within them. By delving into census records, birth, marriage, and death records, private diaries, public documents, medical and educational treatises, and family letters, historians have begun to reconstruct the family patterns of large numbers of anonymous individuals. The history of the family has thus served to reintroduce human intimacy into historical research and, at the same time, to generate a realistic view of the complexities of historical change.[2] An understanding of how individuals and families have responded to historical changes and, at the same time, what their roles were in affecting such changes can considerably broaden our understanding of the process of change itself.

As the field has developed, historians have expanded their inquiry from an earlier preoccupation with the classifications of household and family structure to a broad range of subjects, encompassing marriage and sexual behavior, child-rearing, and relations among kin. In trying to understand the role of the family and its internal dynamics in the past, historians are gradually moving from a concentration on the family itself to an exploration of its interaction with other social processes and institutions. Studies examining the role of the family in migration or the interaction between the family and the industrial process have begun to advance new views about past family behavior.[3]

Particularly important has been a revision of the traditional notion that the family broke down under the impact of industrialization and urbanization. Rather than continuing to view the family as a passive agent, historical studies have revealed that the role of the family was in fact that of an active agent, fostering social change and facilitating the adaptation of its members to new social and economic conditions. The family not only did not break down under the impact of urbanization and industrialization; under certain circumstances, it actually helped to foster those changes.[4] Reacting against earlier studies of family change, especially those advanced by "modernization" theory, students of the family have been able to show that families did not "modernize" automatically in response to sweeping changes in the larger society. Rural families who migrated into urban areas and working-class families already in the cities held on to their traditions, protected their members from drastic dis-locations, and prevented family breakdown. Nonetheless, families did act as agents of change, socializing and preparing their members for new ways of life, facilitating their adaptation to industrial work and to living in large complex urban communities.

These findings have refined some basic conceptions about the adaptations of different groups to changing social conditions and have offered insights into how the *process* of change functions in different levels of society. Particularly impor-tant has been the realization that family behavior was paced differently among different social groups, that people could be "modern" at work and "traditional" at home, and that the family exercised the power of initiative and choice in accepting new ways of life. Even in industrial society, traditional patterns have persisted among families of different cultural and ethnic groups, contradicting established notions that individuals and institutions uniformly shed their tradi-tional customs as the larger society becomes "modernized."[5]

This dynamic approach to family behavior also views the family as a constantly changing entity, as its members move through life. Social scientists have often studied the family as a monolithic institution. In reality, the family is in constant flux. It is the scene of interaction between various fluid individual lives. Individual transitions into and out of different family roles, such as leaving home, getting married, setting up an independent household, com-mencement of parenthood, or—at the other end of the cycle—widowhood are interrelated with changes in the family as a collective unit.

How did individuals time their transitions into and out of various family roles, and how were these patterns of timing related to the family as a collective unit? At issue here is the synchronization of several concepts of time—individual time, family time, and historical time.

This essay examines some aspects of their interaction over the past two centuries in the United States.

Family Time and Historical Time

Most activities in modern life are governed by specific and often rigidly enforced schedules, whether they result from personal relationships or other kinds of social communication. Being early, late, or on time, juggling complicated schedules, and fulfilling a series of conflicting roles within time slots have been essential characteristics of modern society, the product of urban, industrial living. Timing has also become a central feature in the scheduling of family events and the transitions of individuals into different family roles. One of the most fascinating problems is that of the synchronizing of all the different "time clocks" that govern both the movement of individuals and families through life and larger patterns of societal change. Historical time is generally defined as a linear chronological movement of changes in a society over decades or centuries, while individual lifetime is measured according to age. But age and chronology both need social contexts to be meaningful. Social age is different from chronological age: in certain societies, a twelve-year-old is an adolescent; in others, he is already an adult; in certain societies, a person of fifty is middle aged; in others, he is old. How were typical lives "timed" in the past, and how did these life-course patterns fit into their economic, institutional, and demographic setting?

The understanding of "time" patterns along the life course provides an insight into one of the least understood aspects of family behavior—namely, the process of decision making within the family. Since we know that the structure of the family has persisted in its nuclear form over the past two centuries, examinations of how families time their behavior can reveal the important areas in which the major changes in family behavior have taken place.[6]

The concept of "family time" designates the timing of events such as marriage, birth of a child, leaving home, and the transition of individuals into different roles as the family moves through its life course. Timing has often been a major source of conflict and pressure in the family, since "individual time" and "family time" are not always in harmony. For example, the decision to leave home, to marry, or to form one's own family could not in the past be timed strictly in accordance with individual preferences, depending instead on the decisions and needs of the family as a collective unit and on institutional supports. Research has only just begun to sketch some of the basic patterns of the timing of family transitions and to link them with "historical time"—that is, with changing social conditions.

The social values governing timing have also changed under different historical circumstances. For example, the age at which a young man is considered a "drop-out" or a woman an "old maid" varies in different societies and periods. What constitutes a violation of "normal" sequences in the timing of family events also varies among different societies. For example, teenage marriage is under some circumstances, but not under others, considered an act of deviance, and motherhood preceding marriage is considered a violation of social norms in most societies.

Historical changes have impinged upon the timing of family events by providing the institutional or social conditions under which such transitions can be implemented or impeded. It would have been impossible, for instance, to enforce societal requirements for school attendance if public schools had not been readily available; similarly, it would have been difficult to impose compulsory retirement without institutionalized social security or old-age pensions. Institutions of social welfare and social control and public welfare programs have taken over many of the welfare functions previously performed by the family. Under historical conditions where most of the educational, economic, and welfare functions are concentrated in the family, the timing of transitions within the family was more significant than in modern society. In addition to institutional buttresses, a variety of social and economic developments have affected individual and family timetables. Wars and depressions have drastically altered patterns of family timing. Even on a smaller scale, however, such events as migration or the shutdown of a factory, while they do not affect the entire society, can have an important impact on timing for the families involved. Without denying the importance of large-scale transformations, viewing social change from the perspective of the family offers a considerable refinement of our understanding of the interaction between it and individual and family behavior. Migration, for example, could have a greater impact than war upon the behavior of a particular family, despite the larger societal implications of the war.[7]

One of the recurring themes in American history is that of the variation in norms by ethnic cultures within the larger society. "Irish family time" differed in certain respects from "French-Canadian family time," while both differed from native-American family time. These variations result from discrepancies and conflicts between the traditions and practices of different cultural groups and those of the dominant culture. Irish immigrants in late-nineteenth-century Massachusetts, for example, married later than French Canadians or native Americans. Native Americans married earlier and commenced childbearing earlier than Irish immigrants, but they also stopped childbearing earlier, while Irish families had larger numbers of children spread over a longer time period.[8]

A focus on timing enables us to see the point at which family members converge or diverge at different stages of their individual development and how such patterns relate to the collective experience of the family at different points of its development.[9] Even the use of the word "children" within the family is ambiguous, because, in families with large numbers of children encompassing a broad age distribution, an older child will be in an entirely different position within the family vis-à-vis adults and siblings than either the younger ones or those in the middle. As the age configuration of children within the family changes, the status of each child in the family becomes different as well; for example, after the oldest child leaves home, the next child becomes the "oldest" and takes on a new status.

The distinctions are important because individuals fulfill a multiplicity of roles. They can simultaneously be members of their family of origin and their family of procreation. After forming his own family, an individual maintains some ties with his family of origin, but also forms a new allegiance with that of the spouse. The complexity of affiliations casts an individual into various overlapping and, at times, conflicting family roles, which continue to vary at different stations along the life course. Some roles become more active, others recede in importance. A son becomes a father; later, after his own children become independent and his parents have reached the age of needing assistance, he becomes a son again, sometimes even more intensively. The various familial roles held by individuals could come into competition or conflict under different historical conditions, particularly during migration or unemployment, for example.

As Talcott Parsons has pointed out, the kinship system of the United States is loosely structured so that most forms of assistance among kin are informal and voluntary.[10] While the mutual obligations of husbands and wives or parents and children are clearly sanctioned and defined, relationships with extended kin are not. But under different historical and personal circumstances the interaction of individuals both with other members of the nuclear family and with extended kin can vary considerably, because the individual's position in his own family and his relationship to other family members and to more distant kin are entwined with the family's development as a collective unit.

Historical Differences in the Timing of Family Transitions

One widely held myth about the past is that the timing of family transitions was once more orderly and stable than it is today. The complexity that governs family life today and the variations in family roles and in transitions into them are frequently contrasted to this more placid past. The historical record, however, frequently reveals precisely the opposite condition. Patterns of family timing in the past were often more complex, more diverse, and less orderly than they are today: voluntary and involuntary demographic changes that have come about since the late nineteenth century have in fact paradoxically resulted in greater uniformity in the timing of transitions along the life course, despite greater societal complexity. The growing uniformity in timing has been accompanied by a shift from involuntary to voluntary factors affecting the timing of family events.[11] The increase in life expectancy, the decline in fertility, and an earlier marriage age have, for example, greatly increased the chances for temporal overlap in the lives of family members. Families are now able to go through a life course much less subject to sudden change than that experienced by the majority of the population in the nineteenth century.

The "typical" family cycle of modern American families includes early marriage and early commencement of childbearing, but a small number of children. Between 1810 and 1930 the birth rate declined from an average of 8 children per mother to slightly less than 3. Families following this type of family cycle experience a compact period of parenthood in the middle years of life, then an extended period, encompassing one-third of their adult life, without children; and finally often a period of solitary living following the death of a spouse, most frequently of the husband.[12]

This type of cycle has important implications for the composition of the family and for relationships within it in current society: husbands and wives are spending a relatively longer lifetime together, they invest a shorter segment of their lives in child-rearing, and they more commonly survive to grandparenthood. This sequence has been uniform for the majority of the population since the beginning of the twentieth century. In contrast to past times, most families see their children through to adulthood with both parents still alive. As Peter Uhlenberg points out:

> The normal family cycle for women, a sequence of leaving home, marriage, family formation, child-rearing, launching and survival at age 50 with the first marriage still intact, unless broken by divorce, has not been the dominant pattern of family timing before the early twentieth century.[13]

Prior to 1900, only about 40 per cent of the female population in the United States experienced this ideal family cycle. The remainder either never married, never reached marriageable age, died before childbirth, or were widowed while their offspring were still young children.[14]

In the nineteenth century, the combination of a later age at marriage and higher fertility provided little opportunity for a family to experience an empty-nest stage. Prior to the decline in mortality among the young at the beginning of the twentieth century, marriage was frequently broken by the death of a spouse before the end of the child-rearing period. Even when fathers survived the child-rearing years, they rarely lived beyond the marriage of their second child. As a result of higher fertility, children were spread over a wider age range; frequently the youngest child was just entering school as the oldest was preparing for marriage. The combination of later marriage, higher fertility, and widely spaced childbearing resulted in a different timing of family transitions. Individuals became parents later, but carried child-rearing responsibilities almost until the end of their lives. Consequently the lives of parents overlapped with those of their children for shorter periods than they do in current society.

Under the demographic conditions of the nineteenth century, higher mortality and higher fertility, functions within the family were less specifically tied to age, and members of different age groups were consequently not so completely segregated by the tasks they were required to fulfill. The spread of children over a larger age spectrum within the family had important implications for family relationships as well as for their preparation for adult roles. Children were accustomed to growing up with larger numbers of siblings and were exposed to a greater variety of models from which to choose than they would have been in a small nuclear family. Older children often took charge of their younger siblings. Sisters, in particular, carried a major share of the responsibility for raising the youngest siblings and frequently acted as surrogate mother if the mother worked outside the home, or if she had died. The smaller age overlap between children and their parents was also significant: the oldest child was the one most likely to overlap with its father in adulthood; the youngest child, the least likely to do so. The oldest children were most likely to embark on an independent career before the parents reached old-age dependency; the youngest children were most likely to carry responsibilities for parental support, and to overlap in adulthood with a widowed mother. The oldest child had the greatest chance to overlap with grandparents, the youngest child the least. Late-marrying children were most likely to be responsible for the support of a widowed mother, while early-marrying children depended on their parents' household space after marriage.[15] One can better grasp the implications of these differences in age at marriage, number of children, assigned tasks, and generational overlap when one takes into consideration the uncertainties and the economic precariousness that characterized the period; these made the orderly sequence of progression along stages of the family cycle, which sociologists have observed in the contemporary American population, impossible for the nineteenth-century family.

Another comparison between what is considered the "normal" family cycle today and its many variants in the nineteenth century reverses one more stereotype about the past—namely that American society has been experiencing breakdown and diversification in family organization. In reality, the major transitions in family roles have been characterized by greater stability and conformity, because of the greater opportunity for generational continuities. The opportunity for a meaningful period of overlap in the lives of grandparents and grandchildren is a twentieth-century phenomenon, a surprising fact that runs counter to the popular myth of a family solidarity in the past that was based on three-generational ties.

The relative significance of transition into family roles also differed in the nineteenth century. In the nineteenth century, when conception was likely to take place very shortly after marriage, the major transition in a woman's life was represented by marriage itself. But, as the interval between marriage and first pregnancy has increased in modern society, the transition to parenthood has become more significant than the transition to marriage. Family limitation has also had an impact on the timing of marriage. Since marriage no longer inevitably leads to parenthood, postponing marriage is no longer needed to delay it. On the other end of the life course, transitions *out* of parental roles are much more critical today than they were in the past when parental or surrogate-parental roles encompassed practically the entire adult life span.[16] Completion of parental roles today involves changes in residence, in work, and eventually, perhaps, removal into institutions or retirement communities.

Some familial transitions are also more easily reversible today than they were in the past. Marriages can now be ended by divorce, while, prior to the middle of the nineteenth century, they were more likely to be ended by the death of a spouse.

The overall historical pattern of family behavior has thus been marked by a shift from involuntary to voluntary forces controlling the timing of family events. It has also been characterized by greater rigidity and uniformity in the timing of the passage from one family role to another. In their comparison of such transitions in nineteenth-century Philadelphia with the present, Modell, Furstenburg, and Hershberg conclude that transitions into adult roles (departure from the family of origin, marriage, and the establishment of a household) follow a more ordered sequence and are accomplished over a shorter time period in a young person's life today than they were in the nineteenth century. Such transitions to familial roles also coincide today with transitions into occupational roles: "Transitions are today more contingent, more integrated because they are constrained by a set of formal institutions. 'Timely' action to nineteenth-century families consisted of helpful response in times of trouble; in the twentieth century, timeliness connotes adherence to a schedule."[17]

Life-Course Transitions and Family Strategies

What factors guided these transitions and moves into different family roles, what constituted continuities and discontinuities in such transitions, and how did they affect family behavior? Historical research has only barely begun to address these questions. Seemingly "disorderly" patterns in the timing of transitions in the nineteenth century were the result of the special role which the family fulfilled in the society and the prevailing view of its role and organization. The family was a corporate body operating as a collective unit, and the functions of the members within it were defined on that basis.

In modern society, we are accustomed to think of most family and work-career decisions as having been made by individuals. Even marriage is perceived as an individual decision, as an act resulting in independence from one's parents. But until recently these apparently individual transitions were treated as *family* moves and were, therefore, synchronized with other family needs and strategies. Marriage was not seen so much as a union between two freely acting individuals as an alliance between two families. The decision to marry, the choice of spouse, and the timing of the event all depended on calculations relating to the transmission of property, the finding of a job and housing, the support of aging parents, and to a wide variety of other family needs; it was not merely an impulse of romantic love. Collective family decisions took precedence over individual preferences. The careers of individuals were directed by the "familistic" ideology which remained powerful to the end of the nineteenth century, and which persisted in the lives of certain social groups into the twentieth century.

In Western society today, the major burdens of family relationships are emotional, while, in the nineteenth century, they were heavily weighted toward economic needs and tasks. Nor was this situation limited to the rural and urban working classes; the upper class as well maintained a corporate view and organization of family relationships. Family members were valued not only for the way they related to each other and for the degree of emotional satisfaction and nurturing they offered, but also for the contributions they could make to fulfilling familial obligations and maintaining continuity and stability in the family's daily existence. Family and kin were particularly valued for providing assistance during periods of crisis and need, with the understanding that their help could be reciprocated in the future.[18]

Relationships between husbands and wives, parents and children, distant kin, and even family members and strangers were based on socially sanctioned mutual obligations that transcended personal affection and sentiment. Parents raised and supported their children with the dual expectations that the children would start to work as soon as they were able and that they would ultimately support the parents in old age. This "instrumental" view of family relationships has survived the industrial revolution, and it persists in the lives of working-class and rural families today. But in the absence of institutionalized public welfare, such instrumental exchanges between family members in the nineteenth century were essential for survival. They formed the backbone of familial relationships, providing continuity from one generation to the next.[19]

Although the obligations that family members had for each other were not contractually defined, they rested on established social norms, and families had their own methods for enforcing them and for ensuring that the younger members in particular would not put their own interest before that of the family as a collective unit. In rural society, these sanctions were based on the inheritance of land, control of which offered aging parents the necessary leverage for securing old-age support from their sons. In industrial society, sanctions were less formal and were enforced mainly by the need for reciprocity dictated by the insecurities of urban life. Mutual assistance from more distant kin was more apt to entail routine help on a daily basis, such as exchanges of tools, child care, loans, temporary sharing of housing space, and support during crisis situations, such as childbirth, illness, or death. Structured and long-range exchanges across the life course generally involved only close kin—parents and children or siblings to each other.

One of the underlying goals of such reciprocal relationships was the maintenance of familial self-sufficiency. Families preferred to rely on each other for assistance rather than on strangers, even if the strangers were nearer. Individuals were expected to postpone or sacrifice their personal advancement if it jeopardized the family's autonomy as a unit, because the autonomy of the household was felt to be the foundation of family self-sufficiency. Regardless of class, occupation, or ethnic background, most American households in the nineteenth century were nuclear, as they are today, reflecting society's commitment to this autonomy. Families shared their household space with other kin only as a last resort, during periods of housing shortage or severe economic constraint.[20] Co-residence of married children with their parents was generally temporary. Young couples, particularly at the stage of family formation, strove to establish independent households; older couples, as they moved into their later years of life, tried to hold on to the independent household they had. If households became extended, it was usually only late in life. In most situations, even widows tried to maintain their own household by taking in strangers as tenants, rather than live in other people's houses.[21] Autonomy of the household should not be confused, however, with the notion of privacy as we have become accustomed to it. When people had to share their household space they did not hesitate to do so. Households functioned like accordions, expanding and contracting in accordance with changing family needs and external conditions.

Families generally tended to prefer the co-residence of strangers to relatives—at least the boarders or lodgers in most households far outnumbered the kin. We do not know why, and can only surmise that taking in boarders or lodgers represented a clearly defined economic relationship, restricted to a certain period, while sharing one's household with kin could result in a greater and longer-range infringement of the household space as well as in family conflicts. Reciprocity in family relationships was thus more heavily weighted toward exchanging resources and services than toward sharing living space.[22]

Mutual obligations and needs within the family imposed serious pressures on the timing of family transitions, and obviously caused trouble when individual preferences came into conflict with the family's collective timetable. Children had to leave school and start work early to support their younger siblings; sons and daughters often had to postpone marriage, or never marry, to support their aging parents. Individual wishes to leave home or to marry were frequently frustrated in the effort to sustain the family of origin. The types of tensions and pressures arising from such situations were only rarely recorded, and therefore cannot be easily retrieved, but the conflict and frustration individuals experienced when their own plans had to give way to family needs do seep through occasionally, particularly in oral history records. Judging from these occasional statements, family members often reconciled or escaped tensions by drastic moves such as leaving home or migrating. If they did so, they opened up new opportunities for employment and marriage and provided at least temporary escape from family pressures. But marriage or migration rarely broke the magic circle of obligations to kin forever; it extended across the life course.

How conflicts within families were resolved and how the distribution of resources was equalized are still questions in need of exploration. That they existed is itself of importance, however: the emphasis in this essay on the viability of instrumental relationships should not produce a new set of clichés for idealizing the past; rather it should highlight the flexibility in the organization of the household and in the allocation of tasks within the family which served to meet the mutual obligations of family members and to confront the uncertainties of their lives.

Historical Implications

What are the implications of these differences in the timing of individual transitions for the understanding of historical changes in the family generally? Slow and uneven transitions of individuals out of the family of origin and into independent adult roles were the result of a more continuous integration within the family of origin. This meant a greater continuity in the obligations of young people to their parents, which reached more deeply into their own adulthood and often overlapped with their own parental responsibilities. It also entailed a prolonged apprenticeship for future family roles which individuals carried out in their families of origin and, therefore, a less abrupt transition when they did marry and become parents. Closer integration within the family of origin offered greater opportunity for exchange along the life course. In the past, long-term familial obligations were imperative because of mortality, migration, and economic constraints under which the majority of the population functioned. Prior to the "affluent" society and the assumption of important familial functions by the welfare state, the family had mainly itself to rely on to meet its economic needs, to stave off dependency, and to cope with insecurities and disasters. Mutual help by family members was essential for survival. The modern notion of independent autonomous careers, linearly directed toward individual success and an almost exclusive investment in one's conjugal family, is dissonant with conceptions of family obligations in the past. Under earlier conditions when work careers were erratic and unpredictable, the insecurities of the market dictated a tight integration and an interchangeability of the tasks and functions of different family members. When occupational opportunities favored young women, a daughter was sent to work, and when they favored young men, a son was sent. When husbands and wives both found work outside the home, they shared household tasks as well; if only one could find work, the other carried the major burden of domestic responsibilities. This integration of individuals into the family's economic effort is characteristic primarily of rural society, but it also carried over into industrial society in the lives of the working class.[23]

Individualistic patterns of family behavior first appeared in the nineteenth century among the urban middle class, and with them came patterns of segregation in family roles. Middle-class families were the first to follow a clear timing sequence for their children's entry into, and exit from, school, and to promulgate an orderly career pattern that led from choosing an occupation to leaving the parental household, marrying, and forming the new family. Orderly progression along the life course and structured transitions from one stage to the next were related to the "discovery" of childhood and, subsequently, adolescence as distinct stages of life. The segregation of age groups in accordance with their functions also occurred first among middle-class families. The emergence of the private, child-centered family consciously separating itself from the outside world brought about major redefinitions of traditional family roles and functions. This new family type placed emphasis on the family as a center for nurture and affection rather than as a corporate unit. Their wages no longer needed, women and children in the middle class were exempted from the labor force. Wives were expected instead to be the custodians of the family and to protect the home as a refuge from the world of work, and children, although expected to help with household tasks, were freed from serious work responsibilities until their late teens.[24]

Members of middle-class, native-American families were the first to marry younger, to control fertility, and to space their children more closely. In their behavior, as well as in their mentality, they began to approximate the middle-class-family type which has become so common in the twentieth century. Working-class and first-generation immigrant families, on the other hand, continued to hold on to traditional views of family roles, functions, and patterns of timing, at least in the first generation. The various ethnic groups and the working class thus lagged behind the middle class in adopting this new timing and in role segregation among ages. The influx of new groups from rural and small-town backgrounds continued to infuse pre-modern patterns of timing into an increasingly homogenizing society. As state institutions gradually took over the functions of welfare, education, and social control that had previously lodged in the family, there was greater conformity in timing. The gradual introduction of age-related requirements, such as compulsory school attendance, child-labor legislation, and mandatory retirement have all combined to impose more rigid patterns of timing in the larger society and, in the process, have also caused greater uniformity in the timing of family behavior.

Modern American society thus presents a paradox: while, on the one hand, involuntary factors affecting timing of family roles have declined and, on the other hand, voluntary means of manipulating timing, in postponing or reversing transitions, and in juggling a variety of roles have increased, the resulting "liberalization" of timing patterns has been accompanied by a greater rigidity and uniformity in timing of family transitions in modern society than had been experienced in the past. The increase in uniformity in family time has coincided with a growing diversity both in career and opportunity choices and in familial and non-familial arrangements. The broadening opportunity structure, increasing affluence, and a diffusion of obligations previously contained within the family were expected to lead to more flexible timing.

Changes in timing, however, do not always coincide with the availability of opportunity. One of the important sources of historical unrest, as revealed, for example, in the women's movement, has been the incongruity between the norms of timing and the availability of opportunities within the society to conform to those norms. During certain historical periods, individuals who desired to follow the newly established norms were not able to do so because the opportunity was not available. For example, women reached marital age, but were unable to marry because of the imbalance in sex ratios. Young men came of age for the commencement of their first job only to find that there was no job available. This disjuncture between timing and opportunity could also take the opposite form—under certain conditions, changes in the opportunity structure could alter timing patterns, but rigid familial traditions and ideology could prevent individuals from responding to them. In the late nineteenth century, for example, demographic and occupational factors combined to offer optimal conditions for the entry of married women into the labor force, but traditional patterns of timing and ideological constraints prevented middle-class women from taking advantage of these opportunities.[25]

The homogenization and growing conformity in family behavior have not been sufficiently matched by corresponding ideological and attitudinal changes. Demographic stability has been accompanied by psychological and internal conflict within the family. The increased chance for stability in the family as a result of diminishing involuntary disruptions (e.g., decline in mortality) has been counteracted by rising voluntary ones (e.g., increasing divorce rates). What does this suggest? Are families not capable of functioning in a stable and consistent way, as the norms articulated in the larger society expect them to? Or is the family unable to tolerate the demographic stability it has finally achieved?

Stability and conformity, particularly in an affluent society, have led to a greater concentration on the emotional content and function of the family. In periods when the family's economic stability was at stake, emotional gratification had less importance than had instrumental relationships. Parents burdened with the worry of raising numerous children had less time and energy to question personal relationships under conditions of high mortality and economic insecurity. Continuity and survival took precedence over intimacy. By contrast, the emphasis on privacy that characterizes the modern nuclear family has increased isolation and has forced husbands and wives and parents and children to fall back on their own emotional resources within the family, thus eliminating the opportunity for diversity in interaction between kin and strangers that existed in nineteenth-century families.

The decline in instrumental family relationships and the related emergence of privatism as the major ideological base of the family in society have tended to reinforce role segregation along age and sex lines. The modern, private, nuclear family has been frequently characterized as representing progress toward a more rational and equalized family existence. Sociologist William Goode, for example, has linked progress toward sex-role equality to the emergence of the "modern" conjugal family.[26] The historical experience actually shows that the increase in role segregation among family members (a direct product of nuclear-family isolation) has tended to diminish the opportunity for equality within the family. It also shows that sex and age segregations in family roles have been inventions of the past century rather than permanent features of family behavior. Motherhood as a full-time vocation has emerged only since the middle of the nineteenth century. Ironically, its glorification as a lifelong pursuit for women began to emerge at a time when demographic and social factors were significantly reducing the total proportion of a woman's life actually needed for it.[27] The time invested in various family functions and roles over the life course and their significance are still governed by nineteenth-century anachronisms, and are not in harmony with modern demographic and social realities. One major task families face today is bridging that gap.

Advocates of change have invoked historical precedent to reinforce arguments for reform, while custodians of tradition have invoked it to prove that we are threatened by social breakdown. Throughout American history, the family has been seen as the linchpin of the social order and stable governance. When larger societal processes are reflected in the family they have always been viewed with great anxiety. From the early settlers in Plymouth to modern reformers and social scientists, the fear of the breakdown of the family has haunted American society. Every generation seems to be witnessing difficulties and to be predicting the family's collapse. Social science has provided theoretical formulations for these historical anxieties; the breakdown of traditional family patterns under the impact of social change and modernization has been the standard sociological explanation for the "crisis" of the contemporary family.

The discovery of complexity in family behavior in the past, particularly in the area of timing, can provide a new perspective on the problems families face in contemporary society. The model of family behavior which emerges from the past is one of diversity and flexibility, a kind of controlled disorder that varied in accordance with pressing social and economic needs. The complexities, conflicts in roles, and variations imposed on individuals in modern society require an even greater diversity and malleability. If nothing else, history offers proof that families are able to display variety and diversity in their organization and timing and to contain conflicts between the needs of individuals and the collective demands of the family under changing historical conditions.

The family has never been a utopian retreat from the world, except in the imagination of social reformers and social scientists. Some of the major problems besetting family life today emanate from the heavy demands placed upon it by individuals in society who require that it be a haven of nurture and a retreat from the outside world. The modern family's growing discomfort suggests the need for expansion and diversity in what we expect from it and in its adaptation to new social conditions with diverse timing schedules and a multiplicity of roles for its members, rather than for seeking refuge in a non-existent past.

REFERENCES

[1]On the development of the field, see Tamara K. Hareven, "The History of the Family as an Interdisciplinary Field," *Journal of Interdisciplinary History*, 2 (Autumn, 1971), pp. 399-414. Recent research in the field can be found in the new *Journal of Family History, Studies in Family, Kinship, and Demography*.

[2]See, for example, John Demos, *A Little Commonwealth: Family Life in Plymouth Colony* (New York, 1970); Philip Greven, *Four Generations: Population, Land, and Family in Colonial Andover, Massachusetts* (Ithaca, New York, 1970); Philippe Ariès, *Centuries of Childhood*, trans. Robert

Baldick (New York, 1962); Peter Laslett and Richard Wall, eds., *Household and Family in Past Time* (Cambridge, 1972).

[3]The important pioneering work in this area is Neil Smelser, *Social Change in the Industrial Revolution* (Chicago, 1959). More recent works include Michael Anderson, *Family Structure in Nineteenth-Century Lancashire* (Cambridge, 1971); Virginia Y. McLaughlin, "Patterns of Work and Family Organization: Buffalo's Italians," *Journal of Interdisciplinary History*, 2 (Autumn, 1971), pp. 299-314; Tamara K. Hareven, "Family Time and Industrial Time," *Journal of Urban History*, 1 (May, 1975), pp. 365-89.

[4]William Goode, *World Revolution and Family Patterns* (New York, 1963).

[5]William Goode, "The Theory and Measurement of Family Change," in *Indicators of Social Change: Concepts and Measurements*, ed. Eleanor B. Sheldon and Wilbert Moore (New York, 1968), pp. 295-348; Tamara K. Hareven, "Modernization and Family History," *Signs*, 2 (Autumn, 1976), pp. 190-206.

[6]*Ibid.*

[7]An important theoretical formulation of the life course as it changes over time is Glen Elder, "Family History and the Life Course," in Tamara K. Hareven, ed., *The Family Cycle and the Life Course in Historical Perspective* (forthcoming); John Modell, Frank Furstenberg, and Theodore Hershberg, "Social Change and Transitions to Adulthood in Historical Perspective," *Journal of Family History*, 1 (Autumn, 1976), pp. 7-32.

[8]Tamara K. Hareven and Maris Vinovskis, "Marital Fertility, Ethnicity, and Occupation in Urban Families: An Analysis of South Boston and the South End in 1880," *Journal of Social History*, 3 (Spring, 1975), pp. 69-93; Hareven, "Family Time" (cited above, note 3); Howard Chudacoff. "Newlyweds and Familial Extension: First Stages of the Family Cycle in Providence, R.I., 1864-1880," forthcoming in Tamara K. Hareven and Maris Vinovskis, eds., *Demographic Processes and Family Organization in Nineteenth-Century American Society*.

[9]Elder (cited above, note 7).

[10]Talcott Parsons, "The Kinship System of the Contemporary United States," *American Anthropologist*, 45 (January-March, 1943), pp. 22-38.

[11]Peter Uhlenberg, "Cohort Variations in Family Life Cycle Experiences of U.S. Females," *Journal of Marriage and the Family*, 36 (May, 1974), pp. 284-92.

[12]Paul Glick, "The Family Cycle," *American Sociological Review*, 12 (April, 1947), pp. 164-74 "The Life Cycle of the Family," *Marriage and Family Living*, 18 (February, 1955), pp. 3-9.

[13]Uhlenberg (cited above, note 11).

[14]*Idem*, "Changing Configurations of the Life Course," in Tamara K. Hareven, ed. (cited above note 7).

[15]*Ibid.*

[16]Alice Rossi, "Transition to Parenthood," *Journal of Marriage and the Family*, 30 (February 1968), pp. 26-40.

[17]Modell, Furstenberg, and Hershberg (cited above, note 6).

[18]Anderson (cited above, note 3).

[19]*Ibid.*; and Tamara K. Hareven, "The Dynamics of Kin in American Industrial Communities" (forthcoming).

[20]The prevalence of nuclear households has been confirmed by historical demographers for both Europe and the United States and for both the pre-industrial period and the nineteenth century. See Laslett and Wall (cited above, note 2), and Tamara K. Hareven, ed., *Family and Kin in American Urban Communities, 1780-1920* (New York, 1977).

[21]John Modell and Tamara K. Hareven, "Urbanization and the Malleable Household: An Examination of Boarding and Lodging in American Families," *Journal of Marriage and the Family*, 35 (August, 1973), pp. 467-79; Howard Chudacoff and Tamara K. Hareven, "The Later Years of Life and the Family Cycle" (forthcoming).

[22]Modell and Hareven, "Urbanization and the Malleable Household" (cited above, note 21).

[23]Hareven, "Family Time and Industrial Time" (cited above, note 3).

[24]Richard Sennett, *Families Against the City* (Cambridge, Mass., 1970); Barbara Welter, "The Cult of True Womanhood: 1820-1860," *American Quarterly*, 18 (October, 1966), pp. 151-74; Kirk Jeffrey, "Family History: The Middle-Class American Family in the Urban Context" (Ph.D dissertation, Stanford University, 1972); Mary Ryan, "American Society and the Cult of Domesticity" (Ph.D. dissertation, University of California at Santa Barbara, 1972).

[25]Robert Smuts, *Women and Work in America* (New York, 1971), Daniel Scott Smith, "Family Limitation, Sexual Control, and Domestic Feminism in Victorian America," in Mary Hartman and Lois W. Banner, eds., *Clio's Consciousness Raised* (New York, 1974), pp. 119-37.

[26]Goode (cited above, note 4).

[27]Rossi (cited above, note 16).

E. ANTHONY WRIGLEY

Reflections on the History of the Family

HISTORIANS HAVE AWAKENED BELATEDLY to the importance of studying the history of the family. The study of the institutional frameworks that support society has always been a historical preoccupation, because it has the advantage of being at once a valuable device for describing change within a single society and the differences between societies and, at the same time, of representing a first step toward a more fundamental analysis of the structure of the society under study. Thus the nature and function of the manor, guild, church, cabinet, courts of law, firm, chartered company, army, navy, and so on, have all attracted attention as institutions within society. But the family, while not entirely neglected, has never commanded a comparable intensity of study. This is an anomaly the more surprising in view of its central importance in all societies and the attention paid to it by other disciplines such as sociology and social anthropology when studying societies of all types—modern, traditional, and hunter-fisher-gatherer.

In the last fifteen years, however, there has been a striking increase in the number of publications devoted to the history of the family and certain allied topics, particularly historical population studies, the position of women in society, the institution of service, illegitimacy, orphanage, childhood, adolescence, and the position of the elderly. My purpose in this essay is to offer some brief reflections on the scope of this new work, on certain problems of terminology and definition, on available sources and techniques, and on the implications of the substantive material so far published on a limited range of connected topics. There are other questions of the highest interest and importance—especially those centering on the nature and strength of affective ties within the family—that I shall leave largely untouched. This neglect is from choice, but it is not intended to imply that they are any less significant than those on which I shall comment. I have in mind chiefly work on the west European family.[1]

Many of the most taxing and interesting problems associated with the study of the history of the family arise from the protean nature of family life and activities. The sphere of action of other institutions is commonly restricted by a single function or range of functions—political, economic, or religious. Family life, in contrast, has spanned virtually the whole range of human activities. As a result it is far harder to create a satisfactory framework for its study, to model its complexities satisfactorily, and to solve analytic problems. The issues that intrigue scholars vary so widely that it is not surprising they should disagree about their nature and solution. Moreover, though these difficulties exist in all family studies, they are more pronounced in historical than in contemporary studies for two main reasons, in addition to the special problems connected with source materials and their interpretation. First, the family in pre-industrial Europe discharged a far wider range of functions than it has been assigned today. Second, the nature of the historical record frequently allows material bearing on the family to be studied over long periods of time, whereas most contemporary studies are restricted to a comparatively brief period. Change as well as function must therefore be accommodated, at once the prime interest and a major difficulty in historical studies.

The pre-industrial family was to a greater or lesser degree the chief unit of reproduction, production, consumption, socialization, education, and, in some contexts, religious observance and political action. It was the institution to which the individual normally turned to cope with the problems of age, sickness, and incapacity. Effective membership of society at large was attainable in many circumstances only by membership of a family through which a claim could be mediated. But though the concentration of such a wide range of functions within a single institution makes its study especially inviting, it increases the danger that any clarity and simplicity in analysis may prove delusive, obtainable only at the cost of distortion or selection. Take, for example, the question of the bounds of the unit to be studied. What constituted a family unit for reproduction was often a different entity from what constituted a family unit for production. Nor need a unit of production, in turn, coincide with a unit of consumption, and so on. To attempt, therefore, some omnicompetent definition of the family in terms, say, of commensality is to enforce an artificial simplicity and rigidity.

The concept of membership of a family is a frequent and basic source of confusion. In what sense, if at all, for example, does membership of one family preclude membership of another? The act of marriage brings into existence a new family unit, but it does not dissolve—though it may weaken—ties between the two spouses and their respective families of orientation in societies in which a cognatic kinship system prevails. And even in a rigidly agnatic system, the husband in the newly formed marriage will retain close ties with the family in which he grew up. Indeed, as has frequently been observed, in such systems these ties may be so powerful as to make the affective links between husband and wife relatively slight. The wife joins the husband's wider family, and their own marriage may create a family whose functions do not extend much beyond procreation. The concept of family membership must therefore be capable of encompassing simultaneous membership of more than one family.

In western Europe, temporary membership in a family other than the family of orientation or procreation was common, since a substantial proportion of young people of both sexes spent some years in service or apprenticeship. The life cycle of many people therefore included membership of at least three families and frequently of many more. A common period of service with any one family was a year, so that between adolescence and marriage a young man or woman might be a member of several families. The death of a spouse also often meant for the survivor either creating or joining a new family, because he or she remarried or, in later years, because the survivor moved to the family of a married child if such an opportunity existed.

The same point can be made in a different way. The family may be envisaged not as a unit with a single boundary of membership for all its many functions but as a nesting of units, normally with a conjugal unit of reproduction at its core in the case of western Europe, but with a range of overlapping areas around about it, each related to a particular function, so that the whole could be represented in the form of a Venn diagram. The study of the changing composition of such diagrams is one method of describing the changes taking place over time, while a full "library" of diagrams describing different family systems would help to identify any patterns that are universally present from those that are to be found only in particular periods or places.

An individual might be not only a member of several families during his lifetime, but also of more than one type of family—conjugal, stem, extended, and so on. And in this context, too, it is convenient to envisage concurrent membership as possible at least for certain attributes of family life. The point may be clarified by using an example which also illustrates the importance of showing imagination in allowing for the necessary limitations of particular types of source material. In this instance, awareness of the distinction made by demographers between current and cohort methods of measurement is particularly valuable.

In a given community, a typical man or woman may be a member at different times of both conjugal and stem families but may spend much longer in the former than in the latter. In these circumstances, any examination of the family system of the community which springs from a source of a current type (such as a listing of inhabitants) will catch the quantitative dominance of this family type, but it may miss the fact that most people living to adult years have had experience of life in more than one type of family. Yet this aspect of family life would be readily apparent from the use of any source, or combination of sources, that enables an investigation based on the cohort to be carried out—following individuals through their life cycles rather than catching them at a single point in time. The two methods of investigation are, of course, complementary, and, as with current and cohort measures in demography, each will have special relevance for a particular range of questions. If, following the examination of listings of inhabitants, further investigation using cohort methods showed the stem family to be part of the life-cycle experience of most people, younger sons might be regarded as retaining membership of a stem family even after their marriage and establishment of a new conjugal family unit, because the death of an older brother might entail immediate reentry into a stem-family household.

The complexity and diffuseness of the concept of membership of a family, which is reflected in the common usage of the term but is also intrinsic to it, contrasts with the comparative simplicity of the concept of membership of a household, which, if it is defined to connote habitual residence within a single dwelling unit, is capable of a much more exact use. There are difficulties with this term also, but they are minor when compared with those surrounding the concept of membership of a family. The study of household structure in the past, which lends itself to accurate measurement because the household was frequently used as the unit for collecting information by the state and the church, has attracted much attention in recent years.[2] It will be important to the general study of the history of the family to decide whether the household is best treated as an independent feature of the social system (family *and* household), or whether it should be seen simply as one of the dimensions of family life, connoting such topics as co-residence and commensality. Intriguing questions arise in the study of family and household jointly when the household (or, if the distinction is made, the houseful[3]) contains individuals who are not family members, as in the case of lodgers. Is their presence of any social structural, as opposed to economic, significance? For example, does using a room to earn money from letting to a lodger differ in a significant way from using it to house a journeyman weaver at a loom as an alternative source of supplementary income? The first would appear as a member of the houseful, but the latter, living elsewhere, would not.

Within the wide realm of the history of the family, those studies that are feasible cover only a part of the territory, and even within these areas the depth of coverage is variable. As always in historical studies, what can be attempted is largely determined by the range of source materials available. Some aspects of family life can be described and analyzed with considerable precision using sources commonly available. Thus, the functioning of the family as a reproductive unit can be observed satisfactorily using the technique of family reconstitution applied to the entries of baptism, marriage, and burial in parish registers. There are a substantial number of English registers suitable for this purpose and covering 250 years or more between the sixteenth and nineteenth centuries. Age at marriage, age gap between spouses, duration of marriage, length of widowhood, birth spacing, the relationship between what might be called demographic family size (number of children ever born) and existential family size (number of children surviving to some given point in the family cycle, such as the death of a parent), premarital pregnancy, the relationship between the death of parents and marriage of children, the proportion of families childless or sonless at the death of the father—all these and many similar topics can be studied, often in fine detail. Sometimes the extent of differences between groups within the same population can be gauged, as well as differences between different communities or within the same community over long periods of time.

Equally, nominal listings of inhabitants following the general form of a census enumerator's book are commonly available for the recent past, and more sporadically for the period from the sixteenth to the eighteenth century, though rarely for earlier periods. In their classic form, these documents list by name the members of each family or household, identify the head of the family and his or her relationship to other members of it, and provide details of sex, marital status, age, occupation, and birthplace. Some are still more informative, though the majority, especially in earlier periods, are much less detailed. Where good listings exist they permit the study of most of those aspects of family life that are closely tied to co-residence. For example, there was a marked, regular, and consistent positive relationship between social and economic status and the size of the co-resident domestic group in England in early modern times.[4] The better listings both demonstrate the fact of this relationship and reveal how much it depended upon the operation of the institution of service in allowing vulnerable families to release some of their children into the service of families better able to maintain them and afford them employment.

As might be expected, where suitable registers and listings exist for the same community, they both complement and supplement each other. Family reconstitution, for example, does not yield any direct evidence about members of a co-resident family who have not joined it by birth or marriage, nor about those who leave it for reasons other than marriage or death. On the other hand, listings rarely throw any light on kinship links except within the household. Married sisters living next door to each other will go undetected, but their relationship is likely to come to light when information from the two sources is combined.

These illustrations of the value of combining information drawn from different sources suggest a more general point. Even the most informative single source will cover only a fraction of family activities. Hence the attraction of trying to combine information drawn from several sources to produce a picture of the family and its members which, if not "in the round," will at least be less flat than any picture that could be derived from one source taken in isolation—hence, in turn, the importance of developing an appropriate logic of nominal record linkage. Such a logic is fundamental to the full use of many of the chief sources of information about the family in the past. It lies at the heart of family reconstitution, for example, since only by its use can scattered information about individuals be knitted together into family histories in a consistent fashion. And it is likely to prove equally fundamental to the successful articulation of information about the same individual or family drawn from different sources. The identification of individuals in records scattered in many sources over a period which may last a century or more involves taxing problems of logic and of information retrieval, but if the labor is great the rewards are commensurate.[5] When replicated for many individuals and families, the resulting matrix of information is incomparably more informative than community-wide measures of wealth, fertility, marriage age, and so on.

There are, of course, many aspects of family life in the past left largely untouched by the normal range of source material and therefore inaccessible to examination. The attitudes of mind that informed behavior are far more difficult to recapture than those aspects of behavior that can be described and measured from surviving records. Diaries, for example, were not widely kept, and we may assume that most of those that were kept are very likely to have been lost or destroyed. When they do survive, they may be illuminating, but keepers of diaries were a tiny and unrepresentative minority.[6] The dead cannot be directly interrogated; deficiencies in written records cannot be made good in the manner of the social anthropologist.

Where direct evidence about behavioral norms and attitudes is lacking, however, it may sometimes be made good to some extent by the use of indirect evidence. It is fortunate that this kind of evidence often throws light on those aspects of family life least easy to approach from sources which bear chiefly on the family as a reproductive or as a co-resident unit. We need indications of the strength and frequency of contact between kin living in different households, and, if possible, some way of comparing contact with kin and with non-kin—neighbors, friends, members of a joint economic enterprise, and so on, in order to gain some insight into attitudes toward people in these groups. And such information can sometimes be obtained. Evidence about the network of contacts used for various purposes is sometimes to be had, for example, from the proceedings of manorial courts, or, at a later date, from quarter sessional records and similar sources. The circumstances in which kin-based links were invoked in such matters as pledging for debt or compurgation, or the nature of the disputes between kin which came to the attention of the local court, or the examination of the extent to which kin of varying degrees of propinquity figured in testamentary dispositions can reveal a great deal about networks of contact for various purposes if exploited systematically. Indeed, any body of source material that provides information about the selection of one person by another to carry out some ceremonial function, discharge a duty, or undertake an obligation is potentially rich in evidence about the relationship between an individual, his immediate family under the same roof, his kin in other places and his local community. The choice of godparent, for example, has been shown to be a rich vein of evidence in this respect, showing marked variations in different parts of Europe in the eighteenth century that appear to have borne a clear-cut relationship to the social and economic structure of the several communities in question. The use of network analysis to clarify the properties of systems of relationships revealed by records of this type may prove capable of offering for the analysis of the structure and function of the family within the local community the same prospect of fuller information that family reconstitution offers in relation to the demography of communities in the past.

The structure of relationships between individuals who share membership of a family is paralleled by a psychological structure within individuals, the result of internalizing the rules by which family and social life is conducted. To attempt to come to grips with *mentalité* is as important as to examine more directly mensurable aspects of family life. But it has proved an arduous task whether approached on a high level of abstraction or on a more mundane level.[7] Some work of great value has appeared in recent years, however, and it is throwing light on aspects of family life in the past which were almost entirely hidden from view until recently.[8]

Though the history of the family is necessarily of prime interest in the study of any past society, a peculiar importance attaches to it in the centuries during which modern industrialized society first came into being in western Europe. At one time it was commonly supposed that the pressures of the transition from a traditional to an industrial society destroyed an older family type characterized by early marriage, a complex co-resident group, and close ties among kin both within and between households. In its place the industrial revolution produced a new familial system consisting of small conjugal units formed after relatively late marriage and retaining only vestigial ties with any but immediate kin. The work of Hajnal, Laslett, and others in the nineteen-sixties showed this view to be untenable, and also suggested the possibility that the pre-industrial west European family pattern—late marriage for women, a large proportion of women of child-bearing age remaining unmarried,[9] a separate household at marriage, small households comprising only a single conjugal family—was unique among all traditional societies. Suddenly, therefore, the study of the history of the family in western Europe achieved strategic significance for any discussion of the changes that collectively made up modern industrialized urban society. Was it a key to the understanding of the transformations of the eighteenth and nineteenth centuries? If it was not the industrial revolution that had produced the modern conjugal family system, might it not have been the existence of an unusual complex of marriage and co-residential patterns that helped to produce the radical economic changes of the industrial revolution period? A pre-industrial society in which overall fertility is comparatively low because women marry late is one in which a comparatively favorable balance between population and productive capacity is attainable. Once attained, it is easier to sustain where age at marriage is sensitive to economic and social circumstances and not largely determined by a biological event such as menarche. Higher real incomes imply a different structure of demand and a greater chance of provoking the type of changes that precede and accompany an industrial revolution. This line of thinking is sufficiently persuasive to command attention, even though it may require qualification and refinement. There remain, however, not only conceptual problems in assessing the significance of early modern west European family patterns, but also large evidential gaps, though many of them can be filled with further work.

The history of the family in western Europe is, therefore, not yet at a stage where confident generalizations can be made either about the pre-industrial family or about the changes that occurred during industrialization. We have already seen that the industrial revolution did not produce the west European pattern. Even within that pattern, it may prove mistaken to assume that the industrial revolution coincided with great changes. Earlier changes within a still rural society may have been as great or greater. For example, Elizabethan Poor Law legislation in England, which transferred to the parish responsibilities that once had devolved not only upon the conjugal family but also upon a wider circle of kin and neighbors, may prove both to have symbolized and to have expedited a decline in the relative importance of personal and family ties outside the conjugal family greater in scope than any which took place 200 years later.[10]

The store of knowledge about the history of the family is, however, much fuller than it was a decade or two ago, and several misconceptions have been swept away. It may be convenient to expand somewhat on the findings adumbrated earlier. The co-resident family group from Elizabethan times onward normally consisted only of the basic reproductive unit of husband, wife, and children, or of a remnant of the same, supplemented by servants in the households of the more prosperous. Occasionally a grandparent was also present, but lateral extension of the co-resident unit was very rare in the ordinary ranks of society, and vertical extension uncommon. Both men and women married late, with a mean age at first marriage in the middle or late twenties. It seems almost certain that the pattern of late marriage was not new in the sixteenth century; further work on the 1377 and 1381 Poll Taxes has revealed that the same pattern was already to be found by the late fourteenth century.[11] The simplicity of the co-resident domestic group may also have been of long standing by Tudor times. Marriage in early modern England almost always involved the setting up of a new household under a separate roof. Clearly, many features of the "modern" family had been the norm for many centuries before the industrial revolution.

In the period between Tudor and Victorian times, no significant change occurred in the average size of the co-resident domestic group in England, though significant changes did occur in its composition, the most notable of which was probably the decline in the importance of live-in servants in husbandry. Age at marriage also changed substantially over those centuries, reaching its peak in the late seventeenth or early eighteenth century, when it was somewhat higher than it had been a century earlier and a couple of years higher than it was to be a century later. The change was more pronounced for women than for men. Average family size (in the demographic sense) declined during the seventeenth century because of later marriage, and the effect of the change was exaggerated by marked increase in infant and child mortality. But during the eighteenth century, the nuptiality and fertility patterns were reversed so that, by the end of that century, they do not appear to have been very different from those for the Elizabethan period.[12]

In continental Europe, as might be expected from its much greater size, there was far less uniformity than in England, though the lack of uniformity was often to be found in small areas as well as on the continental scale. Even a country as small as Holland, for example, showed a considerable variation in prevailing types of co-resident domestic group.[13] In western Europe generally the small conjugal-family household was very common but far from universal. Married brothers and their families often shared the same house in parts of France and Italy, for example, while stem-family systems were quite widely found in Austria, France, and Germany. In parts of eastern Europe, huge and complex households predominated with extensions both laterally and vertically. The average size of the co-resident domestic group was often twice as great as it was in England. The "eastern" pattern may have reached its most extreme form in serf households on the noble estates of Muscovite Russia, where very few simple conjugal family units were to be found, and households consisting of a single person, common in England and much of Holland, were almost unknown.[14] Eastern Europe also represented a very marked contrast with western Europe in age at marriage. Teenage marriage was so common in Russia that only a minority of either sex passed into their twenties unmarried.

The extreme ends of Europe certainly presented a dramatic contrast. Middle Europe may have displayed less uniformity than either end and a wider prevalence of family forms intermediate in size and complexity, but, though the materials exist to permit comparisons of this type to be made, they have as yet been very little analyzed. Even the description of the eastern and western extremes may prove to be more of a caricature than an epitome when our knowledge has been filled in by a sufficient number of local studies.

Since the dominant forms of co-resident groups in eastern and western Europe appear once to have been so dissimilar though now much more alike, at least in urban settings, it follows that the nature and extent of the changes in familial structures involved in the transition from a rural-agricultural to an urban industrial society must have been very different at the two ends of Europe. To the extent that patterns of co-residence capture familial links and reflect familial behavior, the change was far more extreme in the east than in the west.

To explain the characteristics of the family system of a particular society—or changes in its characteristics—the relationship between its economic, social and demographic functions has to be understood: the data themselves can only be useful in a negative sense by helping to winnow out those theories about this relationship which are clearly at odds with the facts. Empirical data, indeed, hold little meaning unless they are subject to a constant dialectical exchange with a developing body of theory. Progress in work on the history of the family is as much dependent on the formulation of models and hypotheses as it is upon the existence and exploitation of suitable source material. The frequent resort to the ideas of Le Play and Chayanov made by those intent upon giving shape to the plethora of new information now available suggests that recent progress may lack balance in this respect.

The problems of devising helpful models of behavior are not the same for pre-industrial societies as they are for those in transition or already industrialized. In traditional agricultural societies, it is not surprising that much attention has been paid to the system of land tenure, land ownership, and land cultivation in seeking to identify and explain congruences among familial characteristics or between them and other features of community life. In such communities, the characteristics of this system can scarcely fail to be of the first importance. Since the flow of income from the land formed such a large part of the total flow of income generated in pre-industrial economies, and since the size and structure of familial systems were much influenced by their economic circumstances, tenurial and familial systems were necessarily closely related. The inheritance rules by which land passed from one generation to the next and the terms under which it could pass into the land market for sale and purchase were likewise of significance to family constitution and strategy. For example, where land can be bought and sold freely and in units of any size, it is feasible for a family to adjust its holding of land to its labor power as this varies over the life cycle of the family—acquiring additional land as sons grow to adolescence and shedding it again after they leave home. Where, on the other hand, land is inalienable, any symmetry between land and labor on a holding can only be secured by "importing" labor from outside the current co-resident family group whenever the number of able-bodied workers falls short of the number required to work the holding to advantage. Conversely if the family has a surplus of labor, it can only be fully productive if the surplus is "exported" to another holding. There is no necessary connection between inalienable land-holding and particular family characteristics, of course, nor is surplus labor always "exported." Many peasant societies in Asia today, for example, appear to prefer to retain surplus labor on the family holding even when marginal productivity drops below marginal consumption. But the system by which a pre-industrial society attempts to match productive land and productive workers is so important to its general functioning that it is natural to consider the matter when examining family life.

Similarly, partible and impartible inheritance systems may create pressures tending to favor particular types of familial co-residence and characteristic rules about the circumstances in which a marriage may take place, just as they may tend to produce different demographic regimes. A strictly impartible inheritance system, for example, is easier to reconcile with a stable and enduring adjustment of population to its agricultural base than is the case with a partible system.

Within the canons of discussions of this type, there have been elegant and persuasive essays charting both the intricacy and the surprising resilience of th web of relationships that link family behavior with social and economic circum stances to sustain communities without fundamental change over many centurie of ebb and flow of events.[15] Equally, there have been excellent studies of the cir cumstances in which the web may be strained or even ruptured by changes tha overcame the powerful homeostatic tendencies evident in the social, economic and demographic affairs of traditional societies.[16] But the treatment of th family during the transition from an agricultural to an industrial society lack comparable authority. For example, few aspects of family behavior in the las two centuries have changed so fundamentally as the extent and effectiveness o control over marital fertility. This is a change of immense importance, and th timing and extent of the spread of deliberate family limitation can be establishe in outline from easily accessible sources, yet an adequate explanation o observed change is largely lacking.[17] The huge mass of empirical informatio about the family during the industrial revolution and thereafter is not sustaine and given meaning by a matching conceptual framework.

The industrial revolution period is full of apparent paradoxes. In a perio of rapid and radical change in most aspects of economic and social life, i is odd that in many ways the west European family should have changed s little. Perhaps it was the belief that tumultuous change elsewhere *must* hav been paralleled by changes of comparable magnitude within the family tha seduced many scholars into supposing that the modern family pattern was product of industrialization. Some of the changes that did occur (notably in th control of marital fertility) took place only after a long time lag in th populations most affected by economic growth. Major changes did take place The separation of home and work place for those engaged in industry, fo example, affected many aspects of family life.[18] But changes of comparabl magnitude had occurred earlier. The change from husbandman to wage-pai agricultural laborer, for example, also implies changes in family behavior o great importance.

The underlying issue may be approached by noting some of the character istics of change during the industrial revolution and how easily they can prov deceptive. The simplest and most satisfactory way of pinpointing the nature o the *economic* changes brought about by the industrial revolution is to define it as period in which real incomes per head show a strong and sustained tendency t secular growth. Although there has been a prolonged debate about the trend o real wages, during the early stages of the industrial revolution, ultimately th benefits of growing productivity secured by the application of new sources o power to increasingly sophisticated machinery brought an improvement in livin standards that reached the entire population. The change was linear. Equally— and broadly in parallel with the changes in real incomes—there were the pre dictable and often linear changes in many other aspects of social and economi life: in the proportion of the population living in towns and cities, for example and in the proportion of the population engaged in primary, secondary, an tertiary employment.[19] It is easy to assume that in all major aspects of life th immense influence of the industrial revolution must have produced linea changes and that these in turn would ensure sympathetic change in family be navior. The "convergence" hypothesis concerning the family, for example, embodies this assumption, adding to it a view of the final state toward which change moves.[20]

But what if some types of changes were not linear during the industrial revolution? May this not help to explain the complexity and variety of the pressures upon the family which makes its history during this period so difficult to comprehend? It is useful to maintain a distinction between modernization and industrialization when pondering this issue. It is widely supposed that there is a close connection between the cluster of changes which together connote modernization—"rationality," the pursuit of self-interest, universalistic principles of social organization, recruitment by achievement rather than by ascription, functional specialization, and so on—and those features of modern family life that most distinguish it from the family of earlier times. It is also very generally assumed that modernization and industrialization go hand in hand, the latter representing the upshot in the economy of the changes going forward in society more generally.[21] In these circumstances, it is only natural to expect "modern" features of family life to be fostered and furthered as industrialization takes hold.

There are good reasons, however, for thinking that the connection between modernization and industrialization is contingent rather than necessary, and also for supposing that in the early stages of industrialization its progress tended in many respects to impede rather than to expedite modernization.[22] If this is so, it need occasion no surprise if the effects on the family produced by the early decades of the industrial revolution were confused, including some changes which by the general canons of modernization theory would be regarded as regression. The flood of immigrants into towns, for example, often meant an increased dependence upon kin outside the immediate conjugal family who might be able to find or provide employment and accommodation, or who could give aid during illness.[23] The lack or malfunctioning of formal institutions to provide these services left no alternative, whereas, in the rural areas from which the immigrants came, institutional support through the parish was often quite effective in providing help for individuals or conjugal families afflicted by poverty, sickness, or decrepitude. Again, levels of literacy, often taken as one of the key indicators of modernization, fell in areas where the industrial population was growing rapidly while school provision remained largely unchanged. The surge of industrial growth produced many new communities both large and small where the way of life was more *gemeinschaftlich* than that of the older cities and rural areas of much of western Europe. "Rational" economic, social, or demographic behavior had little chance to establish itself in, say, a mining community in Durham, a bucket-making township in the Black Country, or a Manchester slum. Life contained uncertainties far greater even than those forced upon agricultural societies by the vagaries of weather and harvest. Mortality was sometimes high and fertility was often very high in such circumstances. Having a choice between alternatives that can be weighed against one another and reducing the influence of the arbitrary and unpredictable are essential to the conception of "modernization," and these were less easily accomplished for most people directly affected by the early industrial revolution than they had been for a long period before it. Dependence upon daily or weekly wages for access to the resources that sustain life represents a massive increase in uncertainty when compared with the situation facing those in a peasant economy who have a freehold or a secure customary tenure. Bad seasons and high debts may bring heavy burdens to a peasant, but his income is not liable to be cut off without forewarning for a period none can predict. In the country even wage-paid laborers, though more exposed than husbandmen with land of their own, usually had a garden plot to cultivate and could expect some support from the community in times of distress (as under the "Speenhamland" system in England).[24] In new industrial areas, wages were often almost the sole means of access to resources, and they could be stopped at any time.

In circumstances such as these, a web of informal relations with kin and neighbors may be the only resort against disaster, and they may tend to produce changes in family structure and behavior which appear regressive when compared with later changes. Only when real incomes had begun to move upward in a sustained fashion, and when the state had undertaken some responsibility for the provision of education and hedges against sickness, unemployment, and old age was there again opportunity for "rational" behavior to spread among the wage earners. From the last decade of the nineteenth century onward, those most directly involved in the new industrial growth no longer found that industrialization and modernization were at odds with each other. Family structure and behavior began to move once more in a "modern" direction. Nor was it just coincidence that at that period marital fertility rates began to fall rapidly throughout the population. Until there were effective institutional alternatives to family and kin for dealing with the commonest perils of life, the old maxim about safety in numbers made good sense.

Consider the problem of old age, for example. A peasant possessing land had no necessary reason to fear that increasing physical frailty would deprive him of all income since he had a capital asset from which a flow of income would accrue to him whether he worked it himself or not. He could make over his land to his son in return for an undertaking that he would receive food and shelter for as long as he lived. He could rent the land to the highest bidder, or he could sell it and live off the proceeds of the sale. In principle there was no necessary connection between old age and penury. A wage earner in a welfare state also has no necessary reason to fear old age. He will receive a pension after his working days are done even though he may have no personal savings. A wage earner in an eighteenth-century English country parish, though much less secure, nevertheless had a claim on the resources of the parish in which he had a settlement. But a wage earner in one of the communities thrown up by the industrial revolution was dependent in his old age upon his savings, charity, or support from other members of the family. The last was in many cases the most important, and an old man or woman who could depend upon support from his or her children was more secure than someone dependent on charity or diminishing savings.

Much the same was true for the other major sources of insecurity in life. Those with capital or some other source of assured income could afford to be self-reliant. Those who received income only as long as they worked needed outside support when age or illness, economic depression, or local misfortune deprived them of employment. If the state or the parish provided support, a

arge family no longer spread the risks and might prove to be a burden in other
ways, but if the family was the sole or prime source of support, the advantage of
size outweighed its burdens—and where support within the immediate family
was for some reason impossible remoter kin were called upon.

Within the compass of a short essay it is easier to start hares than to run
them down. I have been more concerned with trying to suggest the nature and
range of some of the topics prominent in the study of the history of the family
than in pursuing individual issues to a conclusion. I have also been at pains to
emphasize that both in matters of technique and theory and in the work of
acquiring substantive knowledge much remains to be done. It may be appropriate to conclude by suggesting that each advance in knowledge achieved so far
has served to underline the value of tracing the contrasts between the traditional, industrializing, and fully industrial phases in west European history
through the changing forms and functions of the family as an institution within
society. Many of its activities and characteristics are directly or indirectly
mensurable, and prove to have varied widely in different parts of Europe,
between different groups within the same society, and within the same area over
time. Since the family was responsive to every social or economic change of any
consequence, it forms an excellent vehicle for the study of the development of
the modern out of the medieval world. But its value does not lie simply in its
convenience as a sort of historical litmus paper. No one wishing to explain the
great changes that swept early modern Europe can afford to neglect the
importance of the exceptional nature of the west European family itself.
How far it may be regarded as an independent feature and how far as a
subordinate element in the socioeconomic system as a whole is debatable. But
few if any other features of west European society differentiated it more
clearly from other pre-industrial societies than did its family system. Its
characteristics were in several respects so well suited to the rapid economic
growth that ultimately took place that it would be foolish to ignore the
possibility of an intriguing paradox—that although the immediate impact of the
industrial revolution on family structure and behavior may have produced
changes which made it for a while less distinctively "western," the "western"
features were essential if the industrial revolution itself was to occur.

REFERENCES
[1]See L. Berkner, "Recent Research on the History of the Family in Western Europe," *Journal of Marriage and the Family* 35:3 (1973), pp. 395-405.
[2]See P. Laslett and R. Wall, eds., *Household and Family in Past Time* (Cambridge, 1972). This volume presents a wide range of substantive results and theoretical discussions. For a discussion of the limitations of evidence of this type when used in isolation, see L. Berkner, "The Use and Misuse of Census Data for the Historical Analysis of Family Structure," *Journal of Interdisciplinary History* 5:4 (1975), 721-38; and his empirical study, "The Stem Family and the Developmental Cycle of the Peasant Household: An Eighteenth-Century Austrian Example," *American Historical Review*, 77 (1972), pp. 398-418.
[3]See Laslett and Wall, *Household and Family*, esp. pp. 34-44 and 159-66, for a discussion of the concept of "houseful."
[4]P. Laslett, "Size and Structure of the Household in England over Three Centuries," *Population Studies*, 23:2 (1969), pp. 199-223.
[5]For a discussion of the problems encountered in nominal record linkage using historical material, see E. A. Wrigley, ed., *Identifying People in the Past* (London, 1973).

[6]Detailed diaries are nevertheless immensely valuable, especially when accompanied by subtle and sensitive exegeses. See, for example, the excellent book by Alan Macfarlane, *The Family Life of Ralph Josselin* (Cambridge, 1970).

[7]Among the more interesting essays in the attempt to relate changes in society and economy to the socio-psychological attributes of populations are F. Weinstein and G. M. Platt, *The Wish to Be Free: Society, Psyche, and Value Change* (Berkeley and Los Angeles, 1969); and E. E. Hagen, *On the Theory of Social Change: How Economic Growth Begins* (Cambridge, Mass., 1962). See also the review of the problems of writing on this type of topic in K. Keniston, "Psychological Development and Historical Change," in T. K. Rabb and R. I. Rotberg, eds., *The Family in History: Interdisciplinary Essays* (New York and Toronto, 1971), pp. 141-57. It is a field in which it is singularly difficult to be incisive without at the same time being tendentious.

[8]Especially in recent French writing. See, for example, P. Ariès, *L'Enfant et la vie familiale sous l'Ancien Régime* (Paris, 1960), trans. R. Baldick as *Centuries of Childhood: A Social History of Family Life* (New York, 1962); E. Le Roy Ladurie, *Montaillou, village occitan de 1294 à 1324* (1975); J. L. Flandrin, *Familles: parenté, maison, sexualité dans l'ancienne société* (1976); F. Lebrun, *Les Hommes et la mort en Anjou au XVIIᵉ et XVIIIᵉ siècles* (Paris, 1971).

[9]This pattern, though widely prevalent, was not, of course, omnipresent or invariable. High-status families, for example, sought early marriage for their daughters until a much later date than did the rest of society. See, for example, T. H. Hollingsworth, *The Demography of the British Peerage*, supplement to *Population Studies* 18:2 (1964); or C. Lévy and L. Henry. "Ducs et pairs sous l'Ancien Régime," *Population* 15:5 (1960), pp. 807-30. There were many other exceptional groups, some involving substantial populations. Hajnal drew together and reduced to order much scattered information about west European marriage patterns in J. Hajnal, "European Marriage Patterns in Perspective," in D. V. Glass and D. E. C. Eversley, eds., *Population in History* (London, 1965). Laslett's first major contribution to the revision of earlier views about the family in early modern England may be found in P. Laslett, *The World We Have Lost* (London, 1965).

[10]There is a very persuasive analysis of one aspect of this in A. Macfarlane, *Witchcraft in Tudor and Stuart England* (London, 1970).

[11]See R. Smith, "Some Aspects of Marriage and Household Composition in Late-Fourteenth-Century England," forthcoming in *Proceedings of the XIII International Congress of Genealogical and Heraldic Sciences*.

[12]Evidence substantiating this brief description of demographic trends in early modern England will be published in a forthcoming volume containing the results of the family reconstitution studies undertaken by the SSRC Cambridge Group for the History of Population and Social Structure.

[13]See A. M. van der Woude, "Variations in the Size and Structure of the Household in the United Provinces of the Netherlands in the Seventeenth and Eighteenth Centuries," in Laslett and Wall, *Household and Family in Past Time*, pp. 299-318.

[14]For individual studies of the east European household, see A. Plakans, "Peasant Farmsteads and Households in the Baltic Littoral, 1797," *Comparative Studies in Society and History*, 17:1 (1975), pp. 2-35; and the chapters by E. A. Hammel, "The Zadruga as Process"; by J. M. Halpern, "Town and Countryside in Serbia in the Nineteenth Century, Social and Household Structure as Reflected in the Census of 1863"; and by P. Laslett and M. Clarke, "Houseful and Household in an Eighteenth-Century Balkan City," in Laslett and Wall, *Household and Family in Past Time*, pp. 335-73, 401-27, and 375-400. Professor P. Czap of Amherst College is in the process of analyzing Russian estate listings from the late eighteenth and early nineteenth centuries which are of exceptional interest and quality.

[15]I have in mind here the type of fluctuation without linear trend described by E. Le Roy Ladurie, "L'Histoire immobile," *Annales: Economies, Sociétés, Civilisations*, 29:3 (1974), pp. 673-92.

[16]See, e.g., R. Braun, *Industrialisierung und Volksleben: Die Veränderung der Lebensformen in eine ländlichen Industriegebiet vor 1800* (Zurich, 1960). J. A. Faber and others pursue a similar theme for Holland where the province of Overijssel experienced a period of great difficulty in "Population Changes and Economic Developments in the Netherlands: A Historical Survey," *Afdeling Agrarische Geschiedenis Bijdragen*, 12 (Wageningen, 1965), pp. 47-113, and esp. pp. 72-89.

[17]There is both a useful summary of the current thinking of economists on this issue and a stimulating fresh discussion on conceptualizing the problem in R. Easterlin, "An Economic Framework for Fertility Analysis," *Studies in Family Planning* 6:3 (1975), pp. 54-63.

[18]See N. J. Smelser, *Social Change in the Industrial Revolution* (London, 1959); M. Anderson, *Family Structure in Nineteenth-Century Lancashire* (Cambridge, 1971).

[19]Changes in employment structure were not all, of course, strictly linear. The proportion of the active population engaged in agriculture fell steadily and the proportion in tertiary employment rose; but the proportion in secondary employment, after rising during the early stages of industrialization, usually reached its peak and began to decline as real incomes continued to rise.

[20]See W. J. Goode, *World Revolution and Family Patterns* (New York and London, 1963). This is a very balanced and judicious exposition of a thesis which embraces a "convergence" thesis.

[21]For a fuller discussion of the sense in which the two terms are used and the misconceptions which often arise because of their conventional definitions, see E. A. Wrigley, "The Process of Modernization and the Industrial Revolution in England," *Journal of Interdisciplinary History*, 3:2 1972), pp. 225-59.

[22]This point, too, is discussed at greater length in my article cited above.

[23]See Anderson, *Family Structure* (cited above, note 18), esp. chap. 10.

[24]The enormous value of allotments in improving the lot of the nineteenth-century agricultural laborer and in cushioning him and his family from the worst economic uncertainties comes out vividly in M. K. Ashby's account of her father's life, *Joseph Ashby of Tysoe, 1859-1919: A Study of English Village Life* (Cambridge, 1961).

NATALIE ZEMON DAVIS

Ghosts, Kin, and Progeny: Some Features of Family Life in Early Modern France

How can we talk of family strategies in the sixteenth and seventeenth centuries when even prosperous parents could not be sure of how many children they could bring up to adulthood? How can we talk of a heightened sense of family identity, of the past and present of individual families, when remarriage was constantly creating half-brothers and half-sisters, step-children and step-parents, crisscrossing in-laws—so that it was not always clear where the nuclear family began or ended? How can we insist on the strengthening of parental power when, as in sixteenth-century Lyon, one-third of the teen-agers becoming apprentices and one-half of the young women marrying for the first time were fatherless; when, as in seventeenth-century Bordeaux, more than one-third of the apprentices had neither parent alive?[1] Yet I propose to characterize early modern family life in terms of strategy, identity, and order, as a trend, if not a fact, about every family and as an increasingly persuasive cultural ideal for families above the level of the very poor. As Machiavelli could forge his political rules in the face of fortune's whims, so could families forge their rules as well. In some ways, as we will see, these features of family life were much aided by contemporary political, social, and religious developments; in other ways, they were in tension with them, with interesting long-range consequences for attitudes toward social and corporate solidarity.

I

Let us begin by noting a central concern of many families in the sixteenth and seventeenth centuries: they want to plan for a family future during and beyond the lifetimes of the current parents. Some want merely to pass on the family's patrimony as intact as possible to those of the next generation who will stand for the house or its name in the father's line. Others want to enhance that patrimony; still others want to create a patrimony if it does not already exist. And what is being planned for here is not merely lands, cattle, houses, barns, pensions, rents, offices, workshops, looms, masterships, partnerships, and shares, but also the occupations or careers and the marriages of children. These, too, must be designed so as to maintain, and perhaps increase, the family's store and reputation.

87

This is not, it should be remembered, a "natural" or inevitable way for families to act. It implies a situation unlike that in the early Middle Ages, when wives in some landholding families might have closer ties to their family of birth than to their husbands; when family identity might well extend horizontally out to third and fourth cousins with whom one consulted about immediate issues of vengeance and alliance rather than about distant prospects.[2] It implies a situation in which the family unit, whatever its spread, conceived of its future as requiring invention and effort, rather than simple reliance on traditional custom and providence. Then the family unit must have some power to put its plans into effect, for there were other groups and persons—villagers, lords, guildsmen, city governments, clerics, and monarchs—who had an interest in what parents did with their children and property.

Such long-term planning was, of course, well beyond the possibilities of those who could not bequeath anything because they were serfs (and we must remember that if serfdom had almost disappeared in sixteenth-century England, it could still be the lot of 20 to 30 per cent of the peasants in parts of Burgundy and the Bourbonnais). The best they could hope for was that their children might crowd with them under the same roof and thereby be permitted by custom to succeed to their land when the time came. So a *mainmortable* in the Sologne, trying to buy his freedom, explained that as a serf he could not marry his daughter well, and that his other children had left him and would neither pray for his soul nor pay his debts after he died. Such long-term planning was also beyond the possibilities of landless free peasants and unskilled or ill-paid urban workers. For those without even seed or livestock to pass on, without a trade or art, with little more than a wooden coffer of belongings, their future was made if they could bring even one child to adulthood, rather than seeing offspring all die or abandoning them to a foundling hospital.[3]

But beyond this threshold of thralldom or poverty, already among better-off peasant and artisanal families a habit of mind can be found which, once arrangements for immediate economic and psychological stability have been made, turns toward the future. Listen, for instance, to a sixteenth-century request by eleven families of sharecroppers in the Burgundy, all descended from a household which had opened a farm for an Augustinian abbey some sixty years earlier. They reminded the brothers how they had conserved, increased, and improved the land; how they had multiplied in number of households, children, and separate families; and how they feared that the abbey might decide to contract with some other parties, thus "cutting . . . them off from the fruits for which they hoped from their long and assiduous labor." With such a lack of assurance, their children might have to abandon them and move elsewhere when they were old and feeble. And so they sought—and won— village status and some legal title to the land: "perpetual and permanent habitation . . . for themselves and their posterity . . . born and to be born."[4]

Or see how the process takes place in the family of the printer Jean Barbou. He came to Lyon from a village in Normandy, worked his way up from journeyman to master, married a widow with useful printing connections, if little money, and prudently enlisted a wealthy merchant-publisher as godfather to his son. Then he died at 53, leaving his wife, three unmarried daughters whom he dowered decently, a printing establishment upon which 900 *livres* was still owed, and one son—alas, aged 4—whom he made his heir. Widow Guillemette rallied, married her oldest daughter to a printer richer and more learned than her husband, and saw to it that she and her son were partners in the business. Sister Denise took over; she never faltered, even when her husband was temporarily imprisoned for printing the anti-Trinitarian Servetus (anathema to Catholics and Calvinists alike), and carried on the printing house in her own name after her husband's death. The son, Hugues Barbou, grew up also to become a printer, first in Lyon and then within the safer walls of Limoges, where he purchased an atelier for 1,200 *livres* and founded a publishing dynasty that was to last some two hundred years. From Limoges, in his early thirties, Hugues reflected on the family's rise from that Norman village and on the arrangements made to get him where he was.[5]

To be sure, family strategies for the future were not brand new in Western Europe in the sixteenth century. Careful studies of the nobility of the Mâconnais in twelfth-century France, of patrician families in twelfth-century Genoa, and of burgher families in thirteenth-century Bordeaux (with its newly developed wine trade) have all shown fathers changing the inheritance rights variously of wives, daughters, and younger sons in order to consolidate or enhance their position. In London in the late fourteenth and early fifteenth centuries, there were merchant families who carefully set down a country branch, then waited two or even three generations before moving all the males out of city trade.[6]

Once established, family planning for maintenance and/or acquisition was not always carried on by descendants. In late-sixteenth-century France, Marshal Gaspard de Saulx went against his own good advice to avoid "the ruin of a noble house" by bestowing prodigious dowries on his daughters and dividing his estate equally between his two sons, rather than giving the bulk of it to one. About the same time in England, the aristocracy, more moved by present appetites than future goals, was breaking entails and selling ancestral lands with abandon.[7]

Even with these qualifications, however, it seems likely that family strategies for the future became more generally and consistently used in France and England in the sixteenth and seventeenth centuries (we would expect this earlier in the advanced commercial city-states of northern Italy). Two sets of changes help us understand why this could be so in the French case. First, the powers of feudal lords and of distant kin had been sufficiently eroded by the mid sixteenth century to give better-off families a freer hand. Fiefs were being bought and sold and might well be in the hands of non-nobles; long-term leases were making it easier for some prosperous peasants to think of their holdings as their own. The *retrait lignager*, by which kin out to the sixth or seventh degree might buy inheritance property before it was sold to non-kin, was regularly listed in the French customary-law collections, but actual cases involved only close cousins, nephews, or nieces. As for the continuing constraints on the immediate family from other groups, sometimes they were in competition with private family goals (as with the village assemblies in Burgundy which hindered peasants from turning common lands into inheritable property), but sometimes they supported the interests of the family, or at least the male-line family, as with the ruling of some 300 Lyon silk manufacturers that only daughters and sisters could be female apprentices, lest other women bring in husbands who were interlopers to their art.[8]

Second, with the expansion of the urban economy from the late fifteenth century, with some increase in geographical mobility, and with the multiplication of crafts, careers, and offices, more choices opened up before families—and the response to more choices can be new plans and new forms of control. Now there was more to manipulate as nobles and commoners both aimed to get rents, pensions, annuities, and offices, as even royal jailers and royal sergeants tried to reserve their offices for their sons, and as these finally became part of the patrimony.[9] Now more reflection must be given to the son's career: Will it be in his father's craft, or some new craft just appearing in the city? Should he be a notary or a physician? Now, as the marriage market widens,[10] marriages require more calculation: What job should the future husband have? Should he be a local boy? Might one marry an immigrant? Or what about alliance with a family in another place altogether?

All this planning is done with a curious confidence that it is adequate to the turns and twists of the early modern life mentioned in our introduction. And sometimes the confidence is borne out, as is shown in the case of Louis du Laurens in the mid and late sixteenth century. From a village in Savoie, and then from Turin, subsidized in his Paris medical studies by a former employer, Louis married upward into the notable Provençal family of a fellow student. The dowry of Louise de Castillan was small for her class, but her brother's contacts were extensive. Then the brother died with only one of Louis's ten children provided for. Louise fainted "to lose so good a brother who had promised to do so much for her children." "Get up, my wife," said her husband, "I started from almost nothing and look at my beautiful family. Let's live virtuously and trust in God." So they saved from his medical practice and teaching, invested in land, pushed the boys into school (allowing two sons to switch, because of their aptitudes, from one calling to another) and established connections—until Louis died, having first arranged on his death bed for a son to take over his medical post with the city of Arles, but with several careers still unmade. For the next twenty-four years, his widow followed his schemes and forged her own, contacting, cajoling, obliging, constraining, selling a property every time a son had to pay for a doctor's degree, getting one brother to help the next. When she died in 1598, now scheming for her grandchildren, she was content. "When I was widowed with so many children," she reminisced, "I prayed God to inspire me to govern them . . . so as to follow in the footsteps of so good and wise a father. Now they can all pass through this world honorably." Two sons were archbishops; two distinguished religious; three physicians, including the first physician to Henri IV; one was a lawyer to the privy council; and both daughters had married lawyers.[11]

Planning for the family's future was carried out also in the face of old, slowly changing inheritance customs, some limiting the "liberty" of fathers considerably. In southern France and in part of the Artois, for example, fathers were allowed to "advantage" one child in the inheritance (to make one child "better" or "dearer" as the language went). Some customary laws prescribed the eldest son, others left the choice of child open. In western France, primogeniture was the rule among the nobility, while for all others equality of inheritance was to prevail, either equal division among male children or among all children, female and male. A similar diversity existed with regard to the disposition of property between husband and wife within marriage and when one of them died. Most often, in all classes, the wife brought a dowry, which was returned to her increased by a third or a half if her husband predeceased her. Sometimes (especially in middle level and modest families) the spouses put all their goods and acquisitions together in a "community," in whose profits and losses they shared half and half or in some other specified way.[12]

Was one set of customs and practices clearly the most favorable to private family fortunes? "Never have more than one heir," a Dauphiné lawyer exhorted his son in 1648, "for a good house divided is lost." Many other heads of household would have agreed, as do historians of law and property, who never tire of talking about "the disastrous consequences of division." Thus in areas of equal inheritance, parents in the sixteenth and seventeenth century might get around the customs by "endearing" the "better" son with a gift of most of the patrimony at the time of his marriage. Their other children would have to be satisfied with dowries and smaller legacies.[13]

On the other hand, such a policy had its drawbacks, and it is not always sure that the "one-heir" strategy was the best. Of the psychological costs, we get some inkling from old proverbs ("It is ill waiting for a dead man's shoes"; "the weeping of an heir is laughing under a vizer"), and from the differential treatment accorded the heir, the *dauphin*, in the Occitanien family, with his special nickname, privileges, and responsibilities from childhood a constant reminder to the younger brothers of their status. Sometimes daughters tell us how they feel, as with the seventeenth-century fairy-tale collector Mademoiselle D'Aulnois, an only child until she was eleven. "My Grandmother had that fond love for me which Women advanced in years have many times for Children by whom they expect the continuation of their Name and Family." Then her brother was born, "and my Grandmother lavished all affection on him. There was no more talk of my becoming a Princess. . . . My Brother had bereaved me of all those great advantages."[14]

It was also possible that, rather than accepting their lot, daughters and younger sons might undertake a law suit to increase their share of the patrimony. To avoid such "animosities" and "to nourish peace and concord in [his] family," René Fleuriot, a Breton gentleman and former soldier in the Wars of Religion, left two-thirds of his noble patrimony to his eldest son, but divided his substantial acquisitions equally among the five children. It may be for like reasons that so many prosperous parents in sixteenth-century Paris and Lyon were willing to divide their patrimony among sons, if not always among daughters.[15] At any rate, recent research has suggested how important local context was to the success of an inheritance policy. In Cambridgeshire villages in the sixteenth and seventeenth centuries, for instance, partible inheritance did have a "weakening effect" on families in grain-growing areas but not on families in the fens, where cheese-making and cattle-rearing could be carried on from small holdings. Elsewhere, giving the advantage to one child might not harm the others' prospects, if parents had made adequate provision for careers for them in a nearby town or for a good marriage.[16]

If there were no unfailing rules for the best way of passing on property to the next generation, there was also no certain prescription for the best economic arrangement within marriage. As Denis Le Brun, a late-seventeenth-century jurist, pointed out, either the dowry system or the community in goods could incite the wife to thrift, cooperation, and good management in a family headed by her husband. In the first case, she could hope to be rewarded by extra gifts from her husband in the future; in the second, her gains would depend directly on her effort. What was essential, whatever the strategy, was that authority within the family not be divided. Thus an interesting change took place in the Paris area in the law regarding community goods: by the late sixteenth century the wife had lost all her earlier rights of co-administration. Her husband had become, in the words of one legal historian, "seigneur and master" of the community.[17]

The planning tendency in early modern family life above the strata of the rural and urban poor was, then, expressed in varied ways in different regions and classes; but (I want to suggest) it had certain common consequences for thought and feeling. First, a new sense of the relations between the living and the dead, that is, of the arrow of family fortunes in historical time. Second, a sharper sense of the boundary around the immediate family as a privileged locus for identity, gratification, and reward. And third, a clearer sense of the right ordering of the planning family, with wife and children ideally in accord, but with sovereignty vested in the father. Let us now go on to consider each of these areas of family culture.

II

The relations between the living and the dead can be given cultural expression in varied ways: through funerals and mourning customs, through memories, and through emblems, treasured objects, and beliefs about blood and family stock. In the sixteenth and seventeenth centuries, some of these forms seem to support the sense of family planning and of time that we have been describing, while others make a different statement about social goals and the past.

Catholicism, of course, insisted on the corporate continuity of the dead, the living, and the unborn as they passed through the church militant in this world. It also insisted on the concurrent reality of the damned in Hell and the unceasing exchange between the souls in Purgatory, the saints in Paradise, and the living. Together with popular beliefs about ghosts, Catholic liturgy, art, and devotional practice made of the dead a kind of "age group" to put alongside the children, the youth, the married, and the old.

Now this exchange between the living and the dead sometimes stressed the special link between parents and children. But sometimes it did not, created and sustained as it was by diverse social interests, including a celibate clergy with few legitimate heirs of its body. Let us take as an example the place of burial. Canon law had long guaranteed the freedom of the dying in this regard: wives did not have to be buried with their husbands, minor children were not forced to follow their father's wishes; no one need be interred in his or her parish cemetery so long as a fee was paid. How was this freedom used? Many nobles and wealthy city-dwellers constructed family chapels or acquired at least a piece of stone in the church under which members could be buried: this surely reinforced family sentiment and continuity, especially when the generations lived near each other. So in the seventeenth century in the Limousin, Isaac Chorllon, son of a *fermier* and tithe-collector, father of a local lawyer and royal councillor, "having built for himself and his descendants houses and dwellings for worldly time and mortal life . . . built a house for eternity and for the other life," a family chapel dedicated to Jesus, Mary, and Joseph. So in an eighteenth-century village in the Pyrénées, every house had a distinct burial space in the church and on it the family knelt at every parish mass.[18]

On the other hand, in the earlier period, as Philippe Ariès has suggested, this was not the inevitable choice. At the opening of the fourteenth century, out of all wills registered in the Forez (better-off peasants, burghers, and land-owners), only about one-fourth specified burial "in the tomb of their parents," close relatives, or spouses. Catholics from artisanal, commercial, and legal families in mid-sixteenth-century Lyon had their bodies disposed of in a variety of ways. None of the many newcomers wanted to have a corpse or heart carted back to an ancestral tomb. Men might be buried with their parents, but might also ignore them for an independent burial with a wife, and even an uncle or nephew. Women might be buried with their husbands and pre-deceased children, but might well, if they were natives, choose to rest their bones with their own parents. And finally, there were those for whom the corporate connection with the saints, Christ's poor, or their spiritual brothers superseded their loyalty to family and who sought burial "before Our Lady of Grace," or "under the large holy-water basin," in the hospital cemetery or in a con-fraternity chapel. As late as the eighteenth century in Provence, although there was frequent preference for family tombs, the confraternity burial was still important for the newcomer, and individual notables still placed their remains in the church or cemetery of the poor hospital.[19]

This mixed pattern is seen on other occasions as well. Among those saying prayers at a funeral were orphans and people from the hospitals, praying not as relatives, but as recipients of alms, mourning clothes, and gifts from the departed. The private masses for the repose of a soul in Purgatory, if founded by a family, still had to be said by priests, and often they were established by the confraternity brothers of the deceased.[20] The souls that returned from Purgatory on All Souls' Day, though they especially visited relatives, were a matter of concern to everyone—to the young who danced in the cemetery the evening before, to the men ringing the bells all night and drinking so as to keep the dead at bay, to the parishioners going with the priest next day to sprinkle holy water at the four corners of the cemetery. So, too, when necromancers tried to raise the dead to help them find lost treasure and the like, they did not insist on an affinity to the corpse.[21]

In short, the Catholic mutual economy of salvation—and even its black market—gave scope to ties of family, kin, artificial kin, and sometimes of broader community. The *culte des morts* was certainly not "ancestor worship."

When we turn to Catholic religious events which did conjoin children with their dead parents, we find ritual and folk custom acting to channel feeling and to allow some expression for ambivalence. Most private masses were founded by the beneficiary herself or himself—"for the repose" or "the remedy" or "the

salvation" of the soul, the formulas went; and then the will-maker might go on
to add "and for those of my deceased predecessors and parents." Parents might
enjoin further prayers from their children: "My son," said a seventeenth-
century merchant father in Toulon,

> . . . remember your good mother. . . . Consider what great obligation you
> have toward her . . . how very virtuous she was. . . . Pay attention to all my effort
> to make you a man of honor and parts. . . . Pray the Lord for our souls. . . . That's
> the witness I ask from you after this life.[22]

For the heir, as for any son and daughter who went on to pray for their dead and
to found further masses at the anniversary of death, their act probably blended
love, guilt, and resentment—a way to help parents get on in the next world, but
parents who were, after all, in Purgatory for their own sins.

Relations between children and their parents' ghosts also combined love and
fear, and were restricted in intensity and duration. Right after death, mirrors
were turned and pails of water covered so that the soul might not be caught on
its way to the next world and to limit the danger that might come from the dead.
In certain Pyrénées villages, the family retained bits of finger nails, toenails,
and hair from the deceased father as good luck for the household; but one had to
act quickly lest the dead inconsiderately take his magic with him. If subsequent
visits of the ghost occurred, they usually had precise goals: pay my debts, take
care of the alms I promised, avenge my death, why haven't you founded masses
for me? Usually these demands could be met without the torments of a Hamlet.
Ghosts were not especially beneficent, though they sometimes came back to
cheer up their family or warn members of an impending disaster. Nor were
they busily punitive; they might haunt spouses who had remarried, but they
rarely looked into the careers, patrimonies, and marriages of their children.[23]

How did these feelings and practices relate to the sense of family time,
identity, and control we have talked of earlier? On the one hand, the airing of
ambivalence through ritual may have acted as a useful safety valve for conflict
between the generations about inheritance; and the possibility of the family
tomb may have strengthened the sense of family continuity, especially when
offspring remained in the same place as their parents. On the other hand, I want
to argue that Catholic mortuary customs were even more in tension with the
family arrow moving ahead in the world, with family privatism, and with the
willing adoption or internalization of parental values. Here the living could
mourn the dead without being overwhelmed by the emotional demands of the
past. Here the living distanced their parents by ritual, by a defined set of
exchanges, and by the intervention of corporate values that went well beyond
the interests of the limited family and its future. And the sense of time
engendered was a circular one, permanent converse between the age group of
the dead and the living, as the economy of salvation worked toward the Last
Judgment.

The significance of such a disjuncture between central forms of religious
practice and the aspiration of many families in the early modern period we will
consider a little later. The matter is thrown into relief, however, by the
emergence of Protestant churches which disposed of their dead in quite a
different fashion. All the forms of exchange and communication between souls

in the other world and the living were to be swept away. God had not assigned to the saints the care of our salvation, Calvin said, but only to Christ. As for the dead, they were beyond our help, on their own: "There is nothing more that we can add or take away." The souls of the saved were already present with Christ, those of the damned already suffering torment until the time of the resurrection of the body. The Lord gave them no temporary leave to come back and visit us here. We should bury our dead honestly; we can weep for them with moderation, "in a manly way." This meant no wailing and certainly no ribaldry at funeral feasts, and no ostentatious doles to the needy at the time of interment. The bereaved family itself could wear mourning clothes for a seemly period, so most Protestant preachers thought. But however much our human affection was inclined to show further signs of love for dead parents and friends by praying for them, Calvin warned, we should resist it. Monica's request to Augustine that she be remembered at the altar after her death was "the wish of an old woman." We pray only for each other and ourselves, the living, still in the midst of battle. [24]

Purgatory, then, was just another example of the perverse rule of the priests. They were like skinners, said a Reformed minister, making their living off human hides. French Protestants would bid a final good-by to their deceased at a simple burial, where the pastor, who had consoled them in private, was sometimes not even present. (In Lutheran areas, there was a more elaborate service at which Biblical texts reminded the bereaved of the resurrection and where perhaps a funeral sermon would memorialize the departed.)[25]

Thus the dead were to be done away with as an "age group" in Protestant society. This ritual and devotional break with the dead seemed very cruel to Catholic observers.[26] Perhaps it had been prepared for in some hidden way by a pre-Protestant experience of moving from one's home town and then finding it difficult to enter into the artificial family and sources of grace of the confraternity. But anticipated or not, the transition to Protestant mortuary forms was not made overnight. Ghosts came back to haunt some of the living saints long after Calvin, Ludwig Lavater, and other pastors had told them it was impossible—that such apparitions were angels or devils, and unlikely to appear "to those to whom the Gospel was purely preached." In the late sixteenth century, national synods of the French Reformed Church still had to remind the faithful that there were to be no prayers, exhortations, or public alms-giving at funerals, lest these lead to superstition. And—to give an example from across the Channel—in seventeenth-century Herfordshire and elsewhere, poor people were used as "sinne eaters," consuming bread and beer over the corpse and thus taking upon themselves the sins of the defunct so he need not walk the earth after his death (an eat-now, pay-later variant on the Catholic mutual economy of salvation).[27]

But despite these carry-overs, the new Protestant sensibility took hold. The funeral did become simple: by 1630 even the Anglican aristocrat might be buried quietly at night. In seventeenth-century France, while Catholics were recording family deaths with an added "May God have mercy on him" and "May God give her peace," Protestants were noting that a loved one "professed his faith to his last breath" and adding merely "Adieu," "Goodby." And the living were left, at least in England, with the funeral sermon—now of central importance and printed up for the family if it could afford it—and with the tombstone, less ostentatious now, but more widely used by tradespeople and prosperous farmers, and likely to have carved on it an epitaph or soul-effigy suggesting the deceased was in Paradise. Unfortunately, we as yet know rather little about Protestant graves in late-sixteenth- and early-seventeenth-century France, but what is sure is that burial was to be in a Reformed cemetery, not in a church. In all probability, in the absence of Catholic magical and corporate preferences for special locations, the deceased was placed, as in New England cemeteries of the seventeenth century, next to immediate members of the family. (Indeed, with the banning of all Reformed cemeteries in France in 1685, the alternative for most secret Protestants was a family plot in some concealed place.)[28]

Especially, the living were left with their memories, unimpeded and untransformed by any ritual communication with their dead. Some memories bite the conscience. Paradoxically, in trying to lay all ghosts forever, the Protestants may have raised new ones. It was all very well to dismiss some departed worthy of the parish with "you don't need me; I owe you nothing." But it was perhaps not so easy to erase the inner dialogue with a parent who had reared one for a while, given what we have seen about the actual directions in family life. At seventy-three, the Basel printer and Protestant teacher Thomas Platter was still remembering how his Catholic mother in the mountains of the Valais had nursed him with a pierced horn since she had no milk ("that was the start of my miseries") and how, during a visit home in his student years, she had asked "what the devil brings you here" and then had predicted—as it turned out, accurately—that he'd never be a priest. He went on to establish intimate ties with his own son, Felix, who became the physician Thomas had once wanted to become himself. Felix remembered how, as he left for medical school at Montpellier, his father had promised: "I will never abandon you."[29]

I suggested earlier that the corporate and ritual exchanges of the living and the dead in Catholic piety may have muted such dialogues a little. I speculate now—and it would require a comparative study of many diaries and letters and family records to prove it—that the ending of Purgatory and ritual mourning, whatever energies were thereby freed for other work, may have left Protestants (and especially Huguenots with their reduced ritual and precarious status in France) less removed from their parents, more alone with their memories, more vulnerable to the prick of the past, more open to the family's future.[30]

III

Memories are not, of course, just told to the self, but are passed on to others. This brings us to the most important cultural source for a wholehearted sense of family identity and aspiration, one created by both Catholic and Protestant families—the family history. Unlike tombs, fingernails, and hair, it could move beyond mere conservation to change. Told orally by father and mother to the children, told by fathers who had left their hometown or village and by those who had stayed put, pieced together further by questions from children and overheard conversations ("What was my grandfather doing at Rome for the Cardinal de Bourbon?"; "Who did my late aunt Gabrielle marry?"; "My father's father lived to 126, and before he died I talked to him myself. . ."; "I heard Jean de Lan, aged 85, say that his father said, when he was 85, that in 1331. . ."), the memories usually went back only two or three generations. The words of a Huguenot refugee in the sixteenth century suggest how important a part of family life these conversations were: "The horrible civil wars [in France] have constrained . . . uncountable numbers of families to depart from the kingdom abandoning everything. . . . Many have died leaving no memory to their own about where they came from. Children are not going to know who their parents or predecessors were. . . . The books and papers of my late father are lost, and I must have recourse to what I heard him, my late mother, and my other relatives recount about the origin of our predecessors."[31]

In households with limited literacy, especially among the peasants, such history continued through the early modern period to be passed on verbally, perhaps together with a coffer of notarized family contracts and deeds. But in the fourteenth-century, most notably in Florence, the family history or domestic memoir (called *libro di ricordanze* or *livre de raison* among other names) appeared as a new written genre; by the fifteenth century, notaries and burghers in Provence, the Limousin, and the Lyonnais, and even rural traders were keeping them; and by the sixteenth and seventeenth centuries many such manuscripts were being composed in the middle and upper levels of French and English society.[32]

Spinning off originally from record books in which the household life and economy and the extra-household business were combined, enriched by the details that had been told around the fire, these memoirs have varied forms (some are like diaries; others have entries only for special events; others still tell a consecutive story) and give varied amounts of information about the life of the writer and the times (the ones by husbands tell more about themselves than about wives; the ones by wives usually tell at least as much about husbands and children as about themselves). Some were carried on for generations—by sons or male heirs most often, but by wives, widows, and daughters on occasion, and even by in-laws if the male line died out. Others were completed for a man or a woman's lifetime only and, like Jerômé des Gouttes's "Recital of the House and Origin" of his family in 1588 or the celebrated diary of the seventeenth-century English pastor Ralph Josselin, stayed within the family papers for subsequent reading.[33]

But all were intended to hand on to children some account of the family's fortunes—of the family arrow in time, of the careers and qualities of parents, the training and marriages of children, and the near-escapes and losses. "I have written this discourse," said an old Catholic mother in the early seventeenth century, "so that my children and those that depend on me can see how my ancestors lived, and that parents who live well are always helped by God. Wealth and noble birth did not raise our family, but only virtue joined with divine grace." As for the memoirs of families already elevated by noble birth, they stress virtue nonetheless: "Virtuous fathers leave their children an ardent desire to imitate them," says a son of Marshal Gaspard de Saulx, as he introduces the memoirs of his father. "I put before your eyes the example of your father," says Charlotte d'Arbaleste about her husband, the Protestant nobleman Philippe du Plessis de Mornay, "that you may imitate a man who has done so much to serve God." "I could cite for you four or five houses in our *pays*, including our close relatives," writes a Breton nobleman to his eldest son in his *Advice and Journal*, "who have been shipwrecked by the practice of vices [prodigality, gaming, etc.]. . . . I want to see you and your brothers follow the way of virtue as the path which takes men to heaven and makes them esteemed in the world."[34]

The significance of these sentiments and of the *livres de raison* which accompany them is heightened when we remember other concepts of family time competing with them. Here family time is dominated, not by myths nor by the automatic replication of each generation through old laws of succession, but by the conscious efforts of one generation for the next. Here the role of family virtue, of family planning, is in tension with the idea of "*race*," of "*sang*"—that is, of hereditary qualities—which spread among the nobility at the end of the sixteenth and during the seventeenth century. To establish one's *race*, nobles and would-be nobles drew up genealogies, a blend of fact and fantasy which went back, if possible, to the time before "the memory of man." Even wealthy commoners accepted the notion of "good stock" in order to set themselves off from "the little people" and the poor.[35]

Now such beliefs are usually seen as the defense of position and privilege, while the argument from virtue and effort justifies those who hope to move upward in the social hierarchy or even change its shape a little. This is surely true, but I think it also likely that many families held to both modes of conceiving their past, contradictory though they were. For those stressing "stock," the experience of planning for the family and of recording its history in a *livre de raison* (as opposed to a genealogical chart) argued for the role of effort and led to the formulation of "*bonne race*" as a predisposition to virtue, rather than as virtue itself. For those stressing effort, the argument from "stock" was a useful weapon in persuading children of the danger of misalliance. The memoirs of a late-seventeenth-century canon of a town in Provence illustrate such a mixed perception: the cleric provides his nephews "a little genealogy" of only eight generations because the family papers have been dispersed by marriage, because anything more is useless for a family which has no proof of nobility to defend, and anyway his family is known as one of the oldest and most *honnête* in Cavaillon, having provided canons to the cathedral for four hundred years.[36]

Did *livres de raison* and memoirs tell the truth about families? It is a problem that requires close study, but my impression is that their sins are not those of fabrication, but of omission—some committed innocently enough by persons who lacked any literary training, others by those who had a sense of a "family front," of what must be forgotten and what could be told to the children. For instance, Catholic parents of the mid seventeenth century were usually not willing to own up to earlier Protestant interludes of their ancestors; and mention of children born out of wedlock is very rare. Even then, a considerable range of feeling and fact is passed from one generation to the next: I fell in love with a woman of another religion, a well-born Huguenot says to his children, but her father forbade a marriage, with the result that we both fell ill of melancholy, and she never recovered her health for the rest of her life. My son died of smallpox and my daughters survived it, even though I neglected them to take care of Richard, pens an aristocratic English mother on pages that those daughters later read. My son Alexis died at age five, records a French lawyer, "I had such great hopes for him, seeming to have such wit, judgment, and facility to learn for his age. God took him from me." My sixteen-year-old daughter died in childbirth in my arms, said a Huguenot mother of an artisanal family, where five children had already died. "Would that God had put me in the coffin instead of her; I will never forget her to my last breath." My widowed mother opposed a marriage proposition to my brother Honoré, writes a Catholic woman, because he was a little debauched and without means. But another brother arranged it, and Honoré became a good lawyer and stopped his loose living. "My brother Martial left our house yesterday," a Catholic lawyer said, "having quarreled in ways that I don't dare put here in writing." And finally, a Catholic heir at the opening of the eighteenth century tears some pages from his family's book and admonishes the curious not to guess why he'd done so; it concerned him alone.[37]

Thus, for a few centuries anyway, the family's portrait of itself had some room for conflict, for false steps, for disappointments—enough presumably to be credible and yet not so much as to undermine loyalty to the family's reputation and interests. An additional support for those interests was, of course, the Lord; He appears often in the pages of both Protestant and Catholic *livres de raison*, either thanked for His help or His superior wisdom acknowledged. Some families underscored the message of "virtue joined with divine grace" by adding prayers and hymns. That Reformed families would do this, even binding their memoirs together with Psalters[38] and New Testaments, is not surprising, since the religion insisted so heavily on the household as the arena for Christian instruction and prayer. But the Catholic Church, whatever scope it gave for religious activity to wide kin groups and to the single individual, tended to be suspicious of the household as the center for devotional life. Yet we can find, say, hymns to the Virgin in the fifteenth-century *livre de raison* of a merchant family in the Limousin, while an officer in the royal bureaucracy at Paris in the fifteen-thirties bound his family history together with the sayings of Solomon to his son, a collection of medical recipes of the kind that wives often knew by heart, a little French text on how to confess by oneself, and two Books of Hours. Are we seeing here the independent adoption by lay families of a form of Catholic piety intended by the Church for personal use? Perhaps. If so, this helps explain why the Book of Hours, at first in manuscript and then in printed form, was the most frequently appearing book, and often the only book, in Catholic private libraries in France from the late fifteenth through the sixteenth century.[39]

Having found a form of Catholic sensibility that may integrate rather well with privatistic family sentiments, we are pushed back to the disjuncture described above between the latter and Catholic burial and mourning customs. Now we have seen that Catholic and Protestant *livres de raison* had rather similar values, however much their religious language might differ; but Reformed burial arrangements left much space open for the family arrow in time, while Catholic ritual and ceremony put some impediments in its path. Why did this disjuncture persist? First, because the traditional Catholic forms were connected directly or symbolically with corporate institutions hardly moribund in the sixteenth and seventeenth centuries, such as village assemblies and vestries, professional groups and craft guilds, confraternities and the like. Second, the Catholic system had some give to it: the family chapel or tomb could increase in use by the eighteenth century; Purgatory could more frequently be represented, as M. Vovelle has shown for eighteenth-century Provence, as a less punitive place, from which souls were promptly delivered to Paradise;[40] and all along (as we have just suggested) families could domesticate other features of Catholic piety for household use. Third, there were some contradictions in family experience itself, as between maintenance and improvement, between "stock" and effort. Thus some of the contradictory messages about time and time-lessness and about corporate versus private loyalties communicated by Catholic mortuary customs may have been an effective expression of tension in French family life itself.

In any case, a disjunction between burial and mourning customs and other forms of experience is not peculiar to early modern France. In a remarkable essay on "Ritual and Social Change," Clifford Geertz has described a Javanese funeral feast, well suited to closely knit and religiously uniform villages, but "incongruous" in the jumbled and conflictful urban setting where it was being carried on. So too, Maurice Bloch has shown how the Merina peasants in Madagascar, through a century of "violent social change," have held on to ancestral tombs, often far removed from their existing residence, which link them to a permanent family corporation and to a supposedly unchanging past before the French conquest. Through this connection with ancestors, the Merina can remember independence and experience order, "the element of continuity in a changing situation."[41] Perhaps, like the Merina, some of our French families savored a link with their dead which reminded them of nature's changeless cycle, of the effortless repetition of generations who need not press toward the future.

IV

Along with a new sense of time, many families above the level of the poor were gradually developing a new sense of their boundaries in the sixteenth and seventeenth centuries. Other ties of friendship, association, and patronage remained important, but the interests of the immediate family seemed to emerge as more sharply demarcated from others' interests, especially from those of the wider kinship group and of people with whom one had kin-like relationships. After all, there had been a time when kin out to the seventh degree might be held accountable for crimes and revenge for crimes involving one of their members (as late as 1420, Pope Martin V excommunicated both a bankrupt businessman with debts to the papal court and his relatives out to the fourth degree); but now the criminal law of the monarchical state limited responsibility to no more than the immediate family, and even the duel was triggered only by insults to the self, wives, daughters, mistresses, and the like. (A similar contraction in regard to the use of the *retrait lignager*, the right to buy property lest it pass out of the family, has already been noted.) There had been a time, as Pierre Maranda has shown, when the French kinship terminology was more re-fined for collaterals than for lineals; but now, since the fourteenth century, the terms for lineal relatives (great-grandparent, etc.) were multiplying, while "closer collaterals were distinguished from relatives in the direct line . . . and segregated to marginal positions."[42]

And there had been a time when even families who were not related set up a joint household with common economic enterprise, which called itself a *frérèche* just as if the men had been brothers. By the sixteenth century, when a household was enlarged during one phase of the life cycle or because of economic need, the members were almost always parents or a widowed parent and married children, actual brothers and their wives, or (servants apart) some other member of the inner circle, such as a widowed sister. So, too, in sixteenth-century Lyon, the role of *close* kin—of aunts and uncles, nieces and nephews, brothers-in-law and sisters-in-law and step-parents—continued to be noticeable in bequests, sponsorship of immigrants and apprentices, and in partnerships and advice in contracting marriage, especially in the absence of immediate family; but beyond this degree, the role of relatives dropped markedly. In seventeenth-century Bordeaux, where the common household was still being established by about ten per cent of the newly married children and their parents, the intervention of distant kin in family affairs was infrequent or non-existent.[43]

Surely geographical mobility had something to do with this weakening of connection. "Try to make yourself liked . . . by your neighbors," a Dauphiné lawyer said to his heirs in the mid seventeenth century, "look for every occasion to serve them, since it's very true, as the saying goes, that a good neighbor is worth more than a distant relative, from whom you can get very little help."[44] But such a demarcation of a group and its interests also needs support from cultural symbols and assumptions. In a pastoral society with relatively few forms of economic cooperation, such as Le Roy Ladurie's Montaillou in the fourteenth century, the family house itself—the *domus*—may provide the symbol.[45] When households are caught in a web of economic interchange and cooperative institutions, however, more may be required to set off close family members clearly from the "cousins" and half-cousins and the godparents in the neighborhood. Some of the religious changes of the sixteenth century may have helped. The Reformed insistence on the married vocation as the only vocation certainly intensified the field of sentiment within and around the immediate family. The Counter-Reformation, building on earlier humanist reflection, assigned somewhat more spiritual significance to the married life than had the medieval clergy. At the same time, however, it also refurbished the higher, celibate option by its assault on priestly concubinage and its creation of new religious orders for both sexes.

But what contribution was made to this process by that aspect of Church teaching that had most to do with kinship—the laws on forbidden degrees in marriage and intercourse? Back in the thirteenth century, people remembered the days when one could not marry within the seventh degree, that is, any of the descendants of one's great-great-great-great-great grandparents. Then, at the Lateran Council of 1215, it became and remained within the fourth degree: one was forbidden to marry any of the descendants of one's sixteen great-great grandparents. The prohibition to the fourth degree extended to the relatives of one's spouse, in case of remarriage, and even of a person with whom one had intercourse, so long as there was a "union of flesh," that is, so long as the intercourse had been conducted without unnatural practices. (A man sinned if he buggered a woman or committed *coitus interruptus* with her outside of marriage, but he was still free to marry her sister!) There was also a prohibition established among "spiritual relatives," that is, among all the godparents at a baptism, their own children, and their godchildren. Intercourse or marriage under any of these circumstances was incest, though the sin was worse the closer the relative, and any marriage so contracted was null. The Council of Trent reaffirmed these prohibitions in 1563, except for limiting somewhat the scope of spiritual parentage: godmothers were no longer related to godfathers, and godchildren were no longer related to the children of their godparents.[46]

To enforce such a system to the full degree in medieval and early modern Europe was out of the question. "O mon Dieu," bemoaned a Franciscan in the late sixteenth century, "I'm afraid there are many people living in a state of perpetual damnation with their own relatives." Parish priests might keep charts and diagrams of the prohibited degrees and were supposed to inquire of these matters before allowing the sacrament of marriage; but many of the literate, even those who carefully recorded godparents with each baptismal entry in the *livre de raison*, did not know their genealogy back four generations. Nor was such a web of prohibition necessary for what the Church called "natural" reasons: it surely went beyond what was required for exogamy, biological or social. There was not even clear-cut agreement about whether "monsters" would issue from such a conjunction.[47]

In fact, what happened with prohibited degrees was what happened with the complex prohibitions of canon law regarding usury: exceptions were allowed for cause, such as the impossibility of a female to migrate from a small locality or the possibility of conserving honor in an illustrious family. Couples wanting to marry within the third and fourth degrees sought and paid for dispensation from the Church. Couples or parents wanting to end a union could also discover such hindrances to marriage at a convenient moment—my wife is my third cousin, this marriage must be dissolved. This "abuse" had already been a major reason for the cutting down of the prohibitions from seven to four in 1215, but it continued after that time, at least as an option for wealthy families.[48]

What I think is important for us here, however, is the argument used to defend the scope of these laws and the quality they gave to kinship ties. With the long controversy around Henry VIII's divorce and the subsequent polemic with the Protestants, this was a much discussed subject in the sixteenth century. Augustine was the major proof-text. He had pointed out that if the children of Adam and Eve had had to marry each other out of necessity, once population had multiplied, men and women were obliged by the supreme law of love to distribute their relationships as widely as possible. Eve had been both mother and mother-in-law to her children, but if two women shared that role, then there were "more strands in the bonds of social love," an "increase [in] the community of kinship."[49]

As restated in the late sixteenth century by the Jesuit Emond Auger and others, the reasoning took on a slightly different cast. "Our carnal desires" are by nature strongest toward those closest to us and would be boundless if we married them. "Even allying ourselves with a stranger we can scarce control our eelings." (So much for the frigidity of early modern Europe!) Marrying outside he prohibited degrees, then, enables us both to enlarge the circle of our alliance with more people and to be more virtuous at the same time. Continence within he prohibited degrees creates a holy alliance of friendship and peaceful liaison. Indeed, Auger longed for the days when the Church had been able to maintain hem to the seventh degree.[50]

The Catholic holding to most of the prohibited degrees thus expressed a continued commitment to wide kinship ties as a source of social order and solidarity (even though the Jesuits did not want to revive oath-helpers, blood-money, and blood-avengers) and a continued commitment to marriage as a primary alliance to reduce conflict. The centuries-old image of the *Arbor Consanguinitatis*, distributed now in printed texts to display the forbidden degrees, perpetuated this vision of social amity. There were all the kin held together in the branches of a rooted tree, a popular symbol in Christian thought for Life, Knowledge, Jesse's lineage, and the Cross.[51]

What were the consequences of this Catholic teaching for family attitudes and strategies? It is a subject worth exploring, even though we know there was endogamy in the early modern period. That the Church granted dispensations to marry within "the continent alliance" illustrates the play it allowed to the interests of the immediate family to flourish and compete. Moreover, the Tridentine restriction of spiritual affinity was not a trivial concession to family calculations. Boccaccio might have joked about the special delights of love-making with one's "gossip,"[52] but it was a real advantage for families to have the children of godparents readily available for a marriage with their children, along with the other services expected of *parrains* and *marraines*. On the other hand, he prohibited degrees embedded the family in a network of kin. As the cyclical exchange with souls in Purgatory was somewhat in tension with the arrow of family history, were the branches of the prohibited degrees in tension with the circle around the immediate family?

Here, too, the question is underscored by the contrast with the Reformed position. For the Protestants, the whole mechanism of illicit degrees of marriage and dispensation was just another example of papal tyranny and priestly trafficking. The Calvinists simply prohibited marriage in the immediate family, uncle-niece, aunt-nephew, and between first cousins. In the Church of England, the prohibition did not even extend to first cousins, and Calvin said he had made it "for the time being, only for the sake of preventing scandal." No dispensations were to be allowed. All other marriages, including those involving godparents, were not incestuous. No complicated Tree of Consanguinity needed here; a simple linear list, as in the Book of Common Prayer, would do the trick.[53]

The new ruling attracted much attention in Reformed circles, and well into the seventeenth century cases related to it were being appealed from local consistories up to the French national synod. It certainly did not allow people to get out of marriage by suddenly discovering spouses were cousins: divorce was allowed *only* for adultery or desertion for a long period of time.[54] But the policy did allow for many contingencies in making marriages. It would do for a large city like Geneva filled with refugees and an ample marriage pool, and also for a small embattled Reformed community which might have to turn for survival to marriage between relatives. And it gave an easier hand to families to work out their strategies with no outside interference.

But especially the Protestant rules on incest suggest a view of social alliance different from that of the Jesuit Emond Auger and resembling the Calvinist attitude toward usury. Calvin rejected the Deuteronomic law by which Jews could not take interest on loans to brothers, but could on loans to strangers. "*Notre conjonction*," he said, "our union is entirely different from theirs." Everyone was now a brother, but the sort of brother from whom one could on occasion take interest. Thus, as the great web of continent peaceful kin marrying strangers from without gave way to discrete families competing for property and exchanging children in marriage, so (in Benjamin Nelson's apt phrase) Tribal Brotherhood in usury gave way to Universal Otherhood.[55] All we need add is that the Tribal Brothers and the Universal Others were not isolated individuals, but family units governed by patriarchal fathers.

One form of prohibited degree was discussed very little in the sixteenth century, pro or con, by either Catholic or Protestant polemicists—that created by legal adoption. "Adoption has faded away among us," Pastor Théodore de Bèze commented from Geneva in the fifteen-sixties. It seems to have had some currency in parts of France during the Middle Ages, but by the fourteenth century a French lawyer described adoptions as being rare, and by the late seventeenth century a jurist remarked that "although adoptions have always been in use among most nations, ours has not conserved them." Now this unwillingness to adopt was not due to the absence of childless couples in significant numbers (either sterile or having lost all their offspring through death) nor to the absence of a pool of orphaned children of both sexes, born in and out of wedlock. Nor was it due to an unwillingness to take charge of children who were not blood relatives: domestic service, apprenticeship, helping orphans, godparentage, and guardianship were commonplace. Why then stop short of adoption? Why, in a society where families cared so much about their future, were couples reluctant to bring someone else's child into their household and promise legally to raise it, to give it their name, and to make it their legal heir "as if it had been their own"? Why was the simpler option of making a bequest to an adult male on condition that he adopt the family name used less often than the occasion warranted?[56]

These questions are important ones and much in need of thorough study; here I want merely to suggest how the reluctance to adopt may connect with the sense of close kin and of family stock we have been considering. To begin with, there was the fear, stated long before by certain early fathers of the Church but very much alive in the sixteenth century, that if a child did not know who its true parents were—a possibility when it was adopted, legitimized, or born of an adulterous union—it would grow up and marry a relative. Pastor de Bèze reminded his readers of the calamity of Oedipus, while a contemporary Franciscan casuist warned of the unintentional "mixing of the blood" of brother and sister, father and daughter. Such an outcome hardly seems likely outside the small village, but worry about it reveals once again the strength of the assumptions in early modern France about the natural affinity of close blood relatives for each other. Montaigne might express his doubts, but for many people the folk tales and stories rang true in which abandoned or lost children invariably found their way back to "real" parents. Actual families might quarrel among themselves, favor one child, and disinherit another because of disobedience, but the fairy tale and proverb insisted that it was worse with a stepparent and (by implication) with adopted parents. Perhaps in Thomas More's Utopia it was all right to adopt children from one household to another for demographic or economic reasons, but in everyday life things would not work out so harmoniously.[57]

In Utopia, to be sure, there was no private property, no concern about the family line, and, especially, no belief that the defects or virtues of the parents were passed on through "seed" or "blood" to the children. In the late sixteenth and seventeenth centuries, in contrast, such a belief was deepening in France, even though it could be given no certain support from medical teaching and was in conflict with equally compelling beliefs about how the child could be shaped by anything from maternal impressions and the wet-nurse's diet to proper discipline and education. As for positive qualities, such as wit and intelligence, even as naturalistic a thinker as Juan Huarte, who taught that parents could affect their children's abilities by the food they ate before intercourse and the timing and technique of coition, considered the die had been cast once the child had been born of parents of certain temperaments. And even more, bad traits were inherited: "Bastards resemble their true and natural father," a French lawyer wrote in 1560, "not only in body and lineaments, but also in manners [moeurs] and condition." Over in England, Shakespeare's Leonato regretted his daughter's sexual dishonor in a way which, I think, would not be foreign to some French fathers:

> Why had I not with charitable hand
> Took up a beggar's issue at my gates
> Who smirched thus and mired with infamy,
> I might have said "No part of it is mine;
> This shame derives itself from unknown loins"?[58]

Thus, the reluctance to adopt in better-off families in early modern France may rest in part on the high valuation placed on the *close* blood kin. Once outside that circle, one could not count on the stock. Some support for this contention can be found in a trickle of adoption that did continue throughout the sixteenth and seventeenth centuries—that of orphans from the Aumône-Générale and Hôtel-Dieu of Lyon. Some sixty-eight children were adopted over a period of 142 years by childless couples who ordinarily promised the rectors to give the child the family name, make it their heir, dower it, and the like. About half of the children were born in wedlock of known, sometimes artisanal, families; the rest were foundlings. Virtually all the adopting parents were modest artisans, that is, from the lowest stratum that we have been considering in this essay, or even below. Few rich couples "with no offspring of their marriage" would risk making an heir of a child of artisanal or illegitimate background, any more than they would allow their daughters and sons to marry one.[59]

V

Improved control over marriages in the sixteenth and seventeenth century

was part of a general process by which political and religious authorities and
families tried new techniques to limit the autonomy of the young and guarantee
their growing up with the right attitudes. New youth confraternities, more
systematic use of catechism classes by Protestant and Catholic alike, new
discipline and surveillance at schools and universities, new humanist and Jesuit
techniques of education in which, say, theatrical performances might drum the
lesson home, the multiplication of orphanages, and the invention of the juvenile
prison—all these were intended to strengthen the hand of adults while enticing
the young to accept with alacrity the values of the older generation. The
connection between willing obedience in the family and in society at large was
spelled out by clerics and by kings. Sermons and tracts on the commandment
"to honor thy father and thy mother" moved quickly to honoring ecclesiastical
and political superiors, while Louis XIII reminded his people in a 1639
ordinance on marriage that "the natural reverence of children for their parents is
tied to the legitimate obedience of Subjects for their Sovereign."[60]

As political sovereignty had been dispersed in the Middle Ages, so sovereignty over marriages had been dispersed. Lords had as much interest in the
marriages of women in the families of their vassals and their serfs as did fathers.
Village youth and city neighbors might mount a charivari against ill-matched
fiancés when parents had given their approval. Worse yet, the canon law
ultimately left the decision about marriage up to the young people themselves.
The spouses had to be at the age of sexual maturity at marriage, so the Church
taught; they had to consent freely to the marriage, and there must be no
"hindrances" of the kind we have examined above. A fully licit marriage had to
be preceded by the publication of banns and betrothal and then blessed by some
sort of priestly ritual. From the eleventh century on, that ritual had grown from
a simple domestic affair, such as the priest blessing the marriage bed, to a set of
public ceremonies culminating in marriage in church before mass. For a
marriage to be valid, however, no ceremony was needed, but only the freely
expressed consent of the man and woman to take each other at present in
marriage. It was sinful to marry in this "clandestine" way, but the marriage so
made was a sacrament, and in principle indissoluble until death.[61]

The actual paths followed to marriage before the mid sixteenth century were
various, depending on the social and economic circumstances of the family, the
age and whereabouts of the children, and the like. Most people followed some
or all of the ritual steps, but a surprising number married "clandestinely,"
exchanging formulas of consent and going on to consummate their union. The
latter were likely to be less-well-off peasants and artisans, to be sure, and often
the children of parents who were deceased or far away. But the possibility was
always there that children from families which had plans of their own would
run off and take each other in marriage. Anxious fathers left wills forbidding
inheritance and dowries if the children should marry without permission of the
mother or guardian. The picture of Margery Paston, from a gentry family in
fifteenth-century England, being browbeaten by her parents and the bishop
because she had promised herself in marriage to the bailiff, tells the story well.
Margery did have the power to promise herself in marriage, she did marry the
bailiff, and her family had no legal recourse against her.[62]

This situation drew much criticism in the early sixteenth century. The

hurch courts were weary of breach-of-contract suits when one spouse from a
clandestine consensual union decided to depart. And especially there was
unease in families for whom, as we have seen, the widening of the marriage
market made the calculation of future partners an intricate business. In an
influential treatise, Erasmus argued for another pattern: parents must consent to a
marriage and might well arrange it, but always with the children's best interests
at heart and so as to win the child's consent. Parents would have real authority,
but would not use it tyrannically or inconsiderately. Others echoed Erasmus's
argument with fewer qualifications, such as the Toulouse lawyer who wrote
that marriages contracted without the consent of fathers were in violation "not
only of God's law and nature, but of all law and human reason. Natural reason,
imprinted in our bowels, commands us . . . to obey our parents."[63]

In the next decades, after a spirited debate at the Council of Trent on the
rights of parents and the character of sexual morality, Holy Mother Church
finally reversed three and a half centuries of canon law. The young could no
longer have their own way, though the canons were not exactly what Erasmus
had in mind. Henceforth, to be valid, marriage must be public. Banns must be
read, and especially the couple must be married before their parish priest and
two or three witnesses. That the parents would hear about it if they were in the
vicinity of their child's parish was likely. For them then to put pressure on their
child if they disapproved was easy. That children were sinful if they married
against their parents' wishes was insisted upon. But the parents' consent was not
required (just as it would not be required for a young person over sixteen to take
solemn religious vows, a freedom which the clergy was bound to protect). The
priest stood for the public interest.[64]

As we have come to expect in the course of this exploration, the Protestant
churches assigned more weight to family interests and parental say. The
Ordinances of the Church of Geneva did not allow a man under the age of 20 or
a woman under the age of 18 to marry at all without the father's consent (or if he
were dead, without the approval of the mother and guardian and some
relatives). Beyond that age, they were required to seek paternal consent, and
only after a full hearing by the Consistory to see if the marriage was suitable
would they possibly be allowed to marry on their own. The father could not
force children into marriage either. The Reformed Churches of France adopted
the same ordinances, except for obligingly following French law and setting the
age of majority later.[65]

In fact, neither parents nor government in France were satisfied with the
rulings of Trent and the Reformed Churches. Royal edicts from the mid
sixteenth century on required parental consent for women up to the age of 25
and men up to the age of 30, disinherited children who eloped, and specified
prosecution for one of the parties under the crime of abduction (*rapt*), which
carried the death penalty. By 1639 even children over age could be disinherited
if they married for the first time against their parents' will.

What strikes one in moving from law to behavior is the extent to which
Erasmus's program had been fulfilled by the seventeenth century. Some
elopements continued in aristocratic families, the parties being separated after
widely publicized trials and, if necessary, the threat of a death penalty. Some
Protestants ran off and married Catholics, to the great regret of parents and

pastors. Some clandestine marriage continued in the lowest level of society
though villagers would consider such unions more disreputable than in the day
before Trent.[66] In most families, however, from the prosperous peasants and
artisans up to the landowning *parlementaires*, the *livres de raison* and marriage
contracts suggest agreement between the generations on the goals of marriage,
some area for negotiation about the spouse, and the internalization of the need
for parental consent, perhaps especially by the female children. Charlotte
d'Arbaleste, aged 26, "having lived alone for the five years of my widowhood,"
a refugee in Sedan, where she studies painting and arithmetic, receives a
proposal of marriage from Philippe du Plessis. She writes to her mother and to
all her relations as well as those of her late husband, "for I would go no further
in the matter without their permission. . . . God showed how He had ordained
my marriage for my welfare by the general consent of all those whom we had
consulted." When parents were dead, their progeny often chose, and with care
exactly the kind of spouse their mother and father would have wanted.[67]

The material we have been considering in this essay suggests two interesting
perspectives on historical change. The first has to do with its location. Ordinarily when historians think of change emerging from the decisions of a small
group, that group is made up of a king and his councillors, a party leader and his
inner circle, or some other small elite at the center. When changes are perceived
as emerging from the actions of large numbers of people in the middle and lower
levels of society, they are explained in terms of the forces acting upon them,
such as urbanization, to which they react somewhat automatically. What we see
here, however, is historical change flowing from the decisions of myriad small
groups, some rich and powerful, but many of only middling affluence in
provincial towns and smaller rural centers. Their push toward planning, toward
manipulation of property and persons for private goals, and their blending of
beliefs in virtue with beliefs in stock were assisted by the growth of the state
and of commercial capitalism and the professions, but were also in defiance of
some of the forces of their time, both demographic and social. Some of the tools
for their task, such as the family history, they forged themselves rather than
receiving them ready-made from learned specialists. The extension of family
planning into contraception in eighteenth-century France (in the face of strong
condemnation by canon law) is another example of men and women in small
groups deciding how they are going to conduct themselves.

The second perspective on historical change raised here is that of the
disjuncture between privatistic family values and the more corporate values
often accepted by these same families, which were embodied in Catholic
mourning customs and in beliefs about what constituted incestuous marriage.
Usually such a disjuncture is discussed in terms of cultural lag, of whether and
how much it retarded change toward "modernization." I propose instead that
we consider this disjuncture as possibly a creative one, that we think about how
and why religion or any cultural system can sometimes carry along contradictory values and keep little-used options open for centuries. They may
then be a repository, a "cabinet of remedies," which may be adapted to a new
use when we decide to change things once again. Emond Auger's longed-for
circle of amity out to the seventh degree is not a very strong antidote to the

possessive individualism" that was to become so characteristic of social thought and feeling after his day. But at least it kept open the question of whether property in ourselves is all we want to have.*

*The research for this essay has been assisted by a grant from the Committee on Research of the University of California at Berkeley. I am grateful for criticism received from Marvin Becker, John Bossy, Charles Donahue, Jr., James McConica and Lawrence Stone. I also want to acknowledge the contribution to my thinking made by the participants in my graduate seminar on "Family, Kin, and Social Structure": Sherrill Cohen, David Lansky, Keith Luria, Cynthia McLaughlin, Marilyn P. Miscovich, Dana Morris, Elaine Rosenthal, Frank Schooley, and Ann Waltner.

REFERENCES

[1] For Lyon, percentages based on my analysis of all marriage contracts (286) and apprenticeship and hiring contracts (79) remaining in the Archives départementales du Rhône for the years 1558-79; for Bordeaux, Robert Wheaton, "Bordeaux before the Fronde: A Study of Family, Class and Social Structure" (Ph.D. dissertation, Harvard University, 1973), p. 153.

[2] David Herlihy, "Land, Family and Women in Continental Europe, 701-1200," Traditio, 18 (1962), pp. 89-113. G. Duby, "Lignage, noblesse et chevalerie au XIIe siècle dans la région mâconnaise," Annales: Economies, Sociétés, Civilisations, 27 (1972), pp. 803-23; Jo Ann McNamara and Suzanne Wemple, "The Power of Women Through the Family in Medieval Europe: 500-1100," in Mary W. Hartman and Lois W. Banner, eds., Clio's Consciousness Raised (New York, 1974), pp. 103-8.

[3] Henri Drouot, Mayenne et la Bourgogne: Etude sur la Ligue (1587-1596) (Paris, 1937), I, pp. 39-5; A. Leguai, "Le servage en Bourbonnais aux XIVe et XVe siècles," Cahiers d'histoire, XX (1975), pp. 27-38; Isabelle Guérin, La vie rurale en Sologne aux XIVe et XVe siècles (Paris, 1960), pp. 212-13; Olwen Hufton, The Poor of Eighteenth-Century France, 1750-1789 (Oxford, 1974), chap. 12.

[4] Pierre de Saint Jacob, "Deux textes relatifs à des fondations de villages bourguignons (16e et 7e siècles)," Annales de Bourgogne, 14 (1942), pp. 314-23.

[5] Paul Ducourtieux, "Les Barbou imprimeurs," Bulletin de la société archéologique et historique du Limousin, 41 (1894), pp. 121-308. H. and J. Baudrier, Bibliographie lyonnaise, 12 vols. (Lyon, 1895-1921), V, pp. 2ff; Archives départementales du Rhône, 3E3766, fols. 140ᵛ-142ᵛ.

[6] Duby, "Lignage," pp. 803-23; Diane Owen Hughes, "Urban Growth and Family Structure in Medieval Genoa," Past and Present, 66 (1975), pp. 3-28; Jacques Lafon, Régimes matrimoniaux et mutations sociales. Les époux bordelais (Paris, 1972), pp. 46-58; Sylvia Thrupp, The Merchant Class of Medieval London (Ann Arbor, 1968), pp. 230-31.

[7] Robert Forster, The House of Saulx-Tavannes: Versailles and Burgundy, 1700-1830 (Baltimore, 1971), pp. 4-5; Lawrence Stone, The Crisis of the Aristocracy, 1558-1641 (Oxford, 1965), chap. 4.

[8] Jean Jacquart, La Crise rurale en Ile-de-France, 1550-1670 (Paris, 1974), pp. 68-70, 102; P. Ourliac and J. de Malafosse, Histoire du droit privé (Paris, 1968-71), II, pp. 421-39; R. Mousnier, Les Institutions de la France sous la monarchie absolue (Paris, 1974), I, pp. 62-63. Coutumes de la prevosté et vicomté de Paris (Paris, 1639), pp. 206-10, 548-50; L'Esprit de la Coutume de Normandie (Rouen, 1691), title 17, pp. 138-49; Georges Louet, Recueil de Plusieurs Arrests Notables de Parlement de Paris (Paris, 1712), II, pp. 337 ff., 409-14, 420-21, 463-71, 501-503; J. Salvini, Le chartrier de La Durbelière (Archives historiques de Poitou, 45 [Vienne, 1926]), pp. 141-42; Pierre de Saint Jacob, "Etudes sur l'ancienne communauté rural en Bourgogne, IV: Les terres communales," Annales de Bourgogne, 25 (1953), pp. 236-39. Archives départementales du Rhône, 3E7170, fols. 4ʳ-14ʳ.

[9] Ralph Giesey, "Rules of Inheritance and Strategies of Mobility in Pre-Revolutionary France," American Historical Review, 82 (forthcoming).

[10] The widening of the marriage market is discussed for upper-class families in England in Stone, Crisis of the Aristocracy, pp. 623-26. A like process occurs in France in the sixteenth and seventeenth centuries.

[11] Charles de Ribbe, Une famille au XVIe siècle d'après des documents originaux (3rd ed., Paris, 1879), pp. 35-99.

[12] Jean Yver, Egalité entre héritiers et exclusion des enfants dotés: Essai de géographie coutumière (Paris, 1966); E. Le Roy Ladurie, "Structures familiales et coutumes d'héritage en France au XVIe siècle," Annales: Economies, Sociétés, Civilisations, 27 (1972), pp. 825-46; Ourliac and Malafosse, Histoire, III, pp. 219-86; Lafon, Régimes matrimoniaux, pp. 275ff.

[13] A. Vachet, "Le livre de raison d'une famille de robe au 17e siècle," Revue du lyonnais, 5th ser., 3 (1892), p. 311; R. Aubenas, "La famille dans l'ancienne Provence," Annales d'histoire économique et sociale, 8 (1936), p. 528; Giesey, "Rules of Inheritance."

[14]Michel de Montaigne, *Essais*, Book I, chap. 38; Yves Castan, "Père et fils en Languedoc à l'époque classique," *XVIIe siècle*, 102-103 (1974), pp. 31-43 gives a remarkable portrait of th treatment of the *dauphin* in the Occitanien family; Mademoiselle D'Aulnois, *The Memoirs of tł Countess of Dunois . . . made English from the Original* (London, 1699), p. 2.

[15]Jean Meyer, "Un témoignage exceptionnel sur la noblesse de province à l'orée de XVIIe sièclu Les 'advis moraux' de René Fleuriot," *Annales de Bretagne*, 79 (1972), pp. 324-25. Analysis of nume ous wills of all classes in the Archives départementales du Rhône by the author and of Châtelu records on Paris families by Barbara B. Diefendorf for her doctoral dissertation for the University (California, Berkeley, "Marriage and Patrimony in Sixteenth-Century France: The Families of th Paris City Councillors" (in progress).

[16]M. Spufford, *Contrasting Communities: English Villagers in the Sixteenth and Seventeenth Centuri* (Cambridge, Mass., 1974), pp. 85-87, 104-11, 134-61; Edward Britton, "The Peasant Family i Fourteenth-Century England," *Peasant Studies*, 5, no. 2 (April, 1976), pp. 2-7; Lutz K. Berkner an Franklin F. Mendels, "Inheritance Systems, Family Structure and Demographic Patterns in Wes' ern Europe, 1700-1900" forthcoming in Charles Tilly, ed., *Historical Studies of Changing Fertility*.

[17]Denis Le Brun, *Traité de la communauté entre mari et femme* (Paris, 1709), pp. 4-5; P. C. Timba "L'esprit du droit privé au XVIIe siècle," *XVIIe siècle*, 58-59 (1963), pp. 137-38.

[18]*Summa Sancti Raymundi de Peniafort* (Rome, 1603), Book I, pp. 141-42 ("De sepulturis"); Lou Guibert and A. Leroux, "Livres de raison, registres de famille et journaux individuels limousins u marchois," *Bulletin de la société scientifique, historique et archéologique de la Corrèze*, 8 (1886), p. 668; A Zinc, *Azereix: La vie d'une communauté rurale à la fin du XVIIIe siècle* (Paris, 1969), pp. 234-35.

[19]Philippe Ariès, *Essais sur l'histoire de la mort en Occident du moyen âge à nos jours* (Paris, 1975), pp 132-43; Marguerite Gonon, *Testaments foréziens, 1305-1316* (n.p., 1951); analysis of wills in series 3E B, and G in the Archives départementales du Rhône by the author; Michel Vovelle, *Piété baroque u déchristianisation en Provence au 18e siècle* (Paris, 1973), pp. 102-5; see also P. Chaunu, "Mourir à Par (XVIe, XVIIe, XVIIIe siècles)," *Annales: Economies, Sociétés, Civilisations*, 31 (1976), p. 43.

[20]A. N. Galpern, "The Legacy of Late Medieval Religion in Sixteenth-Century Champagne, in C. Trinkaus and H. Oberman, eds., *The Pursuit of Holiness* (Leiden, 1973), pp. 162-63. From th fifteenth to the eighteenth century, there was also the development of confraternities specializing i helping the dying, in burial, mourning, and devotion to the souls in Purgatory. Guibert and Lu roux, "Livres de raison," *Bulletin de la société scientifique . . . de la Corrèze*, 7 (1885), p. 305, 8 (1886 pp. 152-53; E. Gautier and L. Henry, *La population de Crulai, paroisse normande* (Paris, 1958), p. 23; H Lebrun, *Les hommes et la mort en Anjou aux 17e et 18e siècles* (Paris, 1971), pp. 457-58; Vovelle, *Piéu baroque*, pp. 160-65.

[21]Jacques Toussaert, *Le sentiment religieux en Flandre à la fin du moyen âge* (Paris, 1963), pp. 212 222; Jeanne Ferté, *La vie religieuse dans les campagnes parisiennes (1622-1695)* (Paris, 1962), pp. 332-3 E. O. James, *Seasonal Feasts and Festivals* (London, 1961), pp. 226-27; Keith Thomas, *Religion and tł Decline of Magic* (London, 1971), pp. 230-31; H. Kramer and J. Springer, *Malleus Maleficarum*, trans Montague Summers (London, 1928; reprint New York, 1971), Part I, question 16.

[22]De Ribbe, *Les hommes*, p. 83, n. 1.

[23]Lebrun, *Les hommes*, p. 459; E. Le Roy Ladurie, "La domus à Montaillou et en Haute Arièg au XIVe siècle," in D. Fabre and J. Lacroix, eds. *Communautés du sud* (Paris, 1975), I, pp. 179-8! *Montaillou, village occitan de 1294 à 1324* (Paris, 1975), chap. 26; Noel Taillepied, *Psichologie ou trau de l'apparition des Esprits* (Paris, 1588); Ludwig Lavater, *Of Ghostes and Spirits . . . translated into Englis by R. H.* (London, 1596), Part I, chap. 16; Thomas, *Religion*, chap. 19; see also the remarkable resolu tion of a Florentine father's guilt over the loss of his son in the wake of the father's prayers at th anniversary of his son's death. The son's ghost then visits the father in a dream vision to reassur him. Richard Trexler, "In Search of a Father: The Experience of Abandonment in the Recollection of Giovanni di Pagolo Morelli," *History of Childhood Quarterly*, 3 (1975), pp. 238-51.

[24]Jean Calvin, *Institution de la Religion Chretienne*, ed. F. Baumgartner (Geneva, 1888), Book II chap. 5, p. 10; chap. 20, p. 22; chap. 25, pp. 6, 9; Pierre Viret, *Disputations Chrestiennes, touchan l'estat des trepassez* (n.p. [Geneva], 1552), pp. 26-32.

[25]Viret, *Disputations*, pp. 20-21; R. M. Kingdon, et al., *Registres de la Compagnie des pasteurs d Genève*, 3 vols. (Geneva, 1964-69), I, p. 10; Jean Aymon, *Tous les synodes nationaux des Eglises Reformée de France* (The Hague, 1710), p. 6 (Synod of Paris, 1559, art. 32), p. 26 (Synod of Orléans, 1562, art 15); Louis Spiro, "Saujon: Une Eglise protestante saintongeaise à travers quatre siècles d'histoire, *Bulletin de la société de l'histoire du protestantisme français*, 121 (1975), pp. 180-81; J. Driancourt-Girod "Vie religieuse et pratiques d'une communauté luthérienne à Paris aux XVIIe et XVIIIe siècles, *ibid.*, 119 (1973), pp. 20-22; B. Vogler, "La législation sur les sépultures dans l'Allemagne protes tante au XVIe siècle," *Revue d'histoire moderne et contemporaine*, 22 (April-June, 1975), pp. 191-211

[26]Esprit Rotier, *Responce aux blasphemateurs de la saincte messe* (Paris, 1567), f. 2^v; Antonio Posse vino (an Italian Jesuit who preached in France in the 1560s), *A Treatise of the Holy Sacrifice of the Altar called the Masse* (Louvain, 1570), chap. 30.

[27]Lavater, *Of Ghostes*, Part I, chap. 19, Part II, chaps. 4, 9; Aymon, *Synodes*, p. 143 (Synod o

Figeac, 1579, art. 24), p. 163 (Synod of Vitré, 1583), p. 217 (Synod of Montpellier, 1598), p. 273 (Synod of Gap, 1603); John Aubrey, *Remaines of Gentilisme and Judaisme*, ed. J. Britten (London, 1881), pp. 35-36.

[28]Stone, *Crisis of the Aristocracy*, pp. 572-81; John Weever, *Antient Funeral Monuments of Great Britain* (London, 1767), chap. 3; Allen Ludwig, *Graven Images: New England Stonecarving and Its Symbols, 1650-1815* (Middletown, Conn., 1966), pp. 52-77; Guibert and Leroux, "Livres de raison," *Bulletin de la société scientifique . . . de la Corrèze*, 7 (1885), pp. 596-98, 602-604, 625-26; 8 (1886), pp. 139-55; A. de Barthélemy, "Le journal de René Fleuriot, gentilhomme breton, 1593-1624," *Le cabinet historique*, 24 (1878), pp. 112-13; Claude Longeon, "Le 'Livre de Mémoire' d'un protestant forézien (1608-1646)," *Etudes foréziennes*, 7 (1974-75), pp. 91-106; Driancourt-Girod, "Vie religieuse," p. 18, n. 29.

[29]Thomas Platter, *Autobiographie*, trans. M. Helmer (*Cahiers des Annales*, 22 [Paris, 1964]), pp. 21, 51; Felix Platter, *Beloved Son Felix*, trans. S. Jennett (London, 1961), pp. 25, 30.

[30]An analogous point about the consequences of the Protestant downplaying of the cult of the Holy Family for "investment of feeling and need in the human family" has been made by C. L. Barber, "The Family in Shakespeare's Development: The Tragedy of the Sacred" (The English Institute, Cambridge, Mass., Sept. 3, 1976).

[31]Claude Bellièvre, *Souvenirs de voyage . . . . Notes historiques*, ed. C. Perrat (Geneva, 1956), pp. 68, 71; Platter, *Autobiographie*, p. 20; Guibert and Leroux, "Livres de raison," *Bulletin de la société scientifique . . . de la Corrèze*, 7 (1885), 261-62; P.-F. Geisendorf, *Histoire d'une famille du refuge français: Les Des Gouttes* (Geneva, 1941), p. 13.

[32]Archives départementales du Rhône, 3E343, ff. 210ᵛ-213ʳ, for some of the records kept by a butcher's family in the early sixteenth century; Gene Brucker, ed., *Two Memoirs of Renaissance Florence* (New York, 1967), pp. 9-19; Charles de Ribbe, *Les familles et la société en France avant la révolution d'après des documents originaux* (3rd. ed., Paris, 1874), I, pp. 1-26; Guibert and Leroux, "Livres de raison," *Bulletin de la société scientifique . . . de la Corrèze*, 7 (1885), pp. 143ff.; A. Vachez, "Les livres de raison dans le lyonnais et les provinces voisines," *Revue du lyonnais*, 13 (1892), pp. 231-35. Example of a peasant's family book: A. Vachez, "Le livre de raison d'un paysan du lyonnais au XVIIIᵉ siècle," *ibid.*, pp. 401-17; Paul Delany, *British Autobiography in the Seventeenth Century* (London, 1969); Alan Macfarlane, *The Family Life of Ralph Josselin, a Seventeenth-Century Clergyman* (Cambridge, 1970), pp. 3-11.

[33]Geisendorf, *Les Des Gouttes*, pp. 13-14; *The Diary of the Rev. Ralph Josselin, 1616-1683*, ed. E. Hockliffe (Camden Society, 3rd ser., 15; London, 1908); *Livres de raison* collected in a Provençal family archive: Le baron du Roure, *Inventaire analytique de titres et documents originaux tirés des archives du Château de Barbegal* (Paris, 1903), nos. 216, 377, 937, 1657, 2488.

[34]De Ribbe, *Une famille au XVIᵉ siècle*, p. 98; Jean de Saulx-Tavannes, *Mémoires de Gaspard de Saulx, Seigneur de Tavannes* in J. F. Michaud and Poujoulat, *Mémoires pour servir à l'histoire de France* (Paris, 1838), VIII, p. 23; Charlotte d'Arbaleste de Mornay, *Mémoires*, ed. Madame de Witt (Paris, 1868), p. 3; Meyer, "Les 'advis moraux' de René Fleuriot," p. 324.

[35]Davis Bitton, *The French Nobility in Crisis, 1560-1640* (Stanford, 1969), chap. 5; André Devyver, *Le sang épuré: Les préjugés de race chez les gentilshommes français de l'Ancien Régime (1560-1720)* (Brussels, 1973), part 1; Ellery Schalk, "The Appearance and Reality of Nobility in France During the Wars of Religion," *Journal of Modern History*, 48 (1976), pp. 19-31; Arlette Jouanna, "L'idée de race en France au XVIᵉ siècle et au début de XVIIᵉ siècle (1498-1614)," *Bulletin de l'association d'étude sur l'humanisme, la réforme et la renaissance*, 1 (November, 1975).

[36]De Ribbe, *Les familles et la société*, I, pp. 7-8.

[37]Agrippa d'Aubigné, *Mémoires*, ed. L. Lalanne (Paris, 1889), pp. 37-38; Anne Harrison Fanshawe, *Memoirs*, ed. B. Marshall (London, 1905), p. 92; Guibert and Leroux, "Livres de raison," *Bulletin de la société scientifique . . . de la Corrèze*, 8 (1886), p. 620; C. Serfass, "Autobiographie de Jeanne Céard de Vassy (1666-1668)," *Bulletin de la société de l'histoire du protestantisme français*, 51 (1902), pp. 82-83; De Ribbe, *Une famille au XVIᵉ siècle*, pp. 63-64; L. Guibert, "Livre de raison de Joseph Péconnet," *Bulletin de la société scientifique . . . de la Corrèze*, 9 (1887), p. 316 (cited by Marilyn P. Miscovich in her seminar paper "Expression of Sentiment within the French Family of the 16th and 17th Centuries"); Vachez, "Livre de raison d'une famille de robe," p. 313.

[38]For example, Serfass, "Jeanne Céard," pp. 83-84.

[39]John Bossy, "The Counter-Reformation and the People of Catholic Europe," *Past and Present*, 47 (May, 1970), pp. 68-69; Guibert and Leroux, "Livres de raison," *Bulletin de la société scientifique . . de la Corrèze*, 7 (1885), pp. 150-54; Françoise Lehoux, "Le livre de Simon Teste, correcteur à la Chambre des Comptes au XVIᵉ siècle," *Bulletin philologique et historique du comité des travaux historiques et scientifiques* (1940-41), p. 139 (article called to my attention by Barbara B. Diefendorf); A. Labarre, *Le livre dans la vie amiénoise du seizième siècle* (Paris, 1971), pp. 261-63.

[40]Gaby and Michel Vovelle, *Vision de la mort et de l'au-delà en Provence d'après les autels des âmes du purgatoire, XVᵉ-XXᵉ siècles* (*Cahiers des Annales*, 29 [Paris, 1970]), pp. 37-42.

[41]Clifford Geertz, "Ritual and Social Change: A Javanese Example," in *The Interpretation of Cul-*

tures: Selected Essays (New York, 1973), pp. 142-69; Maurice Bloch, *Placing the Dead: Tombs, Ancestral Villages and Kinship Organization in Madagascar* (London, 1971), pp. 136-37.

[42] Recent discussion of, and bibliography on, issues raised by this section in Mousnier, *Les institutions*, pp. 47-84; Lawrence Stone, "The Rise of the Nuclear Family in Early Modern England," in Charles Rosenberg, ed., *The Family in History* (Philadelphia, 1975), pp. 14-34; Jean-Louis Flandrin, *Familles: Parenté, maison, sexualité dans l'ancienne société* (Paris, 1976), pp. 17-110; Bertha S. Phillpotts, *Kindred and Clan in the Middle Ages and After* (Cambridge, 1913), especially pp. 179-204; E. Forsyth, *La tragédie française de Jodelle à Corneille (1553-1640): Le thème de la vengeance* (Paris, 1962), pp. 17-55; Luigi Passerini, *Genealogica e storia della Famiglia Corsini* (Florence, 1858), p. 27, as cited by Elaine G. Rosenthal in her seminar paper "Patriciate Family Strategies in Quattrocento Milan and Florence"; Pierre Maranda, *French Kinship: Structure and History* (The Hague, 1974), pp. 14-16, 137-39.

[43] Denis Le Brun, *Traité des communautez ou societez tacites*, printed after *Traité de la communauté entre mari et femme* (Paris, 1709), pp. 593-638; Jean Gaudemet, *Les communautés familiales* (Paris, 1963); Henriette Dussourd, *Au même pot et au même feu: Etude sur les communautés familiales agricoles au centre de la France* (Moulins, 1962); E. Le Roy Ladurie, *Les paysans de Languedoc* (Paris, 1966), pp. 162-68; Lutz K. Berkner, "The Use and Misuse of Census Data for the Historical Analysis of Family Structure," *Journal of Interdisciplinary History*, V (1975), pp. 721-38. Analysis of the role of kin in Lyon in contracts of marriage and apprenticeship and in testaments were made by the author, in Bordeaux by Robert Wheaton, "Bordeaux," pp. 120, 143-51. See also R. Muchambled, "Famille, amour et mariage: mentalités et comportements des nobles artésiens à l'époque de Philippe II," *Revue d'histoire moderne et contemporaine*, 22 (1975), pp. 234-37.

[44] Vachet, "Livre de raison d'une famille de robe," p. 309.

[45] Le Roy Ladurie, *Montaillou*, part 1.

[46] *Dictionnaire de droit canonique*, ed. R. Naz, 7 vols. (Paris, 1935-65), V, pp. 262-322.

[47] Jean Benedicti, *La Somme des Pechez* (Paris, 1595), p. 463; Flandrin, *Familles*, pp. 28-38; *Inventaire-sommaire des archives départementales antérieures à 1790. Rhône. Série E supplément: Archives anciennes des communes* (Lyon, 1902), E Suppl. 348: "Manière de connaître les degrés de parenté," belonging to the *curés* of Condrieu; J.-B. Molin and P. Mutembe, *Le rituel du mariage en France du XII⁰ au XVI⁰ siècle* (Paris, 1973), pp. 31, 63. Virtually none of the canonists or theologians refer to deformed children as a possible result of incestuous union, perhaps because of precedents for such marriage in Adam's day. In contrast, the Franciscan Benedicti did mention the danger of monsters or stillbirth when conception followed intercourse during a woman's period—signs of the parents' "incontinence" (*Somme des Pechez*, p. 152). A reference to the *imbecilles foetus* as a possible outcome of incest in Théodore de Bèze, *Tractatio de Repudiis et Divortiis* (Geneva, 1569), p. 36.

[48] Jean-Louis Flandrin, *Les amours paysannes (XVI⁰-XIX⁰ siècle)* (Paris, 1970), pp. 32-36; John T. Noonan, Jr., *Power to Dissolve: Lawyers and Marriages in the Courts of the Roman Curia* (Cambridge, Mass., 1972), chaps. 1, 2, 6; John Baldwin, *Masters, Princes and Merchants: The Social Views of Peter the Chanter and His Circle* (Baltimore, 1970), I, pp. 332-37. Examples of dispensations in family archives: Du Roure, *Archives du Château de Barbegal*, nos. 28, 66.

[49] J. J. Scarisbrick, *Henry VIII* (Penguin Books, 1971), chap. 7; H. A. Kelly, *The Matrimonial Trials of Henry VIII* (Stanford, 1976); Augustine, *The City of God*, Book 15, chap. 16.

[50] Emond Auger, *Discours du saint sacrement de mariage, Livres II* (Paris, 1572), fols. 37ᵛ-49ʳ. Like arguments in Nicholas Harpsfield, *A Treatise on the Pretended Divorce Between Henry VIII and Catherine of Aragon* (Camden Society, n.s. 21; Westminster, 1878), pp. 35-36, 46-47, 144-45, and Cardinal Robert Bellarmine, *Controversiarum de sacramento matrimonii liber unicus*, chap. 29 in *Opera Omnia*, ed. J. Fevre (Paris, 1873), V, pp. 143-44. See also Marguerite of Navarre's story on incest in *The Heptameron*, Third Day, Story 30: "And so great was their love towards one another that never were there husband and wife who loved another better or were more nearly allied, for she was his daughter, his sister and his wife and he was her father, her brother and her husband." A Protestant statement of the strong attraction of those closest to us in John Ford, *'Tis a Pity She's a Whore* (1633), when Giovanni speaks of his love for his sister:

> Say that we had one father; say one womb—
> Curse to my joys!—gave both us life and birth;
> Are we not therefore each to other bound
> So much the more by nature? by the links
> Of blood, of reason? nay, if you will have't,
> Even of religion to be ever one,
> One soul, one flesh, one love, one heart, one all?
>   [Act I, scene 1]

[51] Reproduction in Flandrin, *Familles*, p. 30. See also *Decretalis D. Gregorii Papae IX* (Lyon, 1584) immediately following p. 1966; Silvestro da Prierio Mazzolini, *Summae Sylvestrinae* (Venice, 1591), p. 152; Arthur Watson, *The Early Iconography of the Tree of Jesse* (Oxford, 1934), chap. 3; Marjorie Reeves and Beatrice Hirsch-Reich, *The 'Figurae' of Joachim of Fiore* (Oxford, 1972), pp. 24-29; Harry Bober,

"An Illustrated Medieval School-Book of Bede's *De Natura Rerum*," *Journal of the Walters Art Gallery*, 19-20 (1956-57), pp. 83-84; J. D. Farquhar, "Arbre de consanguinité," *La revue du Louvre et des musées de France*, 20 (1970), pp. 199-202 (I am grateful to Lawrence Silver and Jean Rutenberg for bibliographical suggestions).

[52]J.-M. Gouesse, "Parenté, famille et mariage en Normandie aux XVIIᵉ et XVIIIᵉ siècles," *Annales: Economies, Sociétés, Civilisations*, 27 (1972), pp. 1139-54; André Burguière, "Endogamie et communauté villageoises; Pratique matrimoniale à Romainville au XVIIIᵉ siècle," forthcoming in *Quaderni Storici*; Boccaccio, *Decameron*, Day 7, stories 3 and 10.

[53]"Les Ordonnances ecclésiastiques de l'Eglise de Genève, 1561" in *Calvini opera omnia*, ed. G. Baum, E. Cunitz, and E. Reuss, 59 vols. (Brunswick, 1863-96), X, cols. 109-11; Kingdon *et al.*, *Registres de la compagnie des pasteurs*, I, pp. 33-34. De Bèze, *Tractatio de Repudiis*, Book 1, and a non-figurative chart, pp. 61-62, showing the Protestant prohibited degrees; Pierre Bels, *Le mariage des protestants français jusqu'en 1685* (Paris, 1968), pp. 84-88, 220-33.

[54]Aymon, *Synodes*, pp. 7, 19, 21, 25, 29-30, 39, 41, 46, 79, 91-92, 121, 153, 199, 202-203, 218, 236; Bels, *Le mariage*, pp. 37-49.

[55]Benjamin Nelson, *The Idea of Usury: From Tribal Brotherhood to Universal Otherhood* (2nd ed., Chicago, 1969), pp. 73-82; a related point made in Mervyn James, *Family, Lineage, and Civil Society* (Oxford, 1974), pp. 183-98.

[56]Auger, *Saint sacrement de mariage*, fol. 47ʳ⁻ᵛ; Benedicti, *Somme des pechez*, p. 465; De Bèze, *Tractatio de Repudiis*, p. 204; R. Aubenas, "L'adoption en Provence au moyen age," *Revue historique de droit français et étranger*, 4th ser., 13 (1934), pp. 700-26; Paul Gonnet, *L'adoption lyonnaise des orphelins légitimes (1531-1793)*, 2 vols. (Paris, 1935), pp. 11-32; Ourliac and Malafosse, *Droit privé*, III, p. 79; Robert Wheaton has found that the childless married couple was "common" among those making wills in mid-seventeenth-century Bordeaux ("Bordeaux," p. 137). I am much indebted in this section to the excellent seminar paper of Ann Waltner, "Adoption in Early Modern France, A Study of Attitudes and Cases," now being revised for publication.

[57]Tertullian, *Apologetical Works*, trans. R. Arbesmann *et al.* (New York, 1950), chap. 9 line 17, p. 34; Michel de Montaigne, *Essais*, Book 2, chap. 8: "De l'affection des peres aux enfans" (cited by A. Waltner, "Adoption"); De Bèze, *Tractatio de Repudiis*, p. 36; Benedicti, *Somme des pechez*, p. 118; Perrault's *Cinderella* among many other tales (*Histoires ou Contes du temps passé* [Paris, 1697], story 6). Maranda, *French Kinship*, pp. 63-64, 116 ("*Qui a marâtre a diable en l'âtre*"); Thomas More, *Utopia*, ed. Edward Surtz and J. H. Hexter in *The Complete Works of St. Thomas More* (New Haven, 1965), IV, pp. 126-27, 136-37.

[58]Simon Vallembert, *Cinq livres de la maniere de nourrir et gouverner les enfans des leur naissance* (Poitiers, 1565) for a typical manual stressing nurture and education; Juan Huarte de San Juan, *Examen de Ingenios para las Sciencias*, first appearing in Spanish in 1575 and with editions appearing in French (1580), English (1594), and Italian (1582) in the sixteenth and on into the seventeenth century; Jean de Coras, *Arrest memorable du Parlement de Tolose: Contenant une Histoire prodigieuse d'un supposé mari advenue de nostre temps . . . Prononcé ès Arrestz generaux, le xii Septembre 1560* (Paris, 1560), p. 19; William Shakespeare, *Much Ado About Nothing*, VI, i, lines 133-37.

[59]Cases drawn from Gonnet, *Adoption*, II, pp. 15-52 and from twenty documents kindly transcribed by Mlle Jacqueline Roubert, archiviste of the Archives de la Charité de Lyon. Ann Waltner analyzes these documents fully in her forthcoming publication.

[60]Among other sources on control of the young: Philippe Ariès, *Centuries of Childhood, A Social History of Family Life*, trans. R. Baldick (New York, 1962), pp. 241-69; Lawrence Stone, "Rise of the Nuclear Family," pp. 36-49; I. Pinchbeck and M. Hewitt, *Children in English Society*, 2 vols. (London, 1969); the essays by Richard Trexler, Gerald Strauss, Lewis Spitz, and N. Z. Davis in C. Trinkaus and H. Oberman, eds., *The Pursuit of Holiness* (Leiden, 1974), pp. 200-336; Steven R. Smith, "The London Apprentices as Seventeenth-Century Adolescents," *Past and Present*, 61 (November, 1973), pp. 149-61 and "Religion and Youth in Seventeenth-Century England," *History of Childhood Quarterly*, 2 (1975), pp. 493-516; Yves Poutet, "L'enseignement des pauvres dans la France du XVIIᵉ siècle," *XVIIᵉ siècle*, 90-91 (1971), pp. 87-110; M. Félibien and G. Lobineau, *Histoire de la ville de Paris* (Paris, 1725), IV, pp. 231-34, 265-67 (rulings of 1673 and 1684 on correctional prisons for the young); Benedicti, *Somme des pechez*, pp. 95-102; Catherine Holmes, *L'éloquence judiciaire de 1620 à 1660* (Paris, 1967), p. 76; Ourliac and Malafosse, *Droit privé*, III, p. 66; N. Z. Davis, "Women on Top," in *Society and Culture in Early Modern France* (Stanford, 1975), pp. 124-51; Gordon J. Schochet, *Patriarchalism in Political Thought* (Oxford, 1975).

[61]Joel Hurstfield, *The Queen's Wards; Wardship and Marriage under Elizabeth I* (Cambridge, Mass., 1958), pp. 3-7; N. Z. Davis, "The Reasons of Misrule," in *Society and Culture*, pp. 97-123; *Dictionnaire de droit canonique*, VI, pp. 739-59; Charles Donahue, Jr., "The Policy of Alexander the Third's Consent Theory of Marriage," in Stephan Kuttner, ed., *Proceedings of the Fourth International Congress of Medieval Canon Law* (Vatican City, 1976), pp. 251-81 (includes full bibliography on theory of consent); Molin and Mutembe, *Le rituel du mariage*, pp. 25-48.

[62]Michael M. Sheehan, "The Formation and Stability of Marriage in Fourteenth-Century Eng-

land: Evidence of an Ely Register," *Mediaeval Studies*, 33 (1971), pp. 228-63; R. H. Helmholz, *Marriage Litigation in Medieval England* (Cambridge, 1974), chaps. 1-2; Beatrice Gottlieb, "Getting Married in Pre-Reformation Europe: The Doctrine of Clandestine Marriage and Court Cases in Fifteenth-Century Champagne" (Ph.D. dissertation, Columbia University, 1974); Stone, *Crisis of the Aristocracy*, pp. 594-95; Archives départementales du Rhône, 3E7597, January 16, 1560, for a will in which a woman cuts back her daughter's inheritance if she marries without the permission of her stepfather; *The Paston Letters, A.D. 1422-1509*, ed. J. Gairdner, 6 vols. (London, 1904), V, pp. 36-40; clandestine marriages in England involving a goldsmith, a merchant, and a knight's daughter, in Donahue, "Consent Theory," pp. 269-70 and notes 67-68.

[63]E. V. Telle, *Erasme de Rotterdam et le 7ᵉ sacrament: Etude d'évangelisme matrimoniale* (Geneva, 1954); Bels, *Mariage*, pp. 27-50; Jean de Coras, *Paraphraze sur l'Edict des mariages clandestinement contractez par les enfans de famille, contre le gré et consentement de leurs peres et meres* (Paris, 1579), fols. 2ʳ, 6ᵛ.

[64]*Dictionnaire de droit canonique*, VI, pp. 748-49; Gottlieb, "Getting Married," chaps. 1-2; Auger, *Saint sacrement de mariage*, Book 2, chap. 2; Benedicti, *Somme des pechez*, pp. 70, 455-57, 477-78; Noonan, *Power to Dissolve*, p. 29.

[65]*Ordonnances ecclésiastiques de l'Eglise de Genève* in *Calvini opera*, X, cols. 105-7; Aymon, *Synodes*, pp. 6-7 (articles 34, 38, synod of Paris, 1559), p. 75 (article 16, synod of Vertueil, 1567); Bels, *Mariage*, part 2.

[66]Flandrin, *Amours paysannes*, pp. 36-50; Holmes, *L'éloquence judiciaire*, Book 1, chap. 2; J. Gaudemet, "Législation canonique et attitudes séculières à l'égard du lien matrimonial au XVIIᵉ siècle," *XVIIᵉ siècle*, 102-103 (1974), pp. 15-30; J. Coudert, "Le mariage dans le diocèse de Toul," *Annales de l'Est*, 3 (1952), pp. 72-92; Mark Cummings, "Elopement, Family, and the Courts: The Crime of Rapt in Early Modern France" (Western Society for French History, Reno, Nevada, November 13 1976), forthcoming in the *Proceedings* of the Western Society for French History.

[67]Lucy Crump, *A Huguenot Family in the Sixteenth Century: The Memoirs of Philippe de Mornay Sieur du Plessis Marly, Written by His Wife* (London, n.d.), pp. 140-44.

ISABEL V. SAWHILL

Economic Perspectives on the Family

Introduction

BACK IN THE FIFTIES, a colleague of mine in the economics department of a small college was sitting in his office preparing a class in "money and banking." He was interrupted by a call from an anxious housewife who thought she had been referred to the department of home economics. She wanted to bake bread and was seeking advice on the amount of yeast to use. Partly in amusement and partly in irritation at having been interrupted, he responded: "Madam, I know something about how one raises money but nothing about how one raises dough."[1] Today, even though economists have not gone so far as to study the art of bread-making, there is a whole new literature within the discipline labeled the "new home economics" and devoted to examining such topics as marriage, fertility, and decisions about the use of both time and goods within the household or family.[2] These interests are quite new—dating perhaps from the early or mid sixties and heavily influenced by the development of human capital theory and the theory of the allocation of time.[3] Before their appearance, economists had concentrated almost exclusively on markets and exchange; in such a context, the household or family was only relevant as a final consumer of market-produced goods and services or as a supplier of productive inputs, chiefly labor. What went on *within* the household was largely ignored.

There are several reasons for the economist's newly discovered interest in the family. One stems from the common views of most economists and their own definition of the scope of their discipline, the core of which is that an economic problem exists whenever resources that have multiple and competing uses are scarce. Scarcity requires *choice*, and choices are best guided by comparing the costs and benefits of all the possible alternatives. Once one has defined "resources" and "costs and benefits" broadly enough, there is almost no area of human behavior to which the economic paradigm cannot be applied. More specifically:

—Resources include not only the physical environment (land, other natural resources) and the finiteness of earthly space, but also human resources and the finiteness of human time. Increases in the quantity or quality of either natural or human resources are called "investments" and lead to an accumulation of either physical or human "capital." A major activity which takes place within the family is investment in human capital—e.g., the rearing of children—while the ultimate scarcity for this purpose is parental time.

—It is assumed in economic theory that individuals are rational, that they attempt to maximize their own welfare, and that they have information with which to evaluate and choose among alternative courses of action.

—Individuals begin by deciding whether to marry, and when, and whom to pick from among all possible mates. Once formed, households face a number of additional decisions about how much work to do, by whom (husband or wife), and where (in the home or in the market). They must also choose which set of market goods and home-produced goods to consume, and whether to have children (one type of home-produced good).

All the above decisions are influenced by the costs and benefits associated with the various alternatives. Costs are measured in both time and money and include psychic elements as well as opportunities foregone (e.g., one of the costs of marrying individual A is not marrying individual B). Similarly, benefits may be monetary or nonmonetary in character (e.g., if a woman quits her job to keep house, it is because her time at home is valued more than the income she would have earned). Thus, the broad applicability of economic theory to a wide range of nonmarket phenomena is one reason for the economist's emerging interest in the family.

A second reason is the realization that differences in earnings and in family economic well-being cannot be explained solely in terms of the operation of labor markets. Two of the critical determinants of individual earnings are education and experience, but a great deal of that education either goes on within the home or else is successful because of its interaction with family influences. As for experience, the problem is that those (for example, married women) who devote a great deal of their time to family activities will be handicapped in the labor market as a result of an insufficient investment in marketable skills.[4] Finally, family economic well-being may depend as much on the ratio of earners to non-earners within the household as it does on individual earnings, but this ratio is determined by decisions about marriage, childbearing, and labor force participation (especially by wives).[5]

Specific Contributions

To date, what has the economist's foray into these new areas produced? Most of the literature has been devoted to analyses of (1) fertility, (2) marriage and divorce, and (3) the division of labor within the home and its concomitant effects on labor-force participation and the earnings of men and women. What follows is a brief review of the findings of, and the insights emerging from, this literature. Throughout this review, I shall attempt to reproduce the flavor of the economic writing on these subjects as accurately as possible without commenting on its merits. Later, I shall try to provide an evaluation of the economist's contribution.

A. FERTILITY, CHILDBEARING, AND CHILD REARING

In the "old" economics, the size of the population was occasionally viewed as either a cause or a consequence of the rate of economic growth, but at a microeconomic level, no attempt was made to explain why people had children and why some people had more than others. Children either arrived with the stork (i.e., exogenously) or as the unintended outcome of sexual activity (i.e., almost randomly). In the new home economics all of this has changed.[6] Children are viewed as either "producer durables" (i.e., producing a stream of future income for their parents—perhaps when the latter are old and retired, if not sooner) or as "consumer durables" (i.e., producing a stream of future satisfactions for their parents in the same fashion as does an automobile or a house).[7] In a modern, industrialized country with a well-developed system of social insurance and little or no child labor, children are most clearly analogous to consumer goods. In the rural areas of industrialized nations or in the less developed parts of the world, their value as workers is greater, and this is undoubtedly one explanation for the higher fertility in these areas.

Because of children's value—whether as producer or as consumer goods— parents are willing to invest both time and money in childbearing and child-rearing. They make decisions not only about how many children to have, but also about how much time and money to devote to each child. In other words, the demand for, and supply of, children has both a quantity and quality component, with various trade-offs between the two being possible. In either case, children tend to be extremely time-consuming. Not only is the basic care of children demanding of adult (especially the mother's) time, but the enjoyment that parents are presumed to derive from their companionship, growth, and development also takes many hours, and it must compete with alternative uses of such time, including other leisure-time activities. In a past era, spending time with one's children did not so often have to compete with trips to Europe, Sunday golf games, or evenings at the theater. Nor were women's wages high enough or their employment opportunities sufficient to cause many families to consider a mother's foregone income as an important cost of having children.

In poor societies, alternative uses of time are neither as attractive nor as available. In fact, as Steffan Linder has noted, there may even be "idle time," that is, time which is truly a surplus in that it is not devoted to productive work, to the active enjoyment of leisure pursuits, or to personal maintenance (sleep, etc.).[8] In any case, the time costs of children are low and the (producer) benefits are high relative to what they become in a more affluent and industrialized society. Thus, it is not surprising that fertility declines with economic growth.

In an industrialized economy, the much greater productivity of human resources increases the value of time relative to the value of goods, and it changes people's behavior in subtle but important ways. Rather than bake our own bread, we buy it in the store. Even if valued at the minimum wage, the "time cost" of baking bread is about four dollars while the same product is available for less than one dollar in a commercial bakery or a local supermarket. It will be protested that the quality of the latter is inferior, but it may not be inferior to the tune of the other three dollars or so. Most people, then, bake bread only because they regard it as an enjoyable activity. Even at this level, however, it must still compete with riding a bicycle and playing the piano. In the past, more people baked their own bread not only because the store-bought variety was relatively more expensive, but also because they could less easily afford bicycles, pianos, television sets, and cameras to fill their leisure hours.

In a somewhat similar fashion, the amount of time needed to raise and enjoy one's children has led to a reduction in the size of families. Where possible, there has also been a substitution of market goods and services (analogous to the store-bought bread) for parental time, as when we send children to a day-care center or sit them in front of the television set or buy them records and books instead of talking, singing, or reading to them.[9] The point is that what some have labeled the "dehumanization" of family life or the neglect of children may simply be a matter of the economics of time. As the price of time increases, those commodities the production or consumption of which are time-intensive (e.g., children) will be less in demand than those which are more goods-intensive. Thus, as the parent's (usually the mother's) actual or expected wage rate rises, the demand for children tends to decline. On the other hand, holding the price of time constant, we would expect the demand for children to increase with family income, as is the case with other consumer goods.

Turning to the empirical evidence,[10] the economic literature on fertility has established quite unequivocally that childbearing is negatively related to the price of the mother's time. The effects of income on fertility are much weaker, once the possible confounding influences of education and of the price of time have been removed. One likely possibility is that there is a substitution of quality for quantity at higher income levels—that is, more affluent families may devote more time and money *per child* than their less affluent counterparts in the same way that they buy higher quality food or more expensive clothes. These investments in children, in turn, have important implications for the transmission of inequality to succeeding generations. To date, we have had little success in using extra-family institutions or programs to compensate for these inequalities in family investment.

Finally, it has been found that better-educated parents have fewer children, even after controlling for income. This could be because they have a different set of preferences, because they are relatively more adept at producing high-quality children and thus inclined to make still further substitutions of quality for quantity, or because they are better contraceptors. There is growing empirical support for the last-mentioned possibility. The better educated use more effective contraceptive techniques and also use a given set of techniques with a higher degree of success.[11]

If further improvements in contraceptive efficiency and additional increases in the cost of children contribute to a continuing decline in fertility, what are the implications for marriage?

B. MARRIAGE AND DIVORCE

The economic theory of marriage has been developed by Gary Becker.[12] In his view, a major motivation for marriage is the desire to have one's own children. In addition, the frequent contact and sharing of resources which people who love one another find desirable can occur more efficiently if the individuals share the same household on a relatively permanent basis. Still a third motivation stems from the efficiency associated with the specialization of male and female time within marriage. If women's market productivity and wages are lower than men's, but women are at least as productive within the household as men, then marriage permits a substitution of the wife's less expensive time for the husband's more expensive time in household activities and a corresponding substitution of the husband's time for the wife's time in the labor market. As Becker puts it, "Each marriage can be considered a two-person firm with either member being the 'entrepreneur' who 'hires' the other at . . . [a] salary . . . and receives residual 'profits'. . . ."[13] Men "hire" women to bear and rear children and to do housework because they are physically incapable of the first and because their time is too valuable to devote to the second and third. Women "hire" men to be breadwinners and to earn the wages which they are generally not able to command. Thus, each marriage partner gains by teaming up with the other.[14] On most traits, other than wage rates, husbands' and wives' activities are seen as complementing, rather than substituting for, one another, and in these cases positive assortive mating is predicted to occur, i.e., likes marrying likes. Finally, if spouses love one another sufficiently—if there is what Becker calls "full caring" within the marriage—then each individual will take pleasure in the "consumption" or well-being of the other, effectively doubling the potential gains from the marriage.[15]

The gains from marriage have to be compared with the costs, which include not only such things as wedding ceremonies or license fees, but, more importantly, the costs of searching further for an appropriate mate (or learning more about the present candidate). The net gain, then, will be positively related to a potential spouse's unearned income, to relative *differences* in the earnings (and household productivity) of the two partners, to the desire for children, and to the degree of caring. A general increase (equal for both men and women) in real wages will have uncertain effects, because the cost of time-intensive activities may or may not loom larger in the lives of married than of single individuals.

What kinds of empirically testable implications emerge from this analysis, and where does the evidence support the theory?

Love and caring are not readily observable, and the (ex ante) desire for children is also difficult to measure. Hypotheses about the effects of income on marriage should be a good deal easier to test, although past studies of marriage and divorce have not distinguished earned from unearned income or the wife's earnings from the husband's.[16] However, as a result of the theoretical developments described here and the availability of new data, some evidence is beginning to appear which suggests that the level of earned income within the family is not as important a determinant of marital stability as differences in the earnings of husbands and wives and the level of unearned income. It is also fairly well established that husbands and wives tend to be similar with respect to age, race, IQ, education, and religion and that homogeny along most of these dimensions increases marital stability.[17] All these findings are consistent with the predictions of the theory.[18]

One of the most dramatic and consistent findings has been the greater prevalence of marriage and the lower probability of divorce where women's wages or labor-market participation are relatively low. To understand marital behavior, then, we must pursue these topics further and inquire why women's wages are lower than men's. This exercise will reveal a certain circularity of reasoning, which is an important element in understanding and evaluating the new home economics.

C. SEX ROLES

As we have seen, in the economic theory of marriage, differences in the wages of men and women determine the gains from marriage along with love, the desire for children, and some other factors. And if we refer back to our earlier discussion of fertility, it will be recalled that one of the more important determinants of the demand for children is the price of time which is largely captured by the mother's wage rate. In both cases, female earnings are a key explanatory variable, but one which is treated as essentially "given" for the purpose of these analyses. What happens if we now ask why women earn so little relative to men? The answer, which is derived from human capital theory, is that *because* women marry and bear and rear children, they fail to participate in the labor force as continuously or at the same level as men. As a result they fail to acquire valuable on-the-job experience (a type of human capital) and this lowers their market productivity and their earnings.[19] In this case, it is marriage, fertility, and the division of labor within the household that are treated as the "givens" in the analysis. So we have come full circle. We have seen that women earn less than men because of their special role within the family, but that their special role within the family—and indeed the desirability of marriage and children—are importantly related to the economic status of women.

One place, then, to begin an assessment of what economists have contributed to the study of the family is to ask whether they have done anything more than describe the status quo in a society where sex roles are "givens"—defined by culture, biology, or other factors not specified in the economic model. But this would be only one of many observations which one might wish to make in the broader assessment to which I now turn.

An Assessment

The secret to understanding the family, and particularly variations in family life over time and across cultures, may not be within the grasp of the economist, but then it is not clear that other disciplines have done much better. The difference between economists and other social scientists is that the latter are much more modest. Paul Samuelson has called economics "the queen of the social sciences,"[20] while Gary Becker has argued that "economic theory may well be on its way to providing a unified framework for *all* behavior involving scarce resources, nonmarket as well as market, nonmonetary as well as monetary, small group as well as competitive."[21] Certainly his own work has been extraordinarily influential in moving economics in that direction. The question is, Would some other line of inquiry have been more fruitful?

To anyone who has been trained as an economist, the charms of economic analysis are nearly irresistible. It is intellectually clean, challenging, and rigorously deductive. In addition, the methodological sophistication of most economists, although not essential to good theory, gives them a competitive edge in empirical work. Most importantly, the economic paradigm does have a certain "unifying power" because it is highly general and highly abstract. This power, however, has been purchased at the price of obliterating most of the trees from the forest. Many of the variables found in sociological literature, for example, are included in the economist's household-production function in a formal sense, but they are only occasionally illuminated by being viewed in this context. It might be argued that the trees can easily enough be put back into the forest as extensions of the basic analysis, but the danger is that the forest will turn into a Procrustean bed—the variables and observed relationships from empirical work being forced to fit the received microeconomic doctrine.

Second, many of the assumptions underlying the economic theory of the household could be questioned. Are scarce resources the only constraint on people's freedom to choose from among alternative courses of action? As Duesenberry has put it, economics is all about why people make choices, while sociology is all about why they don't have any choices to make.[22] Preferences are shaped by social norms and by individual psychology, and we must look at both. It is not particularly instructive simply to assume that people do what they want to do. Kenneth Boulding's statement that the economist's indifference curve (representing individual preferences) was "immaculately conceived" gets at the heart of the matter.[23] Finally, the people marching through the economist's household are an enviable group: they are motivated by love and caring and rarely by hate or fear. Very little attention is given to the nature of conflict or to the use of power within the family. In fact, everyone's preferences are swept into one household utility function because different family members are assumed to care enough about one another to weigh each other's preferences in arriving at family decisions. Under these circumstances, it is surprising that divorce ever occurs. Stories of abused children and battered wives together with the statistics that show a large proportion of murders being perpetrated by one family member on another need to be explained. Why is it that marriage sometimes leads to positive and sometimes to negative caring among family members? The economist has no answers.

A third problem with the economist's view of the family is that it is not particularly dynamic. Divorce, for example, is probably best viewed as reflecting a disequilibrium in a relationship, a point at which costs and benefits are out of line and recontracting occurs. In general, many changes in family relationships and behavior occur over the life cycle, and these changes are difficult to explain with existing models.

On the other hand, theory, by its very nature, can never illuminate all reality, so perhaps what has been said thus far should be given less weight than some additional considerations. There will always be (in the social sciences at least) more than one theory or conceptual framework consistent with observed behavior, and there will always be facts that even the best of theories cannot explain. There are, then, other criteria by which we can judge the usefulness of abstract ideas. One of these criteria is the extent to which the ideas, or the additional questions or empirical work they generate, are ultimately a force for positive change. Has the development of an economic theory of the family provided us with new information or insights that give us greater control over our own destinies and the wisdom to make enlightened individual or collective decisions? Much of science, especially the policy sciences, is devoted to this end. The policy analyst begins with the normatively based question, "What do we need to know in order to control and thus improve our lives?," while the more academically oriented social scientist asks, "What are our lives like?" Although the latter may draw out the policy implications of the analysis, these are a by-product rather than a stimulus to work. Let me, then, try to suggest some of the research issues in the area of family life which the more policy-oriented scientist might wish to address.

First, there are questions about the various consequences of individual decisions which often have implications for both personal and social well-being. In economic theory, it is generally assumed that people have sufficient information about alternatives to make reasonably intelligent choices. In some areas, it is easy to obtain such information either before one acts or through experience, and mistakes are not very costly. For example, if one chooses a restaurant and it serves a poor meal, one need not go there again. On the other hand, if one marries or has a child and either decision turns out badly, the situation is not so easily corrected. Furthermore, one's own reactions to it have serious ramifications for the lives of others. Unfrequented restaurants will, and should, go out of business; unloved spouses and children are not so easily written off. Moreover, the costs of these mistakes are often shifted onto the state, as when a mother and children are deserted and forced to seek public assistance, or when an abused child must be institutionalized or a neglected child grows up to be a delinquent.

The mistakes occur, first, because some alternatives are never considered or because current benefits tend to loom large in people's thinking relative to future costs of which they may be only dimly aware. They also occur because, even where the future costs are known, individuals can conveniently ignore the social, as opposed to the private, consequences of their own behavior and will usually act accordingly. Finally, they occur through imitating the behavior of a previous generation which is often codified in a set of social norms. These may once have served as a reasonably inexpensive surrogate for the accumulation of individual wisdom, but they may be inappropriate in a more modern context. Thus, there are essentially three reasons for poor choices: insufficient knowledge of private consequences, failure to consider social consequences, and the obsolescence of social guidelines and mores in a rapidly changing world. Each of these reasons for what I shall call "the failure of individual choice" gives rise to a new set of research issues.

The first is to scrutinize the consequences of individual decisions in the areas of marriage, childbearing, and child-rearing. For example, does having a first child at age 17 rather than at age 21 reduce the probability that one or both parents will finish school and embark on a successful career? What is the "cost" of such early childbearing (if any) in terms of foregone income at, say, age 35? Or, to take another example, does the amount of time one's children spend watching television affect their school achievement or the likelihood that they will enter a life of crime? The number of examples could be greatly expanded, but the point is that decisions are continually being made in the face of great uncertainty about the probable outcomes. Ironically, the objective of research on such questions is to make all human beings more like "economic man"—that is, possessing sufficient knowledge about the consequences of alternative behavior patterns to be able to act rationally and wisely.

The second need is for more information about *social* consequences. Early childbearing, for example, may have no long-term impact on the well-being of parents, but it may impose costs on the child, on the child's grandparents, or on society generally—all of whom may have to compensate in one way or another for the relative immaturity or lack of financial resources of the parents. Such costs (or benefits) need to be estimated in each instance. Then, if the findings suggest an overwhelming public interest in encouraging or discouraging various types of behavior, the appropriateness of providing incentives or disincentives to promote the public good might be considered. This idea will not be popular because the privacy of family life has traditionally been viewed as inviolable. But the time has come at least to examine the implications of a laissez-faire family policy and to consider where decisions not to intervene may be doing more harm than good. Nor should we be lulled into believing that existing policies fail to influence family behavior, even though the effects they elicit may not have been those foreseen or intended. Some effort has recently been made to analyze these effects. For example, the feasibility of developing "family impact statements" is being investigated by Sidney Johnson,[24] while the Urban Institute has given some attention to the effects of existing and proposed welfare programs on family composition, and it has studied the impact of liberalized abortion laws on out-of-wedlock fertility and subsequent public dependency.[25] Still another example is the extent to which rigidities in the work schedules of most employees affect the ability of parents to combine job and family life. These rigidities stem, in part, from government policies that require extra compensation for hours worked in excess of 8 per day or 40 per week, making flexible schedules more costly for employers. They are also related to the structure of social security and unemployment compensation laws, which increase the costs of hiring part-time workers.[26]

A third area of research growing out of "the failure of individual choice" centers on the need to know how the future will differ from the past. In stable societies, the wisdom of prior generations guides the choices of the young and the rules by which they live. In an unstable one, changing attitudes and new technology may quickly make such wisdom obsolete. Perhaps nowhere are public policies and individual decisions as much in danger of being guided by obsolete norms as they are in the area of sex roles. Yet changing sex roles have profound implications for home and family life.[27] These changes need to be understood, so that we can begin to plan for a set of policies that can replace those appropriate only to some earlier time.

This overview of policy-oriented research on the family contrasts quite sharply with the new home economics and suggests that the latter has not yet moved directly into the policy arena. However, as John Maynard Keynes once noted:

> . . . the ideas of economists and political philosophers, both when they are right and when they are wrong, are more powerful than is commonly understood. Indeed the world is ruled by little else. Practical men, who believe themselves to be quite exempt from any intellectual influences, are usually the slaves of some defunct economist. Madmen in authority, who hear voices in the air, are distilling their frenzy from some academic scribbler of a few years back. I am sure that the power of vested interests is vastly exaggerated compared with the gradual encroachment of ideas.[28]

Similarly, the intellectual influence of this new school of home economists is likely to be considerable. Their ideas will find their way into the more practically and empirically oriented work of the policy analyst and eventually into the political domain. Of all of the ideas that have emerged from this body of work perhaps the most central and potentially the most influential is the emphasis on the value of human time. In the past, economists believed that the ultimate scarcity was the finiteness of nature. As the population increased relative to land and other natural resources, standards of living would eventually fall to a subsistance level (although the decline might temporarily be offset by the benefits of technology). Thus, economics was labeled "the dismal science." The popularity of such books as *The Limits to Growth* and *Small Is Beautiful* attest to the modern-day appeal of this Malthusian view.[29] But T. W. Schultz has now given us a more optimistic future to ponder.[30] The ultimate scarcity in his vision of the future is not natural resources but human time. Investment in human capital (e.g., education, health) keeps occurring so that each generation is more productive, and the value of what they can accomplish in an hour or a year increases.[31] But as the value of human time rises, fertility will fall and standards of living will continuously improve. The process will come to a halt when there is no time left to consume the products of an affluent society and thus no reason to seek further increases in per-capita income. There will, in short, be a sufficiency of goods, given the time people will have to enjoy them. It is an interesting, if not entirely credible, view.

For the nearer term, the likely prospect is an increase in the labor-market participation of women as the higher value of their time makes home-based activities, including the rearing of children, more expensive. There will not only be fewer children but also fewer marriages as the wage differential between the sexes narrows. Does this mean that the nuclear family will wither away? I suspect that in a quantitative sense it will diminish in importance, but that the quality of life for children and the relationships between husbands and wives can only improve. In the past, marriage was too often an economic necessity for women, and childbearing either the unintended outcome of sex or an insurance policy against the insecurities of old age. In the future, economics and technology are likely to ensure that the act of having a child and the decision to share life with another adult are freely and consciously chosen for the personal satisfactions they entail rather than as a means to some other end. Personal values and psychological needs met by marriage, children, and family life will be the final arbiters of choice.

REFERENCES

[1]An incident reported by Professor Frederick Reuss, now retired from the department of economics at Goucher College in Baltimore, Maryland.

[2]Several recent publications illustrate the direction of research in this area. One is *Economics of the Family: Marriage, Children, and Human Capital*. ed. Theodore W. Schultz (Chicago, 1974); another is *Sex, Discrimination, and the Division of Labor*, ed. Cynthia B. Lloyd (New York, 1975).

[3]Gary Becker, "A Theory of the Allocation of Time," *Economic Journal*, 75 (September, 1965), p. 512, and *Human Capital: A Theoretical and Empirical Analysis with Special Reference to Education* (New York, 1964).

[4]Jacob Mincer, *Schooling, Experience, and Earnings* (New York, 1974).

[5]*Five Thousand American Families: Patterns of Economic Progress*, I–IV, ed. Greg J. Duncan and James N. Morgan (Ann Arbor, 1973-76).

[6]See Part Two, "Economics of Family Fertility," in T. W. Schultz (cited above, note 2).

[7]For a critique, see Judith Blake, "Are Babies Consumer Durables?," *Population Studies*, 22 (March, 1968), pp. 5-25.

[8]Steffan B. Linder, *The Harried Leisure Class* (New York, 1970).

[9]Some young couples I know view their household pets as partial and inexpensive substitutes for children.

[10]The empirical literature for the United States is summarized in an appendix to an article by T. Paul Schultz which appears in T. W. Schultz (cited above, note 2).

[11]See Robert T. Michael, "Education and the Derived Demand for Children," *ibid.*

[12]See Gary Becker, "A Theory of Marriage," *ibid.*

[13]*Ibid.*, p. 310.

[14]However, as I have suggested elsewhere, it seems clear that the monetary gain generally accrues to the wife and all the compensating non-monetary gains—including greater power and authority within the marriage—generally accrue to the husband. See Heather L. Ross and Isabel V. Sawhill, *Time of Transition: The Growth of Families Headed by Women* (Washington, D.C., 1975), chapter 3.

[15]Another potential gain would come from "economies of scale" which occur when two can live together more cheaply than either can live alone. However, economies of scale also exist in non-married communal households. Both male and female time are viewed as necessary to married living in Becker's model, since it takes both to produce a child and since love and sexual attraction are more common between members of the opposite sex.

[16]For a review of this literature, see Isabel Sawhill, Gerald Peabody, Carol Jones, and Steven Caldwell, *Income Transfers and Family Structure* (Washington, D.C., 1975).

[17]See, for example, Larry L. Bumpass and James A. Sweet, "Differentials in Marital Instability: 1970," *American Sociological Review*, 37 (December, 1972), p. 754.

[18]See Sawhill *et al.* (cited above, note 16); Mary Jo Bane, "Economic Influences on Divorce and Remarriage" (Wellesley College, unpublished paper); Andrew Cherlin, "Social and Economic Determinants of Marital Separation" (dissertation in progress, University of California at Los Angeles), Thomas Kneiser, "On the Economics of Marital Instability (unpublished paper, University of North Carolina at Chapel Hill).

[19]Jacob Mincer and Solomon Polacheck, "Family Investments in Human Capitol; Earnings of Women," in T. W. Schultz (cited above, note 2).

[20]Paul A. Samuelson, *Economics*, (9th ed., New York, 1973), p. 6

[21]Gary Becker, "A Theory of Marriage" (cited above, note 12), p. 299.

[22]James Duesenberry, "Comment on 'An Economic Analysis of Fertility,' by Gary S. Becker," in *Demographic and Economic Change in Developed Countries* (*Universities-National Bureau Conference Series*, 11 [Princeton, 1960]).

[23]Kenneth E. Boulding, *Economics as a Science* (New York, 1970), p. 118.

[24]A grant has recently been made to the Institute for Education Leadership at George Washington University for this purpose.

[25]Sawhill *et al.* (cited above, note 16); and Kristin A. Moore and Steven B. Caldwell, *Out-of-Wedlock Pregnancy and Childbearing* (Washington, D.C., 1976).

[26]Testimony of Isabel V. Sawhill and Ralph E. Smith before the Subcommittee on Employment, Poverty, and Migratory Labor, April 8, 1976.

[27]Implications that I have discussed elsewhere; See Kristin A. Moore and Isabel V. Sawhill, "Implications of Women's Employment for Home and Family Life," August, 1975.

[28]John Maynard Keynes, *The General Theory of Employment, Interest and Money* (New York, 1960), p. 383.

[29]Donella H. Meadow, Dennis L. Meadows, Jørgen Randers, and Willilam B. Behrens, III, *The Limits to Growth* (New York, 1972); and E. F. Schumacher, *Small Is Beautiful* (New York, 1973).

[30]T. W. Schultz, "Fertility and Economics Values," in *Economics of the Family* (cited above, note 2).

[31]These investments continue to be "profitable" because new knowledge improves the *quality* as well as the *quantity* of education, health care, early childhood experiences, and so forth, thus preventing any diminishing returns (e.g., a declining return to higher education) from setting in over the long run.

SUZANNE H. WOOLSEY

Pied Piper Politics and the Child-Care Debate

PUBLIC DISCUSSION OF FEDERAL POLICY toward day care for children has been carried on at high volume for at least a decade with remarkably little progress in either defining the issues or analyzing the evidence. The fervor with which various positions are espoused indicates that this is an issue of great moment, yet a thoughtful listener to the rhetoric on both sides would often be hard pressed to explain exactly what the shouting is about. Indeed, the discussion seems at times to have been translated into a sort of code, to be understood only by the participants.

The day-care debate is in fact about a number of things, many of which are only tangentially related to the extra-familial supervision of young children. Positions on day care have become, for a number of the combatants, proxies for inarticulated beliefs about many other aspects of family functioning. Both advocates and opponents of increased federal subsidies for child care seek to make that particular vehicle carry a very great deal of freight. The result is a jumble of arguments, based on impressions about a number of intractable and complex social problems related to families across the income scale, and about the role of day care in curing those ills.

The cause of day-care supporters has become a banner behind which an unusually diverse coalition has rallied. It includes, among others, "workfare" conservatives, unemployed teachers, the women's movement, professionals in child development and social welfare, and entrepreneurs looking for a new growth industry. Both the underlying philosophies and the specific objectives of these diverse groups differ widely, and in some cases are even in conflict. One of their few points of agreement is that expanded federal support for day care outside the family is a *Good Thing*.

The coalition actively opposing expanded federal day care is also a pot-pourri, although perhaps one with somewhat fewer ingredients. Opponents are generally suspicious that what is being sold them is a nineteen-seventies' version of *Walden Two*. They include fiscal conservatives who are trying to limit federal outlays; those who believe, for a variety of reasons, that mothers should stay at home with their young children; and a reactionary fringe that sees federally sponsored day care as the entering wedge of a government takeover of all children. When President Nixon vetoed the 1972 Child and Family Services Act, his veto message, reflecting these conservative views, complained that the act would place the weight of federal authority on the side of communal child-rearing as against family-centered child-rearing.

When these uncomfortable coalitions mount the arguments on either side, the most immediate casualty is clarity of communication. To specify objectives—what form of day care, for which children, financed through which institutional structure, employing what sort of staff—would undermine team spirit and is thus avoided. Similarly, citing evidence in support of one objective or another is likely to spotlight the deficiencies in the argument of an ally; fuzzy general assertions do not create this problem. Professional politicians also welcome vagueness, especially on an issue related to such a politically delicate and emotionally charged question as the government's impact on the family. Virtually everyone is, or has been, part of a family and therefore considers himself expert on the subject and holds strong opinions about it.

But it is not only the politicians and interest groups who are fuzzy about the issues. Academic research has also found it difficult to come to grips with the complex questions surrounding day care, although for rather different reasons. This might seem surprising because, while it is evident that pluralist politics often require artful generalities, research is supposed to require the clear specification of criteria and the rigorous testing of hypotheses. Perversely, however, this rigor can produce confusion and incomplete treatment of many public-policy issues.

Complex social questions do not readily yield to the scientific method, and they frequently require analyses by different disciplines. Researchers thus commonly assume away large portions of an issue so they can limit their analyses to experimental or theoretical manipulation of a very few variables. Naturally, the variables chosen tend to be the ones more amenable to inquiry by one's own methodological tools, while those assumed away are the ones some other discipline is supposed to be more interested in. The cumulative effect of this is that, the more refined the methods become and the more limited to one specific discipline, the less likely they are to be understandable and applicable to work in other disciplines. Consequently, the assumptions one might use are likely already to have been rendered obsolete by research in other fields. In the minds of otherwise skeptical people the subliminal impression lingers that certain premises have been proven elsewhere when, in fact, they have not. They may either not have been dealt with at all, or they may well be the subject of intense debate.

This interaction between the politics of consensus, which leaves many points unstated, and the conceptual complexity of the issue, which discourages comprehensive and useful analysis, means that very little evidence about day care is brought to bear on federal policy. Existing information on current practice and on the type of child care families prefer—presumably a matter of at least some interest—is ignored. The debate often proceeds as if there were no such data, although the publicly available information on these subjects undercuts much conventional wisdom. Instead, arguments center on broad policy propositions such as the following three examples drawn from those frequently advanced in one form or another by proponents: (1) that day care is critical for giving women the opportunity to enter the work force; (2) that day-care centers are themselves good places to employ welfare recipients, and thus get them off the dole; and (3) that, given high enough standards, day-care centers can significantly enhance children's development. Arguments such as these are clearly seeking to use day care as a tool for achieving some other end—employment of women, reduction of welfare costs, and enhanced achievement of children. But they are rarely assessed in light of the data either. Our knowledge about such matters as the impact of day care on the work force, on welfare policy, and on child development is not perfect, but a great deal of information exists on those questions.

Neither the evidence on parental preferences in day care nor the evidence on day care as part of the solution for other social ills suggests that a single solution to the day-care problem should be promoted. Indeed, both parents' preferences and the various possible objectives of overall social policy seem to point to the importance of a healthy diversity of child-care arrangements. The data do not, however, support the contention that a heavy federal subsidization of institutional day care is desired by parents or would significantly promote other broad social goals.

Parental Demand for Day Care

The problem of estimating latent demand perennially haunts economic analysts dealing with many sorts of issues. To begin to understand that problem with respect to day care, one reasonable—though hardly rigorous—approach is to describe current patterns of child care and the costs which accrue to the parents and to the public now and to compare those data to the kind of child care parents say they would prefer and the price they would be willing to pay. Of course indications of preference and of the level of satisfaction with present arrangements are not as persuasive as actual changes in behavior. Some indication of how parents actually react when offered new day-care arrangements can be extracted from individual research projects.

CURRENT PATTERNS OF DAY-CARE UTILIZATION

Two historically distinct trends in day care have begun to merge in the last few years. One is the nursery school and kindergarten tradition, originally aimed at providing enriched experiences for children of middle- and upper-income families. Enrollment in those programs has expanded steadily in the past few years. A recent *Current Population Report* indicates that 14.5 per cent of 3 year olds and 34.2 per cent of 4 year olds were enrolled in nursery school in 1973.[1] Nursery school remains primarily a middle-class phenomenon, however: 24 per cent of 3-year-old children of white-collar workers were enrolled, but only 16 per cent of farm children and 8.2 per cent of those from blue-collar families.[2] Kindergartens for 5 year olds, on the other hand, have become a well-established part of the public school system in the past twenty years, with between 75 per cent and 80 per cent of all children attending.

The day-care movement traditionally consisted of philanthropic and, later, public support for programs to care for the children of—usually poor—working mothers. Rothman[3] traces the history of day care in the United States. It originated in New York City in 1854 with the establishment of a foundling home and day nursery for the infants of unwed mothers who would then be employed as wet nurses in the families of their benefactors. Interest in day care has been cyclical since then; the program enjoyed a spurt during the early nineteen-hundreds with the settlement-house movement, declined with the widow-pension movement, which aimed to keep mothers at home with their children, and then became important again during World War II, when the government needed to maximize the number of women working in defense production. After the war, federal funds were withdrawn, and the states followed suit, with the exception of New York and California. The late sixties found a revival of interest in group care for young children, largely because of the confluence of interests of the coalition mentioned above.

Recent increases in the labor-force participation of women, especially from middle-class families, has blurred the distinction between nursery school and day care. In addition, school systems are increasingly moving into the provision of services to children below kindergarten age, as the birth rate and school enrollments decline. The most recent national survey of child-care usage, in fact, found that parents used the terms "day care" and "nursery school" to describe places which provided indistinguishable programs.[4] Children build towers, mold playdough, and listen to stories in church basements. If the church is in the South Bronx the basement is a day-care center; if it is in Forest Hills, it's a nursery school. Hours of operation, educational components of the program, and other factors which might once have distinguished the two activities now do not; all these things vary widely in both categories. In fact, different parents using the same facility may place it in one category or the other depending on their reasons for enrolling their children. The distinction, however, between "day care" and "nursery schools" has lived on in people's minds. Therefore, most summaries of day-care utilization and parents' preferences for child care do not include nursery-school enrollments.

In addition to the data on nursery-school enrollment, there are several sources of information on who uses what kinds of day care. In 1965[5] and 1971,[6] major national surveys of the child-care arrangements of working women were conducted. In 1975,[7] a similar survey dealing with *all* babysitting and child care used by employed and non-working parents was done. Finally, the Michigan Panel Study of Income Dynamics, also a national sample survey, included questions on day-care arrangements in its 1973 questionnaire.[8] A comparative analysis of the results of these surveys and other data is contained in a working paper by the author.[9] The 1975 *Child Care Consumer Study* indicates how many people are involved in child care: 15 million or 62 per cent of all households have the children taken care of by someone other than parents or siblings for at least an average of an hour a week. Of those, more than 7 million households include employed mothers or employed single fathers.

The 1965, 1971, and 1973 surveys—dealing only with working mothers—show consistent patterns of utilization, although the questions and samples differed somewhat. Table 1 summarizes the child-care utilization patterns for 1965 and 1971 for women whose youngest child is less than 6 years old. As the table indicates, the patterns of care did not shift much between 1965 and 1971. The percentage of families with children less than 6 years of age who used care provided in their own homes by family members or others increased somewhat:

TABLE 1

DAY-CARE ARRANGEMENTS USED BY WORKING MOTHERS WHOSE YOUNGEST CHILD
WAS UNDER SIX FOR 1965 AND 1971, BY RACE

Day-Care Arrangements	1965		1971	
	Whites	Non-Whites	Whites	Non-Whites
Care in own home:				
By father	16%	9%	15%	9%
By other relative	15	28	17	25
By combination of family and nonfamily members	—	—	17	15
By nonrelative	17	7	7	12
Subtotal	48%	44%	56%	61%
Care in another person's home:				
By relative	13%	24%	4%	9%
By nonrelative	15	18	14	8
Subtotal	28%	42%	18%	17%
Other arrangements:				
Care in group-care center	6%	6%	8%	15%
Child cares for self	1	0	3	0
Mother cares for child at work	16	9	7	4
Mother cares for child after school	1	1	1	2
Other	0	0	8	2
Subtotal	24%	16%	26%	23%
*Total**	100%	100%	100%	100%

*Totals may not add because of rounding.
Source: Shortlidge *et al.*, 1975.

from 48 per cent to 56 per cent for white families, and from 44 per cent to 61 per cent for non-white families. Care in another person's home diminished generally for both relatives and non-relatives: from 28 per cent to 18 per cent for whites, and from 42 per cent to 17 per cent for non-whites. Day-care-center usage went up from 6 per cent to 8 per cent for white families, and from 6 per cent to 15 per cent for non-whites.[10]

The 1973 data also deal only with working mothers and are aggregated for women with children under the age of 12, so one would expect less focus on modes of care designed specifically for younger children. In fact, they found day-care centers and nursery schools used by about 8 per cent of the total population as well, which probably represents a small increase in enrollments. They also found that in 26 per cent of the white and 14 per cent of the black families surveyed, the father and mother managed to split their working hours to cover child-care requirements. Many parents appear to prefer this arrangement; the practice was at least as common among the wealthier families as among the poor. Overall, a little more than half of all working women relied upon family members to care for their children: 34 per cent living in the home 17 per cent living elsewhere. Another 24 per cent used a sitter or friend.

The 1975 *Consumer Study*, dealing with *all* child care, including occasional babysitting, for working and non-working parents, concluded that the most child care is used by families with younger children (2 years is the peak age) employed parents; and single parents, even if not employed.[11] Family structure seems to be very important in what kind of child care is used. Employed single mothers are three times as likely as employed wives to leave their children at home with relatives and about twice as likely to use centers or nursery schools. Relatives not living with the family babysit for nearly half of all families. Day-care centers are used somewhat more by the poor than one would expect from their incidence in the population, and less than one would expect by those just above the poverty line and by the better off. At about the median income, the trends seem to change: relatives are relied upon less—or are not around to be relied on; more people pay unrelated babysitters and housekeepers to take care of the children at home, or they send them to nursery school.

In addition to income distinctions, the 1975 study found some ethnic ones:

—In-home care by non-relatives (especially occasional babysitting) is predominantly a white, middle-class phenomenon.

—Spanish-origin children are looked after by relatives.

—Black families use either relatives or institutional care, but rarely leave their children with unrelated adults.[12]

In sum, parents use a wide variety of child-care arrangements. The modal form of care is still within the family. Parents stagger working hours in order for one of them to be home with the children while the other is at work, and other relatives provide a substantial portion of both occasional and regular full-time care. Among the white middle class, unrelated babysitters often take care of children in the family's home. Unrelated adults provide about 20 per cent of all child care in their own homes. Publicity about day-care centers and about government subsidies of center care has been much more intense over the past decade; the somewhat increased use of centers, especially by poor single mothers, is likely to be in part a result of that attention.

The patterns of utilization do not point the way for policy: they do, however, explode the myth that families are giving up much of their child-rearing responsibility to unrelated or institutional caretakers. The major role of the extended family in these arrangements cannot be overlooked, particularly for poor, near-poor, black, and Spanish-origin families. Reports of the death of extended families are greatly exaggerated.

COST TO FAMILIES

When data about cost to the parent is added to that about utilization, the economic attraction of informal arrangements in the home becomes more apparent. Out-of-pocket expenses for informal arrangements tend to be very small: the 1973 survey found that 49 per cent of working mothers paid nothing at all for day care; most of those were arrangements with relatives. The 1975 survey data show that, while a considerable amount is paid to relatives for child

TABLE 2

PARENTAL EXPENDITURES FOR CHILD CARE COMPARED TO PERCENTAGE OF CHILD
CARE PURCHASED, 1975

	Parents' Expenditures	% Total Child-Care Hours
Relatives, in child's or relative's home	$1.1 billion	45%
Non-relative in child's home	1.7 billion	17%
Non-relative in other home	1.8 billion	20%
Nursery schools and centers	1.6 billion	15%
Other	.2 billion	3%
Total	$6.4 billion	100%

Source: National Child Care Consumer Study: 1975, II, Tables 8-1 and 8-2.

care of all kinds, it buys a lot more child care than the somewhat larger amounts for more formal arrangements. These data are reflected in Table 2.

The out-of-pocket costs to parents are one part of the total cost of child care. Public subsidies lower the price to poor parents of care in a nursery school, center, or the home of a non-relative. Federal reimbursement for child-care expenses pay back some of what parents spend, but these subsidies are not reflected in Table 2. Finally, the opportunity cost if a family member stays out of school or out of the labor market to keep the children may make the real cost of care by relatives higher than it appears to be. The magnitude of these costs is difficult to assess without information on the employment prospects of those taking care of the children.

PUBLIC EXPENDITURES

One might assume that data on the cost to the public would be easier to come by than data on family expenditures, but even a straightforward accounting of federal expenditures for child care is hard to obtain. Some subsidy or another can be found in at least twenty-five federal programs, from SBA loans to firms to set up centers to recomputation of welfare benefits to compensate for child-care expenses. A reasonable estimate is that, in fiscal 1976, about $2 billion of federal funds went to support day care. Approximately $500 million of that is not in federal outlays but in forgone revenue from the tax deduction for child-care expense available to working parents. The remainder includes subsidies for home and neighborhood arrangements, teacher training, experimental pre-school programs, Head Start, and day-care centers. State and local government funds and philanthropies also support child care of various types; these sources probably contribute at least as much as does the federal government.[13]

A final complication in the cost picture is the fact that child care is on the fringes between the home and the money economy. Table 2 indicates that informal day care, even by unrelated adults, is relatively inexpensive; this is largely because the caretaker is usually a housewife—often in her own home—who does not value her services according to market prices. When child care becomes a full-time occupation, rather than a sideline, the price rises significantly if even subsistence wages are paid. This can occur both within and outside the home. The cost of care in the family's home by non-relatives is higher than care by a non-relative in the home of the caretaker, since full-time wages for children's nurses, housekeepers, and professional babysitters must be paid.

The cost of centers, which must include the cost of facilities as well as of personnel, is even higher. In 1971, Edward Zigler, then director of the Office of Child Development, estimated the per-child costs of day-care centers of "acceptable quality" at $1,862 per year and of "desirable quality" at $2,320, based on 1967 prices.[14] Full-time centers with educational programs were estimated in 1975 to cost between $3,000 and $5,000 per child—i.e., in the same range as tuition at Ivy League colleges—and the cost of intensive experimental projects, though rarely calculated precisely, runs twice that.[15]

PREFERENCE

It is difficult to estimate from utilization data alone whether either the cost to parents or a supposed limitation of alternatives is a major determinant in child-care-utilization decisions. Does this pattern of arrangements reflect what families would like to do, or only the exigencies of a day-care market where formal day-care centers are in too scarce supply or are highly desired but beyond the financial means of most parents? There are two kinds of data which could help to answer that question.

First are the preference surveys in which parents are asked how satisfied they are with present arrangements, and what kind of care they would prefer. The Westat survey of 1970[16] found that the type of day care preferred by most parents of all income groups was an informal arrangement in the home or in the neighborhood. This survey reported that parents apply well-defined criteria for choosing among day-care arrangements. These include, in descending order of preference: closeness to home, cost, convenience of hours, sick-child care, and program (i.e., education). This ordering of priorities adds up to a preference for at-home care. Low and Spindler[17] report greatest satisfaction with at-home arrangements, though they did not ask directly about parental preferences.

The 1975 survey also asked parents whether they were satisfied with their current arrangements, what alternatives they might prefer, and a number of questions designed to probe their attitudes toward various forms of care.[18] Sixty-three per cent of the mothers sampled—employed or unemployed, black, white, or Spanish-speaking—prefer to have their children cared for by relatives over any other arrangement. Care in one's own home was preferred over all others by 53 per cent of women. Similarly, care by relatives, whether in the children's homes or the relatives' homes, was almost universally reported to be satisfactory. Greatest dissatisfaction (but still only 11 per cent) was reported for Head Start programs. Not looking a gift horse in the mouth, however, only 9 per cent of Head Start parents indicated an interest in changing to some other program. When asked if they would prefer other kinds of child care, more than three-quarters of the total surveyed said they would not. Those most likely to want to change were sending their children to the home of a non-relative. Of the 24 per cent who thought they might prefer another form of care, about 30 per cent wanted to move to some form of home care, and 45 per cent to nursery schools or centers. The clear loser was the family day-care home. Virtually no one was interested in having her child cared for in the home of an unrelated person.

This study also asked a number of attitudinal questions about various forms of care. The major finding is that parents, unlike politicians, do not hold ideological positions on the subject. None of the questions designed to reflect strong opinions (e.g., "I would rather pay someone to take care of my child than to leave him with a relative," or "I would never send my child to a day-care center") elicited much agreement.

The second kind of information on the care people would use if it were available is more convincing because it is based on behavior rather than interview responses, although it is also based on smaller samples. In a number of experimental programs, parents have been offered—free or at very low cost—expensive day-care centers and other formal types of care. In each case, the number of people who took up the offer was much lower than was expected. An income-maintenance experiment in Gary, Indiana, offered free high-quality day care to the children of welfare mothers at work or in school and subsidized care to others. There were very few takers. At the height of the program, only 15 per cent of the eligible preschool children were enrolled.[19] In Seattle and Denver, income-maintenance experiments also included a day-care subsidy. They divided possible day-care modes into three categories: non-market (in the family, for which no fees are paid), informal market (babysitting by relative or non-relative, either in child's or sitter's home, for which a fee is paid), and formal market (licensed day-care homes and centers). They found that when subsidies are available, the use of paid care increases by as much as 35 per cent for the highest users—employed single mothers. But this was true only for informal market care, and, to some extent, it meant only that arrangements that had been free before were now being remunerated. Use of centers and licensed homes increased about 6 per cent in Seattle and not at all in Denver. This study concluded that one would have to provide heavy differential subsidies to centers and licensed homes if one really wanted to get participants to use them for their children.[20]

Placing a center at a work site does not appear to add to its popularity. In the nineteen-sixties, several corporations set up day-care centers at or near the work site as a service to their employees. When, in 1972, Ogilvie[21] undertook a study of those centers as possible models for expanding the supply of day care, he found that nearly all had already shut down for lack of enrollment. This phenomenon can be attributed in part to the fact that one must have a relatively large work force in order to find enough preschool children of employees at any one time to fill a day-care center of a feasible size. Ogilvie estimated that in 1972 a work-site center for 60–70 children required at least 1,000 women employees. But a second reason for the failure of many centers—at the worksite or away from it—is that many parents favor informal arrangements at home or with relatives.

Thus, evidence accumulates to indicate much less interest on the part of parents in formal day-care centers than the public debate implies. Many parents appear to prefer that relatives take care of their children, and large numbers of them have relatives willing to do it. This finding stands in obvious contrast to the common notion that isolated nuclear or single-parent families predominate.

The preference, cost, and utilization data show that a wide array of methods of day care is in use, most of it informal and outside the market. Overall, parents seem relatively pleased by the arrangements they have, although different modes suit the needs of parents in different circumstances—a good reason for maintaining a system with many alternatives. Preference for change usually reflects either difficulties in finding new arrangements for meeting changed circumstances or the desire for minor changes to make arrangements fit more precisely with the work schedule. Finding care arrangements that are suitable in every respect is not easy. Help in identifying the available possibilities appears to be something parents would welcome enthusiastically. The 1975 survey found parents agreeing overwhelmingly with the suggestion that the government set up an information and referral service on available licensed facilities and caretakers.[22] But, so far as parents are concerned, there is no unanimity about the urgency of expanding the supply of formal day-care centers or day-care homes or any other particular form of care arrangement.

The Larger Debate

Perhaps national policy should rest, however, not on parental desires but on day-care expansion as a way to advance some or all of the larger objectives stated by proponents.

LABOR-FORCE PARTICIPATION OF WOMEN

Lack of available day care is often cited as a major impediment to greatly increased labor-force participation by the mothers of young children. Two very different groups believe that getting women into the labor market is a primary concern: the women's movement and "workfare" conservatives, the latter seeing employment as the only way to reduce AFDC rolls. These two forces focus on distinctly different portions of society and with very different purposes.

The women's movement emphasizes the liberation of women from what they regard as the subservient role of unpaid household labor. The most direct way to accomplish that, they believe, is for women to move from the house into a paying job. There are many benefits, both economic and psychological, to working outside the home. First, of course, is the money. In addition, continuing employment makes a woman eligible for Social Security and other pension systems, and increases her psychological independence and power within her marriage.[23] Moreover, there are good reasons why a woman may want to work while her children are young. One major reason why women in some white-collar professions generally command lower wages than men is their frequently episodic employment history—those who do not stop working for long periods of time command wages more nearly commensurate with those of men.[24] The increasing commonness of divorce, the paucity of child-support payments from bsent fathers,[25] and the concomitant need for women to support themselves all rovide a powerful economic drive to enter the work force.

The social benefits of work outside the home are also becoming more nportant to some women. Social contacts with peers and reinforcement of ne's feeling of accomplishment by colleagues one respects provide important sychic income which was perhaps once otherwise available in more closely knit ommunities, but is now more apt to be found through the job. Measures of uccess may often seem a lot easier to come by on the job than at home with the hildren, where a beatific "I love you, Mommy" can be followed within minutes y a temper tantrum and a plateful of spaghetti thrown against the wall.

The focus of these arguments is primarily on improving the economic and sychological status of women as individuals, and secondarily on helping them dd to their children's welfare. Though the arguments could apply to women cross the income scale, those who advance them focus primarily on the elatively well educated and the middle class. This is in many ways a con-ervative position: no radical change in the structure of employment is sug-ested, only increased participation of one segment of society, for whom a few upport services are necessary—such as day care. The women's movement is ertainly not unanimous on this issue; more psychologically oriented feminists nay question the value of adopting the essentially male definition that one's vorth is defined by a wage rate. But advocates of labor-force participation tend ot to discuss, or even to consider, whether there might not be some non-conomic costs connected with a mother's working full time.

The workfare conservatives are also interested in getting women to work, ut a different group of women and for very different reasons. Those who hold his position regard with chagrin the inequities of a system that provides welfare o some people for doing nothing, while giving no support to equally impover-shed neighbors who work long hours for poverty wages. The conservatives see utting the welfare mothers to work as accomplishing two ends: reducing this norizontal inequity and saving the government some money in welfare outlays. Since a woman would not be on AFDC if she didn't have children, some rrangement to care for them is felt to be necessary if she is to be required to vork. Like their distant cousins in the women's movement, workfare con-ervatives concentrate on economic arguments and view day care as an adden-dum to their primary mission: employment of mothers. They share with feminists the assumption that combining mothering and employment is in some vay superior to mothering alone. Ironically, the AFDC program was initiated on precisely the opposite premise: that the public interest is best served by subsidizing mothers to stay at home and take care of their children rather than going to work.

But even assuming what a large part of the population does not—that it is best for a mother with young children to work—one can ask at least two central questions with regard to increasing women's labor-force participation: (1) Is the public interest served, in macroeconomic terms, by inducing more women to join the labor force? (2) Is the provision of day care by the government an important prerequisite to mothers', and especially welfare recipients', becoming employed?

The answer to the first question is far from obvious. In the short run, and

especially today, in 1976, "joining the labor force" often means swelling th
rolls of the unemployed. In the longer run, economic forecasters are of tw
minds: given the apparent secular trend toward lower birth rates, such analyst
as Drucker[26] argue that within ten to fifteen years there will be a labor shortag
if the economy continues to expand only at its present rate. Others contend tha
automation, the increased use of low-cost overseas labor by American corpora
tions, and the natural limit of resources portend a stagnant or diminishe
demand for workers in the next few decades. The macroeconomic rationale fo
encouraging women—or anyone else—to enter the labor force turns in part on
the resolution of these contending arguments.

The second question is easier to answer. The evidence to date indicates tha
offering day care has relatively little effect on a woman's decision to work. Th
best estimate is that the availability of even free day-care centers explains only
about 10 per cent of mothers' decisions to enter the work force.[27] What matter
most is the existence of a job—when that is available, most mothers find som
way to cope with the child-care problem. Welfare mothers are no different from
the large mass of working and lower-middle-class women in this regard
Decisions are made largely in terms of economic necessity; if net income goe
up, employment is worth it.

Welfare mothers can be distinguished from upper-middle-class well-edu
cated women who work because they want to. For the latter, the availability o
precisely the sort of child-care arrangement they judge best for their childrer
may be a factor in the decision to work or not. It would be nice if society hac
arrived at the point where parents at all income levels were equally free to
consider non-economic benefits to the family when making employment deci
sions. In fact, the workfare conservatives have engineered the economi
incentives at the bottom of the income scale so that for AFDC recipients there is
never a point where the economic incentive to work is relaxed. Only those
whose families can live relatively well without the mother's income have the
luxury of making that sort of choice.

Further, as the utilization and preference data show, when mothers become
employed they most frequently turn to informal home- or family-based arrange
ments, which the government can subsidize but cannot create. There is also
evidence that when formal day-care arrangements break down, alternatives are
readily available. A 1973 study in South Carolina of low-income mothers whose
day-care center was no longer available to them found that nearly everyone
continued to work and in the same job, and that they found other arrangements
for their children within a few days.[28] Moreover, only 3 per cent of the women
in the Seattle-Denver income-maintenance experiment who did not work cited
lack of day care as a reason.[29]

To summarize, provision of federally funded day care—especially day-care
centers—does not appear to be critical to the labor-force participation of
women; the need for and availability of employment is overwhelmingly more
important. This does not imply that child care is an unimportant national policy
question, only that the day-care tail should not be expected to wag either the
Great Dane of federal employment policy or the St. Bernard of welfare reform.

But how, then, can one deal with the problems pointed out by those
advocating day care to increase the employment of women? The first step is to

face directly what is being said: work at home is not valued. The feminist message is that women should get into the labor market in order to receive their due. The conservative message is that welfare mothers should be improved by the discipline of working and their children through surrogate care.

Steiner[30] and Rivlin[31] have analyzed proposals to reduce welfare expenditures by obtaining jobs for mothers and providing day care for their children. Both conclude that the expense of formal market day care is likely to overwhelm any welfare savings for all but a very small portion of AFDC recipients.

Steiner concludes that the real motivation for such proposals is that not simply a zero valuation but a negative valuation is placed on the work AFDC mothers put in raising their children. He observes:

> There is no political conflict over the proposition that a young mother suddenly widowed and left dependent on social security survivors' benefits should be supported with public funds so that she can stay home and take care of her children. Nor is there congressional discussion or any HEW proposal for day care for those children. If 94.5% of AFDC dependency were attributable to death of the father, there would be no congressional interest to speak of in day care. But, in fact, 94.5% of AFDC dependency is not attributable to death of the father; only 5.5% of AFDC dependency is so attributable. Most of the political conflict and a good deal of the interest in day care is over whether the public should subsidize those women whom Senator Russell Long once called "brood mares" to stay home, produce more children—some of them born out of wedlock—and raise those children in an atmosphere of dependency.[32]

Interest seems to center much more on the proper role of the husband and wife in marriage, discrimination against women, sex, race, and freeloading than on the economic relationship between the availability of formal child care and employment.

DAY CARE AS AN EMPLOYMENT OPPORTUNITY

The different value placed on work at home and in the market is also apparent in proposals to expand federal day-care subsidies in order to increase the supply of jobs. There are two discrete interests advanced by those who make this argument. The first is that of the AFDC mother who wants to work but cannot find employment. Why not put her to work caring for the children of others? There is a certain irony to the definition of caring for other people's children, but not one's own, as work. However, if a welfare mother wants to do that, it seems a laudable objective. How might it be accomplished?

The part of the government subsidy that might have some direct impact on hiring practices in day-care programs operates through state and local governments or quasi-governmental groups such as Community Action Projects. It includes Title XX social services, Head Start, and preschool projects for the handicapped. Unfortunately, using federal leverage—including money—to create genuinely new jobs in the state and local public sector is a very tricky enterprise. A political shell game frequently ensues, in which states and localities fire some of their employees and rehire them with federal employment funds, expanding the supply of positions not at all but adding a bit to the state or local treasury. This problem would have to be overcome to bring about any

genuine increase in the number of publicly supported day-care jobs open to
AFDC mothers. Enriched tax credits to private firms for hiring AFDC recipients in day care have also been proposed; even if successful, the benefit is likely
to be small because private firms comprise a very small proportion of the day-
care market. Another obvious possibility is to provide more generous subsidies
to individual families for day care, hoping that the increased demand will
produce more jobs for welfare recipients. Unfortunately the likely efficiency of
that strategy is also very limited. There are several obstacles, including the
competition faced by welfare mothers trying to get jobs in centers, the way day-
care quality is currently defined, and the fact that most of the demand is for day
care by relatives or at home for little pay.

Untrained AFDC mothers face fierce competition in the formal day-care
market. The most powerful comes from the increasingly numerous ranks of
unemployed teachers. They and the powerful national associations which
represent them are the second major force pushing for new federal day-care
funding as a job-creation device. Recently the AFL-CIO has placed its political
weight behind the position that new federal day-care legislation must give
control to the schools. Clearly the teachers and the AFDC mothers have
competing interests. Under traditional definitions of staff quality (education and
work experience) the teachers would win hands down. And those traditional
definitions are now used to define "quality" day care.

Day care is an example of an industry where professionalization is just
beginning to take place. In order to make it a more appealing employment
possibility for its members, the education lobby wants to move day care out of
the status of a cottage industry. Parents, by and large, want to keep it there.
The Office of Child Development, in an attempt to dilute the impact of
traditional educational credentials judged by many to be generally irrelevant to
the effective provision of child care, initiated in 1970 a Child Development
Associate project designed to provide credentials based solely on demonstrated
competence in dealing with young children. To date this project has confined
itself mainly to testing and certifying persons already at work in day-care
centers or family day-care homes in order to provide them with a basis for
advancement. If such efforts as the Child Development Associate project are to
meet the original objective of establishing operationally defined competence as
the primary basis for certification in child care, however, potential workers
must be found, certified, and placed in initial jobs.

But the probability is fairly small that such efforts will, by themselves,
successfully turn around the trend toward staffing federally subsidized day-care
centers with people who have professional degrees. The pressure of school
systems with unused facilities and surplus teachers is powerful; in California,
the public day-care system is administered by the state education agency and
has already come closely to resemble the primary schools, with certified
elementary school teachers as senior staff and former principals as administrators.[33] But whether or not such projects as Child Development Associates were
successful in making less-educated poor women competitive in the race for jobs
in day-care centers, one must face the fact that—California's experience aside—
neither the present pattern of day-care arrangements in this country nor the
expressed preference of parents at all income levels places much emphasis

n formal center-based day care for young children. Thus the greatest demand
or AFDC mothers as child-care workers is likely to come from relatives or close
iends on a barter basis or for very little money.

The conflict is clear; the easiest way to justify paying market wages is to
nake child care more like other service professions: institution-based. Parents
ither do not perceive that the benefits that come to them and their children
ustify the higher price or they are simply unable to pay it. So government
ubsidies must be increased to keep the enterprise afloat.

The reason for the high cost of centers is that we are paying the price—with
dditional overhead, fringe benefits, and amortization costs—of remunerating a
art of the work mothers do at home. Keepers of the federal treasury should be
hankful that most families would still prefer to keep the kids around the house.
)ther ways to redress the unequal value placed on work at home and in the
narket need to be considered.

CHILD DEVELOPMENT

There is one remaining and extremely important argument for formal day
are: possible benefits to children. Public policy decisions should not be guided
y parental preference alone; millions of research dollars have been spent
nvestigating the vital question of how to improve the welfare of the nation's
hildren. One should not be too blithely confident that parents will make the
visest choice. Every reported incident of child abuse is a poignant reminder of
arental fallibility. And experiences outside the home can provide important
ntellectual and emotional experiences for young children.

The world of research in child development has not been closely attuned to
he day-care policy debate. The single most furiously debated question regard-
ng the impact of day care on children is that of staff-child ratios. Only recently
large experiment has begun testing the effects of varying the number of
hildren per adult on the children's development. Until then, no research
ddressed that issue. Research has concentrated on the possible negative effects
f separation from the mother and on possible intellectual and social benefits for
hildren in group settings. Virtually all the research uses experimental, university-
)ased preschools and centers, not ordinary day-care arrangements.

Regarding the emotional tie to the family, even parents who are alert to how
hildren are reacting to care arrangements could use some help. It is hard to
eparate behavior changes due to developmental phases from those that signal
erious distress. An eighteen-month-old starts having occasional nightmares: is it
something about the new babysitter, the fact that mother is gone all day, or that
eighteen months is about the time children start to have nightmares?

There is a massive research literature on mother-child attachment and
separation anxiety, and on their effects, particularly on the child's reaction to
strange adults. Results from such studies vary, but generally suggest little or no
difference in the emotional bonds between mother and child whether the child
is in a center, at home with mother, or at home with a babysitter.[34] Nor does
the evidence show that whether or not the mother works when a child is young
determines the development of later difficulties; mental health and behavior
problems can be traced to serious conflict between parents and children, not to

employment status. In fact, one study concluded that if the mother is satisfie
with whatever she is doing—working at home or in the labor market—th
children are likely to be better off psychologically.[35] Day care is not tl
beginning of the end for close family ties. Eighteen months is about the tim
when children first have nightmares, whether their mothers work or not.

Research on the child-development centers is more mixed. Significant shor
term gains in cognitive abilities or applied skills are found only in the fe
university-based experimental projects which apply structured sequences c
learning activities for the children.[36] Experimental parent-training project:
especially those combined with centers in which mothers are trained as chilc
care staff, produce short-term effects.[37] Researchers have not yet overcome th
difficulty of transplanting the techniques that are successful in these hothous
research environments to larger-scale programs. There is very little correlatio
between early gains in a preschool environment and later success in school, c
between early school achievement and later success in life. Children's lives ar
subject to too many complicated influences to expect an early experience t
immunize them from later difficulties. There do seem to be some differences i
social behavior between children reared at home and those with extensiv
group-care experience. The day-care-center children are often more aggressive
physically active, and peer-oriented than the children accustomed to care a
home.[38]

There are enough intriguing findings to justify continued curiosity an
research investment in the field. One would hope, with Bronfenbrenner,[39] tha
the research effort might concentrate more closely on typical experiences c
children—informal care at home or in the neighborhood by parents an
relatives—and less on those university-based laboratory preschools that are s
convenient for researchers.

In sum, the research findings do allay some fears about the emotional impac
of day care, but do not provide one with much confidence that children'
development is markedly improved by one form of care or another.

Conclusion

The day-care debate has proceeded with very little consideration of th
evidence on current practices and parental preferences in the area. One canno
help wondering why the principal method of child care used most by workin
mothers—within the household and the extended family—comes so little int
the spotlight of public discussion. There is yet one other possible explanatio
for this phenomenon: spokesmen for the various positions are generally whit
and upper middle class. They are the least likely group in society to hav
functioning extended families, and they may forget that the poor and the lowe
middle class do.

Aggregate data sources such as the census tend to reinforce the illusion tha
there are no extended families by using households as a unit of analysis. A
decline in the number of adults in the household is read as a decline i
functioning kinship networks. The fact is, as Hareven has indicated elsewher
in this volume, that extended families in the United States have throughou

istory maintained separate but closely tied nuclear households. Oft-touted mobility figures (e.g., the average American moves once every five years) also mask important class differences. The poor and the working class move within he same area to find better housing; long-range moves to new cities are relatively rare.[40] The postwar migration from the South to northern cities largely followed kinship lines: one went where friends or relatives were already established.[41] In contrast, the probability of long-distance moves increases sharply with income and educational level. Those at the upper end of both scales are the least likely to live near relatives—and the most likely to be making public policy. A policy maker or academic who lives in Bethesda or Cambridge, with parents in Fort Lauderdale and a sister in Berkeley, is not predisposed to think of relatives caring for his or her children. It is easy to forget that for those who live in South Boston or Harlem a child's grandmother or aunt is more likely to be a few blocks away.

But whatever the reason, the data seem to show that there is far more interest in informal care in the home or the extended family than anyone would gather from the public debate. Federal policies to help make this sort of care more affordable are lost in the cacophony of contesting arguments over one method of care—formal centers—and one way of funding it—federal support to those centers. What we need is closer concentration on what people need and want to help them cope with their child-care problems. Instead, policy makers are importuned by ideological and interest group pied pipers, promising to rid us of various forms of pestilence: oppression of women, a thoroughly unworkable welfare system, emotional disturbance, and school failure.

A focus on the parents and children might simply produce some modest tinkering at the margins of the system. Information services to enable parents more efficiently to make their own arrangements would be welcomed; flexible work hours and allowing leave to care for sick children would help a number of families. But such changes hold no utopian promise; women would continue to find job scarcity the main deterrent to employment, poor and working-class families would continue to supervise their own children, and the educational system would not be given major new responsibilities. Some children would still do better in school than others. Life would be slightly eased for those millions of families who do need and use various day-care arrangements.

Such a view relegates day care to that most undignified of political categories: a secondary issue. This move would considerably diminish the political appeal of day care as a cause, but the level of federal investment would probably remain more stable if less were expected of it. Some federally funded centers are needed, but their status and the grand objectives some envision for them should not dominate the question of the government's role in child care. In Browning's Hamelin, the children were forfeit to a policy dispute among adults over the law of contracts and the social benefits of rat extermination. Then and now, children and parents are not helped by having the child-care question unnecessarily entangled with other issues of public policy. Those who seek to help parents solve their child-care problems—narrowly defined—can make a valuable contribution to the public weal. But they should not take their pipes to town.

REFERENCES

[1]*Current Population Reports*, "Nursery School and Kindergarten Enrollment, October 1973, series P-20, no. 268, U.S. Department of Commerce, Bureau of the Census, August, 1974.

[2]*Ibid.*

[3]Sheila M. Rothman, "Other People's Children: The Day-Care Experience in America," *The Public Interest*, no. 30 (Winter, 1973).

[4]Office of Child Development, DHEW, *National Child Care Consumer Study: 1975*, II.

[5]S. Low and P. G. Spindler, *Child Care Arrangements of Working Mothers in the U.S.*, U. Department of Health, Education, and Welfare, Children's Bureau (U.S. Government Printing Office, Washington, D.C., 1968).

[6]C. L. Jusenius and R. L. Shortlidge, *Dual Careers: A Longitudinal Study of Labor Market Experience of Women*, 3 (Center for Human Resource Research, Ohio State University, Columbus, Ohio, 1975).

[7]Office of Child Development, *National Consumer Study*, 1975.

[8]Katherine Dickinson, "Child Care," in *Five Thousand American Families—Patterns of Economic Progress*, ed. Greg J. Duncan and James N. Morgan (Institute for Social Research, University of Michigan, Ann Arbor, 1975).

[9]Suzanne H. Woolsey and Demetra S. Nightingale, "Day Care Utilization Trends: Socioeconomic Status, Ethnicity, and Mobility" (unpublished paper, Urban Institute, Washington, D.C. 1976).

[10]A startling, though statistically insignificant, rise among the white population of children reported to "care for self" below the age of 6 (from 1 per cent to 3 per cent) deserves greater attention, as it might possibly indicate a serious problem for a small group of youngsters. The corresponding figure for non-whites is zero. The form of these data, in which the family is the unit of analysis, does not yield readily to closer analysis of this question—one cannot tell, for example, whether families were reporting such arrangements for only one child under 6 or the entire sibling group.

[11]*Child Care Consumer Study* (cited above, note 4), II, pp. 5-6.

[12]*Ibid.*, pp. 5-12.

[13]Meredith A. Larson, *Federal Policy for Preschool Services: Assumptions and Evidence* (Stanford Research Institute, Menlo Park, Calif., 1975), p. iv.

[14]H.R. 9803, *Congressional Record*, March 9, 1976, p. H1711.

[15]Larson, (cited above, note 13), pp. 19-20.

[16]Westinghouse Learning Corporation and Westat Research, Inc., *Day Care Survey—1970*, Office of Economic Opportunity, Evaluation Division (Washington, D.C., U.S. Government Printing Office, 1971).

[17]Low and Spindler (cited above, note 5).

[18]*Child Care Consumer Study* (cited above, note 4), III.

[19]Lois B. Shaw, "The Utilization of Subsidized Child Care in the Gary Income Maintenance Experiment: A Preliminary Report" (mimeo, 1974).

[20]Mordecai Kurz, Philip Robins, and Robert Spiegelman, *A Study of the Demand for Child Care by Working Mothers* (Stanford Research Institute, August, 1975), p. 37.

[21]D. G. Ogilvie, *Employer-Subsidized Day Care*, Inner-City Fund (Washington, D.C., 1972).

[22]*Child Care Consumer Study* (cited above, note 4), III, pp. 6-14.

[23]Heather L. Ross and Isabel V. Sawhill, *Time of Transition: The Growth of Families Headed by Women* (Urban Institute, Washington, D.C., 1975).

[24]Thomas Sowell, "Affirmative Action Reconsidered," *The Public Interest*, 42 (Winter, 1976).

[25]Ross and Sawhill (cited above, note 23), p. 46.

[26]Peter Drucker, "Pension Fund 'Socialism,' " *The Public Interest*, 42 (Winter, 1976).

[27]Jack Ditmore and W. R. Prosser, *A Study of Day Care's Effect on the Labor Force Participation of Low-Income Mothers* (Office of Economic Opportunity, June, 1973).

[28]Sonia R. Conly, "Subsidized Day Care and the Employment of Lower Income Mothers, A Case Study" (Ph.D. dissertation, University of South Carolina, 1975).

[29]Kurz, Robins, and Spiegelman (cited above, note 20).

[30]Gilbert Steiner, *The State of Welfare* (The Brookings Institution, Washington, D.C., 1971).

[31]Alice M. Rivlin, "Child Care," in C. L. Schultz et al., eds., *Setting National Priorities: The 1973 Budget* (The Brookings Institution, Washington, D.C., 1972).

[32]Steiner, *The State of Welfare*, p. 71.

[33]Joan Bissell, *Current Issues in Public Subsidized Child Care* (Legislative Analyst, State of California, Sacramento, December, 1975).

[34]Urie Bronfenbrenner, "Research on the Effects of Day Care on Child Development," in *Toward a National Policy for Children and Families* (National Academy of Sciences Advisory Committee on Child Development, Washington, D.C., 1976).

[35]Lois W. Hoffman and F. Ivan Nye, *Working Mothers* (San Francisco, 1974)

[36]M. S. Stearns, *Report on Preschool Programs: The Effects of Preschool Programs on Disadvantaged Children and Their Families*, U.S. Department of Health, Education, and Welfare, Office of Child Development (U.S. Government Printing Office, Washington, D.C., 1971); and Sheldon H. White *et al.*, *Federal Programs for Young Children: Review and Recommendations*, 2 (The Huron Institute, Cambridge, Mass., 1972), pp. 112-21.

[37]Mary Robinson, "An Experiment with Strategies of Intervention and Innovation," a paper prepared for a symposium on Parent Child Development Centers at the 1973 meeting of the Society for Research in Child Development.

[38]Bronfenbrenner (cited above, note 34).

[39]*Idem*, "The Experimental Ecology of Education," AEFA Award Address, American Educational Research Association, San Francisco, April, 1976.

[40]Julie S. DaVanzo, "A Family Choice Model of U.S. Interregional Migration Based on the Human Capital Approach" (Ph.D. dissertation, University of California at Los Angeles, 1972).

[41]Stanley Masters, "Are Black Migrants From the South to the Northern Cities Worse Off Than Blacks Already There?," discussion paper 86-70, Institute for Research on Poverty, University of Wisconsin (undated).

COLIN C. BLAYDON AND CAROL B. STACK

Income Support Policies and the Family

THE PROGRAMS FOR DISPENSING PUBLIC WELFARE have been growing piecemeal ever since the Great Depression. The product has not been a coherent "system," but a collection of overlapping, confusing, and sometimes contradictory programs that offer a diverse array of cash and other benefits. But, to get these benefits, recipients must run a maze of requirements, inconsistent and arbitrary criteria for eligibility, and perverse provisions that manage both to discourage work and to encourage the formation of female-headed households among the poor. On two points, then, there is general agreement: American welfare policies are unfair, and their implementation is inefficient. Yet, although critics can agree on the need for change, they find it harder to concur on what the changes should be. The result is a constant debate over welfare policy—a debate that reflects deeper divisions in the society as a whole. New proposals for welfare reform are based on opposing, and possibly irreconcilable, assumptions about the nature of the American economy, society, and government. They produce complex, and possibly irresolvable, disputes over our most basic values.

The outcome to date has been deadlock over reforms. The essential contours and categories of our welfare policies have been left unchanged, except for the recent massive growth in the food-stamp program. "Progress" has taken the form of tinkering—occasional changes in benefit levels, eligibility requirements, or bureaucratic procedures. The reform debate has typically focused on several themes—the overall costs of welfare, the need to preserve incentives to work, the division of responsibility between the federal and state governments, and the requirements for child support.

One major problem—the impact of welfare programs on family stability—has been widely debated. Critics have begun to examine both historical and contemporary data concerning the degree to which welfare policy has disrupted marital and household patterns among the poor. Most recently, for example, in the *Promise of Greatness*, social critics Sar Levitan and Robert Taggart joined those who have begun to cite evidence calling into question the popular notion that welfare is responsible for "family deterioration." Levitan and Taggart argue not only that the impact of the welfare system on family dissolution is much less serious than is popularly believed, but also that the social effects of any "family deterioration" seem to have little consequence. This really should not have been a surprising discovery. Other recent studies, mainly

147

about black families, have begun to point out the strengths of the highly adaptive, resilient kinship networks and patterns of mutual help among the poor.

Herbert G. Gutman, in *Black Family in Slavery and Freedom, 1750-1925*, shows that patterns of intense loyalty to kinsmen and mutual aid arose early, even before the Civil War. Slave couples, according to Gutman, tended to stay together for many years, and their obligations to their families were intensely felt. Following the Civil War, and into the twentieth century, family traditions that developed under slavery broadened to include obligations to distant kin. In the urban environment, low wages, unemployment, and discrimination made necessary the extension of kin ties to distant kin and even non-kin, patterns of co-residence and of mutual aid, and a highly adaptive dependency upon ties of kinship rather than upon marital bonds. Other studies of contemporary black urban families, including some of the evidence cited later in this paper, show that these families are embedded in cooperative domestic exchange and that they have continued as organized, tenacious, active, lifelong networks.

But, while it is a fact that the welfare system has not been able to disrupt the cooperative strength and collective survival of poor urban blacks, that is not the crucial issue. The important point is that we have developed a welfare system that treats many low-income families and individuals unfairly. In our welfare system, persons with identical economic needs may receive different welfare payments, or even no welfare at all, depending on their family structure. Thus, even though our welfare programs may not have destroyed the cooperative patterns of poor families to the extent that we once thought, there is little doubt that existing welfare policies, and even proposals for reform, undermine that life.

Welfare policy can be analyzed from many perspectives, but the starting point must be a close look at the evolution of our welfare arrangements—at the social and economic assumptions that underlie our income-support policies. Comparison of these assumptions with the findings of recent research on poor families suggests that our current policies are sadly misguided and that even the most forward-looking proposals for reform still do not constitute a sufficiently comprehensive "family policy." The modern welfare policy, as it was designed, misreads not only the nature of the American economy, but also the social structure of poor families. Reform proposals should remedy this, not perpetuate it, and a reassessment of these assumptions can be used to develop guidelines for reform.

The Development of Social Insurance Policies

People derive income from several sources. Most, of course, rely primarily on their jobs for income. This may be supplemented by assets, and by gifts from other people—perhaps cash, possibly goods or services. Most people are also enrolled in either a social or private insurance scheme. Finally, some people are on welfare.

Government plays a major role in this system by taxing the income and gifts of some persons, and transferring part of that tax to others in the form of social insurance and welfare. Social insurance programs are the least controversial of our income-transfer schemes. This is largely because the benefits appear to have been "earned" by the persons who receive them. The programs began in the nineteen-thirties with the aim of replacing earnings that were lost through temporary unemployment, disability, or retirement, and replacing support lost to survivors at death. They required people to set aside money for retirement while they were still working, and to contribute to funds for unemployment, disability, and life insurance. Thus, it was thought, money would become available to cushion the impact of the Great Depression and of other similar crises in the future.

Three main programs comprise our social insurance system: First is the program of Old Age, Survivors, and Disability Insurance (OASDI), commonly known as Social Security. It is designed to replace earnings lost through retirement and disability, and support to survivors at death. Second is Workman's Compensation, which replaces earnings lost through job-related disability. Third is unemployment insurance, which replaces earnings lost through involuntary and temporary unemployment. Since these programs are designed to replace lost earnings, people become eligible by working and making (mandatory) contributions from earnings. Thus, benefits under these programs are a "right," not a privilege; work-related earnings, not welfare. Over the years, however, many welfare features have been introduced into these programs. As a result, benefits may be little related to the contributions made from earnings. The best example of this is the minimum benefit level found in both Social Security and unemployment insurance. In fact, all pretense of tying benefits directly to contributions was dropped from Social Security in 1939, only four years after the enabling legislation was first passed. Still these liberalized welfare-like benefits are much less controversial than are other income transfers, in part because they help the "deserving poor"—those who worked at least enough to gain entry into the program—in part because benefits go to non-poor persons as well.

To be eligible for social insurance benefits a person must either have been a wage earner or closely related to one. The emphasis is on legal relationships, not living arrangements. In general, social insurance is concerned about a wage earner's legal responsibility for his primary relatives, regardless of whether he has lived with them or has in any way supported them. Eligibility is based on the initial legal marriage; it ignores subsequent non-support, desertion, or divorce. Such a "legalistic" bias is well demonstrated in cases involving the elderly. Widowed persons often find that they cannot remarry without suffering a reduction in their Social Security survivor's benefits, yet they face no penalty if they live together unmarried.

Social insurance, then, is based on work. It assumes a steady flow of personal earnings. It was designed to replace only those earnings that were unavoidably interrupted or terminated. The programs themselves were to be paid for from the earnings of workers. In an economy with ample employment opportunities, adequate wage levels, and generous social insurance benefits, this would leave only a small task for welfare. That task would be to provide a minimum standard of living for those who have little income and not enough work-force participation to be eligible for social insurance benefits, and who, moreover, society agrees could not be expected to earn normal wages.

Development of Welfare Policies

These assumptions generated the programs of Aid to Dependent Children (ADC), Old Age Assistance (OAA), and Aid to the Blind (AB) as part of the Social Security Act of 1935; in 1950, Congress added Aid to the Permanently and Totally Disabled (APTD). These programs, all of which gave cash payments, covered those who have low incomes and cannot be expected to earn regular wages.

Programs that provide benefits in kind (food, housing, health care, education) also emerged to supplement cash assistance. The political support for these programs comes from those who supply the benefits (farmers, home builders, doctors, educators) as well as from those who feel that welfare recipients should be required to spend their publicly provided resources on certain especially worthy commodities. The major welfare programs of both types (cash and in kind) are listed in the table below:

Programs	*Recipients and types of support*
Aid to Families with Dependent Children (AFDC)	Cash payments to families with children who have lost support of parent through death, incapacity, or absence.
Supplementary Security Income (SSI)	Cash payments to the aged, blind, disabled (combined and federalized OAA, AB, and APTD).
Food Stamps	Food vouchers for households that purchase food in common.
Medicaid	Health benefits for welfare families.
Housing	Public housing, rent, and purchase subsidies for the poor.
Day Care	Day-care payments for poor families under three programs: Social Services, WIN, and Head Start.

Since the original purpose of welfare was to provide a minimum level of subsistence, it was not surprising that eligibility and benefits were based on need, taking into account both income and actual living arrangements. Welfare programs did not rely to any great extent on the concept of legal responsibility that is found in social insurance. Instead, it relied on a concept of "deservedness." Policymakers have adopted welfare programs that exclude persons who seem able to earn income through the employment system, while providing welfare to those who "deserve" it because they are not employable. These deserving persons include children who are not supported by a wage earner (and the mothers or other relatives who must care for them), the aged, the blind, and the disabled. Left out of the system are the working poor, and unemployed or low-income adults who may be part of families, but who are not considered part of the AFDC unit.

American views about the adequacy of our economy and our social insurance system have led us to adopt welfare programs that contain some notoriously odd incentives. This is most apparent to our major cash-benefit welfare program, Aid to Families with Dependent Children (AFDC), which is the expanded and renamed version of the original ADC program. When ADC began, it was supposed to benefit dependent children in families in which the male wage earner had died or had been totally disabled before earning enough to provide sufficient social insurance coverage or other private benefits to support his family. At that time, the typical beneficiary was thought to be the young child of a deceased miner. The program was later expanded to include mothers, or other female or elderly relatives who were responsible for the child's care. The presence of an able-bodied father in the household automatically excluded that family from the program, regardless of how little the father earned. The assumption was that this father could earn an income adequate to support his family. In the early sixties, states were given the option of providing benefits to families with unemployed fathers (though the father himself did not receive any benefits), but fewer than half of the states did.

The impact of these provisions is clear. Able-bodied, but unemployed, fathers have an incentive to leave their homes so that their children can receive AFDC benefits. Thus, this country finds itself supporting a major cash assistance program designed to preserve a family setting for children, but in fact offering encouragement to divorce, separation, and desertion.

Another perverse feature of AFDC is its lack of any strong incentive for the recipient to work. Because the program was intended to help only those persons who were not expected to work, the benefit is based strictly on need. If the AFDC family finds itself with other sources of income, then the family's "need" is less and the AFDC benefit is reduced accordingly (although recent program changes allow families to keep some portion of any increase in income and to deduct work-related expenses). Thus there is small incentive for an AFDC mother to look for a job because her wages would add little to her family's overall income. Lack of work incentives may have been desirable when the typical beneficiary was conceived of as a miner's widow with young children. It seems much less acceptable, however, when welfare critics characterize the typical beneficiary as a "lazy black woman with illegitimate children." As a result, strongly worded, but generally ineffective, work requirements have been added to the program without strengthening the work incentive.

The major in-kind welfare program—food stamps—should be briefly mentioned here, because it avoids many of the less attractive features of AFDC and is often seen as a possible model for reforming all welfare. With food stamps, benefits are awarded to households, not to families, thus avoiding those conflicts about the role of fathers which AFDC promotes. Furthermore, the food-stamp program reduces benefits only slightly (no more than 30 per cent) as income increases, and thus does not so severely discourage employment. While it generally avoids the particular incentives that plague AFDC, it introduces an odd incentive of its own: it encourages higher-income persons or groups to leave the household, an unavoidable feature in any program that reduces benefits a income increases and assumes that all members of a household pool resource (an assumption that may not in fact be true).

Our description of welfare-policy development has generously given our society the benefit of the doubt. It attributes the failure of our welfare designs to a misperception regarding the adequacy of employment opportunities available to the conscientious, responsible, and able-bodied poor. A less generous view would be that, on the one hand, our society has fully recognized the inadequacy of those employment opportunities, but that, on the other, society also recognizes the benefits of having a sizable poor population that consumes large amounts of marginal housing and provides a pool of cheap, unskilled, and immediately available labor.

The Policy Debate

In the last decade, the debate over welfare policy has changed a great deal. but the policies themselves have not. The landmarks in this continuing debate have been proposals to provide a single, nationally uniform, cash benefit program along with elimination of most in-kind benefits. The major proposals have been:

The Family Assistance Plan (FAP): This proposal would have provided cash benefits to all families, but employable adults would not have received benefits unless they were part of a family. There would have been only partial reduction of benefits as family income increased (thus reducing the work disincentives), and the proposal contained strong language regarding requirements for work. Proposed by the Nixon administration in 1969, the plan was finally defeated in 1972, although the portion of the bill that reformed and federalized welfare programs for the aged, blind, and disabled did pass as the Supplemental Security Income program (SSI). This proposal was the first serious consideration of the "negative income tax" approach to welfare, although it was restricted only to families with dependent children, and it left many working poor outside the system.

The Long Plan: Toward the end of the three-year congressional debate that began with the introduction of FAP, the Senate Finance Committee, chaired by Senator Long, introduced a proposal for wage subsidies for the working poor. This plan would have brought low-income adults with no dependent children into the welfare system for the first time, but it also would have retained a revised AFDC program principally for families headed by mothers of very young children. By retaining the basic elements of the old AFDC program in the plan, substantial incentives for families to separate remained, even though work incentives were increased and coverage was broadened.

Subsequent Comprehensive Cash Benefit Reform Proposals: Since the final defeat of a modified FAP in 1972, there has been no serious consideration of legislation for a comprehensive reform of cash welfare benefits. However, detailed proposals have been developed that have served as a basis for continuing debate. Among the more comprehensive proposals are the Income Supplement Plan (ISP) announced in the President's State of the Union Message in January, 1974, but never sent to Congress, and the proposal introduced by Congresswoman

Griffiths in 1974, before her retirement, and reintroduced by Congressman Cornell (HR 6430) in slightly modified form in 1975. All these plans would replace the current welfare system with a comprehensive negative income tax that would extend eligibility to all needy persons regardless of whether or not they had any income or were responsible for dependent children.

An evolution in the policy debate is evident in the proposals described above. Each of them would have provided greater incentives to take jobs by requiring less drastic reductions in benefits as income increased. Yet the first proposals retained many of the early misconceptions about who should be expected to work and about the job opportunities available to employable adults in our economy. Thus FAP would give benefits only to adults who had responsibility for dependent children, and the Long plan, while extending benefits to all needy low-income persons, still retained the AFDC program (for those non-intact families where the household head was not expected to work). Only the most recent proposals have eliminated family membership as a condition of eligibility, and have also extended benefits to the working poor in a way that preserves the incentive to work.

Yet even these proposals do not take the final step in the form of a comprehensive policy that sets equitable guidelines for the sharing of resources among members of a separated family. This is not just a failing of our policies toward welfare families, but a reflection of the total absence of any general family policy.

How Poor Families Function

Our original welfare designs had a vision of the typical welfare recipients as being unemployable dependents (children and mothers) of a hard-working wage earner who had been unavoidably deprived of his livelihood. As the programs grew, and as more was written by journalists and social scientists describing the persons actually receiving welfare, the portrait of these poor families, especially the large number of black families, changed. They came to be described as "disorganized," "broken," "fatherless," and "pathological," presumptions that formed the tone and structure of AFDC eligibility requirements which sought to improve the family structure of the recipients.

Recently, social scientists have undertaken long-term case studies of black families; unfortunately comparable studies of poor white families have not been done. These researchers have found a vitality, stability, and flexibility among black cooperative kin networks in cities and rural areas that had been heretofore ignored. These studies suggest that black families have survived poverty and unemployment primarily through tight kinship bonds and mutual aid that provide benefits to poor families and indirectly to society generally. Our welfare policy should recognize these bonds and encourage them. The following section summarizes how these sharing patterns work among the poor.

Welfare and Sharing Patterns: According to several recent studies, black families are part of a larger social and economic environment to which they have relatively little access or control, but which influences their daily lives in many ways. Owing to unemployment, segregated housing, and educational patterns, as well as social patterns (e.g., bans on interracial marriage), blacks are not well integrated into the overall economy. Despite these hardships, they have developed economic and social mechanisms quite different from those of the predominantly middle-class white society surrounding them. They have learned to survive external conditions which they view as highly unpredictable and arbitrary. These external forces are totally unresponsive to their daily needs and fluctuate so greatly as to require continual rearrangements in household composition. Irregular employment unpredictably alters an individual's ability to contribute to the household income. Although welfare provides a meager but steady income, the regulations tend to discourage two of the necessary requirements for social mobility: formation of a stable nuclear family unit and ability to develop a base of financial resources that can be called on in an emergency. In order to cope with all these disruptive external influences, the poor have developed extended networks of economically cooperating kin and friends. These networks extend well beyond household boundaries and represent relatively stable social relationships which are maintained throughout periods of uncertainty and economic fluctuation, providing a reasonable degree of stability and economic security. While the individual cannot control the amount of income available to him, he can, through reciprocal exchange, compensate for the fluctuations and the short-term economic hardships that would otherwise ensue.

These sharing patterns thus provide the security necessary for a family to withstand income fluctuations due to chronic underemployment and the resulting lack of a sound financial base. These networks also serve to regulate the distribution of goods and services within the community to ensure that no individual is significantly worse off than anyone else. Contrary to appearances, they are expressions of considerable economic forethought on the part of the members. They form a differentiated subsystem within the overall economy that mediates the effects of the fluctuations imposed by the surrounding social and economic system and regulates the distribution of goods and services.

The strength of a particular domestic network is dependent upon cooperation among adult females, between male and female kin, and between females and their childrens' fathers and fathers' kin. Close cooperation among male and female siblings who share the same household or live near one another has been underestimated by those who have isolated the female-headed household as the most significant domestic unit among the urban black poor. A man and his kin contribute positive, valuable resources to his children and enlarge the circle of people both families can count on for help. All these strategies tend to maximize and to maintain long-term relationships within domestic networks.

Whether black culture and these particular familial patterns derive from African forms, from patterns established during slavery, or from adaptations to urban poverty is not at issue here. The important question is how information concerning the existence of these sharing networks should influence policy. In the next section we will review some of the results or unintended consequences of existing welfare policies, and provide an analysis of the impact of welfare requirements on fathers of AFDC children.

Fathers and Families: Any effort by welfare policy to strengthen family bonds has always been undermined by two requirements concerning the biological father. First, by excluding the father from the household, AFDC discourages him from exercising his nurturing rights and obligations. Second, AFDC rules about family income make it difficult for a low-income father, particularly one separated from his family, to use his wage to raise the standard of living for his AFDC-supported family. These problems arose originally from the highly criticized "man in the house rule," from the regulation that did not let an AFDC family keep any of its earnings (the latter was amended slightly in 1967 to permit recipients to retain one-third of earned income above $30 per month), and from the Child Support and Establishment of Paternity legislation that Congress passed on January 4, 1975 (42 U.S. Code, Sect. 651, et seq.). In January of 1975, the Government began large-scale efforts to obtain child-support contributions from non-supporting fathers of AFDC children in an effort to reduce the public cost of welfare. Only a small portion of any payment recovered from the father could be passed on to the child in increased benefits, and often the payment accrues solely to the state, with the child receiving nothing.

Not only do many AFDC children gain little or nothing from this vigorous pursuit of their fathers, but the net effect of the program may be an actual reduction in the total resources available to the children. One study of welfare-supported black families in a midwestern city found that many children receive financial and psychological support from the absent fathers and their families on an informal and voluntary basis. The actual financial support involved may be small, or even nonexistent, and the expectation of such support is low, but a variety of material and psychological resources is nonetheless obtained by the child from the father's kin if the father openly accepts the child. These resources cannot be easily measured in terms of dollars: they include child care, food, furniture, clothing which circulates among children in the network, and social and recreational activities. On occasion, the father's kin may assume complete care of the child. Moreover, a substantial number of AFDC fathers maintain close relationships with their children and play an important parental role, providing affection and discipline, even though offering no financial support.

The importance of the supportive role of the father's kin must also be evaluated in terms of the low levels of AFDC payments. The strengthening and expansion of kin networks can be an important contribution to the well-being of poor families. A child's network can be doubled in size by including its father's kin. Even if it reduces public costs, then, a program that actively seeks legal sanctions against low-income black fathers who are not voluntarily contributing to the support of their children is likely to deprive some poor children of sorely needed material, psychological, and social support that would otherwise have been forthcoming. Because of welfare sanctions, some fathers may refuse to acknowledge paternity, for poor communities will soon learn that open acknowledgment of paternity increases the speed and certainty of legal requirements for support.

In some cases, the pursuit of low-income fathers to reimburse the state for public-assistance payments may cause a loss of additional financial benefits available to a child. A father may not offer regular support, but he may make occasional gifts of money, pay some rent in a crisis, or buy the child clothing. Such cash outlays may occur when the father gets a job after some time without one. The amounts may appear small to the more affluent, but a gift of $30 is a great deal to a welfare family—and is more than welfare authorities budget to feed a child for an entire month. In many states, small gifts at irregular intervals are not considered resources or income and do not reduce the amount of public assistance payment; if they are technically a resource, they are unlikely to be reported. Should a father be saddled with a sizable reimbursement order, on the other hand, he would be unlikely to have the funds or to want to use them to make an additional payment to his child.

Vigorous support programs can have additional negative effects on poor families. Because, under current policies, the amount taken from the father will generally accrue mainly to the state, increasing the contributions demanded of a low-income father may only hurt the father's current family without helping his children from a prior union. Some low-income AFDC fathers are supporting, or contributing to the support of, children other than their AFDC children, and they are often living with those non-AFDC children and married to their mothers. A division of the father's income to reimburse the state for its AFDC payments to a child by a prior union may result in adding his present family to the welfare roll, or in driving that second family deeper into poverty. Or it may be the last straw which leads the already overburdened father, struggling at a thankless job at low pay, to give up entirely. As Gellhorn has suggested, the financial return on support actions is achieved at the cost of "later social expenses for institutionalization of the parties, for lawlessness by men whose latent grudges against society are aroused, and for the economic and emotional wounds that may be suffered by the defendent's other family. In short, there are hidden as well as direct costs in collecting these moneys."

All this is not to suggest that fathers should be freed from any requirement to support their children, but simply that it is better done in a uniform and equitable way, with incentives as well as requirements for compliance. If this were done, the father would be less likely to see support payments as harsh and arbitrary and the system would be less likely to undermine the extended kinship and informal support systems that now exist.

Guidelines for Income Support Policies

The impact of income support policies on poor families has a parallel in our tax system. Working taxpayers often complain about the welfare system they help to finance, yet they rarely appreciate the underlying similarities between hidden incentives in the welfare system and those in the tax system. Just as welfare programs have provided financial incentives for divorce or separation, especially when couples have children, tax laws have, to a lesser degree, offered incentives to dissolve marriages of higher-income people. In fact, over the past thirty years, income-tax law has seesawed between imposing tax penalities and offering tax bonuses for marriage. This suggests that the same principles should be applied to the evaluation and reform of both welfare and tax policy. Families should not be encouraged to dissolve. They should be allowed the freedom to choose how they will function. These goals alone represent an imposing agenda of reform. They cannot be attained, however, until policy makers become more sensitive to the impact of both income taxation and income-support programs on the nature of family life.

Future welfare policies and tax laws must be designed to increase the freedom of choice of the recipients. Welfare recipients should have as much freedom to choose where and with whom they live as do other adults. Families should be able to choose how they will function. The tradition of sharing that the poor have developed should not be undermined. Future policy should rely more heavily on cash as opposed to in-kind benefits. Programs offer in-kind benefits (surplus commodities, food stamps, social services) at least in part because policy makers distrust the poor. They think that recipients squander cash, and they want to influence the behavior of the poor by limiting their freedom of choice. There is no evidence, however, that the poor are less thrifty than the rest of us, and they are entitled to the freedom the rest of us have, which would be provided by cash benefits.

Perhaps the most difficult issue for reform is child support in families that have already separated. Absent, but employed, fathers should contribute to the support of their children, but the demands made of them should not be so severe as to tempt them to deny their paternity and stop voluntary support. To achieve these ends, several steps are called for. First, the requirements for child support must be specified in income support policies; provisions for child support should be a factor in setting benefit levels. Second, the structure of these requirements should not—insofar as possible—influence the functioning of the family. Thus the separated families should receive no more in total benefits than they would if they were intact. Similarly, the total income of the separated family should be taxed at rates no lower than those for the intact family. If more equitable child support were an explicit part of the benefit calculus, less damage would be done to existing traditions of informal and voluntary mutual aid.

Today, we recognize that there are two primary family forms among the poor: the nuclear family and the extended kinship network. Current welfare policy undermines both of them. AFDC first encourages fathers to leave the home, child-support laws then discourage them and their kin from continuing whatever material and psychological support they can give to the children. Thus, while aggressive child-support programs may reduce public welfare costs, the children may find themselves worse off, both financially and in other important ways.

The recent proposals for comprehensive welfare in the form of a nationwide system of cash benefits would do much to alleviate these two problems. First, these proposals would more fully extend welfare benefits to intact needy families, reducing the financial incentives for separation. Second, the proposals would extend benefits to low-income adults who are not part of a family unit. This would increase the resources of many separated fathers and make it easier for them to provide support to their children, reducing the burden of child-support payments. However, even these reform proposals contain the seeds of further "unintended consequences" for family life, because they do not spell out the support relationships in separated welfare families. Three consequences of current proposals are:

1) An incentive for low-income wage earners to separate from their families in order to escape the high income-tax rates that would be part of the welfare system.

2) An inability for separated fathers to improve the situation of their children because of the way the welfare system would tax such support.

3) A disincentive for a separated father to remarry because the resources that the welfare system would make available to his new family would be too low.

In order to assure that these effects do not generate a new set of "unintended consequences," any comprehensive cash-benefit reform must include explicit and equitable support arrangements. The objectives for such support arrangements should be that:

1) The income of members of a separated family should not receive more favorable tax treatment than that of an intact family.

2) Families should benefit from the increased income of absent parents.

3) The determination of welfare benefit levels should take into account all the support responsibilities of a low-income parent and not harshly penalize a "new family" in favor of a previous family.

This will not be easy. It will require explicit decisions, specified in law, about what equitable support arrangements are and how much the family should share in any improvement in the financial situation of a parent who has left it. These decisions will be further complicated if an absent parent has become part of a new family.

In addition to the difficult task of deciding how to allocate a parent's income among his dependents, there is one other problem, namely, retaining adequate work incentives. If support payments are to vary with the income of an absent welfare parent, it will effectively increase the tax rate on that parent (see Appendix). Because welfare tax rates would already be very high (typically 50 per cent in most proposals), a sizable support payment could be the final straw that removes any incentive for a parent to work. On the other hand, reducing the burden of support payments (perhaps by lowering the welfare tax rate for parents who pay support or by giving a "welfare credit" for support payments) would make it easier for families to separate. If this were done, it could then appear that absent parents were being treated more favorably than parents who stay with their families, or that the government was subsidizing support payments. Neither characterization would make the program popular.

If incorporating support standards directly into the welfare law is likely to be difficult and to require a compromise between two worthy goals, why do it at all? The main reason, of course, is that these decisions and trade-offs will have to be made in any case. The only question is whether they should be left to administrative whim or debated in Congress and clearly spelled out in the law. If legislation establishes a uniform national standard that is based on an open and public attempt to achieve a fair compromise between the needs of children and the needs of separated parents, then all parties to the compact are more likely to see the arrangement as fair and non-arbitrary. The welfare system would then be less likely to undermine the rich but informal patterns of support that are of real importance to children who otherwise have so little. This logic can be extended. Our national system for taxing the incomes of working people now offers some incentives to dissolve families and undermines child support. Thus a focus on the problem of child support (in welfare reform) can provide a basis for an equitable family policy in our tax system as well.

APPENDIX

This appendix gives examples of three problems that can arise when support payments are not an explicit part of the determination of benefits.

Example 1: Incentives for Separation

An incentive for a low-wage earner to separate from his family could still exist under a negative-income-tax approach as is shown below:

Consider a system that allows benefits of $1,750 for a head of household, $1,325 for a married adult, $375 for each dependent child, and $875 for a single adult, and that reduces benefits by fifty cents for each dollar in income. (This is similar to the Cornell bill except that it omits the personal-credits provision.) Under this approach, the maximum grant (at zero income) for a family of four would be $3,825. When separated, the single filer would get $875 and the three-person family would get $2,500. Together this would total $3,375, that is, less than the amount received if the family remains intact.

However, the tax rates in the negative-income-tax system at 50 per cent are high. Thus the four-person family would find its welfare payment reduced as its other income increased until the grant became zero when family income reached $7,650. At incomes above that, the family income would be taxed at rates applicable in the regular (positive) income-tax system. But if the father separated from his family, he would be dropped from the negative-income-tax system when his earned income reached $1,750, and any income above that amount would be taxed at the lower rates applicable in the regular tax system. If, the low end of the tax schedule retained its current rates, then it would be possible for the separated family to have greater total income than the intact family.

As an example consider a family of four with the father earning $7,000. The family would get welfare payments of $325 to bring their total income up to $7,325. If the father were separated from his family, he would pay some taxes (assumed for this example to be at the current low rate of 14 per cent on all income that was above the $1,750 amount) leaving him with income of $6,265. His family would still receive welfare payments of $2,500 for a combined income of $8,765 or $1,440 more than the income of the intact family. Of course this does not take into account any required support payments, and these could change this picture, as demonstrated by the next example.

Example 1:	*Intact Family*	*Separated Family*
Father's income	$7,000	$7,000
Family grant	325	2,500
Father's grant (tax)	—	(735)
Total income	$7,325	$8,765

Example 2: Lost Income Due to Child Support

Suppose that the father in the last example were required to pay $3,000 in child support to his family. His remaining income after taxes would be $3,475. His family would not get the full $3,000, however, because support payments are taxed as income. In fact, because they are considered "unearned" income, they would be taxed at higher rates, typically 67 per cent in most reform proposals. This means that the family would now have an income of $3,500 and the combined income of the separated family would be $6,975. This is $350 less than the income of the intact family.

Example 2:	*Separated Family*	
Father's income		$7,000
Family grant		2,500
Father's grant (tax)		(525)
Support payment from father	(3,000)	
Support payment to family	1,000	
(Net tax loss of support payment)	(2,000)	(2,000)
Total income		$6,975

Example 3: Pressure of Child-Support Payments on a "New" Family

If the separated father in the last example became the head of household in a new four-member family, that family would get welfare benefits of $325. The father would have available resources of $7,000 in income, less the $3,000 that he owed in support payments. Thus the new family would have total resources of $4,325 instead of the standard $7,325 they would have had in the absence of the required support payments to the father's "old" family. The old family, on the other hand, still receives the same amount as before, namely $3,500. If the welfare system recognized that support payments were not available to the father's "new" family (i.e., if support payments were deductible), then the "new" family would increase its welfare payment by $1,500 bringing total family resources up to $5,825.

Thus, there are four possible situations for the "new" family. First, if the father is absent entirely they will get welfare benefits of $2,500. If the father is present and his support payments are not deductible, they will have resources of $4,325. If the support payments are deductible, they will have resources of $5,825. And finally, if he has no responsibility to make support payments, their resources will be $7,325.

Example 4: Work Disincentives

The effects that are noted in these examples come partly from two factors that could easily be altered: the non-deductability of support payments by the absent parent who is also on welfare, and the high tax rate on the support payments coming to the family. The problem that will be hard to resolve will be the setting of equitable standards for the sharing of income among the "old" and the "new" family responsibilities of low-income workers.

There is one final comment to be made about tax rates, which can be illustrated by the following example:

Suppose a low-income father with both an old family and a new family is ordered to make support payments of 20 per cent of his income, leaving 80 per cent for his new family. When his income increases by $1, the welfare grants to the two families will be reduced by a total of 50¢ (since that is the meaning of a 50 per cent tax rate). The old family would get 20¢ more in support payments but their welfare grant would be reduced by 10¢—for a net increase in income of 10¢. The new family would get the 80¢ that is left of the increased income and its grant would be reduced by 40¢ for a net increase of 40¢. Note what the tax rate is from the father's viewpoint, however. From where he sits in his new family he sees himself retaining only 40¢ out of the extra $1 of income—a tax rate of 60 per cent. Thus the child-support payment effectively raises the tax rate and further reduces the father's incentive to work. If this father were to have an effective tax rate of 50 per cent, as do other welfare fathers, his welfare tax would have to be reduced to 37.5 per cent.

This example illustrates a basic problem concerning support payments that are tied to income levels—namely, that for fathers on welfare such payments increase effective tax rates to a level high enough to be a serious work disincentive. On the other hand, the remedy would appear to reward fathers for leaving their families.

SUGGESTED READING

Much of the discussion of the history of the policy debate is found in greater detail in the following works:

Henry J. Aaron, "Why is Welfare So Hard to Reform?," staff paper in *Studies in Social Economics Series* (Washington, 1973).

Harvey Brazer, "The Tax Rate Structure," in *American Families: Trends and Pressures, Hearings of the Subcommittee on Children and Youth*, Ninety-Third Congress, 1973.

Priscilla Burbank, "Food Stamps," *National Journal*, 7:36 (September 5, 1975), pp. 1259-88.

Vincent J. and Vee Burke, *Nixon's Good Deed: Welfare Reform* (New York, 1974).

Congressional Budget Office, *Growth of Government Spending for Income Assistance: A Matter of Choice* (Washington, 1975).

Irene Cox, "Treatment of Families Under Income Transfer Programs," *Studies in Public Welfare*, 12 (Washington, 1973).

Walter Gellhorn, *Children and Families in the Courts* (New York, 1953).

Robert I. Lerman, "The Family, Poverty, and Welfare Programs: An Introductory Essay on Problems of Analysis and Policy," in *Studies in Public Welfare*, 12 (Washington, 1973).

Sar A. Levitan and Robert Taggart, *The Promise of Greatness* (Cambridge, Mass., 1976).

Laurence E. Lynn, Jr., "A Decade of Policy Developments in the Income Maintenance System," paper presented at a conference on "A Decade of Federal Anti-Poverty Policy: Achievements, Failures and Lessons" in Racine, Wisconsin, 1975.

Theodore R. Marmor, *Poverty Policy* (Chicago, 1971).

Joseph A. Pechman and P. Michael Timpane, eds., *Work Incentives and Income Guarantees* (Washington, 1975).

Robert Plotnick, "Poverty and the Public Cash Transfer System," in *Poverty Report: A Decade Review* (Madison, Wisconsin, 1975).

Felicity Skidmore, "Welfare Reform: Interest Wanes But Problem Remains," *Institute for Research on Poverty Reprint Series*, 166 (Madison, Wisconsin, 1975); *idem*, "Welfare Reform: Some Policy Alternatives," *Institute for Research on Poverty Reprint Series*, 167 (Madison, Wisconsin, 1975).

Timothy Michael Smeeding, "Measuring the Economic Welfare of Low Income Households, and the Anti-Poverty Effectiveness of Income Transfer Programs" (Ph.D. dissertation, University of Wisconsin, 1975).

The detailed discussion of the functioning of kin networks among the poor draws from the following recent contributions:

Herbert G. Gutman, *Black Family in Slavery and Freedom 1750-1925* (New York, 1976).

Joyce Ladner, *Tomorrow's Tomorrow: The Black Woman* (New York, 1971).

Carol B. Stack, *All Our Kin: Strategies for Survival in an Urban Black Community* (New York, 1974).

Carol B. Stack and Herbert Semmel, "The Concept of Family in the Poor Black Community," *Studies in Public Welfare*, 12 (Washington, 1973).

Carol B. Stack, "Social Insecurity: Breaking Up Poor Families," in Betty Reid Mandell, ed., *Welfare in America: Controlling the Dangerous Classes* (New York, 1976).

Charles Valentine, "Blackston: Progress Report on a Community Study in Urban Afro-America" (mimeographed, 1970).

ANTHONY DOWNS

The Impact of Housing Policies on Family Life in the United States since World War II

Introduction

How GOVERNMENT HOUSING POLICIES since World War II have affected American families is not only an interesting issue in itself, but it also illustrates certain intriguing aspects of how social policies operate in America. Housing policies and actions carried out by both governments and the private sector have achieved two major results since the end of World War II. One is the elimination of the initial postwar housing shortage and the accommodation of subsequent growth through the construction of new dwellings on a massive scale. The other is the achievement of an urban development process that has suburbanized the majority of our metropolitan-area populations. Both these accomplishments have greatly improved the standard of living for millions of American families; at the same time, they have imposed great social and personal costs upon many others.

Although the group suffering from the costs is numerically much smaller than the group enjoying the benefits of improved housing, it nevertheless also includes millions of people. More important, it includes many of the poorest and most disadvantaged households in the nation—precisely those persons least capable of bearing the costs thrust upon them. To put it bluntly, a majority of American urban families have enjoyed the fruits of "social progress" in housing that have been purchased at the expense of a minority who can ill afford to pay the price.

This outcome, which I will describe in detail below, belies several widely believed myths about the nature and effectiveness of recent housing and other urban policies in the United States. The first myth is that all urban social policies sponsored by governments—especially the federal government—have "failed." The alleged proof of their failure is the continuation of major social and economic problems in the poorest parts of our largest and oldest cities. I believe, however, that these problems have resulted in large part from the very success of American urban policies since World War II. After all, should not any set of policies that greatly improves the standard of living for a preponderant majority of urban American families be considered a success? That is precisely what our housing-related policies have accomplished. True, those policies certainly cannot be considered an unqualified success, because their benefits have been accompanied by significant costs borne by persons other than those receiving the benefits. But that is no reason to deny that those benefits exist, nor to minimize their major importance in our national life.

On the other hand, the impact housing policies have had on families since World War II also disproves the myth that the problems of the urban poor are almost entirely their own fault. It is always morally comforting to those profiting from existing social institutions to claim that the people who appear to be harmed by them really "deserve their fate." That fate is usually attributed to some type of immoral behavior that the suffering group "could change if they really wanted to." This myth rationalizes the advantageous position of the beneficiaries, and shields them from the disquieting thought that perhaps their success is a result of chance or even exploitative behavior, rather than of moral superiority. It also excuses the beneficiaries from taking any action to help those harmed by the system—especially action that might impose costs upon the beneficiaries. But, in reality, the urban development process we have institutionalized in America since 1945 unjustly exacts substantial costs from the poorest urban families in order to benefit the non-poor majority, and it does so in ways that are hidden from the consciousness of most participants in the process. That lends credence to the erroneous belief of the beneficiaries that they have nothing to do with the problems of low-income big-city neighborhoods. After all, they live many miles away and rarely venture into these neighborhoods, so how can they be in any way responsible for the undesirable conditions that obtain there? A major part of this essay seeks to answer that question concerning the impact of housing policies upon families.

A third myth that prevails concerning American social policy in general is that it could be vastly improved if only we would develop a single comprehensive and cohesive "national strategy" for closely coordinating the actions of all relevant public and private agencies. As regards housing, dozens of well-known political, and other, leaders have recently been calling for the development—by someone else, of course—of a "national land-use policy," or a "national urban strategy," or for one all-encompassing, unified plan under some other name. But experience with the relationship between housing policies and families proves the futility of this demand. America's decision-making and action machinery—in both the public and private sector—is far too decentralized and fragmented to make the implementation of a single plan possible—especially where such fundamental items as housing or family life are concerned. Every fundamental social reality is influenced by dozens, or hundreds, of policies and actions carried out by various specialized agents, each focused upon some narrowly defined subject.

"Housing" in the broad sense in which it is usually used by the average person is thus influenced by transportation policy, national fiscal and monetary policy, the effectiveness of local criminal justice systems, racial integration policy, the levels of unemployment and real incomes, and myriad other factors seemingly remote from the actual construction and maintenance of dwelling units. Each aspect of life relevant to housing is the province of a different set of specialized organizations and actors. Moreover, the powers of government in the United States are astonishingly fragmented among its levels (federal, state, county, and local) and among many agencies at each level. As a result, it is virtually impossible for the United States to develop a single highly coordinated approach toward housing, families, or any other fundamental social unit. Too many different people are involved, and they are organizationally embedded in too many different structures with widely varying perceptions, goals, constituencies, and responsibilities. This means the whole concept of dealing with social problems through carefully planned "social strategies" is probably not possible in this country.

Instead, the process we must employ in grappling with our social problems is basically one of "muddling through" with an intellectually messy collection of disparate policies only loosely related to one another. The analysis in the remainder of this essay does not focus upon the specific housing policies adopted since World War II in sufficient depth to prove this assertion, since it concentrates upon the impact of those policies upon families. I believe, however, that the almost accidental way in which those many uncoordinated policies have affected families—rather than affecting them through some cohesive "grand strategy"—illustrates the "disjointedly incremental" nature of our system of social-policy formation and implementation. [1]

Attempting to assess the impact of housing policies upon families is an intellectually risky enterprise, given the lack of careful studies and relevant data on the subject. The term "housing policies" covers a multitude of laws, programs, and actions undertaken by governments at many levels in pursuit of diverse and often conflicting goals. Moreover, in our complex society, it is impossible to separate the effects of housing policies from those of many other variables—especially since programs such as public housing and welfare aid are often highly correlated. Under these circumstances, dealing with the subject of this essay requires both arbitrary assumptions and conjectural links between variables; consequently, the conclusions arrived at will necessarily be judgmental rather than purely scientific. Within that limitation, I shall try to support the general conclusions set forth above by analyzing what I believe have been the effects upon families of both the elimination of initial postwar housing shortages and the urban development process that has created our enormous suburban settlements.

Impacts of the Expansion of the Total Housing Supply

A. WHAT HAPPENED TO TOTAL SUPPLY

Production of new housing units in the United States dropped sharply during the nineteen-thirties as a result of the Great Depression, and during the first half of the nineteen-forties as a result of our concentration on war production. That same concentration drew millions of households into American urban areas, and this had, by 1945, created an acute housing shortage. Thousands of large urban housing units were cut up into smaller apartments to accommodate burgeoning city populations. The number of additional housing units occupied consequently greatly exceeded the number of new units built for the period 1930 through 1945—in contrast to the periods both before and after. This can be seen from the following table:

TIME PERIOD	TOTAL ADDITIONAL UNITS (IN THOUSANDS)		ADDITIONAL OCCUPIED UNITS AS PER CENT OF NEWLY BUILT UNITS
	Occupied	Newly Built*	
1921–30	5,552	6,915	80.3%
1931–40	4,950	3,007	164.6%
1941–45	2,745	1,721	159.5%
1946–50	5,266	7,071	73.9%
1951–60	10,198	14,435	70.6%
1961–70	10,426	14,595	71.4%

*Not counting mobile homes.
Source: U.S. Bureau of the Census, Historical Statistics of the United States, Colonial Times to 1970, Bicentennial Edition, Part 2 (Washington, D.C., 1975), pp. 639–40, 646.

As the table indicates, the number of additional housing units occupied from 1931 through 1945 exceeded the number of new units built by about 63 per cent, whereas in all other periods shown the reverse was true by from 24 to 42 per cent. From 1950 onward, for about a decade, American housing policies were in part directed at remedying the resulting housing shortage. About 16 million new units (including mobile homes) were built in the ten years from 1950 to 1959. As a result, for households with reasonably good incomes, an approximate balance had, by 1960, been restored between housing supply and demand in most metropolitan areas. Further production, averaging about 1.6 million units per year, retained this balance until 1966, when there was a sharp drop in new starts as a result of our full-scale entry into the Vietnam war. The urban riots of 1965-1968 then focused attention upon the continuing problems of low-income urban households, shifting federal housing policies once again toward expanding production with a whole new set of subsidy programs in the Housing and Urban Development Act of 1968. From 1969 through 1973, new housing production soared to record levels. About 11.9 million new units (including mobile homes) were built in those five years—an average of 2.4 million per year, or 49 per cent more than the average from 1950 to 1967. By the end of 1973, major surpluses of housing had emerged in nearly every large metropolitan area (at least in relation to the number of households who could afford to occupy unsubsidized units).[2]

This dramatic shift in the nation's housing markets from an acute shortage in 1945 to a widespread surplus three decades later was one manifestation of the tremendous rise in real incomes that occurred during this period. Moreover, it had occurred in spite of a large increase in the nation's total population and in the face of a massive migration from rural to urban areas. Rather than describe the battery of housing policies that helped the highly competitive private housing industry to achieve this result, I will focus upon its likely impact upon American families. That requires first looking at the effects of the initial urban housing shortage upon family life.

B. EFFECTS OF AN ACUTE HOUSING SHORTAGE UPON FAMILIES

During housing shortages, families are compelled to "double up" by sharing a single housing unit or common facilities, such as one kitchen or bath, that serve several units. This tends to encourage the maintenance of extended-family households in which members of the same family regardless of age remain living together in the same unit, or in adjacent ones. The resulting age heterogeneity in the household provides a breadth of experience to children as they grow up that may help contribute to their sensitivity and understanding of others. It also provides built-in babysitters for parents of young children. On the other hand, individuals in households crowded into small quarters lack privacy, and they may experience heightened tension from constantly being "on top of each other": parental sexual activity is hard to conceal from children; school-age children find it difficult to do their homework; and family arguments can be intensified.

Under housing-shortage conditions, young people may postpone marriage if they cannot find separate living quarters; married couples may postpone having children; individuals or couples who would like to live separately cannot do so. Hence, the formation of new households is definitely inhibited by a shortage of housing. It is thought, for example, that some Eastern European nations experienced relatively low birth rates after World War II primarily because they lacked adequate housing. Thus a prolonged housing shortage can affect the demographic structure of a nation, including its population growth rate.

When many households are crowded into all the available housing, urban population densities become relatively high. Local facilities, such as schools, stores, and streets, are often congested beyond their most efficient capacity (on the other hand, public transportation systems operate much more efficiently in high-density areas than in low-density ones). If this congestion is viewed as permanent, it may influence social customs as people get used to tolerating crowded conditions—possibly producing less individualistic social customs and outlooks than would prevail under non-congested conditions. I strongly believe, however, that housing has far less impact upon traditional customs than customs on housing—witness the bewildering variety of cultures that flourish in very similar crowded urban conditions in cities such as London, Cairo, Calcutta, Bangkok, Tokyo, Lagos, and Rio de Janiero.

Another consequence of extended housing shortages accompanied by large-scale population migrations (such as our postwar rural to urban movement) is an inescapable increase in the proportion of "substandard" dwellings. Either existing structures must be divided up and overloaded to the point where they break down and wear out rapidly, or new, very inexpensive dwellings (often little more than shacks) must be rapidly built to accommodate large numbers of people. Hence the quality of accommodations almost invariably declines below what it would have been in the absence of shortage.

I am confident that housing shortages have these effects, but I am not very confident that I can describe the influence these effects in turn have upon family behavior patterns. They will vary widely, depending upon three key factors. The first is the prevailing culture of the society in which the shortage occurs. Observing housing conditions around the world, one is amazed at how easily some people accommodate to congestion and cramped quarters that would be considered intolerable elsewhere. Japanese society, for example, seems to have developed a whole set of mores and customs far less individualistic than those in the West—and far better suited to living in crowded conditions without excessive tension. The second factor is the housing standard to which the persons enduring the shortage were previously accustomed. If they came from tiny rural shacks, cut-up urban apartments may not be as intolerable as they would be if they came from large suburban homes. The third factor is what people believe the chances are of the shortage ending. Observation of experiences in concentration camps shows that individuals can learn to tolerate almost any conditions if they believe they have no alternative, and refugees entering Hong Kong from China in the nineteen-fifties were at least initially happy to occupy seven-story-walk-up public housing buildings containing 120-square-foot units with no heat, no plumbing, and no water because those units were still superior to the alternatives.

C. EFFECTS OF MOVING FROM SHORTAGE TO SURPLUS CONDITIONS

In the United States, housing policies since World War II have largely eliminated shortage conditions. What effects has moving from a shortage to a surplus in most housing markets had upon American families? Because housing was available in big cities, a large-scale migration of low-income families from country to city took place, especially during the nineteen-fifties and early -sixties. These households came mainly from the rural South, Puerto Rico, and the Latin American nations. Their arrival greatly increased the diversity of ethnic groups in many northern and midwestern cities, influencing the flavor and nature of the neighborhoods in which they lived. The immigrants themselves usually improved the quality of their housing in their move from rural shack to urban slum.

The massive expansion of suburban housing construction after 1950, combined with the outlawing of racially restrictive covenants and the rapid growth of minority-group populations within big cities, resulted in a "decanting" of previously bottled-up black and other minority-group populations. They spread out from very high-density neighborhoods into surrounding lower-density—and better quality—housing areas. This would not have been possible if the housing shortage had continued. It caused a huge fall in densities in what had formerly been the most crowded neighborhoods. It also opened up a large supply of good housing to such households—though still in racially segregated neighborhoods. This expansion was accompanied by the withdrawal of millions of white households from formerly all-white neighborhoods. The transition process itself probably produced family tensions among both the white and the minority-group households involved.

Another "up-grading" impact of the rapid expansion of the nation's urban and suburban housing supply in the nineteen-fifties and -sixties was its provision of relatively high-quality homes for the millions of newly formed families in environments considerably more spacious and healthful than those most their parents had lived in. Federally guaranteed mortgages and other government financing policies also ensured that many could buy their own homes. This relatively favorable environment for family life was one of the factors that generated record levels of new babies in the late fifties and early sixties, when the number of births exceeded 4 million per year. Thus, in terms of both quality and quantity, the increased total supply of housing certainly was a

ositive factor benefiting millions of American middle- and upper-income
amilies. Some quantitative measures of this increase are:

HOUSING UNIT MEASURE	PERCENTAGE		
	1950	*1960*	*1970*
Over 30 years old	45.7	46.5	40.6
Lacking complete plumbing	35.4	16.8	6.9
Overcrowded	15.8	11.5	8.2
Dilapidated	9.8	5.0	4.5

ource: U.S. Department of Housing and Urban Development, *Housing in the Seventies* (Washington, D.C., 1973), pp. 6ff.

All these negative quality indicators declined substantially from 1950 to 1970.
Moreover, the *number* of substandard units dropped significantly in this period,
oo—though it is impossible to estimate by just how much because in the 1970
ensus the Census Bureau stopped trying to measure what constituted a
"substandard" unit.

Large-scale housing construction even affected the size and age-composition
of American households. The construction of 11.9 million new housing units in
he five years 1969 through 1973 coincided with a rapid increase in the
ormation of new households, partly because the progeny of the early postwar
"baby boom" were entering young adulthood. This was also a period of
prosperity (except for the recession of 1970–71), so many young people could
afford to move out of their parents' homes and occupy separate housing units as
ndividuals, couples, or groups. At the same time, the easy availability of new
apartment units led many elderly individuals and couples to occupy separate
dwellings as well. Thus, the existence of a large supply of housing units
encouraged the separation into small households or groups of related persons
who might well have lived together in periods of housing shortage. This greatly
reduced the number of extended families in the United States, and increased
hat of small nuclear families. The surplus of apartments in particular may also
have aided the rapid growth of female-headed households (and single-parent
households generally) during this period, because husbands and wives wishing
o live separately could more easily do so.

According to some analysts of family trends, the increasing percentage of all
children living in single-parent (mostly female-headed) households is probably
eading to greater emotional instability, juvenile delinquency, and other nega-
ive conditions among American families as a whole.[3] The extent of the current
"break-up" of the family is shown by the following statistics: (1) from 1970 to
1974, 87 per cent of the net increase in number of households in the entire
nation consisted of a net increase in one-person and two-person households. (2)
The average number of persons per household declined 5.7 per cent (3.33 to
3.14) from 1960 to 1970, but dropped 5.4 per cent (to 2.97) in just the four years
1970 to 1974.[4]

The tendency for related persons to establish separate households was further encouraged by the development of "new communities" aimed at specific age groups. The most obvious of these are the large "retirement communities" created by real-estate developers in warm-climate areas, such as Florida. Arizona, and Southern California; small-scale versions of them are the apartment buildings—including public housing developments—restricted to the elderly that are found throughout the nation. By the late nineteen-sixties, real-estate developers had also created specialized apartment colonies exclusively for young "swinging singles." All these specialized developments reflect the abundant housing supply in the nation. They are both a response to, and a further cause of, the tendency for traditional extended families to break up into smaller groups living separately over a greater and greater part of their lives.

Over time, this tendency toward familial separation and toward living by age group is probably contributing to a general decline in the solidarity and importance of family ties in our society. Though this conclusion is purely speculative, it is consistent with observations about family trends made by many experts not directly concerned with housing patterns. Living in separate dwellings reduces contacts among family members, and it also reduces the ability of some members to obtain help and services (such as housing repairs and babysitting) from others. Middle-income households with a single parent who must work, or two working parents, can afford to hire professional babysitters to carry out the functions that live-in relatives may once have performed, but low-income households cannot. They are therefore often frequently driven to leaving young children unattended, or forsaking job opportunities that might help raise their incomes, or using such (often low-quality) day-care facilities as they can find in their neighborhoods. These outcomes tend either to reinforce their poverty or to provide relatively low-quality care for their children. The latter in turn reduces the ability of those children to escape from poverty and its attendant maladies as they grow up.

One clearly beneficial impact of the large increase in housing supply relative to demand during the past three decades has been a significant improvement in the possibilities for individual privacy within families. Not only are there fewer persons per dwelling unit, but the average dwelling unit has also increased substantially in size since 1950. From 1940 to 1965, the median square footage of FHA-insured new single-family homes increased by 40 per cent.[5] This expansion continued at a slower pace until 1970, and then stabilized or reversed slightly with the introduction of smaller "townhouses" and "quadruplex" ownership units. From 1960 to 1970, the median number of rooms per unit rose from 4.9 to 5.0; whereas the median number of persons per unit fell from 3.0 to 2.7; the median number of persons per room declined by 12 per cent.[6]

A final impact of high-level housing production upon families was a substantial reduction in the acute overcrowding of neighborhood facilities during the housing-shortage period. In fact, there was significant underutilization of many facilities after 1970, resulting from the gradual spreading out of population groups—especially black—whose members had been "bottled up" during the shortage period. Overcrowding of public schools and other neighborhood facilities continued in some areas undergoing racial transition even after 1970. In most large cities, however, residential densities in the formerly most crowded areas fell sharply as those areas "emptied out" and sometimes became plagued by abandonment. The impact of this change upon family life is intimately related to the resulting bifurcation of population growth and social forces within metropolitan areas (discussed at length in the following section). The spreading out of minority groups did not, however, result in much racial desegregation of residential areas. Instead, it seemed to provide more opportunities for the spatial separation of the various groups by giving those with superior mobility more places to "flee to" where they could establish relatively homogeneous enclaves of their own.

The Dualistic Impact of the Postwar Urban Development Process upon Family Life

In 1950, there were 46.1 million housing units in the United States; in 1973, there were 76 million units—a net gain of 29.9 million units or 65 per cent in 23 years. In the same period, the number of households rose 56.7 per cent and total population went up 38.2 per cent. This net housing gain was achieved through the construction of some 42.5 million new units in that period including mobile homes)—an amount equal to 92.2 per cent of the entire inventory in 1950. About two-thirds of all existing units in 1973 were located within metropolitan areas, and a somewhat higher fraction of all new units built from 1950 through 1973 were constructed in those areas. Thus, during this period, there was an immense surge of urban development within the nation's metropolitan areas, mainly in their suburbs. In fact, the nation's suburban housing inventory went from 11 million units in 1950 to 27 million units in 1973—a net increase of 16 million units, or 145 per cent. That was two-thirds of the entire net increase that occurred within metropolitan areas during that period.[7]

The tremendously increased emphasis upon suburban living that resulted from this "explosion" of housing construction has undoubtedly affected the nature of family life in America. In order to analyze its effects, however, it is first necessary to understand the basic nature of the "trickle-down" process that has dominated American urban growth.

A. HOW THE TRICKLE-DOWN PROCESS WORKS

All newly built urban housing in the United States[8] (except mobile homes, which are not allowed in most parts of metropolitan areas) must meet relatively high standards of size and quality set by local building codes and zoning regulations. The cost of meeting those standards is high. Consequently, less than half of all American households can afford to occupy newly built housing without either receiving a direct subsidy or spending over 25 per cent of their incomes on housing. Hence, only households in the upper half of the income distribution normally live in new housing.

This pervasive exclusion of low-income and moderate-income households from new units has a profound impact upon our housing markets—and upon American society in general. Throughout the world, new urban housing is mainly constructed on vacant land around the edges of already existing neighborhoods. Therefore, all urban areas normally expand outward. Most of the

newest housing is on the outer edge, most of the oldest housing is in the center
and moderately aged housing lies between them.

Outside the United States, households of all income levels may be found a
any given distance from the center of urbanization. Both poor and rich live i
older housing near the center—the poor in deteriorating units, the rich in unit
they have maintained or remodeled. Similarly, both poor and rich live in new
housing on the urban periphery—the poor in shacks they have built themselves
and the rich in new units constructed to high-quality standards. Middle-incom
groups concentrate in the rings between the center and the outer edge
occupying "used" housing that is still in good condition.

In the United States, it is illegal both to build new low-quality housing unit
and to allow older units to deteriorate into low-quality status. But the law
against these two types of substandard housing are not enforced to the sam
degree. Laws against building low-quality units are rigorously enforced in al
urban areas. Therefore, only households in the upper half of the incom
distribution can afford to live in much of the urban periphery where new
growth is concentrated. But laws that apply to old low-quality housing ar
much less rigorously enforced in most older neighborhoods and they are almos
totally ignored in areas where the most deteriorated units are found. This is no
an evil conspiracy between local officials and landlords. Rather, it is a necessary
recognition of the inability of very poor households to pay for high-quality
housing. No such recognition, however, is extended to the poor in newly buil
areas. There, local officials zealously exclude the poor by enforcing high-quality
housing standards to the letter.

This process has resulted in a sharp separation of households by income
group in urban areas in this country. The most affluent urban households reside
mainly around the suburban periphery; the poorest urban households are
concentrated in the oldest structures near the center (sometimes in older suburb
as well); and middle-income groups live between them. Each variety of neighbor
hood goes through a typical life cycle. When it is first built, the new housing
units are occupied by relatively affluent households. Then, as these housing
units age slightly, the most affluent households move on to still newer area:
farther out. Other households move in that are somewhat lower in the relative
income distribution, but still have good incomes. This trickle-down process
continues as the housing units age. But they still provide excellent shelter sc
long as their occupants can maintain them.

Eventually, however, the people who move in are too poor to maintain these
units—especially since maintenance costs have by then risen, and lending
institutions are reluctant to risk funds for building renewal. Then the housing
deteriorates markedly, and the neighborhood becomes a slum. This cycle
normally takes from 40 to 60 years. (Some older neighborhoods never experience it because, for various reasons, wealthy households remain and maintain
the property in good condition.)

For the majority of households in American metropolitan areas, this
trickle-down process works very well. It furnishes good-quality housing in
neighborhoods free from the vexing problems of extreme poverty, since nearly
all very poor people (except some elderly residents) are excluded. But for the
poorest urban households, especially poor minority-group households, this

rocess is a social disaster. It compels thousands of the poorest people to
oncentrate together in the worst-quality housing located in the older neighbor-
oods near the urban center. This concentration of the poorest households
ogether should be distinguished from overcrowding, poor-quality housing, or
igh-density settlement patterns, since it has effects different from those other
onditions. Spatial concentration of the poor tends to produce neighborhood
redominance of certain conditions associated with poverty—such as unemploy-
nent, very low incomes, instability of job tenure, incidence of one-parent
ouseholds, and large numbers of children per family. The prevalance of these
onditions among poor and non-poor families is shown in the following table:[9]

ITEM	INCIDENCE AMONG U.S. FAMILIES IN 1974	
	Among Poor Families	Among Non-Poor Families
Percentage of family heads working full time year around	19.2%	65.6%
Percentage of family heads not working	46.8%	21.8%
Percentage of family heads in the labor force unemployed	18.0%	5.8%
Percentage with female heads	46.0%	9.7%
Percentage with three or more children	35.5%	15.3%
Percentage with five or more children	11.1%	2.3%
Average number of children	2.63	2.03
Average household size in persons	3.81	3.38

Neighborhoods containing a high proportion of poor households thus tend
o have large numbers of young children, many of whom live in above-average-
ized households with only one parent. Limiting destructive behavior among all
he children in a big household is hard enough with two parents and a relatively
ood income; with only one parent and very low income—particularly in a
eighborhood where other similar households are very common—it is almost
mpossible. It is easy to understand why rates of crime and vandalism are high
n such neighborhoods, since both these types of acts are, in our society,
ommitted largely by young people.

Moreover, some poor households become so discouraged by their failure to
make it" in our success-oriented society that they adopt anti-social behavior
patterns:

The concentration of poor thus generated contains two different types of poor
households: the mainstream poor and the left-out poor. Since both share the basic
values and aspirations of middle-class Americans, both want to escape from
poverty. The mainstream poor—except for the elderly—believe they are capable
of escaping soon. Their behavior is almost the same as middle-class behavior,
except they lack money. The left-out poor, who no longer believe they can escape
from poverty in the foreseeable future, may shift to adaptive behavior that differs
from middle-class behavior and often creates negative spillover effects upon
surrounding households. As sociologist Kenneth Clark has pointed out, " 'Cashing

in' and the 'hustle' reflect the belief that one cannot make a living through socially acceptable vocations." Robert Weaver, the first Secretary of Housing and Urban Development, has also linked negative behavior patterns with feelings of being left out: "It is . . . unrealistic . . . to expect most of those who are denied middle-class rewards to strive for what experience has demonstrated to be unobtainable to them. . . . The social pathology of slums and blighted areas will persist as long as elements in our population are relegated to what seems to their members as an institutional submerged status."[10]

Thus, the concentration of large numbers of very low-income households tends to produce a negative "critical-mass" effect that multiplies the impact of many problems associated with poverty. Such neighborhoods become dominated by high crime rates, vandalism, unemployment, drug addiction, broken homes, gang warfare, and other conditions universally regarded as undesirable. Most households with incomes high enough to have a choice move somewhere else; so do many employers and retailers. This withdrawal of economic and other resources further weakens the neighborhood and removes many possible checks upon the negative forces mentioned above.

Although overcrowding within individual housing units and high-density residential patterns often contribute to the concentration of poverty, they are not the crucial causes of the resulting negative neighborhood conditions. This is clear from the comparative absence of these conditions in high-density neighborhoods occupied by affluent households, even though individual units there might also be overcrowded. It is local neighborhood dominance by poverty conditions that is crucial—and this dominance can occur even when the fraction of poor households is less than 50 per cent. In fact, only a minority of the people living in these areas of concentrated poverty engage in destructive behavior, so the primary victims are the nondestructive majority who live there. They are prevented from moving out by the exclusionary barriers erected in most middle-income and upper-income neighborhoods. They must stay and bear the social costs of providing the fine-quality neighborhoods enjoyed by the upper two-thirds of the income distribution.

Yet prosperous households have strong arguments against opening up their neighborhoods to unrestricted entry by low-income households. They have observed the destructive environments in concentrated poverty areas, and they do not want those conditions where they live. They have no way of screening low-income households entering their areas to keep out destructive individuals while admitting the nondestructive majority, so they prefer to keep *all* poor households out. This attitude is reinforced by their experience that nearly all non-poor households stop moving into a neighborhood whenever many poor people start moving in. As normal housing turnover proceeds, the area inevitably becomes mainly poor, because only other poor households are willing to settle there. This causes a temporary decline in property values that threatens the major investment residents have made in their homes. Thus, many powerful forces pressure middle-income and upper-income households to persist in exclusionary behavior—in spite of its unjust consequences for the nondestructive majority of low-income households "trapped" in concentrated poverty areas.

B. THE DUAL IMPACT OF THE TRICKLE-DOWN PROCESS UPON FAMILIES

From the above analysis, it is clear that the trickle-down process of urban development has opposite effects upon family life for two different categories of American families. For those middle-income and upper-income families who can occupy new or relatively new housing, it has in most respects improved the neighborhood environment for family living during the past 25 years. Some of that improvement stems from better physical conditions: larger and better-quality housing units, more yard space, more open space, and newer schools and other facilities. Other aspects of the improvement come from the greater social homogeneity of the local public schools and environment. This is prized by many parents because it makes passing their own values on to their children easier than it would be in areas of greater cultural diversity—and hence more conflicting viewpoints. Many parents would, of course, consider that same social homogeneity to be a serious disadvantage, because it reduces contacts with others that better prepare children for adult life in our pluralistic society. Nevertheless, millions of American parents have elected to move to the burgeoning suburbs, partly because they believe conditions there provide a much better environment for rearing children than do big-city neighborhoods. It might be argued that these parents had no real choice. After all, the vast majority of all relatively inexpensive new single-family homes built in this period were located in the suburbs, not in the cities. Yet numerous surveys of persons moving into suburban areas indicate that most feel they are improving their housing and their environment. Consequently, housing vacancy rates have been consistently higher in city neighborhoods than in the surrounding suburbs—even though most new units are being added to the suburban supply.

Since 1945, for millions of low- and moderate-income families living in concentrated-poverty neighborhoods within large cities, the trickle-down process—in conjunction with many related factors—has probably worsened the neighborhood environments in which they must live and rear their children. True, the general increase in housing supply relative to demand greatly reduced population densities in these areas, and it also improved the physical quality of dwelling units occupied by the average urban family—even among the poorest households—as compared to that prevalent in 1945. But these gains have been substantially, or even wholly, offset by rising rates of delinquency, drug addiction, violent crime, broken homes, child suicide and homicide, and other deleterious conditions.[11] For example, the rate of violent crimes known to the police per 100,000 inhabitants in cities with populations of 250,000 or more soared from 294 to 1,108 in 1974, an increase of 276.9 per cent in 14 years, or 9.9 per cent per year compounded. The rate of increase was 6.8 per cent per year from 1960 to 1965; it then accelerated to 11.7 per cent per year from 1965 through 1974.[12] Within large cities, crime rates are invariably much higher in very low-income neighborhoods than anywhere else. Of course, these deleterious conditions did not arise solely, or even primarily, because of government housing policies. Yet those policies surely aggravated the situation in concentrated-poverty areas by making poverty the dominant condition there. These negative environmental changes have been an especially heavy burden on minority-group families for two reasons. First, a much higher proportion of minority than of white families are poor and live in urban concentrated poverty areas. In 1974, the fractions of different groups with incomes below the "official" poverty level were 8.9 per cent among whites, 31.4 per cent among blacks, and 23.3 per cent among Hispanics.[13] Second, because of racially segregated housing markets, it is more difficult for middle-class minority-group households to "escape" from concentrated poverty areas and their effects than it is for middle-class white households to do so. In 1970, the non-poor households within the 50 largest cities living in concentrated poverty areas were 56.1 per cent black, but only 11.7 per cent white. The negative impact of concentrated poverty is obviously felt by a much larger part of the black community than of the white community.

It is crucial to recognize that these two opposite effects of housing policies upon family life in different groups are not unrelated. Rather, they are inherently linked because they result from the same urban development process. To a significant (but immeasurable) extent, the environment for family life has worsened among many low- and moderate-income urban households—especially minority-group households—precisely *because* middle- and upper-income households—especially whites—have deliberately excluded the former from sharing in the improved quality of the neighborhood environment they have enjoyed.

This causality is rarely recognized among the suburban and other beneficiaries of the trickle-down process. They prefer to think of themselves as spatially and socially isolated from, and unrelated to, the ills they perceive in distant inner-city poverty neighborhoods, rather than as major contributors to those ills. To some extent, this erroneous view is based upon ignorance. But it also reflects the "law of cognitive dissonance." After all, recognition of their responsibility would put moral pressure on the beneficiaries of the trickle down process to help counteract the ill effects of their own good fortune. That would in turn require allowing at least some low- and moderate-income households to enter their own neighborhoods. Since they want to avoid that at almost any cost, it is morally more comforting to deny a connection between their exclusionary behavior and the deleterious family environment in urban concentrated-poverty neighborhoods.

C. SOME REINFORCEMENTS OF THIS DUAL IMPACT

The dual impact of the urban development process described above has been reinforced by other government policies that are not inherent parts of that process. One set of these policies has enhanced opportunities for middle- and upper-income households to move out of large cities into higher-quality suburban environments. This includes provision of FHA insurance and mortgage terms for suburban developments, but not inner-city housing (especially in the fifties and early sixties); the construction of federally supported urban highway systems linking suburbs and central business districts—and, later, of high-speed "beltways" around large cities; the development of new federally funded financial institutions supporting home-mortgage markets; and, finally, the continuation of tax advantages for home ownership as opposed to rental tenancy (in 1973, the proportion of owner-occupants was 49.3 per cent in the central cities and 70.8 per cent in the suburbs).[14]

A second set of government policies has intensified the isolation of very low-income households in concentrated poverty neighborhoods, thereby worsening the quality of their family environment. Prominent among them have been the public housing programs carried out in most large cities in the Northeast and Midwest. In the fifties and early sixties, thousands of public housing units were built in massive clusters of high-rise buildings. This design was used to reduce costs and provide open space between structures. Up to then, most public housing projects had involved low-rise buildings, and had been occupied mainly by the "working poor," for the most part, two-parent-family households. Under those conditions, most public housing had provided desirable shelter at low cost. But the displacement from poverty areas of single-parent households, especially those on welfare, was accelerated by urban renewal and highway construction in the fifties and early sixties. These households had to be relocated somewhere, and court decisions compelled local governments to place many of them in public housing, even if some of their members exhibited destructive behavior patterns. As the concentration of troubled households within public housing projects increased, social conditions there began to deteriorate, reflecting the difficulty both of controlling the behavior of children in large, single-parent, and poor households and of monitoring behavior in high-rise buildings not well designed for security. Drug addiction, crime, and delinquency rates in these projects soared. Consequently, more and more two-parent households withdrew as soon as they could afford quarters elsewhere. This further increased the concentration of broken homes on welfare in public housing—thus intensifying the maladies of the environment there. In most large cities, big public housing projects are widely regarded as the most dangerous and unhealthy family environments in the entire society. Yet millions of persons live in those environments, most of them black and other minority-group households with children.

Several other programs, in addition to public housing, contributed to this outcome, and to the formation of relatively "undesirable" family environments in other concentrated poverty neighborhoods. The welfare system provides much higher aid payments for female-headed households with children than it does for two-parent households. This encourages the actual, or at least ostensible, breaking up of "normal" households, and thereby increases the difficulty of providing caring environments for, and effective social controls over, children in large poor households. Urban renewal and highway construction programs in the fifties and early sixties involved massive clearance and displacement of low-income neighborhoods without compensation sufficient to cover moving costs. This uprooted established social relationships and caused rapid neighborhood turnover both there and in the surrounding neighborhoods. Slums therefore spread outward from their original locations into adjacent areas. In the late sixties the FHA began to insure inner-city home loans in deteriorating areas because of pressure from federal officials reacting to urban riots. Ironically, this program actually quickened the pace of racial transition in many inner-city areas because it allowed white homeowners to sell out to incoming blacks and then "flee" to the suburbs—a practice that formerly had been effectively prevented by the weak market for those units. The concentration of publicly subsidized housing projects in low- and moderate-income neighborhoods further contributed to spatial segregation between middle- and upper-income groups and poor households.

In northeastern, midwestern, and western cities, adherence to neighborhood school policies, linking the enrollment of each school with the population composition of the surrounding neighborhoods, reinforced the tendency for expansion of minority-group populations to occur through "massive transition." Whole neighborhoods shifted from white to non-white occupancy en masse, since most whites refused to move into areas once blacks or Latinos had begun to do so. With only minority-group households moving in to occupy vacancies created by normal turnover, these areas "inevitably" became mainly non-white. This has led to marked deterioration in the relative quality of big-city public school systems, especially in those schools serving concentrated poverty neighborhoods. Enrollments in such schools in northeastern, midwestern, and western cities are heavily dominated by children from low-income households. Hence inadequacies of their home and neighborhood environments are transferred directly into the school, preventing it from acting as an effective offsetting force to help its students overcome those inadequacies. As a result, public school arrangements in these regions both reflect and reinforce the dualistic impact of the housing policies described above. This outcome is somewhat less prevalent in the South because the school districts there that were desegregated by court orders in the sixties and seventies were much larger.

Implications for Future Social and Housing Policies

It is impossible to present in this short essay a detailed discussion of the various future social and housing policies implied by the preceding analysis. However, I can summarize what I believe are the most important general policy implications as follows:

(1) The average annual production of new units should remain high enough to enable the housing standards of American families to continue to improve. That means producing enough new units to accommodate future population growth and inter-regional migration, and to replace the many existing deteriorated and dilapidated units in older portions of our metropolitan and rural areas. Although annual levels of new housing production will inescapably vary within each general business cycle, they should certainly be high enough to avoid future shortages. That probably implies average annual production somewhere between the recent high levels of 1971, 1972, and 1973 and the relatively depressed levels of 1974 and 1975.

(2) Specific policies should be undertaken to help deconcentrate low-income households from the areas where their dominance now produces negative neighborhood conditions. Such policies could include the following:

    a. Help raise the incomes of the poor by reducing unemployment and improving income-maintenance systems. Poor households will disperse from poverty areas as soon as they earn high enough incomes to move somewhere else. In my judgment, raising the incomes of the poor deserves far higher social priority than any policies specifically aimed at improved housing.

b. Provide housing assistance to low-income households so that they can occupy housing in non-poor neighborhoods. This could take the form of a housing allowance paid to households to obtain their own units, or rent supplements paid to landlords for accepting low-income households into units in non-poor neighborhoods. (Both of these devices are incorporated in the present Section 8 housing program.)

c. Create specific housing opportunities for low- and moderate-income households throughout the non-poor portions of metropolitan areas, especially in the suburbs, through various subsidies and zoning policies.[15] Considering the political unpopularity of such a strategy among the middle- and upper-income majority in each metropolitan area, this must be viewed as a long-range goal rather than one likely to be pursued vigorously in the near future.

(3) Immediate efforts should be made to improve the standard of living in older neighborhoods now dominated by concentrations of poor households. In addition to raising the incomes of the poor, as noted above, these efforts should include improving the effectiveness of the criminal justice system, providing economic aid for rehabilitation of older housing units, improving the flow of private capital into housing rehabilitation (especially in areas not yet in advanced stages of decay and abandonment), and providing good-quality local government services on a day-to-day basis. In view of the fiscal squeeze faced by many older cities with declining populations, some added federal economic assistance may be necessary to achieve these goals.

Just how these recommended policies should be carried out cannot be considered apart from formulating an overall strategy for future urban development in our metropolitan areas. But that complex subject is far beyond the scope of this essay.

Conclusion

The net impact of American government housing policies upon family life in the past 30 years is rather ambivalent. On the one hand, they have helped overcome the acute housing shortage prevalent in 1945, and provided the greatest expansion in numbers of families in the nation's history with its highest quality dwellings. On the other hand, the urban development process through which this immense increase in total supply took place had a dual impact. It was favorable to family life for a majority of Americans, but terribly harmful to the neighborhood environments in which millions of others had to live. Since the latter consisted mainly of poor and minority-group- households, the basic "trickle-down" urban development process tended to aggravate the already existing major social, economic, and familial inequalities.

It appears from recent data that American family life is becoming less stable and more subject to serious deficiencies than it was right after World War II. I suspect this is occurring in spite of a large improvement in the quality of dwelling units, and, at least in part, because of a marked deterioration in the quality of neighborhoods in concentrated-poverty areas. Thus, housing policies have had a significant impact upon family life, even though it is undoubtedly less important than the impact coming from many other key social, cultural, and economic variables.

REFERENCES

[1]"Disjointed incrementalism" is a term coined by Charles E. Lindblom in his extensive discussion and defense of the general "muddling through" method of decision-making. See Charles E. Lindblom and David Braybrooke, *A Strategy of Decision* (New York, 1963).

[2]Housing-starts information taken from Anthony Downs, *Federal Housing Subsidies: How Are They Working?* (Lexington, Mass., 1973), p. 11.

[3]This is the contention of Urie Bronfenbrenner as stated in his speech, "The Next Generation of Americans," presented at the 1975 Annual Meeting of the American Association of Advertising Agencies at Dorado, Puerto Rico, March 20, 1975. For a contrasting point of view, see Heather L. Ross and Isabel V. Sawhill, *Time of Transition: The Growth of Families Headed by Women* (Washington, D.C., The Urban Institute, 1975).

[4]U.S. Bureau of the Census, *Statistical Abstract of the United States: 1975* (96th ed., Washington, D.C., 1974), p. 40. I will refer to this volume hereafter as *Statistical Abstract 1975*.

[5]President's Committee on Urban Housing, *A Decent Home* (Washington, D.C., 1968), p. 119.

[6]*Statistical Abstract 1975*, p. 718.

[7]Data in this paragraph are taken from U.S. Bureau of the Census, *Annual Housing Survey: 1973*, Part A, "General Housing Characteristics" (Series H-150-73a), XIV-XXII. I will refer to this volume hereafter as *Annual Housing Survey 1973*.

[8]This section is quoted directly from my article "The Success and Failures of Federal Housing Policy, 1960-1974," in *Urban Problems and Prospects* (Chicago, 1976), pp. 89-91.

[9]U.S. Bureau of the Census, *Characteristics of the Population Below the Poverty Level: 1974* (P-60, No. 102), January, 1976, Table 4, pp. 24-33.

[10]Anthony Downs, *Opening Up the Suburbs* (New Haven, 1973), p. 90.

[11]Urie Bronfenbrenner (cited above, note 3).

[12]*Statistical Abstract 1975*, p. 152.

[13]U.S. Bureau of the Census, *Characteristics of the Population Below the Poverty Level: 1974* (P-60, No. 102), January, 1976, p. 2.

[14]*Annual Housing Survey 1973*, XIX.

[15]This strategy is described in detail in my *Opening Up the Suburbs* (cited above, note 10).

HIROSHI WAGATSUMA

Some Aspects of the Contemporary Japanese Family: Once Confucian, Now Fatherless?

IN MARCH OF 1975, an adolescent girl from a middle-class Tokyo family became seriously depressed as day and night, like tens of thousands of other Japanese high school students, she prepared for her college-entrance examinations. Tormented by anxiety and terrified that she would fail, in the end she could not face the ordeal. So far, there is nothing very unusual about this story in contemporary Japan, where many young people suffer from "examination hell,"[1] but the situation took a bizarre turn when her father decided to help her. On the day of the examination, disguised as a young girl with wig, cosmetics, and costume, he went to the women's college and took her examinations for her. As he was leaving the room, however, he was stopped and questioned by a professor who thought "she" was not only a little too old for a high school student but behaving strangely as well. The father's identity was revealed, and the story was spread. The media sensationalized the incident to the point where this one small case of individual pathology became a *cause célèbre* and the subject of a good deal of discussion and criticism. One of the comments most frequently heard was: "Such a thing could *never* have been done by a father before the War!"

In prewar Japan, the family system (*kazoku seido*) was regarded as being of the utmost importance, as the embodiment of all that was fine and noble in the national tradition, as the only suitable moral training ground for patriotic and loyal citizens, and the core of the national polity.[2] A passage frequently quoted from *Greater Learning*, a Confucian textbook, went: "Their persons being cultivated, their families were regulated. Their families being regulated, their states were rightly governed. Their states being rightly governed, the whole kingdom was made tranquil and happy." In the original text, the passage referred to the rulers of principalities under the feudal Chou dynasty in China (737 B.C.-251 B.C.). It was, however, an axiom of Chinese political philosophy generally that stable families ensured a stable society and that filial piety was a civic duty.

The Japanese family, as a system of legal and political organization, was based upon these Confucian political principles. Under the family system, the "house" (*ie*) was the major unit of social organization. However, the "house" was not comprised simply of the actual living members of the family. It was an entity that continued through time with changing personnel but with an unchanging identity. The "house" included dead ancestors, living members,

181

descendants yet to come, and the name, occupation, property, and actual house and the graveyard belonging to that group. Some "houses" among the upper classes had a "constitution" (*ka-kun*) that governed the behavior of their members. The "house" was of greater importance than the individuals who temporarily dwelled in it. It was a legal personality in which property rights and duties were vested, and it was represented by its "househead" (*ka-chō*). Under the old civil code, the continuation of the "house" was not only a moral but also a legal duty.

The power of the househead over other family members was great. His decisions affecting its members were final in such matters as marriage and choice of occupation. He was explicitly given the power to determine where members of his family might live. His authority was backed by the old warrior institution of expulsion from the family (*kandō*), which was a formal act removing the offender's name from the family register. When a househead was also a parent, he could force the dissolution of a marriage of a son until the age of 30, and of a daughter until the age of 25. However, the objective of the househead's authority was to promote the good of the house, not to indulge personal whims. His duty was to look after the family under his jurisdiction.[3]

Japanese social scientists, under the influence of Max Weber, tended to define the "house" under the family system as a "patriarchal" organization.[4] For example, one noted authority of the Japanese family wrote: "The 'house' (*ie*) was a historicosocial institution that was based on the patriarchal rights of the househead; it was grounded in the selfless piety (*Pietät*) of its members toward traditional authority."[5] The family system was often regarded as synonymous with the ethical system, or at least as a conceptualized set of behavior patterns that had normative implications.[6]

These patterns strongly reflected Confucian ethical notions. Emphasis was placed on the individual's respect, obedience, and "piety" toward his parents, especially toward his father, and upon the observance of rank order within the family. Respect was required from a person of lower rank to a person of higher rank, that is, from children to parents, from younger siblings to older ones, from wife to husband, and generally from younger members to older members. The picture of a family governed by Confucian ethics often took on a "patriarchal" quality, although the benevolence of parents and a harmonious solidarity among family members were equally emphasized. A father was often described as "strict" (*kibishii*) and "awesome" (*kowai*), while a mother was generally said to be "loving" (*yasashii*). The notion of ideal parents was of "a strict, stern father and an affectionate, protective mother" (*gen-pu, ji-bo*); this was believed to be the pattern most conducive to the growth of a healthy, virtuous Japanese citizen. The following is a description of such an ideal father and mother in the "constitution" of a warrior family of the mid-eighteenth century:[7]

> The father raises children strictly, corrects their manners, teaches them arts and techniques, educates them in all matters, scolds them for, and warns them against, wrong doing, cultivates their good character, looks after them so that they grow up to be praiseworthy in the opinion of others, and disciplines them for their own sake. Such is the father's benevolence and duty.

The mother cares for her children gently and quietly, calms them down and explains to them in detail and reasonably why their father is strict, so that the children will not become angry and resent their father's attitudes. Such is the mother's benevolence and duty.

No one could be more distant from this "stern and strict father" than the paternal transvestite taking the entrance examination to the women's college!

It is now claimed that Japanese fathers lost their previous dignity and authority after the war and that they have become "nobodies" in their homes. Responding to an opinion survey of the *Asahi News Press*, University of Tokyo students ranked their mothers at the top of the "list of people they respected the most."[8] Clinical psychologists observed that children who were morbidly afraid of attending school (a pathology called "school phobia" in Japan) often came from families in which the father was either absent or played no important role and/or the mother was dominant. Another clinician found that mother-dominated homes tended to produce immature children whose social development was considerably delayed.[9] These studies often imply that the number of such children is on the increase.

On Father's Day, June 17, 1973, in a Tokyo survey, 542 junior high school students were asked, "Does your father tell you what kind of life he wants you to lead both now and in the future?" Only one-fourth (25.4%) answered "Yes," while more than two-thirds (74.6%) said their fathers never talked about such things. Of those whose fathers did talk to them about life, only 3.2 per cent said they would accept and follow their father's advice. Nearly half (46.5%) of 1,584 men and women (aged 20-60) interviewed in 1973 thought the father's authority was definitely weaker than it had been in the past, while only 8.8 per cent thought it had become stronger (the remaining 44.7 per cent could not decide).[10] Of 100 male and 100 female university students in Tokyo living with their parents, only 18 per cent of the males and 15 per cent of the females thought their fathers were "awe-inspiring" (*kowai*), and only 8 per cent and 9 per cent thought their fathers were too strict. The father was looked upon as "too indulgent" (*amai*) by 27 per cent of the male and 44 per cent of the female students.[11]

The appearance of the Japanese translation of *Auf dem Weg zur vaterlosen Gesellschaft* by a German psychoanalyst[12] proved timely; it was a best-seller, widely read and frequently quoted. The "fatherless society" (*chichi naki shakai*) became a catch-phrase. The Japanese father was said to have become a nobody who played no significant role in the home; he had become "shadowy" (*kage ga usui*). It was almost as if the concern, worry, and resentment, long dormant among the Japanese since the "democratization period" of postwar Japan, had suddenly surfaced on this issue. The nuclear family, the weak father, the dominant mother, and the loneliness of old age joined the list of social problems, alongside pollution, traffic jams, housing shortages, and juvenile delinquency. Some even began to say that it had become necessary to "reevaluate" the old family system of Japan. Whether the Japanese father has actually become "weak and insignificant" is a question to which we shall return later. Let us first look at the reasons proposed to explain the alleged changes.

It has been said that Japanese fathers have become "almost non-existent" because of postwar changes in values, the increased number of nuclear families, crowded housing conditions, the influence of the media as a source of information, and the father's relatively weakened financial position. Under the new constitution, the "house" ceased to be a legal entity. The legal rights and duties of the househead no longer exist. Marriages are now expected to be based on the mutual consent of a man and a woman, legally defined as equal. The importance of communication between parents and children is constantly emphasized as a sign of "democracy" in families. The teaching of Confucian ethics in the schools is a thing of the past. Changes in values after the war were drastic, and they have since become even more far-reaching. As the traditional warrior-Confucian ethics were abandoned, it is argued, the authority of the father was destroyed as well. Two different fathers are quoted in the following passages:

[A 74-year-old man:] Ever since we lost the war, whatever I say is condemned as "feudal." Nobody in my home listens to me any longer. I carry no weight.

[A 55-year-old man:] Until the end of the war, the father's role was clearly defined. It was our duty to protect our family members, to raise our children, to be loyal to our emperor, and to fight for our country. Filial piety at home and patriotism outside the home: clear and simple. When we were defeated and we had to start all over again, the fathers were blamed for all that happened. They were condemned as no good. Since then all Japanese fathers have been blamed and condemned as no good.[13]

The second reason proposed to explain the decline of the father's authority is the rapid increase in the number of nuclear families in postwar Japan. It has been suggested that in order to maintain the paternal (or househead's) authority, there have to be many family members, all maintaining "pious attitudes" (or *persönliche Pietätsbeziehungen*, as Weber called it) toward the father. When there are only a few people, such as a wife and a child or two, the authority of the head is bound to weaken. As Table 1 indicates, the average size of a Japanese household in 1972 was 3.52 people (it was 3.06 in the United States); in 1975 it was 3.6; in 1940, it was 5.01 (in the United States, 3.8). The increase in the number of nuclear families has been very rapid in postwar Japan. In the United States, for example, it took the average-household size fifty years (from 1880 to 1930) to decrease from five individuals to four, while in Japan the same change took place in twenty-five years (from 1940 to 1965). The proportion of nuclear families among all types of households was 60 per cent in 1920, 69 per cent in 1964, and 78.4 per cent in 1965. The proportion of lineal extended families decreased from 30.2 per cent in 1920 to 25.2 per cent in 1964. The extended families, including collateral members, decreased from 9.8 per cent in 1920 to 5.8 per cent in 1964.[14]

One may argue against the nuclear-family explanation for the loss of paternal authority by pointing out that extended families—assumed to be a necessary basis for paternal authority—were far less numerous in the past than is commonly believed, nor has their decrease at present been particularly drastic (from 40 per cent in 1920 to 31 per cent in 1964). The nuclear families shown in Table 1 merely represent a cross section of Japanese society at a given time; the data do not reflect the cycle within each household. When the history of each family is followed longitudinally, and the question is asked if a family has ever

TABLE 1

THE AVERAGE SIZE OF A HOUSEHOLD

Year	U.S.A.	Japan
1880	5.0	—
1890	4.9	—
1920	4.3	4.89
1930	4.1	4.98
1940	3.8	5.01
1950	3.37	4.97
1960	3.33	4.56
1965	3.29	4.08
1970	3.14	3.63
1971	3.11	3.56
1972	3.06	3.52
1975	—	3.35

included three-generational members, a different picture emerges: the number of families in which grandparents have never lived with their children and grandchildren is relatively small.[15]

This is important for any consideration of old age in Japanese society. The postwar change of values and the increase of nuclear families combined to cause many commentators to dwell on the misery and loneliness of old people who now live apart from their children. Under the Confucian family system of the past, they would have been respected and cared for by the eldest son and his family and dwelled under the same roof. It seems, however, that the present situation is not so different from the past as commentators tend to imagine. In spite of changes in values, a majority of young Japanese still intend to support their parents in old age. When the Office of the Prime Minister interviewed 160,000 young people, 83.5 per cent of them indicated their intention to support their parents unconditionally ("no matter what," 29.8%) or with some qualification ("as much as my financial situation allows," 53.7%). Those who wanted their parents to support themselves or to rely upon public facilities and welfare programs were very few in number (2.8%). The remaining 13.3 per cent could not make up their mind, and 0.5 per cent gave no answer.[16] Compared with German or American adults and youths, the Japanese seem to approve of the idea that aged parents should live together with their children. When the Office of the Prime Minister studied the attitudes toward social norms among 700 youths and 300 of their parents in Japan, the United States, and Germany, one of the questions asked was: "Is it preferable for parents to live with their adult children?" While 71.2 per cent of the Japanese youths and 70.2 per cent of the adults answered "Yes," 21.3 per cent of the youths and 25.1 per cent of the adults answered "No" (the remainder did not answer the question), only 23.0 per cent of the American youths and 11.5 per cent of the adults answered "Yes," and 72.9 per cent of the youths and 86.6 per cent of the adults answered "No." Similarly, only 13.3 per cent of the German youths and 17.7 per cent of the adults thought living together with parents was a good idea, while 86.1 per cent of the youths and 81.3 per cent of adults did not think so.[17] Unfortunately, we do not know if these figures reflect any postwar change in attitude, as no comparable data are available from before the war. Regardless of their children's attitudes on the subject, however, many old people apparently do not intend to depend upon their children, at least if they can afford not to. Of 350 older people interviewed in a study, about one-third (37%) intended to live separately from their children and to support themselves. Another third (34%) wished to live together with their children, but did not want to be financially dependent upon them. Presumably they would share food and utility bills with their children—a pattern that already seems to be widely practiced in Japanese urban middle-class families. Those who intended to live together with, and depend financially upon, their children constituted only 15 per cent, and those who intended to live separately from, but depend upon, their children constituted only 5 per cent. A very small number (2%) expected to enter a home for the aged.[18] In fact, however, more people in old age seem to be living with their children or relatives than not. According to one report, only a very small number of people above age 60 (14.3% male and 10.2% female) live either alone or with their spouse in Japan, while more than 50 per cent, perhaps as many as 70 per cent, do so in Western societies (see Table 2). A majority of elderly Japanese (80.3% male and 82.7% female) live with their married or unmarried children, while comparable figures for Western societies run around 30 per cent or less.[19]

A third reason offered for the assumed loss of paternal authority is "overcrowding." It is argued that a certain distance between the father and other family members is a necessary condition for the maintenance of his authority.

TABLE 2

LIVING ARRANGEMENTS FOR THE ELDERLY
IN VARIOUS COUNTRIES

	U.S.A. 1957		England 1962	Germany 1958		Denmark 1962	Japan 1960	
	Man	Woman	Man-Woman	Man	Woman	Man-Woman	Man	Woman
Married old person living								
with spouse[a]	47.8%	27.7%	33.0%	49.0%	25.0%	45.0	11.3	4.2
with married child	17.6	7.7	13.0	17.0	8.0	8.0	40.7	18.1
with unmarried child							14.5	3.5
with relative(s)	4.2	2.7	3.0	—	—	2.0	2.4	1.3
with non-relative(s)							0.0	0.0
Single old person living								
alone[b]	14.5	25.1	22.0	13.0	30.0	28.0	3.0	6.0
with married child	8.0	22.7	19.0	14.0	25.0	9.0	21.0	50.8
with unmarried child							4.1	10.3
with relative(s)	7.8	14.0	10.0	7.0	12.0	8.0	1.8	4.5
with non-relative(s)							0.7	1.1
Household of old person(s) only [(a & b)]	62.3	52.8	55.0	62.0	55.0	73.0	14.3	10.2

The father needs to remain aloof in his own private domain and not to mingle casually with the family; familiarity tends to undermine authority. But the population density in homes has been higher in postwar Japan than ever before, particularly in large cities, where overcrowding has become a chronic problem. In a Japanese-style room, the floor is covered with straw mats called *tatami*. The size of a tatami is standardized (6 feet by 3 feet), and each room is measured by the number of tatami it can contain. Typical rooms are of 2 tatami (that is, 6 by 6 feet), 3 tatami (6 by 9 feet), 4½ tatami (9 by 9 feet), 6 tatami (9 by 12 feet) and 8 tatami (12 by 12 feet).[20] In one prewar and one postwar year, the average number of tatami for a house in three major cities was as follows:

	Kyoto	Tokyo	Yokohama
1941	20.43	18.23	16.58
1965	19.15	14.22	15.01

In other words, residents in a house of average size had less than 32 square yards of space for dining and sleeping in Tokyo and Yokohama in 1965 (the kitchen, toilet, and bath are excluded).[21] According to a report by the Ministry of Construction's Bureau of Housing, in 1968 nearly 42 per cent of the total Tokyo population lived in houses where two- or three-member households had less than nine tatami (18 square yards), and four-or-more-member households had less than 12 tatami (24 square yards) for living space. According to another source, the average number of tatami per person in different cities and various types of housing in 1965 varied from five and a half (10 square yards) to two and a half (5 square yards) as shown in Table 3.

In these very small houses and apartments, where family members live crowded together, no father can be physically distant from the rest of the

TABLE 3

AVERAGE NUMBER OF TATAMI PER PERSON IN
VARIOUS CITIES AND DIFFERENT TYPES OF HOUSES

	Average	Owned House	Public Rental	Private Rental A	Private Rental B	Company Housing
National	4.91	5.42	3.42	3.74	2.75	4.13
Tokyo	3.87	4.51	3.27	3.21	2.42	3.82
Yokohama	3.80	4.22	3.56	3.03	2.40	3.81
Nagoya	4.57	5.30	3.53	3.91	2.91	4.39
Osaka	3.69	4.27	3.31	3.44	2.44	3.68
Kobe	3.94	4.73	3.23	3.38	2.22	3.93

Public Rental: House or apartment for rent, operated by Japan Public Housing Corporation.
Private Rental A: House or apartment for rent, operated by private owners.
Private Rental B: House or apartment for rent, operated by private owners, in which some facilities such as kitchen or toilet are commonly shared with neighbors. Often there is no bathroom and the tenants go to a public bathhouse.
Company Housing: House or apartment owned by a company or a firm to house its employees.
   Note: Most Japanese wish to live in a public rental home or apartment because the rent is reasonable and facilities are good. However, those on a long waiting list must live in a private rental home or apartment with less satisfactory facilities and with by far higher rent.
   Source: Information obtained from the Department of City Engineering, School of Engineering, University of Tokyo (1967).

family, and he therefore has no physical space to use for maintaining his authority. A taxi driver who was interviewed for a report was quoted as saying: "A father, lounging around the house in only his underwear on Sunday morning, sits down to the dinner table and suddenly wants to begin to lecture his children on the meaning of life and their plans for the future. Who will take him seriously? The children will simply laugh."[22] Once again, however, one could argue that the figures indicate that dwellings in prewar Japan were not that much less crowded than they are today and that, inversely, fathers living in spacious houses today should still be able to maintain their authority. But that does not seem to be the case.

The fourth reason for the alleged loss of paternal authority is said to be the increasing influence of television and the press as sources of information for the young. According to this argument, in the traditional society the father was often an important, sometimes the only, source of information and instruction for his children. Especially when a son took over his father's occupation (as in farming, fishing, or store-keeping), the father was often the only teacher and model his son had to follow. In recent Japan, however, children do not so frequently take over the father's occupation, while technological innovations and rapid changes in fads and fashions have also served to eliminate fathers as the childrens' sole source for instruction and information.

Statistics support the belief that young people are more strongly influenced by the media than they are by parents. For example, the Office of the Prime Minister found that, among 160,000 youths interviewed, television, radio, newspapers, and weekly magazines ranked highest in importance as sources of information, while parents, siblings, and relatives ranked only sixth in importance, coming after friends, supervisors at work, and teachers.[23] Still another study indicated that few fathers have any opportunity to teach their children through working together or discussing their work. Of the 13,361 fathers interviewed in 475 different locations in 1969 and 1970, nearly half had "no opportunity to work with the children." Those fathers who actively told their children about the difficulties and rewards of their jobs constituted only one-third. The chances of communication between fathers and their children through the father's work are thus very small.[24] This argument is certainly applicable for contrasting feudal Japan (before 1868) and industrial Japan (after 1868), but it is much less successful in explaining pre- and postwar differences. Such "discontinuities" between father and son were already prevalent by 1945.

The last reason given for the alleged lack of authority among today's fathers is their now weakened economic position. In contrast to the past, younger workers are relatively well paid, and they are particularly well off so long as they remain unmarried, because the bread-winners for four- or five-member families do not receive correspondingly better salaries. In 1969, the average monthly income for the head of a four-member household was 68,424 yen ($190), while that for an unmarried young worker was 41,500 yen ($115). Among white-collar workers (who now number about 30 million), a husband aged 40 has to support a wife and two children with his monthly income of about 70,000 yen, while an unmarried young man has more than 40,000 yen all to himself.[25] Young unmarried workers are consequently much better off than middle-aged family heads. According to the argument, then, working sons are less and less dependent on their fathers, and consequently fathers have less and less basis for maintaining their authority over their children. If this explanation is correct, the wealthier fathers should be found to have more authority than the poorer ones in today's Japan. However, according to the data on decision making (to which we shall refer again later), this does not seem to be the case.

Now let us look more closely at how Japanese men actually are behaving, first in their role as husband and then as father. Ruth Benedict once wrote that the Japanese woman walks behind her husband, symbolizing her lower status.[26] Today, most young husbands and wives in Japan walk side by side, if not hand in hand, or body to body. The Japanese wives described in the following quotation make a striking contrast to the stereotyped image of the "Oriental wife," quietly subservient and gently obedient:

> Usually babies are brought to me for the first check-up about a month after birth. In the past, the mother-in-law commonly carried the newborn baby. The baby's mother followed behind. Nowadays, it is the young mother herself who carries the baby into the clinic. She is usually followed by her husband, who carries a plastic bag with diapers. When I take the clothes off the baby for his checkup, the baby's diapers may be wet. Noticing the wet diapers, the young mother quickly says to her husband in a tone of voice that sounds almost peremptory, "Get diapers!" The husband immediately takes diapers out of the bag and hands them to his wife. In order to find out the baby's height and weight at its birth, I need to take a look at the mother's notebook for nursing, given to every mother by the ward office. Often the mother says, "Oh, I left it in the car," and she turns to her husband, "Go and get it quickly!" The husband dashes out of the clinic and comes running back with the book. I cannot help but feel that these mothers speak to their husbands in the same way as a daughter of an aristocratic family in prewar Japan would once have talked to her chauffeur.[27]

It ought to be added that the young mothers visiting the clinic of this pediatrician (referred to as "Japan's Dr. Spock") are the women of Kyoto, the ancient capital of Japan, where women still have a reputation for grace and conservatism.

Japanese social scientists have been interested in finding out who plays the crucial role in handling the household budget and making the major decisions. Based on the answers to a questionnaire asking whose opinion was the more important or effective regarding various matters in family living, a social psychologist classified married couples of Kobe City into (A) husband-wife cooperative, (B) husband-wife independent, (C) husband dominant, and (D) wife dominant. The couples were classified into these four categories as follows:

(A) Husband-wife cooperative	16%
(B) Husband-wife independent	70%
(C) Husband dominant	4%
(D) Wife dominant	10%

In homes of type B, which were in the majority, the division of labor was clearly worked out, and the husband and wife made decisions independently about those things for which each was responsible.

Cross-cultural comparisons in this respect are not always easy to make because definitions of roles and especially the psychological implications of specific roles tend to vary from culture to culture. For what its worth, however, the results of studies in Detroit by University of Michigan researchers indicate that "husband dominant" marriages constituted 25 per cent in Detroit (in Japan only 4 per cent), and "wife dominant" types only 4 per cent (in Japan, 10 per cent). Another Japanese researcher found "husband-dominant" types more often among less-educated people and "wife-dominant" types more frequently among the better educated.[28] Other studies also indicate that in most families the wife is in charge of, and manages, the family budget, and this tendency is particularly strong among those on a high educational level (see Tables 4-A and 4-B). When a Japanese wife manages the household budget, the family income, usually the husband's salary, is handed to the wife, and she then doles out whatever is needed to other members of the family—for example, the husband receives back his monthly allowance. It was found that the higher the educational level of the husband, the more frequently the wife alone made decisions regarding the purchase of major items of expense. Among the better educated and wealthier couples, the wife seems to have considerable autonomy in managing the economic life of the family (see Table 4-C).[29] This is in contrast to findings in Germany, although, as mentioned before, such cross-cultural comparisons can sometimes be misleading. Two studies done there show that, among families of wealth and high social status, it is the husbands who tend to make important decisions regarding income management, leisure activities, and various other family matters.[30]

TABLE 4-A: WHO MANAGES THE FAMILY BUDGET?

Type of Household	Husband, Wife Together	Wife Alone	Others	Number of Individuals Interviewed
Husband-wife	5.1%	94.9%	—	118
Husband-wife-children	5.7	92.6	1.7	818
Three generations	4.9	74.4	20.4	183
Extended family with non-lineal relatives	—	82.2	17.8	73
Total	5.2	89.5	5.3	1,203

TABLE 4-B: WHO MANAGES THE DAILY BUDGET?

Educational Level of the Husband	Husband, Wife Together	Wife Alone	Others	Number of Individuals Interviewed
6-9 years	6.8%	89.8%	3.4%	355
11-12 years	3.4	93.6	3.0	640
15-16 years	3.0	95.0	2.0	201

TABLE 4-C: WHO IS THE DECISION-MAKER REGARDING
THE PURCHASE OF EXPENSIVE ITEMS FOR THE FAMILY?

Level of Education of the Husband	Decision-Maker				Number of Individuals Interviewed
	Husband	Husband and Wife	Wife Alone	Others	
6-9 years	44.1%	11.6%	24.4%	19.9%	336
11-12 years	44.1	11.2	28.0	16.7	600
15-16 years	33.5	12.0	36.2	18.3	191

According to the comparative studies by the Office of the Prime Minister on social attitudes described above (surveying 700 young people and 300 of their parents in Japan, the United States, and Germany) the Japanese seem most inclined to expect their wives to manage the household economy. Responding to the question, "Suppose you are a white-collar worker receiving a monthly salary and your wife stays at home, would you hand over all your income to your wife and ask her to manage the household budget?," more than half of the Japanese youths (62%) and adults (77.1%) answered "Yes," while only one-third of the youths in the United States (33.4%) and in Germany (35%), and half of the American (54.1%) and German (54.3%) adults answered the same way.[31]

Unfortunately, no comparable data are available for prewar Japan. Accordingly, we have no way of knowing whether or not the trends reflected in these figures regarding the wife's role in today's Japanese families are the consequences of postwar changes, including "women's liberation," for it is possible that similar trends existed in prewar Japan. It has, however, been shown that Japanese men tend to be emotionally dependent upon women (a son upon his mother and elder sisters, a husband upon his wife),[32] and it is entirely possible that this was also the case with Japanese men before 1945 (although another possibility is that they were less attached to their mothers and, therefore, less dependent upon women generally—this is a point to which we shall return). If it is an indication of a husband's dependency upon his wife to want her to manage the household budget, it follows that a Japanese housewife has considerable authority. One can also argue that it is entirely possible that Japanese women enjoyed much the same authority even under the old family system, in spite of their officially lower status and legal (though not necessarily psychological) inequality.

The problem is of considerable importance for the study of the position of women more generally. Feminists may consider Oriental women as "enslaved" and "subjugated." But, if Japanese housewives are found to be more economically (and emotionally) autonomous than their Western counterparts and to play a more significant role at home, it might be necessary to reexamine the whole notion of the low status of women in Japan. I do not, however, want to leap to the conclusion that Japanese women in the past were not at a disadvantage; even today, Japanese society is male oriented in many respects. There are also data suggesting that Japanese women were more unhappy in the past than they are today. For example, the suicide rate, very high among young women in the past, has dropped since the war. In addition, according to nationwide attitudinal surveys of more than 4,500 individuals, the answers given by women to the question, "Supposing you can be reborn again, would you like to be born as a man or a woman?," have changed in the past twenty years. In 1953, only 27 per cent of women answered that they wanted to be reborn as women, while 64 per cent wished to be reborn as men. In 1973, as many as 50 per cent of women wanted to be reborn as women, while those wishing to be reborn men had decreased to 43 per cent.[33]

The physical and emotional closeness of Japanese mothers to their children is well documented. Many researchers have pointed out the great importance of the mother in the socialization of Japanese children.[34] How do the Japanese fathers now fit into this picture? Who, for example, is the major disciplinarian?

According to one report on the disciplining of children, the importance of father and mother seems almost equal, with a slight tendency for the father's role to become more important as the child grows older. From a sample of 13,631 fathers and 11,590 mothers drawn from both rural and urban Japan, approximately half saw the final authority as being the father, and the other half saw the final authority as being the mother.[35] At the same time, both fathers and mothers were apt to consider themselves as the authority, and were unwilling to acknowledge that role for the spouse. For example, while 45 per cent of the fathers considered themselves to be the authority, only 41 per cent of the mothers considered their husbands to be so. While 49 per cent of the mothers considered themselves to be the authority, only 43 per cent of their husbands acknowledged it. The father seemed slightly more important to the older children than he did to the younger children. For example, while 45 per cent of fathers whose children were aged 3 to 8 said they were in charge, 53 per cent of those with children in junior high school gave that answer (see Table 5).

Other studies, however, seem to indicate that the mother is overwhelmingly more important than the father in disciplining the children. Among 300 parents of preschool children studied in a rural community in Japan and in the Shitamachi and Yamanote communities of Tokyo,[36] the mother was the "main scolder" in a majority of cases (65.3 per cent in the rural community, 73 per cent in the Shitamachi, and 71 per cent in the Yamanote, community). The father is slightly more important in the rural community (17.8%) than in Tokyo (15.3% and 14%). This may indicate that rural areas still maintain the traditional authority of the father to some extent (see Table 6-A). In addition, despite the

TABLE 5

WHO MAKES THE FINAL DECISION REGARDING
THE BASIC POLICIES FOR DISCIPLINING THE CHILD?

Child's Age	GRANDFATHER Fathers' Answers	GRANDFATHER Mothers' Answers	GRANDMOTHER Fathers' Answers	GRANDMOTHER Mothers' Answers	FATHER Fathers' Answers	FATHER Mothers' Answers	MOTHER Fathers' Answers	MOTHER Mothers' Answers	OTHERS Fathers' Answers	OTHERS Mothers' Answers	NUMBER OF INDIVIDUALS CONTACTED
Three yrs to 2nd grade	2%	1%	3%	3%	45%	41%	43%	49%	7%	6%	4,504 (father) 4,227 (mother)
Third to 6th grade	1%	1%	7%	3%	48%	46%	44%	46%	0%	4%	4,813 (father) 3,859 (mother)
Junior high	0.7%	0.8%	1%	1%	53%	46%	41%	47%	4%	4%	4,214 (father) 3,504 (mother)

fact that the mother does most of the scolding, the children still seemed to be more obedient to their father. In the rural town, this was most clearly the case; in Tokyo, the mother remained the "authority figure" for smaller children in Shitamachi and for the older children in Yamanote[37] (see Table 6-B).

TABLE 6-A

WHO DOES THE MOST SCOLDING?

	Rural Community	Shitamachi Community	Yamanote Community
Father	17.8%	15.3%	14.0%
Mother	65.3	73.1	71.0
Father & Mother	2.0	7.4	7.4
Grandfather	3.0	3.2	0.9
Grandmother	3.0	—	2.8
Others	8.9	1.9	3.7
Total Couples	101	94	107

TABLE 6-B

TO WHOM IS THE CHILD THE MOST OBEDIENT?

	RURAL		SHITAMACHI		YAMANOTE	
Child's Age	2-3	4-5	2-3	4-5	2-3	4-5
Father	42.2%	60.7%	35.4%	45.5%	50.8%	34.0%
Mother	33.3	23.2	47.8	39.1	35.3	46.4
Father & Mother	2.4	0	2.1	2.2	0	7.1
Grandfather	0	8.9	4.2	4.4	2.0	1.8
Grandmother	4.4	1.8	6.3	4.4	2.0	7.1
Others	17.7	7.3	4.2	4.4	0.9	3.6
Total Couples	45	56	48	46	51	56

In the same three communities, other researchers asked the parents of older children who the major disciplinarian was. The responses again indicated the definite importance of the mother. For example, 76.4 per cent of the mothers, as compared with 7.8 per cent of the fathers, were the major disciplinarians for the fifth-grade boys in the rural town. However, the father seemed to join the mother in disciplining the children in junior and senior high school. In 41.7 per cent of the cases, the father and mother together disciplined the boys of senior high school age in the Yamanote community, while, in 58.3 per cent, the mother alone was the disciplinarian. As the child grows up, the father tends to play a more important role as disciplinarian, but he joins his wife in doing this, rather than taking over her role (see Table 7).

TABLE 7

WHO IS THE MAIN DISCIPLINARIAN?

			Father	Mother	Father Mother Together	Other	Number of Individuals
R	Fifth	Boy	7.8%	76.4%	11.8%	4.0%	39
U	grade	Girl	2.4	80.5	9.8	7.3	41
R	Junior	Boy	12.9	35.5	51.6	0	31
	high	Girl	15.0	60.0	20.0	5.0	20
A	Senior	Boy	24.0	52.0	24.0	0	25
L	high	Girl	13.8	55.2	27.6	3.4	29
S	Fifth	Boy	3.8	49.0	35.8	11.4	42
H	grade	Girl	6.0	60.0	28.0	6.0	44
I	Junior	Boy	2.7	35.1	59.5	2.7	27
T	high	Girl	5.6	63.8	30.6	0	36
A	Senior	Boy	6.1	42.4	51.5	0	33
M A C H I	high	Girl	8.7	43.5	47.8	0	23
Y	Fifth	Boy	2.2	73.9	19.6	4.3	41
A	grade	Girl	5.6	75.8	14.8	3.8	40
M	Junior	Boy	10.4	31.1	58.5	0	29
A	high	Girl	0	65.5	34.5	0	29
N O	Senior	Boy	0	58.3	41.7	0	36
T E	high	Girl	2.6	61.5	35.9	0	39

Children in high school in these communities were asked who the strictest person was in their home. In the rural and Shitamachi communities, more children (53% and 34.9% respectively) thought their father was the stricter, while fewer children (20% and 28%) thought their mother was the stricter. However, for many children the mother *was* regarded as more strict than the father. In the Yamanote families, an equal number of children (37.1%) indicated the father and the mother as the more strict, but the children who said "nobody" was strict were the most numerous in the Yamanote community (16.1%) (see Table 8).[38]

These results indicate that mothers apparently play a very important role as disciplinarians, often completely replacing their husbands as the authority figure. The traditional images of the stern father and the protective mother are apparently no longer the reality in many homes: the Japanese father seems in fact to have become "insignificant." This tendency is particularly evident in urban homes. In the rural community, the father is frequently still the disciplinarian. If one assumes that traditions are usually retained in rural communities longer than in urban ones, then this finding should suggest that the father was more important as an authority figure in the past. That this was once the norm in Japan is also suggested by another study of "role expectation"

TABLE 8

WHO IS THE STRICTEST PERSON?

	Rural	Shitamachi	Yamanote
Father	53.0%	34.9%	37.1%
Mother	20.0	28.0	37.1
Others	4.0	6.2	2.9
No one	5.0	7.7	16.1
Don't know	18.0	23.2	6.8
Number of Children interviewed	100	129	132

and "actual role performance" in the disciplining of children. More than 12,000 couples were asked, "When a child does not obey, who do you think should best scold the child? Who in your home actually does scold the child in such a situation?" In the answers, the father was expected to do the job more often (53.8%) than he actually did do it (30.8%), while the mother actually did more scolding (46.3%) than she was expected to do (36.3%) (see Table 9-A).

The same study shows that the older the parents are, the more often it is the father who does the scolding. While only 23.3 per cent of the fathers in their twenties scolded the child, 46.7 per cent of those in their sixties did so, and while 68.5 per cent of the mothers in their twenties scolded the child, 45.0 per cent in their sixties did so (see Table 9-B). Although older parents presumably have older children to discipline, in which case the father might well be needed, it is also possible that among older people the father's traditional role as disciplinarian has been better maintained. This "traditional" tendency is also stronger among those with lower educational levels and lower incomes. The higher the educational and income levels, the more frequently the mother is the scolder.[39]

With regard to the management of the household budget, as well as the disciplining of the children, the present-day Japanese wife plays a very important role in the family, particularly among urban, younger, better-educated, and better-off people. If these are the people among whom the postwar values of egalitarianism and "democracy" are strongest, then the wife's playing an important role and, perhaps, the husband's playing a less significant role are indeed postwar phenomena. That there has been a change, especially in the attitudes of the fathers, is the opinion of the majority of the fathers themselves. In all three communities mentioned, more than two-thirds of the fathers of grade-school children said, "In the past the father used to discipline and scold children strictly, but now I talk to the child calmly, listen to it, respect its autonomy, and accept its wishes." They also said, "I used to think my father was strict and fearsome, but my child does not seem to feel that way toward me at all."[40] Another study asked the fathers to compare their attitudes toward their children with the attitude of their own fathers toward them. They found themselves to be more affectionate, more understanding, more companionable

TABLE 9-A

WHO SHOULD SCOLD AND WHO ACTUALLY DOES SCOLD?

	Father	Father Mother Together	Mother	Others	Number of Couples Studied
Expectation	53.8%	3.9%	36.3%	6.0%	12,000
Reality	30.8	3.6	46.3	19.3	

TABLE 9-B

WHO ACTUALLY SCOLDS THE CHILD?

Parents' Age	Father	Father Mother	Mother	Other	Number of Individuals Contacted
20s	23.3%	1.4%	68.5%	6.8%	73
30s	31.9	6.3	57.9	3.9	304
40s	36.8	3.3	55.6	4.3	299
50s	41.7	2.6	48.7	7.6	230
60s	46.7	3.7	45.0	4.6	109

and helpful, and less punitive toward their children than their fathers had been toward them.[41] In another study, nearly 3,000 parents with children under the age of three were asked, "When your child falls down what do you do?" More fathers (28%) than mothers (17%) said they would help the child get up, and more mothers (63%) than fathers (46%) said they would wait until the child got up by himself. The remaining 25 per cent of the fathers and 18 per cent of the mothers did not answer either way.

In the same study, 1,000 parents of children in kindergarten, grade, and junior high school were asked about physical punishment. It was found that mothers were more often punitive (55%) than were fathers (49%), stating that they "occasionally" punished their children physically. Fifty-one per cent of the fathers and 45 per cent of the mothers said they did not punish their children physically at all.[42]

Many of these fathers liked to think of themselves as being more affectionate, less punitive, and more communicative with their children than their own fathers had been with them. However, other data indicate that fathers still fall far behind their wives in contacts with their children. The Office of the Prime Minister found that the 160,000 youths (aged 15-24) talked much more often with their mothers than with their fathers: while 45.6 per cent said they talked frequently with their fathers, 78.6 per cent said they talked frequently with their mothers (the figures include some who answered that they talked frequently with both).[43]

The comparison of "role expectation" with "actual role performance" in "helping the child with homework" and "counseling" indicated that neither father nor mother lived up to expectation. However, the mother's interaction with the children in these matters was by far greater than the father's: 11.6 per cent of the fathers versus 39.2 per cent of the mothers helped their children with homework, and 8.1 per cent of the fathers versus 39.8 per cent of the mothers counseled their children. Older fathers (30.8%), however, counseled their children more often than did younger ones (3.4%)[44] (see Table 10-A-B-C).

By now it seems apparent that at least some changes have in fact taken place in the attitudes of Japanese fathers toward their families since the end of World War II. Questions remain, however, regarding how extensive these changes

TABLE 10-A

WHO SHOULD BEST HELP WITH THE CHILD'S HOMEWORK, AND WHO ACTUALLY DOES
SO IN YOUR FAMILY?

	Father	Father Mother	Mother	Himself Herself	Tutor	Other
Expectation	19.6%	5.0%	57.0%	0.9%	2.0%	15.5%
Reality	11.6	2.0	39.2	2.8	4.5	39.9

TABLE 10-B

WHO SHOULD BE THE COUNSELOR FOR THE ADOLESCENT CHILD, AND WHO IS THE
ONE IN YOUR FAMILY?

	Father	Father Mother	Mother	No One	Other
Expectation	25.5%	12.3%	51.7%	0.2%	10.3%
Reality	8.1	3.7	39.8	1.1	47.3

TABLE 10-C

WHO ACTUALLY COUNSELS THE
ADOLESCENT CHILD?

Parents' Age	Father	Father Mother	Mother	Other
30s	3.4%	10.3%	79.4%	6.9%
40s	16.8	8.7	67.3	7.2
50s	13.5	9.8	69.7	7.0
60s	30.8	2.8	53.3	13.1

have been. Were the majority of husbands/fathers in prewar Japan really so
strong, strict, autocratic, and authoritarian, and are the majority of them now
really so weak, lenient, insignificant, powerless, and irresponsible? We reported
elsewhere that we found among lower-class couples many wives who were
strong-willed and many husbands who were dependent.[45] Their existence
cannot, however, be attributed solely to postwar changes. One finds in the
traditional culture many comic stories and anecdotes about life among the
common folk in the Tokugawa period that describe impulsive and somewhat
careless husbands who act as foils for their more realistic, practical, and
dependable wives. Some people have proposed that not only low-income
husbands, but Japanese husbands generally, were "never really strong." Chie
Nakane, a well-known anthropologist at the University of Tokyo, supports this
view: "Although people say that the Japanese father has lost his authority," she
says, "there were in fact not many families in which the father had any real
authority. In most families, the father only pretended an authority he did not
actually possess."[46] Later she stated that, under the old family system, there
was househead authority (*kachō-ken*), but there was no paternal authority (*fuken*):[47] "When a father had authority, it was not because he was a father but
solely because he was a househead." According to Nakane, in Japanese families,
unlike the large extended families of ancient China and India, paternal authority
was never firmly established. She is correct in differentiating between the two
kinds of authority: the civil code of prewar Japan did draw a distinction between
parental authority and househead authority. In most cases the househead's
authority and the father's authority coincided in the same individual, but this
was, of course, not always so, and, when it was not (many younger sons became
fathers without becoming househeads), the father qua father had no authority.
Nakane implies that there were many such fathers, although she seems unable
to make up her mind regarding just about how many (a majority? a minority?),
since her views on the subject seem to vary over time. However, she concluded
that: "Although the basis for their authority may seem to have been firm and
real, often it was not really very substantial, or it was maintained at the expense
of the freedom of other family members. Consequently, I see no necessity for
lamenting the loss of the father's authority." Nakane seems here to be all for the
"weak father," and she continues in the same essay:

> I was once interested in what sorts of fathers socially active [meaning profes-
> sional and career] women had, so I looked into the subject. I was impressed with
> the fact that most of these women had, or have, liberal fathers; their fathers bear
> no resemblance to the image of the feudal father in prewar Japan. It is significant
> that when there were fathers like those once considered ideal by society, there
> were not many daughters with independent aspirations. It might be, then, that
> many of today's fathers, who lament the loss of their authority and who are looked
> upon as insignificant and unreliable, are actually contributing to the growth of
> women with promising futures, although the father who lacks self-confidence and
> allows himself to be treated with contempt also runs the risk of raising self-
> important daughters.[48]

Nakane is differentiating here between an *authoritarian* father and a *liberal*
father: the former might well have been domineering and repressive toward his
children, while the latter might well have been guiding and encouraging.

However, she does not even mention the third type in her argument—the *weak* father, the one who is said to play an insignificant role in the upbringing of his children. The liberal father might well produce a daughter "with independent aspirations"—like Nakane herself—but it is the weak and insignificant father about whom so many Japanese are now concerned.

Kazuo Aoi, one of Nakane's Tokyo University colleagues, supports her thesis when he says: "Japanese fathers in the past, especially those among the common people, did not have as much authority as one might think. When a father was at the same time a househead he had authority, but when he was not, he had none. Conversely, it has often been said that Japanese women were weak, but, again especially among the common folk, they had much more authority than one might think, particular when they were a househead's wife." His conclusion is: "Although it is said that Japanese fathers have lost their authority and suffer a lack of self-confidence, this is not at all new."[49]

Because of the lack of data on prewar Japanese husbands/fathers comparable to those results we have reported here, we do not really know how most Japanese fathers behaved before the war. Social norms certainly expected fathers (and not only househeads) to be responsible disciplinarians with unquestioned authority. Research seems to suggest that these norms were, and to some degree at least still are, being observed by older people, especially in rural areas. Declaring that Japanese fathers were "never really strong" would ignore the stern and strict fathers who actually existed, and we know they existed although we do not know how common they were.

In 1974, the *Asahi News Press* serialized reminiscences about the fathers of seventy well-known Japanese. Many of them recalled their fathers as "strict" and "stern," and made it clear that the father was the source of instruction and was a model of behavior with which identification was firm. The following are some examples:

[*A novelist:*] Both my father and grandfather were strict with themselves and with their children as well. I received a Spartan education. . . . The way my father continued his scholarly work in Manchuria after Japan's defeat was really worthy of respect. . . .

[*An actress:*] He was affectionate but also strict in disciplining us children.

[*A news commentator:*] He taught me a lesson through the way he lived his own life. . . . He taught me the virtues of hard work. As long as one works hard there will eventually be a reward.

[*An ex-governor of a prefecture:*] In my own old age, I often dream of my father. He was stern like a warrior of the past. He told me how to commit *seppuku*, and he told me to kill myself if I realized that I had done wrong.

[*A stage director:*] He was very strict in teaching us manners and etiquette. Morning and evening we children bowed to our father in the traditional fashion with both our hands on the tatami. . . .

[*A president of an automotive company:*] Once his anger was over he did not nag or complain, but when he was angry I was really afraid of him. His scolding was like thunder. . . . I learned from my father how to live independently, doing everything on my own. He was the greatest model for my life.

[*A former Sumo champion:*] He did not nag, nor did he even scold us often. But his authority was always felt. We used to feel ill at ease when our father was with us at the dinner table. He was authoritarian. Our mother was always protective of us. A typical Japanese family of the time.

[*The principal of an elite high school:*] I could never criticize my father, who was stern but wise. He was a strong influence in my life. He was a strict disciplinarian. I was scolded severely when I failed to sit properly while studying at my desk. . . . Now I feel that my father approves of the way I live and the way I think.[50]

It is possible that the internalization of norms of Confucianism colored these reminiscences. It is also possible, however, that many fathers actually were stern, strict, and awe-inspiring.

Mokichi Saito, a physician and a prominent poet, was recalled by his son, also a physician-novelist, as being a fearsome patriarch:

> Looking back at my childhood, I can say that my father was, above all, an awesome, frightening being. He was often enraged. When he became angry, it was with all his physical and spiritual strength. Even when I overheard my father reprimand somebody in the next room, a cold shiver used to run down my spine, not to speak of the times when I was chastised. . . . And yet, he was truly a support as I grew up.[51]

In quoting this reminiscence, Matsumoto, a scholar of religion, remarks that "until August, 1945, the Japanese father to a greater or lesser extent had such an aspect." He insists that, in the traditional Japanese society, there was a commonly shared notion that the father was fearsome and strict, as shown in a very common proverb describing terrifying objects as "earthquake, thunder, fire, and father" (jishin, kaminari, kaji, oyaji). Matsumoto says that such a strict father no longer exists in today's Japan. He refers to the *Yomiuri Press* survey of May, 1975, according to which more than 60 per cent of the parents now bring up their children on a "leave them alone" principle; the survey found the trend to be especially evident among fathers in their twenties. Nor does Matsumoto approve. He asserts that, for healthy children, Japanese society needs a strong father.[52] There are others who share this view.

In his discussion, Matsumoto differentiates between religions based on "paternal principles" and those based on "maternal principles." Those resting on paternal principles represent the normative world and serve as a guide for people; like a father toward his children, they are punitive toward disobedience or failure. The maternal principles represent the natural world; they are unconditionally forgiving and receptive toward people as a mother is toward her children. In the "paternal religions," emphasis is placed on the principles of the world "that should be" (das Sollen), and the gods are often powerful rulers, transcending this world. In "maternal religions," the emphasis is placed on the principles of the world "as it exists" (das Sein): tolerance and acceptance are its characteristics, and the gods are often seen as aiming toward the harmony and integrity of the community. According to Matsumoto, religions are in practice neither purely paternal nor purely maternal. Every religion mixes and blends paternal and maternal elements in varying degrees. When one element becomes dominant, the other tends to become suppressed. In Judaism, Christianity, and Islam, the paternal religious elements have tended to suppress the maternal elements. The maternal symbols have repeatedly been rejected, although they have survived in secret rituals among the common people and in the tenets of mysticism. In China, the "paternal" Confucianism thrived as an orthodoxy, while the "maternal" Taoism languished. In Matsumoto's opinion, "in the

Japanese cultural and religious tradition, the maternal elements have always been very strong," and "traditionally, the images of deities in Japanese religious consciousness have been those of the mothers. The father images have never been very strong."[53] For this very reason, Matsumoto believes, the Japanese need a strong father.

Matsumoto differentiates three aspects of the paternal role. The first is that the father represents sociocultural norms to his children. A son, successfully resolving his oedipal complex, internalizes his father's image and the norms he represents, and this results in the formation of his superego: "The severe trials to which a father subjects his son are, after all, part of the process through which he properly transmits the spiritual and material property he owns." The second aspect is that the father may become restrictive when his normative powers assume a negative form: "The cultural norms and values of a society represented by the father may, in a dynamic and changing period or for an exceptionally creative child, be understood as coercively stabilizing and restricting. The father's order of prohibition may then be met with disobedience and rebellion, the response to which will be expulsion or some other form of punishment." And the third is that the father also supports, encourages, and guides his children in their growth toward autonomy and independence. "For the establishment of his identity, the child needs to be accepted by his benevolent mother, but also to be supported, encouraged, and guided by his father." In order to establish his own autonomy, a Japanese son needs to cut himself off from his ties with his mother and to stand on his own. For this, he needs a father's guidance. Like Moses, Jesus, Buddha, and Muhammad, who all left their "maternal" home behind, guided and supported by the "paternal" power, the Japanese youths need strong paternal religious principles in order to leave their home-mother behind and become independent. The establishment of an independent identity is difficult for the Japanese youth not only because of the traditional predominance of maternal elements in Japanese culture, but because Japanese fathers have become weak and insignificant in their influence. Thus, Matsumoto concludes, "What is needed in today's Japan, I think, is the reestablishment of a strong and powerful paternal principle."

Hayao Kawai, a well-known Kyoto University Jungian psychologist, says that the human mind contains opposing principles of paternity and maternity. Referring in the Bible to Matthew 12 and Luke 11, in which Jesus denies his mother,[54] Kawai states that Western culture is based upon "a fierce denial of the mother," while the Japanese mind is "maternally dominated." In his opinion, contemporary Japanese are caught between paternal ethics (with its individualism, division between "subject" and "object," and emphasis on individual autonomy and achievement) and maternal ethics (with its group orientation, tolerance, acceptance, and egalitarianism). The cause of the confusion in present-day society lies in the fact that people cannot decide which ethics they should follow. Although he does not explicitly propose the reestablishment of the father's power, Kawai seems to imply that it should be done when he contrasts the American situation with the Japanese: "The American problem is how to restore the mother who has for too long been rejected and ignored, whereas the Japanese problem is how to become independent of the mother with whom contact is maintained for too long."[55]

Takeo Doi, a Freudian psychiatrist at Tokyo University, widely known fo his analysis of dependency among the Japanese, recognizes the "fatherlessness of postwar Japanese society, and finds that the younger generation is looking fo a value system by which it can live. Yet these young people feel frustrate because the older generation cannot provide them with values. In his opinion the "fatherlessness" of Japanese families has been caused by the postwa rejection of all traditional values, authority, and order. These changes actually began to take place soon after 1868, when Western civilization was introduce into Japan. However, the father's authority was maintained until the end o World War II. In defeat, all the ethical standards of old Japan were throw away and, with them, the father's authority.[56] Doi also says that in Wester countries, which have long served as the model of modernization for Japan, confusion of values also prevails, and that the ideological currents in the worl generally are moving toward the denial of paternal authority; these trends ar both directly and indirectly influencing the Japanese situation. When a father i weak and insignificant, he cannot help his sons repress their rebellious impulse and internalize the social norms which the father should represent. Accord ingly, sons rebel against any authority or "establishment," even when they ar grown. Doi thinks this is the major reason for the irrational rioting that occur in Japan from time to time among radical students. He refers to the old Japanes folk tale about Peach Tom (*Momotaro*), who is born out of a big peach that i picked up along a river by an elderly couple. Momotaro grows up, and, followed by his retainers, a dog, a monkey and a pheasant, he attacks the devils island and brings back their treasure. Doi says Momotaro needed to attack devils because he did not have a powerful father at home, and he calls the radical students "the Momotaro of the twentieth century."[57]

Evidently Doi disapproves of the situation: "Generational conflicts between parents and their children are often interpreted as inevitable historical phenome-na created in the shift from the lineal family to the nuclear family. However, I do not agree with this interpretation." The idea behind the Japanese proverb, "Children never know how and what their parents think" (*oya no kokoro, ko shirazu*), is, in Doi's opinion, very important for the children's proper growth. Precisely because their parents appear somewhat mysterious, children respect and obey them. If the parents' thoughts were transparent to their children, the children would have no illusions and would be led astray by whoever else appeared to them as mysterious: "Human beings need to have somebody whom they cannot fully understand and in front of whom they cannot help but bow," says Doi. "In my opinion, no proposition is more foolish than one that emphasizes the necessity of verbal communication between parents and their children as a remedy for the so-called generation gap. Communication is not what is needed."

What, then, is needed? In the following passages Doi, as a Catholic rather than as a psychoanalyst, answers:

> What is needed is for parents to harbor profound feelings toward their children. . . . Parents cannot possibly have such profound feelings if they regard their relationship with their children as something assumed or inevitable. In the past, parents thought of their children as gifts from Heaven. But parents nowa-days think they "make" their children—as if children were objects they could

manufacture. Parents cannot be parents unless they are mature enough to see the extraordinary world behind the prosaic world. Parents should be sufficiently sensitive to feel the mystery of life and the mystery of human existence that are hidden behind mundane things.[58]

Here Doi seems to be advocating a deep and strong sense of responsibility on the part of the parents, especially fathers, that should spring from religious awe regarding the value of human life. Perhaps he is saying that the solution for the "pathology" of the contemporary Japanese household and society does not lie in the argument over whether or not Japanese fathers have become weaker or whether or not they should become stronger again; the answer is to be found on a philosophical and religious level that transcends the sociological level of roles and powers.

We have seen that since around 1970 a general concern has grown up among the Japanese over the "insignificance" of the father/husband in postwar families. I have quoted a number of research findings by Japanese social scientists which seem to indicate that the fathers, especially the younger ones, do not play a very significant role in their children's upbringing. I have also mentioned the reactions of several well-known scholars to the "pathology of the fatherless society" in postwar Japan. Those scholars—Nakane, Aoi, Matsumoto, Kawai, and Doi (there are also others)—express convictions one' way or another regarding how Japanese fathers do or should behave, without, however, considering any empirical data. Because we do not have data on the behavior of the father/husband for the prewar period to compare with postwar research findings, we do not know whether or not—or how much—Japanese fathers have actually changed. Not only do we not know what they were like before the war, but we do not as yet know enough about what they are like now to discuss with any exactitude the "fatherlessness" of present-day Japanese society. Consequently, what follows in these concluding remarks can only be speculation that has still to be empirically checked.

The question we are facing is this: Has there actually been so drastic a transformation of the Japanese father from an authoritarian, strict, stern, and "thunderous" figure into an irresponsible, overindulgent, weak, and "shadowy" one? The picture of the "thunderous" father is based upon reminiscences and upon our knowledge of Confucian norms regarding father/husband roles. The picture of the "shadowy" father is based upon general impressions and upon the results of numerous sociological studies.

In my opinion, the reality of the Japanese father lies somewhere between these two extremes. I have two reasons for this conjecture: First, the "shadowy" father of postwar Japan can very well be an exaggerated picture, reflecting not so much the actuality as the contemporary norms of "democracy." It will be recalled, for example, that the wife is most apt to play an important role in the management of the household budget and in child-rearing in the homes of urban, better-educated, better-off, younger people most strongly committed to the postwar norms of egalitarianism, individual freedom, and democracy. This often happens when questionnaires are used to study people's attitudes and behavior. Especially in regard to such subtle, delicate, and often unconscious

processes as husband-wife and parent-child interactions, people tend to confus
in their minds what they think they should do and what they think they do a
what they actually do, when these are not the same. Indeed one can only repo
what one is aware of. What a researcher obtains in the responses to h
questionnaire, then, is a mixture of those three different levels, and it
difficult, if not impossible, to differentiate between them.[59] Nor is this probler
limited to Japan. When a lower-class American says the husband makes th
decisions, this often reflects nothing more than an expression of norms or eve
of wish fulfillment.

It is possible, then, that while both the husband and wife think, or like t
think, that the wife is doing all the scolding, she is actually using her husband a
the final authority when she deals with her children, and that they, in turr
might very well know this. When children do not obey their mother, th
husband may be called upon to handle the situation, without even thinking c
himself as scolding or disciplining his children. Furthermore, the wife may no
notice, or may soon forget, that the problem has actually been handled by he
husband. The "division of labor" between a husband and wife[60]—their dec
sions regarding who is in charge of what and who takes the initiative in what—i
usually worked out through the processes of marital adjustment. These proces
es may take a long time, starting with discussions and conflicts, then perhap
going through a phase of semi-conscious struggle and maneuvering, and ever
tually leading to unconscious compromises or divisions into territories for eac
to control. It often happens that the husband thinks he is in charge, while hi
wife actually is, or that both the husband and the wife think of a certai
function as belonging to the wife, while the husband handles it in fact. In short
the husband and the wife may believe one way about their conjugal and parenta
roles, while behaving in another.[61] Such subtle, delicate, and even touch
processes of which the people themselves may not be aware cannot be accurate
ly ascertained by questionnaires. They need long and careful observation b
highly trained, sensitive, and perceptive researchers who can somehow manag
to avoid interrupting the natural flow of these marital interactions.

The second reason for my conjecture is that the "thunderous" father c
prewar Japan can also be an exaggerated image in many instances. Man
fathers, observing the Confucian norms, might have played the role of "authori
tarian" father while being totally non-authoritarian by nature. When rol
behavior is clearly defined and required by a society, an individual may behav
in compliance with its norms even though they may run counter to hi
personality. A father who was "thunderous" in his children's eyes may ver
well have been tender-hearted, but successful in hiding that characteristi
behind the performance of his role. When a son rebelled against his father an
his disobedience was serious, his father was obliged to "disown" him, or at leas
order him to leave the home, as punishment. The son would go away to live hi
life somewhere else. So far as the father was concerned, he lost his son
However, the wife very often kept in contact, corresponding with the son an
even sending him money. The husband might be perfectly aware of this, an
even silently grateful, although he would never say so—he could not, as
matter of principle. It is also possible that such a "thunderous" father wa
emotionally dependent upon his wife backstage, as it were. I do not intend t

propose that there were no fathers in prewar Japan who were authoritarian and "thunderous" in their personality; there certainly must have been at least some, and for them being a proper Confucian husband/father must have come naturally.

A change has certainly taken place in postwar Japan: The Confucian definition of the father/husband role has disappeared, and an egalitarian, "democratic" definition of the new father/husband role predominates. Consequently, non-authoritarian fathers are no longer required to act "thunderously." There must also now be some young Japanese men whose personality is authoritarian, but who may no longer express that trait in their behavior toward wife and children because the new norms disapprove of it. They may be behaving that way at home, but they would certainly not reveal it when answering questionnaires! In short, what have changed are the cultural norms rather than the psychological characteristics of the Japanese fathers. In their personalities, I am inclined to see more continuity than change.

In any case, we need to know much more about the effects of the father's behavior on the socialization of Japanese children.[62] What precisely are the effects on the children's growth of so-called "weak" fathers? When a father actually plays "no significant role" in their upbringing, do his sons remain tied to their mother? Do they fail to develop an adequate superego? In prewar Japan, when lower-class fathers presumably had much less authority than upper-class fathers, were lower-class Japanese youths more like Peach Tom than their upper-class cousins? Or did the rigorous and even brutal treatment of young men by their superiors in the imperial army and navy have an effect upon them comparable to that of a strict father? When most fathers are in fact inadequate, which sons become Momotaro and which do not? How different are fathers of delinquent or neurotic children from those of normal, healthy ones? How do the father's attitudes influence his daughter's character? Are Japanese girls also changing because their fathers have changed (if they have)? Until and unless we have answers to these and many other questions based on empirical data, we will not be able to discuss very meaningfully the question of "fatherlessness" in Japanese society.

REFERENCES

[1]Ezra Vogel, "Entrance Examinations and Emotional Disturbances in Japan's New Middle Class," in R. J. Smith and R. K. Beardsley, eds., *Japanese Culture: Its Development and Characteristics* (Chicago, 1962), pp. 140-52.

[2]Ronald P. Dore, *City Life in Japan: A Study of a Tokyo Ward* (Berkeley and Los Angeles, 1958), p. 91.

[3]*Ibid.*

[4]Max Weber, *Wirtschaft und Gesellschaft: Grundriss der Sozialökonomik*, III, 3 (Tübingen, 1922), chapter 7.

[5]Seiichi Kitano, "Nihon no Ie to Kazoku" ("Japanese *Ie* and Family"), *Osaka Daigaku Bungakubu Kiyo (University of Osaka, Faculty of Humanities Bulletin)*, 11 (1965), pp. 5-49.

[6]Dore (cited above, note 2), p. 95.

[7]Shigeru Matsumoto, "Atarashiki Chichioya Zō o Motomete" ("In Search of a New Father Image"), *Chūō Kōron* (August, 1975), pp. 60-72.

[8]Takeo Doi, *Amae no Kōzō (Structure of Dependency)*, (Tokyo, 1971).

[9]For example, Shusuke Tamai, "Iwayuru Gakkō Kyōfushō ni Kansuru Kenkyū" ("A Study of the So-Called School Phobia"), *Seishin Eisei Kenkyū (Mental Health Studies)*, Japan National Institute of Mental Health, 13 (1964); Kikuo Uchiyama, "Tōkō Kyohi Ji no Hatsubyō ni okeru Katei Yōin no

Bunseki" ("An Analysis of the Family Factors Underlying the Onset of the Refusal to Go to School"), *Tokyo Kyōiku Daigaku Kyōiku Sōdanjo Kiyō (Tokyo University of Education, Educational Counseling Center Newsletter)*, 9 (1970); Koji Kashikuma, *Tokyo To Seishōnen no Shakaisei no Hattatsu ni kansuru Kenkyū: Nichijō Seikatsu ni Mirareru Mondai Kōdō (A Study of the Development of Social Attitudes Among the Tokyo Metropolitan Youths: Problem Behavior Observed in Daily Life)*, Tokyo To Seishōnen Taisaku Honbu (Tokyo Metropolitan Government Headquarters for Youth Problems), 1973.

[10]Nihon Hōsō Kyōkai (Japan Broadcasting Corporation), *Oyaji: Chichi Naki Jidai no Kazoku (Father: Families in the Era Without the Father)* (Tokyo, 1974).

[11]Taketoshi Takuma, *Oya to Ko no Aida (Relations Between Parents and Children)* (Tokyo, 1974). According to this study, more students respected their fathers (47% male and 54% female) than respected their mothers (30% male and 35% female). The results differ from those of another study mentioned earlier which indicated that the mother was at the top of the list of respected people among the students of the University of Tokyo.

[12]Alexander Mitscherlich, *Auf dem Weg zur Vaterlosen Gesellschaft (On the Way to the Fatherless Society)*, (Munich, 1963), an English translation by Eric Mosbacher was published under the title *Society Without the Father: A Contribution to Social Psychology* (New York, 1969).

[13]Nihon Hōsō Kyōkai (cited above, note 10).

[14]Haruo Matsubara, *Kaku Kazoku Jidai* ("The Era of the Nuclear Family") (Tokyo, 1969); "Gendai no Kazoku" ("Contemporary Families"), *Tokyo Daigaku Kōkai Kōza (University of Tokyo Public Lecture Series), Ie (House)* (Tokyo, 1974), pp. 29-65. Sōrifu Tōkei Kyoku (Statistical Bureau, Office of the Prime Minister), *Showa Yonjushichinen Junigatsu Jinkō Suikei Geppō (Monthly Report on Population Estimates)*, December, 1972; Kōseishō Tōkei Kyoku Jōhō Bu (Public Relations Department of the Statistical Bureau, Ministry of Health and Welfare), *Report*, 1975.

[15]Kazuo Aoki, "Gendai Nihon no Oyako Kankei" ("Parent-Child Relations in Contemporary Japan") *Tokyo Daigaku Kōkai Kōza (University of Tokyo Public Lecture Series), Oya to Ko (Parents and Children)* (Tokyo, 1973), pp. 23-75. Befu rightly makes a distinction between the "conjugal, nuclear family" of the West that always remains "nuclear" and the "stem nuclear family" of Japan that may become a three-generational household in some phase of its cycle. See Harumi Befu, *Japan: An Anthropological Introduction* (San Francisco, 1971), p. 45.

[16]Sōrifu Seishōnen Taisaku Honbu (Headquarters for Juvenile Affairs, Office of the Prime Minister), *Gendai no Wakamono Tachi (Contemporary Youths)* (1970).

[17]Sōrifu Seishōnen Taisaku Honbu, *Seishōnen no Rūru Kan—Shakai Kihan Chōsa Hōkokusho (Youthful Views on Rules—A Research Report on Social Norms)* (1975).

[18]Nihon Hōsō Kyōkai (cited above, note 10).

[19]Table 2 was adapted from Hiroshi Oikawa, "Kazoku ni okeru Rōjin" ("Old People in the Family"), in S. Yamamuro and T. Himeoka, eds., *Gendai Kazoku no Shakaigaku (The Sociology of the Contemporary Family)* (Tokyo, 1970), pp. 117-40. Although I am indicating that, compared with the Western countries, a large number of the aged still do live with their children, I am not suggesting that old age does not constitute a social problem in Japan as well. The expectation of life at birth in 1973 in Japan was 70.7 for males and 76.02 for females, while in the U.S. in 1972 it was 68.3 for white males, 76.0 for white females, 61.3 for non-white males and 69.9 for non-white females. People above age 60 constituted 11.64% of the total Japanese population in 1975, and, by the year 2000, they are expected to constitute 19.32% of the total population (Japan Information Service, Consulate General of Japan in New York, *Japan Report*, 20: 7 [1975]). The number of older people is increasing, and the suicide rate among the aged remains high, although the suicide rate for the whole nation has much decreased. According to the World Health Organization report, the suicide rate in Japan from 1955 to 1959 was 45.5 per 100,000 population for men and 29.3 for women. In 1971 however, it was 25.1 for men and 18.8 for women. Nevertheless, the suicide rate among those above age 65, and especially among the women, remains high. In 1970, the suicide rate for Japanese men was 57.7 per 100,000, the seventh highest rate in the world (it was 41.1 for white American males, 10.8 for non-white males, and for Japanese women it was 45.9 per 100,000, the highest rate in the world (it was 8.5 for white American females and 3.6 for non-white females). Why are so many elderly Japanese unhappy? One of several possible reasons seems to be related to an important difference regarding older people between the Western and Japanese societies: in Western societies many old people, although they live by themselves, still live near, or maintain close contact with, their children, while in Japan when they live alone they are totally alone. For example, in Denmark, England, the U.S., and rural Germany, more than 80% of the aged were reported to be living within an hour's distance of their children, and more than 60% of them saw their children at least every two days.

	LIVING WITHIN AN HOUR'S DISTANCE FROM A CHILD	SEEING A CHILD AT LEAST EVERY OTHER DAY
Denmark	88%	62%
England	89%	69%
U.S.A.	84%	65%
Germany (rural)	82%	67%

Even in large cities like London, Detroit, or San Francisco, half of the aged maintained daily, or at least once-a-week, contact by seeing or phoning their children or other relatives. In Japan, on the other hand, those aged who live away from their children maintain contact only once a month or, in the worst cases, once a year. Those aged who kept contact with their children or relatives more than once a week constituted only 10% of those living away from their children in rural areas and only 6% of those living in Tokyo. It is probable, then, that in Japan those aged who live alone are genuinely lonely, and it is among those lonely people that the suicide rate is high. See Haruo Matsubara, *Kaku Kazoku Jidai (The Era of the Nuclear Family)* (Tokyo, 1969).

[20]In wealthier families, one finds larger rooms with 10 or 12 tatami, but rooms of that size are very rare in ordinary homes.

[21]Shigeo Tani, *Jūtaku Mondai Nyūmon (An Introduction to Housing Problems)* (Tokyo, 1968).

[22]Nihon Hōsō Kyokai (Japan Broadcasting Corporation) (cited above, note 10).

[23]Of the 160,000 youths, 36.9% indicated television and radio to be the most important source of information influencing the formation of their opinions regarding recent events, 19.7% indicated newspapers and magazines, 11.8% mentioned friends, 6.6% their supervisor at their place of work, 7.2% their teachers, 4.3% their parents, siblings, and relatives, 3.9% books, 2.2% an organization or union they belonged to, 1.4% some scholars' opinions, and 7.9% referred to various other sources. Sōrifu Seishōnen Taisaku Honbu (cited above, note 16).

[24]Masanori Hiratsuka, *Nihon no Katei to Kodomo—Konnichi ni Okeru Katei no Kyōiku Kinō o Saguru Japanese Home and Children—An Inquiry into the Educational Function of Contemporary Families)* (Tokyo, 1973).

[25]Sōrifu Tōkei Kyoku (Statistical Bureau, Office of the Prime Minister), *Shōwa Yonjūyon-nen Zen-koku Shōhi Chōsa Hōkoku (Research Report on National Consumption Patterns in 1969)*. When adjusted to 1976 conditions, these figures would be something like 180,000 yen ($600) for a 40-year-old man, and 120,000 yen ($400) for a younger worker.

[26]Ruth Benedict, *The Chrysanthemum and the Sword: Patterns of Japanese Culture* (Boston, 1946), p. 63.

[27]Michio Matsuda, *Oyaji Tai Kodomo (The Father Versus the Children)* (Tokyo, 1966).

[28]Kunio Tanaka, "Fūfu no Seiryoku Kōzō—Dochira ga Tsuyoku Natte Iruka" ("Power Structure Between Husband and Wife—Which is Actually Stronger?"), *Hoiku (Nursing)*, 20:9 (1965), pp. 48-49; Kokichi Msauda, "Gendai Toshi Kazoku ni Okeru Fūfu Oyobi Shūtome no Seiryoku Kōzō" ("The Power Structure Among Husband, Wife, and Mother-in-Law in Contemporary Urban Families"), *Konan Daigaku Bungakubu Kiyo (Konan University Publications in Humanities)*, 27 (1965), pp. 49-66.

[29]Takashi Koyama, et al., *Gendai Kazoku no Yakuwari Kōzō (The Role Structure in Contemporary Families)* (Tokyo, 1967).

[30]G. Baumert, *Deutsche Familien nach dem Kriege* (Darmstadt, 1954), René Koenig, "Family and Authority: The German Father in 1955," *American Sociological Review*, 5:1 (1957), pp. 107-27.

[31]Sōrifu Seishōnen Taisaku Honbu (cited above, note 17).

[32]William Caudill and H. Weinstein, "Maternal Care and Infant Behavior in Japan and America," *Psychiatry*, 32 (1969), pp. 12-43; W. Caudill and C. Schooler, "Child Behavior and Child Rearing in Japan and the United States: An Interim Report," *Journal of Nervous and Mental Disease*, 157:5 November, 1973), pp. 323-38; Hiroshi Wagatsuma, *Korekara no Ikuji to Shitsuke o Kangaeru (Essays on Child Rearing and Disciplining from Now On)* (Tokyo, 1971); *idem*, "Ishiwara Shintaro's Early Novels and Japanese Male Psychology," *Journal of Nervous and Mental Disease*, 157:5 (November, 1973), pp. 458-69.

[33]Chikio Hayashi, "Nihonjin no Kokoro wa Kawatta ka—Chōsa kara mita Nihonjin no Koku-minsei" ("Has the Japanese Mind Been Changed? Japanese National Character as Seen Through Empirical Data"), in Nihonjin Kenkyū Kai (Association for the Study of the Japanese), *Nihonjin Kenkyū (The Study of the Japanese)*, 1 (Tokyo, 1974), pp. 1-80. To the same question, 94% of men in 1953 and 89% of men in 1973 answered they would want to be reborn as men. Those who wished to be reborn as women constituted only 2% in 1953 and 6% in 1973. When a similar question was asked in a Gallup survey in 1959 and 1970, unlike the Japanese women, the majority of the American women (83% in 1959 and 84% in 1970) wanted to be reborn as women. Only 17% (1959) and 16% (1970) of them wished to be reborn as men. Those men who wanted to be reborn as men constituted 96% in both years, and only 4% of them wished to be women. See Sumiko Iwao, "Onna no Manzokukan, Onna no Ikigai" ("The Sense of Gratification and Goal of Life Among Women") in Nihonjin Kenkyukai, ed., *Nihonjin Kenkyu (The Study of the Japanese)*, 3 (1975), pp. 42-68. According to another source, 74% of unmarried men aged 19-25 said they were happy that they were born as men, while 6% were unhappy (20% did not know which). Of the unmarried women of the same age range, 30% answered they were happy being born as women, 16% said they were unhappy, and 54% could not answer. Of the men, 75% wanted a son while 24% wanted a daughter, and, of the women, 58% wanted a son and 42% wanted a daughter. Asahi Shinbunsha, ed., *Otoko to Onna (Men and Women)* (Tokyo, 1973). It seems that many women are either negative or ambivalent about their being women and that this does not seem equally true of men. Also more men and women want sons than want daughters. These figures should indicate that Japanese society is still male-centered, in

spite of the overwhelming importance of the mother in Japanese life and the general emotional dependence of men upon women. Although the percentage of women in the total population of the gainfully employed is somewhat larger in Japan (39%) than in the U.S., England, and West Germany (36% in 1970), a large number of them are in relatively low-status jobs, and there are notable differences in this regard between Japanese and American working women. In 1970, of working American women, 4.2% were in managerial positions (as compared with 0.5% of Japanese women), 13.5% were professionals (in Japan 6.3%), 34.1% were secretaries and clerks (17.7% in Japan), 17.6% were blue-collar workers (25.1% in Japan), 21.7% in service industries (11.2% in Japan), 7% in sales (13% in Japan), and only 1.9% in primary industry (26.2% in Japan). Another difference between the U.S. and Japan is that, while there are more married American women (62.2%) than unmarried women (22.8%) among the gainfully employed (1964), many more Japanese working women are unmarried (50.5%) than married (39.1% in 1968). Divorcees and widows constituted 15% of American working women and 10.4% of Japanese women. See Shoko Fuse, "Tomobataraki Kazoku no Ningen Kankei" ("The Relationships Between Working Husbands and Wives"), in S. Yamamuro and T. Himeoka, eds., *Gendai Kazoku no Shakaigaku (Sociology of the Contemporary Family)* (Tokyo, 1970), pp. 77-100. In Japan, a wife's social status is linked to that of her husband, and when the linkage is broken by divorce or by her husband's death, she becomes "statusless" until and unless she links her status to her next husband or, more commonly, to her grown-up son. Linda Perry, "Being Socially Anomalous: Wives and Mothers Without Husbands," in David W. Plath, ed., *Adult Episodes in Japan (International Studies in Sociology and Social Anthropology, 20)* (Leiden, 1975), pp. 32-41.

[34]For example, W. Caudill and D. Plath, "Who Sleeps by Whom—Parent-Child Involvement in Urban Japanese Families," *Psychiatry*, 29 (1966), pp. 344-66; W. Caudill and C. Schooler (cited above, note 32); W. Caudill and H. Weinstein, "Maternal Care and Infant Behavior in Japan and America," *Psychiatry*, 32 (1969), pp. 12-43; G. DeVos, "Relation of Guilt Toward Parents to Achievement and Arranged Marriage Among the Japanese," *Psychiatry*, 23 (1960), pp. 287-301; G. DeVos and H. Wagatsuma, "Status and Role Behavior in Changing Japan," in S. H. Seward and R. C. Williamson, eds., *Sex Roles in Changing Society* (New York, 1970), pp. 334-70; Takeo Doi, " 'Amae,' A Key Concept for Understanding Japanese Personality Structure," in R. J. Smith and R. K. Beardsley, eds., *Japanese Culture: Its Development and Characteristics* (Chicago, 1962), pp. 132-39; E. Vogel and S. Vogel, "Family Security, Personal Immaturity and Emotional Health in a Japanese Sample," *Marriage and Family Living*, 23 (1962), pp. 161-66; H. Wagatsuma, "Ishiwara Shintaro's Early Novels" (cited above, note 32).

[35]Masunori Hiratsuka, *Nihon no Katei to Kodomo (Japanese Homes and Children)* (Tokyo, 1973).

[36]*Shitamachi* or "low town" is the area in which the townsmen (merchants and artisans) developed their communities in Tokyo, when it was called Edo; it was until 1868 the site of the Tokugawa feudal government. *Yamanote* or "hillside" is the area where the feudal lords and the retainers had their residences. In the modern era, Shitamachi continues to be predominantly industrial and commercial, and the residential area for people in such enterprises. Yamanote has largely become the residential area for white-collar and professional people. Certain "sub-cultural" differences—in speech, dress, habits, and temperament—existed between the people of Shitamachi and Yamanote. The Shitamachi people have tended to be more traditionally oriented in their values and tastes, more community centered and conservative, while the Yamanote people have tended to be more Western oriented and individualistic in their values and tastes. Although such clear differences are quickly disappearing, and have been since World War II, the two areas in the minds of Tokyo residents are still very different. For these reasons, the researchers selected a community from each of these areas, expecting the Yamanote people to be more individualistic and less tradition-bound, and the Shitamachi people to be more conservative. For the differences in sub-cultures between the two areas, see R. P. Dore (cited above, note 2), chapter 2.

[37]Akira Furuya, "Yōjiki no Shitsuke" ("Child Rearing and Discipline"), in T. Koyama, ed.,*Gendai Kazoku no Oyako Kankei—Shitsuke no Shakaigaku-teki Bunseki (Parent-Child Relationships in Contemporary Families—A Sociological Analysis of Child Rearing and Disciplining* (Tokyo, 1973), pp. 67-127.

[38]Kiyomi Morioka and Kenji Tamura, "Yōdōki no Shitsuke" ("Rearing and Disciplining in Infancy"), T. Koyama (cited above, note 37), pp. 128-78; Kenji Tamura, "Seishōnenki no Shitsuke" ("Rearing and Disciplining in Youth"), *ibid.*, pp. 179-258.

[39]Takashi Koyama*et al*. (cited above, note 29).

[40]K. Morioka and K. Tamura (cited above, note 38).

[41]Taketoshi Takuma (cited above, note 11).

[42]*Ibid.*

[43]Sōrifu Seishōnen Taisaku Honbu (cited above, note 16).

[44]T. Koyama*et al*. (cited above, note 29).

[45]G. DeVos and H. Wagatsuma (cited above, note 34).

[46]Chie Nakane, "Bunka ni Okeru Oyako Kankei no Sōi" ("Cultural Differences in Parent-Child

Relationships"), *Tokyo Daigaku Kōkai Kōza* (University of Tokyo Public Lecture Series), *Oya to Ko (Parents and Children)* (Tokyo, 1973), pp. 3-22.

[47]Chie Nakane, "Ie no Kōzō—Shakai Jinruigaku-teki Bunseki" ("The Structure of the Family—A Social Anthropological Analysis"), *Tokyo Daigaku Kōkai Kōza (University of Tokyo Public Lecture Series), Ie (House)* (Tokyo, 1974), pp. 3-27.

[48]Chie Nakane, "Fuken no Kiso to Yakuwari" ("The Basis and Function of Paternal Rights") in *Nihon Hōsō Kyōkai (Japan Broadcasting Corporation)* (cited above, note 10), pp. 23-42.

[49]Kazuo Aoi, "Gendai Nihon no Oyako Kankei" ("Parent-Child Relations in Contemporary Japan"), *Tokyo Daigaku Kōkai Kōza (University of Tokyo Public Lecture Series), Oya to Ko (Parents and Children)* (1973), pp. 23-75.

[50]Asahi Shinbun Kokoro no Peiji (the editorial staff of the *Asahi News Press* "Hearty Pages"), *Chichi Ariki (There Was a Father)* (Tokyo, 1974).

[51]Asahi Jānaru Henshubu (the editorial department of the *Asahi Journal*), *Oyaji (Father)* (Tokyo, 1964).

[52]Shigeru Matsumoto (cited above, note 7).

[53]Shigeru Matsumoto, "Fusei-teki Shūkyō to Bosei-teki Shūkyō—Nihon Bunka Dentō e no Ichi Shiten" ("Paternal Religion and Maternal Religion—An Approach to Japanese Cultural Tradition"), *UP* (newsletter of the University of Tokyo Press), nos. 8 and 9 (1974), pp. 1-10. An interesting proposition was made by the literary critic, Eto, that, toward the end of a contemporary novel entitled *Silence*, Jesus Christ is described almost as if he were a Japanese mother (Jun Eto, *Seijuku to Sōshitsu—Haha no Hōkai [Maturity and Loss—Dissolution of the Mother Image]* [Tokyo, 1967]). The novel was written by Shusaku Endo (the English translation by William Johnston was published in 1969 by Sophia University and Charles Tuttle). In the novel, a Portuguese Catholic priest arrives in Japan in the seventeenth century after the feudal government has banned Christianity. He is quickly arrested, imprisoned, tortured, and forced to give up his religion. As a sign of the sincerity of his conversion, he is told to step on an image of Christ, called a *fumie* or "a stepping picture." The *fumie* was a copper medal, depicting either Christ or Mary, tied onto a plank of wood. It was also used to detect hidden Christians among the Japanese. The priest looks at the face of Christ and hears the voice gently allowing him to step on it. The author, Endo, is a Catholic and has long been concerned with the question of what happens to Christianity when it is brought into the entirely different climate of Japanese culture. William Johnston's translation of this very significant novel tends to be rather free, and the original flavor of this particular passage is not at all conveyed in the English. Accordingly, I am contributing my own translation: "Upon the same *fumie* I, too, put my foot. At that time, this foot of mine was on his face. His face, which I had thought of innumerable times. His face which I had never forgotten while wandering in the mountains and while confined in prison. The face of that person who remains good and beautiful as long as humans live. The face of that person whom I had wished to love all my life. That face, worn off inside the wooden frame of the *fumie*, looked at me with sad eyes: 'Go ahead and step on me,' that was what the sad eyes in that face told me. . . ." Eto, the critic, believes that the author was describing an ever-forgiving and accepting Japanese mother when he had the priest in his novel reflect upon the face of Christ, and that Endo is symbolically suggesting how Christianity had become transformed under Japanese influence. On October 15, 1976, I had an opportunity to discuss this subject with Mr. Endo himself, and he admitted that Mr. Eto was accurate in his interpretation. In Endo's opinion, Christianity has become "maternal" in the Japanese mind.

[54]"Then one said unto him, Behold, thy mother and thy brethren stand without, desiring to speak with thee. But he answered and said unto him that told him, Who is my mother? and who are my brethren? And he stretched forth his hand toward his disciples, and said, Behold my mother and my brethren! For whoever shall do the will of my father which is in heaven, the same is my brother, and sister, and mother" (Matthew 12). "And it came to pass, as he spake these things, a certain woman of the company lifted up her voice, and said unto him, 'Blessed *is* the womb that bare thee, and the paps which thou hast sucked.' But he said, 'Yea rather, blessed *are* they that hear the word of God and keep it' " (Luke 11).

[55]Hayao Kawai, "Bosei Shakai Nihon no Eien no Shonen Tachi" ("The Eternal Youths in the Maternal Society of Japan"), in H. Kawai, *Bosei Shakai Nihon no Byōri (Pathology of the Maternal Society of Japan)* (Tokyo, 1976), pp. 8-34.

[56]There is another opinion, however, that the decline of the father's authority in Japan began in the twenties, rather than after 1945, under the influence of Western ideas such as democracy, individualism, socialism, unionism, etc., especially among urban intellectuals. In his excellent psychological study of novelists who spent their formative years in the period of the so-called Taisho Democracy, the critic, Jun Eto, points out that these authors have as a theme in their novels the strong attachment of a son to his mother (or wife, strongly identified with the mother). There is also a curious lack of oedipal conflict between son and his father; Eto says, "In modern Japanese society as time went on, the father's image unavoidably became weak and fragile." Jun Eto, *Seijuku to*

Sōshitsu—Haha no Hōkai (cited above, note 53). Eto seems to suggest that in the early-modern era, when Confucianism was still strong, the Japanese fathers were so powerful and authoritarian that their sons had to give up their oedipal attachment to the mother and internalize the father. However, after the introduction of democracy in the nineteen-twenties, the image of the strong father began to fade and sons became more and more attached to the mother. In many modern Japanese novels written by the authors whose formative years dated from before the twenties (i.e., authors much older than those Eto studied in his book), the protagonist's struggle for autonomy often takes the form of a terrible conflict between the father (or the household) and his rebellious son. Such conflicts are lacking in the novels written by the authors, such as Endo, Yasuoka, Yoshiyuki, and Kojima, whom Eto analyzed. See, for example, Yukio Miyoshi, "Kindai Shōsetsu ni Okeru Ie" ("House in Modern Novels"), *Tokyo Daigaku Kōkai Kōza (University of Tokyo Public Lecture Series), Ie (House)* (Tokyo, 1973), pp. 119-35.

[57]Takeo Doi, *Amae no Kōzō (Structure of Dependency)* (Tokyo, 1971).

[58]Takeo Doi, "Oyako Kankei no Shinri" ("Psychology of Parent-Child Relationships"), *Tokyo Daigaku Kōkai Kōza (University of Tokyo Public Lectures Series), Oya to Ko (Parent and Children)* (Tokyo, 1973), pp. 107-20.

[59]The difference between what people think they should do and what they think they actually do is observable in the studies of role expectation and actual role performance mentioned earlier in this essay; for example, see Table 9-A.

[60]In addition to "conjugal division of labor," another concept, "interference," can be used to describe marital interaction processes. Interference is to be defined as "setting standards for, criticism of, supervision over, or negation of a spouse's performance so that he or she changes that performance to meet the other spouse's approval." Linda Perry, "Mothers, Wives and Daughters in Osaka—Professionalism, Autonomy, and Alliance" (Ph.D. dissertation, University of Pittsburgh, 1976). To what extent and in what areas one spouse grants the other this ability of interference has to be worked out between them through the processes of their marital adjustment.

[61]In a study of decisions with regard to child-rearing reported in this essay, both the husband and wife thought they were more responsible for decision-making than their spouse acknowledged. What people tell others does not necessarily express what they unconsciously wish. While one researcher stated that the dissatisfaction that was reported by the Japanese wives interviewed was focused on their wish that their husbands assume a greater share of responsibility in disciplining and helping the children with school work (Karen Smith, "Attitude Toward the Maternal Role and Child Rearing in Japan and the U.S.," a paper presented at the annual meeting of the Association for Asian Studies, Toronto, Canada, March 21, 1976), another researcher has the impression that even when the wives complain about the lack of participation by their husbands in family matters—management of household budget, rearing, and counseling of children—they actually do not want their husbands to "interfere" with their activities at home, because it is their domain (Linda Perry, personal communication, April 15, 1976).

[62]Before discussing the effects of a "weak" or a "strong" father upon the children's socialization, it may be necessary for us to think about the basic nature of the father's influence in general upon his children's upbringing, for it may be different from that of the mother. An interesting proposition has been made that a son's identification with his father tends to be "positional"—that is, with aspects of the male role—rather than with the father as an individual, because the father in general rarely plays a major caretaking role due to the physical separation of his domestic and public spheres. In contrast, a daughter's identification with her mother is "personal," and is not based upon imagined or externally defined roles of the mother. See Nancy Chodorow, "Family Structure and Feminine Personality," in M. Rosaldo and L. Lamphere, eds., *Women, Culture, and Society* (Stanford, California, 1974), pp. 43-66.

BEATRICE B. WHITING

Changing Life Styles in Kenya

FAMILY LIFE IN KENYA has many styles. Traveling from the coast of this relatively new East African nation west to Lake Victoria, north to Lake Turkana, and south to the great Mara and Serengeti plains is like taking a trip through time. It is as if the history of the Western world in microcosm were passing rapidly before one's eyes. In the Rift Valley, on the eastern and western highlands, along the coast of the Indian Ocean, and in the burgeoning cities of Nairobi, Nakuru, and Kisumu, in every corner of Kenya the family is in transition. So fast is this transition that a description of the Kenyan families today will become dated within a decade.[1]

The major thrust of the change is in the economic sphere. At the time of the arrival of British settlers, which took place in the early part of this century, Kenya was occupied by farmers in the well-watered savannah highlands, by herdsmen in the drier grassy plains, and by fishermen and traders on the coast. The farmers were for the most part Bantu speakers who had migrated to Kenya from the west and south bringing with them a type of shifting hoe agriculture with maize as their principle crop. Traditionally each family had a small herd of cattle and a few sheep and goats. The pastoralists came from the dry steppe country to the north, from the Sudan and Ethiopia. Some of these groups were in the process of adopting agriculture while others depended entirely upon their herds of zebu cattle, sheep, goats, or camels. The coastal people were a Swahili-speaking mixture of Arab and Bantu.

The British took over the so-called "white highlands," the fertile savannah and steppe north of Nairobi, and introduced modern agriculture which, after a shaky start, prospered, so that at the time of independence (1963), there were huge ranches with four bottom plows drawn by diesel tractors, combines for harvesting wheat, dairy herds of Jersey, Guernsey, and Holsteins with the most modern milking machines, cross-bred zebu and Angus or Hereford beef-cattle herds, and great flocks of Merino and Shropshire sheep. The inevitable concomitant of these changes in subsistence methods was the growth of commerce, industry, and urbanization.

The British and other European ranchers and farmers needed laborers. They introduced a hut-tax system which forced the Kenyans to seek wage labor, thus plunging them into a cash economy.[2] In order to pay the taxes and buy the new products introduced by the colonials, many Kenyan men sought

211

temporary employment on the new estates, sometimes moving their families into company housing, but often leaving their wives and children behind to tend the family crops and herds.

All these economic changes have been documented in numerous books and articles, but what has been less often described is the effect of these economic changes on family life. How have the roles of men and women been transformed? How has the relation of husband and wife to each other and to their kin and to other men and women been altered? How has the life and development of the children been affected? These are questions which should be of concern to policy makers, questions that are too often neglected and left unanswered as new nations struggle toward improving the economic well-being of their people.

Traditionally the ideal form of marriage among the various cultural groups in Kenya was polygyny, one man with several wives. This form of marriage occurred in most of the world as recorded in the early historical and ethnographic reports. As I worked among the Kenyan polygynists, especially the Bantu agriculturalists in the Central Province, I was often struck by their similarity to the families of the Old Testament, a similarity which is perhaps not surprising as there is evidence of people living in the highlands of Kenya before the Bantu invasion whose language, Cushitic, was similar to Semitic.

The polygynous families were embedded in extended family units consisting of a man, his wives, and their married sons and children, and into patrilineages. Every man, woman, and child was identified as belonging to a named group whose members were the descendents of a male progenitor, real or eponymous. The polygynous families tracing descent from this named progenitor lived together in areas which were identified as lineage lands. When the area became crowded, the lineage divided and some families migrated to new land.

Among the herdsmen, the traditional polygynous families were semi-nomadic, living in temporary or semi-permanent settlements. Among some groups the households were patrilineally related, in others, co-resident family heads were not necessarily related. An age-grade system with elaborate initiation ceremonies and elaborate changeover ceremonies bonded men into named groups that moved as a cohort from junior warriors to senior warriors, thence to junior and senior elders. The status and role of each group was clearly defined. General polygyny was possible since men did not marry until they became junior elders, typically in their thirties, while girls married soon after menarche.

It is difficult to be anything but an economic determinist when reviewing the changes that have occurred and are in progress in Kenyan family life. The new cash economy is associated with the demarcation of traditional lineage lands into individually owned farms. It is associated with a demand for a Western type of education which is valued as a key to economic success. Changes in the division of labor have been dramatic as the child-labor force disappears into schools and men leave the farms for wage-earning jobs.

The relation between husband and wife is changing as polygyny decreases and the prevalence of monogamy increases. The importance of the extended family and patrilineage declines as families migrate from their home areas and settle in urban centers where the support of kin groups is less essential. A national court system is replacing the family and lineage elders in settling disputes, a national police force replacing relatives in the protection of life and property. Parental expectations and values change, as mothers and fathers prepare their children for a new life. All these transformations are associated in a predictable fashion with changes in the subsistence base of the society, the system of land tenure, and the social structure of rural and urban settlements. Similar changes have occurred in other periods of history in other parts of the world. But here one can watch the changes as they occur in a single community.

The rate of change among the various groups was, and still is, a function of their distance from the former colonial estates and the administrative and trade centers. The early British colonials, agriculturalists and animal husbandmen, favored the cool, fertile highlands to the east and west of the Rift Valley, land reminiscent of their native isles. They built up large tea and coffee estates on the highlands and large ranches on the lower escarpments and adjacent land in the Rift Valley. The tribal groups which traditionally used these lands either migrated out of the areas or were isolated on reserves. Some families chose to live and work on the tea and coffee estates and on the sheep and cattle ranches. Other men and women commuted from the reserves or from their remote home areas to work on the estates for limited periods of time.

The impetus to work at wage labor for the colonials was influenced by both proximity and poverty. Residents of relatively non-productive areas, for example Luo groups in the Lake Victoria region, took wage-earning jobs to pay their hut tax. The groups who lived in close proximity were motivated both by the need for cash to pay this tax and by a desire to gain access to some of the material goods owned by their neighbors—labor-saving devices such as farm tools, lanterns, charcoal and paraffin stoves, tin roofs and water barrels, bicycles and automobiles. They admired the purebred stock and the new crops that could be traded for cash. Working in the colonial houses, they learned to appreciate soap, tea, coffee, and other luxury products.

Various missionary groups contributed to the pressure toward social change. Confident of the superiority of their beliefs and values, they attempted to "educate" the "natives" to the right way of living, inculcating habits and aspirations often at odds with the existing culture. Some of these mission groups laid more stress on education than others, and their schools were more successful in teaching literacy and inculcating Western styles of thinking and associated beliefs and values. Kikuyu in the Central Province and Maseno in the Western Province had two of the finest mission schools.

The herdsmen of the Mara plains and northeastern Kenya were the most remote from these modernizing contacts. Their nomadic life made it difficult for the British government to collect taxes or the missionaries to establish schools. The Samburu and Masai are representatives of the herdsmen tradition, a tradition which is now also fast disappearing as the Kenya government strives to turn much of the area which served as grazing land for the large herds of native zebu cattle into wheat and alfalfa farms, fenced ranches for purebred stock, or game preserves for the tourist trade. Today, however, there are still some of these families in the northern and southern areas of the Rift Valley whose main subsistence is derived from these large native-cattle herds.

The families of these savannah herdsmen live in thorn-bush-enclosed compounds (*boma*) which serve both as cattle corral and living area. Several adult males and their wives build their low, turtle-back houses within this enclosure, and each adult male has his own gate through which his cattle pass in the early morning as they move out to pasture and in the evening as they return. The men who share a *boma* are not necessarily related. Furthermore, since the *boma* is moved from time to time, the same men may not continue to live together. There are two aspirations shared by most of these herdsmen: to have many cattle and many sons. To this end they also seek several wives to help care for the cattle and to bear children.

The marriage with each woman requires a contract with her family, sealed by the payment of cattle. Men cannot marry until they have been initiated into the proper age group; the initiation follows a period of six or more years spent as a *moran*, or young warrior, living most of the time in separate camps (*manyattas*). These young men traditionally were in charge of pasturing the large animals, taking them many miles from the base camp when the pastures began to dry up and feed and water ceased to be adequate. They protected the herds from both human and animal predators.

Since women marry as soon as they become capable of child-bearing, the discrepancy in age between husband and wife can be ten years or more. From early childhood—as early as eight or nine—young girls have warrior lovers who initiate them into sexual life. This is considered essential for growth into adulthood. What Westerners might consider romantic love affairs, or certainly adolescent crushes, are part of growing up for these young women, and it is difficult for them to give them up when they are married by arrangement to older men. Marriage is for reproduction.

A married Masai or Samburu woman's well-being depends on her ability to get on amicably with her co-wives and the other women in the *boma*, on the number and health of the cattle her husband allots to her at marriage, and on her success in bearing children and raising them to maturity. Each wife has her own house and hearth and the milk from her cows to feed to her children.

The women are responsible for milking their cows, caring for their calves, and for inspecting the animals in the morning for ticks and signs of poor health. They are responsible for supplying their house with wood and with water, a task which in the dry season may require walking six or more miles. Each wife is responsible for keeping the roof of her house tight and for cooking and caring for her children. A good lieutenant, she organizes her children from a young age to help her in these tasks. In her leisure hours in the afternoon, she sits with her co-wives and the other women of the *boma*, gossiping and doing bead work. She sings and dances with them on ritual occasions. There are often open expressions of hostility, but in the end they are usually forgotten as it is to everyone's advantage to get along.

A good polygynist moves among his women carefully so as not to cause jealousy by favoring one too much over another, seeing to it that each wife gets pregnant when she wishes, and that she has a large enough milking herd to ensure the health of her children. He finds it advantageous to discuss new marriages with his wives before he contracts them. To keep peace in the compound, the husband must be authoritarian but just. It is his responsibility to be equitable in his treatment of all, and, to do this, he remains aloof and rarely becomes intimate with any of his wives or their children. He controls his wives (if need be) with physical force. A successful man is fearless and aggressive in defending his family and herds. He is dependent not only on his sons, but on the men of his own age to whom he is bonded in an elaborate initiation ceremony to help him protect his cattle from raiders and from animal predators.

Both the Masai and Samburu have resisted being drawn into the new forms of economic life. They have been loath to give up their large herds for a few grade cattle even though the latter would produce more milk. The young men have been unenthusiastic about attending school, preferring the pleasant life in the warrior camps with their young mistresses.

The Kipsigis of the western highlands provide an example of a group in transition between herdsmen and agriculturalists. Several members of the Child Development Research Unit have worked in the area around Sotik and Bomet and among Kipsigis groups as far south as the Tanzanian border. Within this area there are, on the one hand, families still living primarily as semi-nomadic herdsmen with clan lands, zebu cattle, and rudimentary subsistence agriculture, while, on the other hand, there are farm families living on large settlement schemes developed by the government on lands that were formerly European farms. These families own land individually, sell milk from grade cattle, and raise cash crops such as pyrethrum, tea, potatoes, and maize.

A comparison between these groups gives insight into the consequences of introducing the cultivation of crops into a cattle economy. When sorghum, millet, and maize are cultivated in fields adjacent to the living areas, it is the women who do the agricultural work. They work the soil with a mattock, plant the crops, and thresh and winnow the grain. The division of labor is clear— agriculture is women's work. The more these grain crops become important in the diet, the greater the workload for the women. Their leisure hours decrease rapidly. When the land for pasturing becomes scarce and the number of cattle is drastically reduced, settlements become permanent, the ownership of land is allotted to individual families, and the division of labor becomes even more inequitable. Men continue to consider agriculture primarily women's work and, since they have few cattle, find themselves with little to do and frequently seem to suffer from loss of self-esteem. Their chief duties remain the keeping of peace within the homestead, the protection of property, now crops as well as livestock, the making of major decisions, and the discussing of legal and political affairs with other men in the community.

Although the bullock-drawn plow has been introduced on the farms where cash crops are grown and men see to the preparation of the soil and help with the planting and harvesting, agricultural work such as planting and weeding are still considered women's province. Furthermore, women here—as among the Masai and Samburu—are responsible for providing food for their children. The fields in which cash crops are grown are considered the men's fields, but each woman has her own plot which she works with a mattock. On this land she attempts to raise sufficient surplus to furnish cash for buying staples such as sugar, tea, cooking fat, and clothes for herself and her children. She joins with neighboring women in groups that work together, rotating from field to field, when the season requires heavy labor.

Kipsigis men, by the time our studies were done, still preferred to have a house of their own where they could eat, sleep, and entertain their men friends.

They were still warrior herdsmen at heart; the actual transition to agricultural-ists and dairymen preceeds the men's emotional acceptance of their new role. Some, no longer called upon to be the rulers of large polygynous families and the protectors of herds against lions and cattle thieves, do not seem able to find satisfaction in their new way of life. They spend many aimless hours drinking beer and discussing politics. Although the practice of polygynous marriage has decreased, many men still consider it ideal to have several wives. Even in monogamous families, husband and wife still live essentially separate lives, men bonded emotionally to their age mates, women to their close neighbors. Men are forbidden by custom to handle infants. They delegate the care of their young to women until the boys are old enough to move out to the men's world and the children have become important contributors to the family work force.

The Gikuyu, among whom I have spent the most time, have been primarily agriculturalists for many generations. Within Gikuyuland, there are few, if any, families left who do not raise cash crops. The Gikuyu have been involved in coffee, tea, and pyrethrum cultivation since they won the right to raise these crops from the colonials who had previously maintained exclusive rights to their production. Living in close proximity to the British colonials, working on their estates, the Gikuyu developed an admiration for the European farmers' ability to make money from the land. They compared the milk production of the grade cattle with that of their own zebu cows. And, most important, they witnessed the luxurious life style of the Europeans and developed the covetousness which accompanies such exposure. With few exceptions, the Gikuyu have adopted, or are seeking to adopt, the complex, specialized culture that is associated with the industrial world.

In the village of Ngecha, twenty miles north of Nairobi, where my colleagues and I worked off and on for five years, I was able to observe families in various stages of transition and to record the details of their life. A few men in the village are still polygynous. These men are without exception the owners of comparatively large holdings of land for this area (five or more acres). Their wives are the agricultural laborers, the polygynists are the supervisors, man-agers, and sometimes part-time workers. The sons of these men, however, realize that with land demarcation and individual ownership, unless they are able to purchase more land, agriculture is not a viable economic pursuit for more than one or two members of their large families. As a consequence, these men are trying various alternatives. Some are buying grade cattle and hoping to produce enough surplus milk to pay for taxes and school expenses, and to build a modern house. Others are raising chickens and eggs for the Nairobi market, raising flowers or attempting intensive truck gardening on small plots of land. Some are setting up small stores or trucking businesses. Almost all the young men aspire to wage-earning jobs in the neighboring town of Limuru or in the capital city of Nairobi. Most want to buy land, and those who have learned how and have sufficient means are becoming shareholders in cooperative-settlement schemes in the Rift Valley.

The profile of family life changes with the occupation of the husband. Life in the homesteads of the polygynists is similar to that already described, although in Ngecha there seems to be less spontaneity and shared leisure pleasures among the men and women than among the Masai and Samburu. The competition among the wives for school expenses for their children and for a share of the shrinking land increases rivalry. On the homesteads where there is enough food and a reasonable amount of cash, and where the co-wives are friendly, there is a sociability among the adult women which makes visiting with them a pleasure. The women work together, combining with neighbors into groups which, like their Kipsigis counterparts, rotate between gardens preparing the soil for planting, weeding, and in general cooperating whenever there is heavy work to be done. They still sing as they work, each providing the meals in turn as the work groups move from one farm to the next. These women are strong support for one another in times of crisis. If the polygynist husband owns a store or a restaurant or has a wage-earning job, all the agricultural work and many of the day-to-day decisions fall to the women.

There are many new cultural innovations, however, which are discouraging the practice of polygyny. As early as the turn of the century, the Church of Scotland Mission set up a school in Thogoto, eight miles southwest of Ngecha. Some of the men and women left home to attend this school, often without the consent of their parents. In 1911, a mission school was started in the village. In 1926, the first schoolhouse was built, and a small number of the youth of the village attended classes regularly. In the mid forties, a large stone schoolhouse was built. By the mid sixties, this building proved too small to provide for the ever increasing number of village children whose parents decided that education was essential for economic well-being. At the same time, a nursery school was built, and young children were sent off to learn their letters, counting, and simple English phrases.

The introduction of school has had a dramatic effect on family life. Although education is now universal and free, for many years a man who wished to educate his children had to pay school fees for each child. If he valued education he began to realize that if he had many children he could not afford to send them all to school. Since it was also obvious that with land demarcation and laws restricting the division of land the family could not support many married sons and their wives, the viability of farming as a way of life became questionable. Some men would need to seek wage-earning jobs, and the best guarantee of success in the labor market was a certificate of having completed at least six years of school. As time went on and competition for the scarce and highly coveted white-collar jobs became stiff, four to six years of secondary education became necessary, and by 1973 even college graduates were beginning to worry about their chances of finding prestigious positions.

The combination of these school expenses and shrinking acreage is probably one of the chief deterrents to polygyny which, from all one can see, is decreasing rapidly. A very wealthy and powerful man may still attract more than one wife, but with few exceptions the young women we interviewed stated that they did not want to marry polygynists. They want the best for their children, and they recognize that where there is a scarcity of land for each wife to cultivate and raise food for her own children, polygyny is economically unsound. For many women this seems to be the first consideration in opting for a monogamous union. Other women speak of their desire to have a new kind of relationship with their husbands, one which is more intimate and exclusive of others, both co-wives and patri-kin. They speak of spending leisure time with their husbands, visiting friends with them on Sundays. They expect their husbands to take more of an interest in young children. But first and primarily, they are interested in the economic well-being of themselves and their children.

Some of the monogamously married young women who have wage-earning husbands have settled into the role of managing an acre or so of land and one or two grade cattle. They use the money from the sale of milk and surplus vegetables for their own and their children's needs. They expect their husbands to provide funds for school fees, taxes, and major investments. If they live on the homesteads of their husbands' families and the land they cultivate still belongs to the patriarch, they are bound into the lives of other families and, depending on the peacefulness of the compound, share the supervision of children and some of the agricultural work with their in-laws. There is a ready-made support group for these women and a large, multi-aged play group for their young children.

Other young couples are far more ambitious. The men strive to get their fathers to grant them title to a portion of the homestead land. The couple then attempt to use this small acreage to advance themselves in the new society. Some of the wives are driving themselves beyond belief. One woman I know with four children under seven years old manages 600 chickens as well as two grade cows on a quarter-acre plot. Pasturage for the cows is on separate land owned by her father-in-law. This woman carries water for the chickens and cows from the town pump. Since the pasturage is inadequate for the cows, she gathers and carries fodder for them. She works from early morning to late night, her husband helping her wash and box the eggs each evening so that he can take them to the Nairobi market on his way to work. This couple are achieving things for themselves and their children. They would not think of keeping a child home from school to help care for the youngest children or to help with the farm work. Like their equally ambitious neighbors, they see education as essential; they enter their children in nursery school as soon as they are old enough to be accepted. The seven- and eight-year-olds who were once considered ideal child nurses are no longer available to play this role. Now mothers who must be out of the house working in the garden or pasture are using preschool children as young as four to supervise even younger siblings.

Children who formerly were performing many tasks essential to the family economy are now only available after school in the late afternoons. They are receiving less training in thinking of the welfare of others, more training in competitiveness and individual achievement, the fare provided by the Western-style schools they attend.

This young family with its 600 chickens and other families like it are breaking some of the bonds with their kin. The women have no co-wives, or sisters-in-law who are co-resident, to share their heavy work. Kinship bonds are strained as one nuclear family succeeds and becomes wealthier than closely related families. Successful families face a dilemma: should they share their wealth with poorer relatives or reinvest it to increase their income? The preoccupation in many such families is getting ahead. The motive for economic success overrides all other concerns.

Values are changing. Traditionally generosity, goodheartedness, respect-fulness, obedience, and responsibility were the five most admired traits—the characteristics one would hope for in one's child. Now cleverness and curiosity, which are considered essential for success in school and in the new society, are valued by many more than are generosity and goodheartedness.

There is a new style of architecture which reflects the increasing autonomy of the nuclear family. Traditionally Gikuyu houses were round mud and wattle structures with thatched roofs. Each woman had her own one-room house. Adolescent boys and adult males all aspired to have separate dwellings. Men not only frequently slept apart but also ate apart from the women and children. Now houses are almost exclusively rectangular metal structures with metal roofs, with two bedrooms and a central living area, which may serve as a kitchen or may be furnished with a table, chairs, and sometimes a couch. In the latter case, there is a separate building or an addition which serves as the cooking area. Husbands and wives now have some privacy from a master bedroom shared only with the youngest children.

Such living arrangements lead inevitably to an increase in the intimacy of husband and wife. Cross-culturally it has been found to be true that where husbands and wives sleep together, they tend to eat together and the husband is more apt to help with daily child care.[3] This is also the case in Ngecha. Some of the men seem to find the new role awkward, others to accept it as part of being "modern."

I have often wondered whether the acceptance of the monogamous family would have come about so rapidly without the introduction of Christianity. Most of the residents of Ngecha are members of either the Protestant Church of East Africa or the Kikuyu Orthodox Church, a branch of the Greek Orthodox Church. The former has not accepted polygynists into its congregations. The model of the Holy Family is that of the nuclear family as we know it in the Western world. Although this ideology has undoubtedly had its influence, it seems probable that economic factors would inevitably have led to the decrease in polygyny. Along with Christianity, the cost of schooling, the demarcation and granting of individual titles to land subject to restrictions on subdivision, the decrease in the available farm land, the desire for modern houses of wood or stone, for radios, bicycles, cars, and all the other technological accoutrements of the industrial world combine to discourage polygyny and undermine the joint patrilineal farm family.

But these are not the only factors to consider when predicting the fate of the corporate extended family in developing countries and assessing the role of urbanization on the increase and the prevalence of autonomous nuclear families. Changing values and aspirations are also decisive. So long as the nuclear family is embedded in a larger kinship group through co-residence on undivided land, the pressure to share and to get along with relatives is strong. Rivalries close beneath the surface are kept at bay. In training their children these families must emphasize generosity, goodheartedness, and respectfulness. They must repress and deny feelings of hostility which are generated within the home-stead. It is safer to project aggression onto others, a mechanism often identified as the explanation for the widespread belief in "poisoning" among Kenyans. These families, when they become involved in disputes, still need the members of their extended families and their lineage to act as advocates. They may still need them as protectors of their land and possessions.

It is true that kin are of less use in the city as defenders of rights and property. Unlike the villages, which still have a dual system of conflict settlement, both traditional and modern, legal disputes in the city are adjudicated in the national courts, and the protection of property is in the hands of a professional police force. An urbanite needs money to hire a lawyer, friends in the government to ensure that he procures proper protection. If he is lucky, these men may be relatives or age mates, or acquaintances from his native district, but in many cases they are strangers.

But families do not necessarily give up their extended-family and lineage connections. Two of our colleagues studied families who maintained two households, one in their extended-family compound, the other in Nairobi.[4] A husband who finds a job in Nairobi rents a room. He usually leaves his wife or wives to care for the garden, returning to visit for a weekend from time to time. Some wives, when they are not needed on the farm, move to the city, bringing their young children and crowding into the husband's small quarters. These women find child care much more difficult. Not only is there inadequate space in the house, but the yard is often pocket-handkerchief size with no fence to protect the very young from automobiles and other dangers. There are no farm chores to occupy the children's time. Neighbors are strangers, often speak a different language, and their trustworthiness is unknown. A woman has no garden where she can produce food for her children and hence is dependent on her husband's generosity or the food she brings from home. Temporary jobs are hard to find, and, if she does find employment, there is seldom anyone she can trust to care for the children. If she stays at home in the country she assumes sole responsibility for all the farming, but she is able to feed and clothe her children and has help from her kin.

There are obvious trade-offs, advantages and disadvantages of the various styles of family life. Where the mother, father, and children share a house to the exclusion of others, there are two adults who are able to talk in privacy, to discuss problems, make plans, and jointly reach decisions. Eating and sleeping together, they are able to help each other with the routines of living. If the woman is ill or for some reason needs an extra hand, the man is familiar with the details of her activities and can substitute for her. Where the family is embedded in an extended unit, there is frequently greater segregation of the sexes; a mother depends on other women of the household or compound and her husband joins with other men to form male solidarities. This kind of life requires cooperation with more individuals. There are many children in the house or compound. Since rivalry among nuclear family units must be minimized to prevent strife, individual children are not singled out for praise or special attention. One is never without company. In exchange for loss of privacy and autonomy, the husband, wife, and children have the security of knowing their relatives are at hand to help them in emergencies and stand behind them if they have conflicts with outsiders. They are also available for all types of emotional support.

Nowhere is the problem of choosing between the life paths more obvious than among the successful urban families. Through the hard work of their parents and older siblings, many of these men and women were sent to the best secondary schools at considerable cost. Some of the most successful were accepted into the university or provided with specialized training. They are now among the most powerful and wealthy citizens of Kenya, and most are living in Nairobi. But their expenses are great. Both housing and food are costly. They have high aspirations for their children and want to send them to the best schools, some of which are private and have high entry fees. Some families whose older siblings have helped pay their school fees are faced with a difficult dilemma: should they share their income with their siblings who now need help with their children's school fees, or should they use what extra income they have to help their own children and increase personal family holdings? Another problem is created by country relatives who flock into Nairobi hoping to find jobs. They move in and expect to be housed and fed. They have little realization of the cost of food and the financial burden they are placing on their city cousins. What should the Nairobi family do?

Most want to maintain their kinship bonds. Kenyans are still farmers or herdsmen at heart, and there are few who would feel complete without owning land, and preferably land in their home area. If their family of origin owns a large tract of land, they still have an heir's interest in their native homestead. In a new nation with a history of inter-tribal dispute, individuals feel most secure when they are in their native territory. The dilemma is therefore a very real one. Few families sever kin ties completely, but some remain more closely embedded in their extended family than others do.

How does the relation between husband and wife in the city fare? There are many strains. Housing in Nairobi is scarce and expensive. Most units were designed by Western architects for nuclear families. A man finds himself sharing a small apartment with his wife and four or more children. There is no space in which to retire from the world of women and children. For many the confinement is smothering, and some men escape to clubs and bars where they can enjoy male company as they would in their rural villages. In the process they make serious inroads into the family budget. Others, however, settle into a style of life similar to that of urban families in the United States, and adjust as best they can to the evening confusion.

Most of the women who are living in the city permanently are working long and exhausting hours. The traditional ideology as to the division of labor lingers on, and women try to earn the money for the food and clothing for their children. The income they earn is their security against the vagaries of husbands who have not been raised in a monogamous tradition. Unfortunately, along with other aspects of Western culture we have exported the eight-hour work day,[5] and working wives must leave before eight o'clock in the morning, rarely returning until around five in the afternoon. There is no institutional care for infants, and the few preschools are expensive. Women must find household help who are reliable and, as in other parts of sub-Saharan Africa, this is a major problem. Young women who are relatives are too much of a responsibility in a city which does not furnish them with the type of supervision provided by kin in the village. Too frequently young girls return home pregnant. Unrelated women, on the other hand, are apt to be jealous of the more affluent city women. Older women who come into city homes as servants may find the new standards of child-rearing too permissive and mete out more severe punishment than the parents approve of. The new city mothers are unsure of how to deal with hired help, and they vacillate between extremes of pseudo-kinship behavior and authoritarianism.

Developing new styles of family life and child rearing are not without stress. A visitor to Nairobi households will often be reminded of households in the United States during the forties when the new look in American child care was influenced by a mixture of John Dewey and misinterpreted Freud. The advice to mothers was to love their children, stimulate them, and meet their needs as immediately as possible. Their curiosity was to be encouraged, their every question answered. Households who followed this advice were child-centered, parents giving priority to the needs of the young, dedicated to understanding each individual child, judging its potential and ensuring its proper development. In the new Nairobi households, similar doctrines are now influencing parental behavior. Children may be underfoot late in the evening, demanding attention from parents and other adults, behavior that is not tolerated in most rural families.

Exposed to Western psychology and educational theories, thoughtful parents are concluding that good performance in school is essential for financial success and prestige as an adult. They are concerned as to how they should train their children if school achievement is fostered by curiosity and autonomy. To what extent will the family become child-centered? To what extent can parents require respectfulness to adults and obedience and responsibility without impeding the cognitive development of their children? These are indeed painful dilemmas, made even more difficult if the husband is a reluctant co-resident, unused to an ideology demanding so much concern on his part for the care and, training of the very young.

My observations in both Ngecha and Nairobi families convince me that, as individual achievement becomes more important, sociable interchange between adults becomes less frequent. In New England, in the child-centered homes with which I am acquainted, the life of parents is scheduled around what they perceive to be the educational, social, and emotional needs of their young. Adult conversations are only possible when young children have finally been put to bed and older children taken to educational or social appointments. An unplanned visit to such a home is frequently frustrating, as every attempt at conversation is interrupted. A visit to most families in Ngecha is a very different experience. Children are present but, as in the early tradition of New England homes, seen but not heard unless called upon.

Visiting is ceremonious. Used to quick greetings, I learned during my years in Kenya what a truly neighborly conversation would cover, the importance placed on communicating to others that one is genuinely concerned with their welfare and values their friendship. One should take care to greet all members of the household each morning. When I asked the students living in our house why this was customary, they explained that it was important that every individual know that one feels about him each morning as one felt about him the night before. The greetings include the conventional "How are you?," but one stops to hear the response and to assure the individual that one is interested in the answer. I learned what gift exchange and sharing of food can mean. These rituals are constant reassurances that one is willing to take time and to give both substantive and emotional support to others.

In my eyes, the Kenyan men and women are models of civilized sociability. These skills are taught from an early age by both example and instruction. Traditionally, children are not supposed to initiate interaction with adults, and, indeed, our observations indicate that after they reach the age of two they seldom do. They are allowed, and expected, to be silent observers of adult social life. There are many adults about, sharing gossip and good humor. Children are expected to sit silently and listen to the conversation and share in the laughter.

Strict etiquette concerning greeting and appropriate, respectful behavior are taught from infancy. I have frequently visited homes in Ngecha when the women were working in the garden or fetching wood or water to be greeted by a young male or female child-nurse, five to eight years of age, carrying an infant on his or her back and supervising other young siblings. With all the mannerisms of their mothers, these children would greet me, offer me a chair, and sometimes even prepare the tea that is customarily offered to visitors.

The privacy and isolation of the nuclear family which have so often been discussed in the literature on family life seem to me to be related to child-centeredness and the associated pressure on parents to equip their children for a world where personal achievement is perceived as the prerequisite to a successful life, a world which values the sort of egoistic behavior encouraged by Western education.

Will the new Kenyan family life be able to perpetuate its sociable tradition, or will the increase of nuclear households turn the family inward to the detriment of interaction with other adults? Will husband and wife devote the hours of the day to personal achievement and the training of their children in the skills that seem to be most advantageous in a capitalistic industrial society? Will the women devote too little time to bonding with other women, the men too little time to socializing with their age mates? Will the Kenyans lose their fine art of sociability?

There are pressures pushing the members of the new nation now one way, now another. Some, anxious to succeed in a competitive, capitalistic society, have loosened their ties with the extended family, have become less generous to individuals who are not in their immediate family and less concerned with the welfare of others. Other citizens of the new nation, particularly those who have spent time abroad and studied other societies thoughtfully, are not willing to give up the old ways completely. Kenyan students who have spent the year at Harvard and observed Cambridge family life comment on the loneliness of the families, the frantic pace of life with its lack of sociability, the seriousness of the interaction within households, the absence of laughter, the paucity of interaction among young siblings, and the dependency of the young upon interaction with their parents. The women among them cannot understand the dependence of young American wives on their husbands. Why do the women not work and establish their autonomy?

Kenyan women who have stayed longer periods in the States and had children while pursuing their studies have greater awareness of the problems of the mother who has no help in infant and early childhood care. One African student, who had been perplexed by young American mothers and who tried to continue her doctoral work after having a baby, told me, "I now understand why many American mothers do not work. Without helpers it is hard to study at home. It is difficult to have big thoughts when constantly interrupted by a baby's cry." She observed how few young parents had relatives or close female friends to help with the children, and noted the expense of hired help and the lack of child-care facilities. The student was at Harvard in the late sixties. Now, returned to Africa and the mother of four young children, she shares many of the problems of American mothers. She has found it difficult to find adequate help in the city, when she is away from home from eight in the morning to five at night. Having been exposed to the manuals of child psychology used in American universities, she also worries that she is not giving adequate attention to the development of her children.

There are many influences familiar to historians of American family life which may force Kenyan women to relinquish a certain amount of their economic independence and adopt the role of the helpless housewife so familiar to the Western world. Although it is theoretically possible for individual families to choose how they are to live, there are economic and social pressures that are difficult to counteract; competition for scarce jobs for one thing, inadequate mother surrogates or institutional provisions for infant and child care for another.

As a woman, I hope that my Kenyan counterparts will not lose their fine sense of competence and autonomy that has been their reward for successfully providing their children with food and clothing. Their ability to play the dual role of economic provider and mother is a valuable heritage. Their rural mothers taught them how to care for the young and made them confident little mothers to their younger siblings at the age of eight. Young girls learned how to grow food and cook meals. By twelve they are competent women with a sense of personal worth. Provided a woman had a piece of land on which to grow crops and was bonded to other women with whom she joined in cooperative work groups, she had security for herself and her children.

Once a family chooses to get on the modernization escalator, the young mother is overworked as a farmer until the family is rich enough to hire much-needed help. If a woman takes a wage-earning job in the country, she has the dual role of subsistence farmer and wage earner. If she moves to the city and takes a job, she is bound into the eight-hour day and has problems getting adequate help. She returns home in the evening to work till midnight with little or no time for sociability.

It is to be hoped that Kenya can avoid repeating the mistakes of the West and so organize its economy that women can continue to share, as in the past, the responsibility for themselves and their children. It is hoped that they can so arrange things that they will be able to maintain the personal autonomy and self-esteem that has characterized their lives. It is hoped that they can enter the international industrial world without severing their ties with kin and neighborhood and adopt a pace of life that does not preclude traditional African sociability.

REFERENCES

[1] The data on which this essay is based were collected by the personnel of the Child Development Research Unit in the Faculty of Education at the University of Nairobi in Kenya during the years 1967-1972, when the author and her husband, John Whiting, were co-directors.

The Unit was financed by the Carnegie Foundation and by a grant from the National Institute of Mental Health—MH01096. Research teams included graduate students from the United States and undergraduates from the University of Nairobi. Below are listed, by linguistic groups, some of these researchers (for a complete list, see the annual reports of the Child Development Research Unit [now the Bureau of Educational Research]): Masai: Melissa Llewelyan-Davies; Samburu: Judith and Michael Rainey; Kipsigis: Robert Daniels, Sara Harkness, Michael Saltman, Sarah Sieley, Charles Super, Kathleen Wilcox; Gikuyu: Susan Abbott, Jane Chisiano, Frances Cox, Dorothy and John Herzog, James Kagia, Beatrice and John Whiting.

[2]For a discussion of the hut tax and its effect on the life of Kenyans, see Ann Seidman, *Comparative Development Strategies in East Africa* (Nairobi, 1972).

[3]See John W. M. and Beatrice Whiting, "Aloofness and Intimacy of Husbands and Wives: A Cross-Cultural Study," *Ethos*, 3:2 (1975).

[4]Susan Abbott, "Full-Time Farmers and Week-End Wives: An Analysis of Altering Conjugal Roles," *Journal of Marriage and the Family*, 1976, pp. 165-74; Thomas Weisner, "The Primary Sampling Unit: A Non-Geographically Based Rural-Urban Example," *Ethos*, 1, pp. 546-59; and *idem*, "The Structure of Sociability: Urban Migration and Urban-Rural Ties," *Urban Anthropology* (in press).

[5]Edward O. Edwards of the Ford Foundation has commented on the consequences of the exportation of the eight-hour day.

PHILIPPE ARIÈS

The Family and the City

I SHOULD LIKE TO MAKE SOME OBSERVATIONS in this essay* about the relationship between family history and urban history. My central theme will be that when the city (and, earlier, the rural community) deteriorated and lost its vitality, the role of the family overexpanded like a hypertrophied cell. In an attempt to fill the gap created by the decline of the city and the urban forms of social intercourse it had once provided, the omnipotent, omnipresent family took upon itself the task of trying to satisfy all the emotional and social needs of its members. Today, it is clear that the family has failed in its attempts to accomplish that feat, either because the increased emphasis on privacy has stifled the need for social intercourse or because the family has been too completely alienated by public powers. People are demanding that the family do everything that the outside world in its indifference or hostility refuses to do. But we should now ask ourselves why people have come to expect the family to satisfy all their needs, as if it had some kind of omnipotent power.

Life in Traditional Societies

First of all, let us take a brief look at Western traditional societies from the Middle Ages to the eighteenth century, that is, before they had been affected by the Enlightenment and the industrial revolution. Every individual grew up in a community made up of relatives, neighbors, friends, enemies, and other people with whom he had interdependent relationships. The community was more important in determining the individual's fate than was the family. When a young boy left his mother's apron strings, it was his responsibility to make a place for himself within the community. Like an animal or a bird, he had to establish a domain, a place of his own, and he had to get the community to recognize it. It was up to him to determine the limits of his authority, to decide what he could do and how far he could go before encountering resistance from the others—his parents, his wife, his neighbors, and the community as a whole. Securing a domain in this way depended more on the skillful use of natural talents than on knowledge or savoir-faire. It was a game in which the venture-

*This paper was written for presentation, on February 24–25, 1977, at the University of Southern California, during a colloquium on "The American Family: Its Changing Images and Social Implications," jointly sponsored by the University's Division of Humanities, the National Endowment for the Humanities, and the Rockefeller Foundation.

some boy gifted in eloquence and with a dramatic flair had the advantage. All life was a stage: if a player went too far, he was put in his place; if he hesitated, he was relegated to an inferior role.

Since a man knew that his wife would be his most important and faithful collaborator in maintaining and expanding his role, he chose his bride with care. On her part, the woman accepted the domain she would have to protect along with the man with whom she would live. Marriage strengthened the husband's position, as a result not only of his wife's work, but also of her personality, her presence of mind, her talents as player, actress, story-teller, her ability to seize opportunities and to assert herself.

The important concept, then, is that of *domain*. But this domain was neither private nor public, as these terms are understood today; rather, it was both simultaneously: private because it had to do with individual behavior, with a man's personality, with his manner of being alone or in society, with his self-awareness and his inner being; public because it fixed a man's place within the community and established his rights and obligations. Individual maneuvering was possible because the social space was not completely filled. The fabric was loose, and it behooved each individual to adjust the seams to suit himself within the limits set by the community. The community recognized the existence of the empty space surrounding people and things. It is worth remarking that the word "play" can mean both the act of playing and freedom of movement within a space. Perhaps, by the act of playing, the free space to play in was created and maintained. The state and society were forces that intervened in a person's life only infrequently and intermittently, bringing with them either terror and ruin or miraculous good fortune. But for the most part, each individual had to win his domain by coming to terms only with the men and women in his own small community.

The role of the family was to strengthen the authority of the head of the household, without threatening the stability of his relationship with the community. Married women would gather at the wash house; men at the cabaret. Each sex had its special place in church, in processions, in the public square, at celebrations, and even at the dance. But the family as such had no domain of its own; the only real domain was what each male won by his maneuvering, with the help of his wife, friends, and dependents.

Three Important Changes in the Nineteenth and Twentieth Centuries: A New Way of Life

In the course of the eighteenth century the situation began to change. It is necessary at this point to analyze what the major trends were that produced this change. I find at least three important phenomena that caused and directed it. The first of these stemmed from the fact that, in the eighteenth century, society—or, more properly, the state—was loath to accept the fact that there were certain areas of life beyond its sphere of control and influence. Earlier, the situation had been just the reverse: such free areas were allowed to exist, and adventurous individuals were permitted to explore them. In American parlance, we might say that the community had a "frontier"—or rather several frontiers—which could be pushed back by the audacious. But following upon the

Enlightenment and industrialization, the state, with its sophisticated technology and organization, wiped out those frontiers: there was no longer an area beyond which one could go. Today, the state's scrutiny and control extend, or are supposed to extend, into every sphere of activity. Nothing is to remain untouched. There is no longer any free space for individuals to occupy and claim for themselves. To be sure, liberal societies allow individuals some initiative, but only in specific areas, such as school and work, where there is a pre-established order for promotion. This is a situation totally different from the way things were in traditional society. In the new society, the concepts of play and free space are no longer accepted; it must be too well regulated.

The second phenomenon that produced this change is directly related to the first: this is the division of space into areas assigned to work and areas assigned to living. The working man now leaves what had been his domain in traditional society, the place where all his activities had taken place, to go to work far away, sometimes very far away, in a very different environment, where he is subject to a system of rules and to a hierarchy of power. He enters a new world, where he may, for all we know, be happier and more secure, and where he can become involved in associations with others—for example, through trade unions.

This specialized place devoted to work was invented by the new society in its abhorence of the void. Running industrial, commercial, and business enterprises requires systems of tight control. Free-enterprise capitalism has demonstrated its flexibility and ability to adapt. But this flexibility has nothing in common with the old concept of free space; rather it depends on the precise functioning of the unit as a whole. Although enterprises in a free-market economy may not be controlled by the state, they are no less controlled if by society at large.

One could reasonably argue that this displacement of workers was a form of "surveillance and punishment," as Foucault phrased it, similar in nature to the locking up of children in school, madmen in asylums, and delinquents in prison. In any case, it was certainly, at the very least, a means of maintaining order and control.

The third and last important phenomenon that affected the transformations of the eighteenth and nineteenth century is of a very different order than the first two; it is psychological in nature. But the chronological correlation with the other two is nonetheless impressive. The era witnessed not only the industrial revolution but an emotional revolution as well. Previously, feelings were diffuse, spread out over numerous natural and supernatural objects, including God, saints, parents, children, friends, horses, dogs, orchards, and gardens. Henceforth, they would be focused entirely within the immediate family. The couple and their children became the objects of a passionate and exclusive love that transcended even death.

From that time on, a working man's life was polarized between job and family. But those people who did not go out to work (women, children, old men) were concerned exclusively with family life. Nor was the division between job and family either equal or symmetrical. Although there was no doubt some room for emotional involvement at work, the family was a more conducive setting; whereas the working world was subject to constant, strict surveillance, the family was a place of refuge, free from outside control. The family thus acquired some similarities to the individual domain in traditional society, but with an important distinction: the family is not a place for individualism. The individual must recede into the background for the sake of the family unit, and especially for the sake of the children. Furthermore, the family had become more removed from the community than it was in earlier times, and it tended to be rather hostile to the external world, to withdraw into itself. Thus, it became *the* private domain, the only place where a person could legitimately escape the inquisitive stare of industrial society. Even now, industrial society has not given up trying to fill the gaps created by the decline of traditional society; it does, nevertheless, show some respect for the new entity—the family—which has grown up in its midst as a place of refuge.

Thus, the separation of space into work areas and living areas corresponds to the division of life into public sector and private sector. The family falls within the private sector.

New Forms of Social Intercourse in the Nineteenth Century: The City and the Cafe

These, then, were the main features of the new way of life. They evolved slowly in the industrialized West, and were not equally accepted in all places. Two important periods must be distinguished: the nineteenth century before the automobile conquered space, and the first half of the twentieth. The difference between these two periods lies in the degree of privacy that people enjoyed and in the nature of the public sector.

During the first period, roughly the whole of the nineteenth century, family life among the bourgeoisie and the peasantry was already much as it is today, that is, it was a private domain. But—and this distinction is very important— only women (including those who worked) were affected by the increased privacy; men were able to escape at times, an outlet they no doubt considered a male prerogative. Women and children had virtually no life outside the family and the school; these comprised their entire universe. Men, on the other hand, had a lively meeting place outside their families and jobs—to wit, the city.

I would like at this point to focus my attention on the city, disregarding those peasant societies where age-old tradition and the innovations of the industrial era are so intertwined that it is difficult for the analyst to distinguish between them. Still, it should be noted that historians today agree that, thanks to the agricultural prosperity in Western Europe during the nineteenth century, a flourishing rural civilization developed there. This was no doubt true of the United States as well. Is it not said that in certain regions of the Midwest immigrants have maintained traditions which have long since disappeared in their original homelands? These flourishing subcultures testify to the enormous vitality of the peasant communities at a time when privacy, the family, and the school were making great inroads upon them.

The rural exodus had not yet destroyed peasant life; rather, it had made it easier. This was the era of the beautiful costumes and regional furniture we find today displayed in folk museums. It was a time when folk tales were easily collected. It was also, however, a time when, thanks to the schools, many peasants were trying desperately to force open the doors to government careers for their children (who by then had grown fewer in number). The elementary-school teacher was an important person in nineteenth-century rural communities; today he is no longer. But it is the urban, not the rural, development that I should now like to discuss.

The long nineteenth century marked a high point in the development of the city and its urban civilization. No doubt urban populations had already increased to frightening levels; the poor immigrants who descended en masse upon them from the villages appeared as a threat to the bourgeois property-owners, who watched them encamp in their towns, and viewed them as an army of criminals and rebels. But this image born of fear need not deceive us today. To be sure, the large city was no longer what it had been in the seventeenth century, that is, a group of separate neighborhoods or streets, each constituting a community with a character of its own. In eighteenth-century Paris, the arrival of a transient population without a fixed placed of residence upset this way of life. Traditional patterns of social intercourse based on neighborhoods and streets began to disappear. But new ones replaced them that maintained and developed the city's basic functions.

Central to these new patterns were the cafe and the restaurant, public meeting places where conversation flowed as abundantly as food and drink—the cafe was a place for discussion, an invention of the late eighteenth century. Previously there had been eating places, inns, and hostels, places to serve meals in the home or to provide food and lodging for transient guests. There were also taverns and cabarets where people went to drink, and often for the low life to be found there. But they were places of ill-repute, sometimes brothels. Cafes, on the other hand, were something completely new and different. They were strictly an urban phenomenon, unknown in rural areas. The cafes were meeting places in cities, which were growing very rapidly and where people did not know one another, as they had before. In England the cafes were enclosed like cabarets, but the name "pub" describes their function well. In continental Europe, cafes opened onto the street and came to dominate them, thanks to their terraces. Cafes with their large terraces were in fact one of the most striking features of nineteenth-century cities. They were all but non-existent in the medieval and Renaissance sections of the old cities, such as Rome, but made up for it by being very much in evidence in those same Italian cities around the large public squares that owe their existence to Cavour's vast urbanization and Italian unity. In Vienna, too, cafes were, and still are, the heart of the city. In Paris the opening of the cafes was probably the reason behind the shift of public life from closed places, like the famous gallery at the Palais Royal, to the linear, open space of the boulevard, the center of the city's night life.

Cafes no doubt originally served the aristocracy, rather than the bour-geoisie. But they were quickly popularized and extended to all classes of society and to all neighborhoods. In nineteenth-century cities, there was not a neighborhood without at least one cafe, and more often several. In working-class neighborhoods, the small cafe played a vital role; it enabled communication that would otherwise have been impossible among the poorly housed residents who were often away at their jobs: the cafe served as message center. That is why the telephone became so immediately accessible after its advent. The cafe became the place where steady customers could make and receive telephone calls, leave and receive messages. It is easy to understand Maurice Aguilhon's surprise at the extraordinary number of small cafes in a city like Marseilles, each with its little network of neighbors and friends gathered around the counter and the telephone. The number and popularity of these cafes suggest that a new public sector had spontaneously developed in the nineteenth-century city.

Needless to say, the state's desire for control extended even to this new public sector. The state immediately understood the danger represented by the cafes and sought to limit it by establishing and enforcing codes or regulations. But it never completely succeeded. In addition, self-righteous people, concerned with order and morality, were suspicious of the cafes, which they considered to be hotbeds of alcoholism, anarchy, laziness, vice, and political wrangling. In France even today urban planners relegate cafes to shopping districts in residential areas and at a good distance from any elementary or secondary schools. But the mistrust of the authorities and of the self-righteous has still failed to diminish the popularity of the cafes. In the nineteenth century civilization was based on them.

Now let us compare the role played by the cafe in that era to that played by the family. The family was a private place; the cafe a public one. But they had one thing in common: they both managed to escape society's control. The family did so by right; the cafe in actual fact. These were the only two exceptions to the modern system of surveillance and order which came to include all social behavior. Thus, alongside the growing privacy of the family during the nineteenth and early twentieth centuries, a new and lively form of social intercourse developed in even the largest cities. This explains why the cities of the era were so full of life, and why the increased amount of privacy did not weaken the forms of social intercourse, at least among males.

The Decay of the City in the Twentieth Century

Toward the middle of the twentieth century in Western industrialized societies, these forms of social intercourse began to break down. The social and socializing function of the city disappeared. The more the urban population grew, the more the city declined. I am reminded of the words of the comedian who suggested moving the cities to the countryside. That, in fact, was exactly what happened.

Immense continuous urban areas have developed in all countries, but especially in the United States where they have replaced the city. There, cities have ceased to exist. This phenomenon, one of the most important in the history of our society, must be seen in the light of what we know about the family and the ways it has changed. I should like to show how the decay of the city and the loss of its socializing function have affected contemporary family life.

From the late nineteenth century, even before the advent of the automobile, rich city-dwellers began fleeing from the crowded cities, considering them unwholesome and dangerous. Far from inhabited areas, they sought purer air and more decent surroundings. En masse they began to settle in those neighborhoods on the outskirts of cities that were still sparsely populated, such as the sixteenth and seventeenth arrondissements in Paris near the greenery of the Parc

Monceau and the Bois de Boulogne. Later, thanks to the railroad, the streetcar, and, in time, the automobile, they pushed farther and farther out. This well-known phenomenon applies to all Western industrialized societies, but it is in North America that it developed most fully and reached its most extreme proportions, so we shall examine it there.

Neighborhoods are segregated not only by social class but also by function. Thus, just as there are rich, bourgeois neighborhoods and poor, working-class ones, so, too, there are business districts and residential ones. Offices, businesses, factories, and shops are found in one location, houses and gardens in the other.

The means of transportation most often used to get from one place to the other is the private car. In this scheme of things there is no longer room for the forum, the agora, the piazza, the corso. There is no room, either, for the cafe as meeting place. The only thing there is room for is the drive-in and the fast-food outlet. Eating establishments are to be found in both business and residential districts; depending on their location, they are busy at different times of the day. In business and industrial districts, they are humming with activity at lunchtime; in residential neighborhoods they do most of their business at night. During the off-hours, in both places, they are empty and silent: the only sign of life amidst the furniture and electric lights is the bored face of the cashier.

What is truly remarkable is that the social intercourse which used to be the city's main function has now entirely vanished. The city is either crowded with the traffic of people and cars in a hurry or it is totally empty. Around noontime, office workers in business districts sometimes take an old-fashioned stroll when the weather is nice, and enjoy a piece of cake or an ice cream cone in the sun. But after five o'clock the streets are deserted. Nor do the streets in residential neighborhoods become correspondingly crowded, except around shopping centers and their parking lots. People return to their homes, as turtles withdraw into their shells. At home they enjoy the warmth of family life and, on occasion, the company of carefully chosen friends. The urban conglomerate has become a mass of small islands—houses, offices, and shopping centers—all separated from one another by a great void. The interstitial space has vanished.

This evolution was precipitated by the automobile and by television, but it was well underway before they had even appeared, thanks to the growth of the cult of privacy in the bourgeois and middle classes during the nineteenth century. To people born between 1890 and 1920 (now between 50 and 80 years old), the green suburb represented the ideal way of life. They wanted to escape from the bustle of the city and to live in more rural, more natural surroundings. This shift to the suburbs, far from the noise and crowds of city streets, was caused by the growing attraction of a warm private family life. In those areas where private family living was less developed, as in the working-class areas along the Mediterranean, i.e., in societies dominated by obstinate males, community life fared better.

During the nineteenth and early twentieth centuries, the results of the increased privacy and the new family style of living were kept in check, it seems, thanks to the vitality of community life in both urban and rural areas. A balance was achieved between family life in the home and community life in the cafe, on the terrace, in the street. This balance was destroyed and the family carried the day, thanks to the spread of suburbia as a result of the unexpected help it received from the new technology: the automobile and television. When that happened, the whole of social life was absorbed by private, family living.

Henceforth, the only function of the streets and cafes was to enable the physical movement between home and work or restaurant. These are no longer places of meeting, conversation, recreation. From now on, the home, the couple, the family claim to fulfill all those functions. And when a couple or a family leave the house to do something that cannot be done at home, they go in a mobile extension of the house, namely, the car. As the ark permitted Noah to survive the Flood, so the car permits its owners to pass through the hostile and dangerous world outside the front door.

Not long ago I found myself in Rome at midnight in the working-class neighborhood of Trastevere. There were still crowds of people in the streets, but there were no adults, only *ragazzi* of 18 or 20. They were mostly boys, because people there have not yet gotten into the habit, at least in working-class neighborhoods, of letting girls run around at night. Although children and adults are content to sit in front of the television, adolescents are more interested in the life around them, in personal, spontaneous experiences. The young people of Trastevere were greeted by the marvelous Roman street, still the warm, picturesque setting of their daily life. But what about places where the setting no longer exists? Where do adolescents gather then? In the basements of houses, in underground garages, in the rooms of friends. They are always enclosed. They may very well reject their families, but they still retain their tendency to seek seclusion. Today's frontier is this internal wall: it continues to exist even though it no longer has much to protect.

Conclusion

In the so-called post-industrial age of the mid twentieth century, the public sector of the nineteenth century collapsed and people thought they could fill the void by extending the private, family, sector. They thus demanded that the family see to all their needs. They demanded that it provide the passionate love of Tristan and Yseult and the tenderness of Philemon and Baucis; they saw the family as a place for raising children, but, at the same time, as a means of keeping them in a prolonged network of exclusive love. They considered the family a self-sufficient unit, though at times they were willing to enlarge the circle to include a few close friends. In the family they hoped to recover the nostalgic world of Jalna and to experience the pleasures of family warmth; from the private fortress of the family car they sought to discover the world outside. And they cherished the family as a place for all the childish things that continue even beyond childhood. These trends were intensified by the baby boom. Since then, the family has had a monopoly on emotions, on raising children, and on filling leisure time. This tendency to monopolize its members is the family's way of coping with the decline of the public sector. One can well imagine the uneasiness and intolerance that the situation has created.

Although people today often claim that the family is undergoing a crisis, this is not, properly speaking, an accurate description of what is happening. Rather, we are witnessing the inability of the family to fulfill all the many functions with which it has been invested, no doubt temporarily, during the past half-century. Moreover, if my analysis is correct, this overexpansion of the family role is a result of the decline of the city and of the urban forms of social intercourse that it provided. The twentieth-century post-industrial world has been unable, so far, either to sustain the forms of social intercourse of the nineteenth century or to offer something in their place. The family has had to take over in an impossible situation; the real roots of the present domestic crisis lie not in our families, but in our cities.

Epilogue

WHEN STEPHEN GRAUBARD INVITED JEROME KAGAN, Tamara Hareven, and myself to serve as coeditors of this volume, his charge to us was twofold: to discuss what we see as the major elements in the ferment that has characterized theory and research on the family over the past decade, as illuminated in the essays included in this collection, and to speculate about the probable or desirable direction of theory and research on the family in the decade ahead.

That charge seemed eminently reasonable, but its execution has not proved to be easy. We have been contributors to this ferment ourselves: indeed, the three essays we have written for this collection are evidence of the dissatisfaction we have felt with our disciplines, I with sociology, Kagan with child psychology, Hareven with family history. We have followed a common logic, moving from dissatisfaction with our discipline's treatment of a family issue to a reformulation with the aid of other disciplines. In my case this has involved a venture into the biological sciences from a base in family sociology; for Kagan, a move from child psychology into cultural anthropology and sociology; and for Hareven, a move from social history into human development and role theory in sociology.

Indeed, one of the common characteristics of the essays in this collection is the frequency with which their authors work across disciplinary boundaries, not as social scientists tended to do a few decades ago, by collaborating with a colleague in another discipline, but by the more difficult but perhaps ultimately more fruitful if lonely route of submerging themselves in another discipline and attempting to reformulate an issue or theory in light of this exposure to new perspectives and knowledge. Thus, historians have learned the tools of demography and survey analysis, studied the theories of economics and kinship in social anthropology, and have reworked the field of historical demography and family history, deepening our understanding of family behavior in the process, as Wrigley describes in his review of recent work in his field. The impact of cultural anthropology is apparent in the historical research represented by Davis and in contemporary research on child development reported by Kagan. An appreciation of historical processes of social and economic change is evident in Whiting's essay on the family in Kenya, as it is in Wagatsuma's piece on the Japanese family. In all these instances, the authors use knowledge of other disciplines to sharpen and lend depth to the analysis of an issue in their own disciplines. In Sawhill's essay, by contrast, we can examine the contribution made when economists apply their theoretical tools to problems traditionally analyzed by other fields, in this case, the application of the economist's mode of analyzing decision making to family decisions concerning divorce or childbearing.

A critical component of the intellectual ferment taking place concerning the family would therefore seem to be the painful effort to break down the barriers among disciplines, by individual efforts by social scientists to reeducate themselves and then to reformulate problems of importance to the understanding of family systems and family relations. The three disciplines represented by the coeditors, however, vary in the extent to which this is a modal or an exceptional development. In history, the family was a neglected topic of investigation for a long time, enjoying a renascence of serious inquiry only in the past few decades. The basic question of how the family system articulates with the economic system was the stimulus for Hareven's turning to sociology and human development for concepts that helped to illuminate the materials she worked with in the study of Manchester workers and their families; and her historical research has contributed to the growing evidence that industrialization per se has not had as powerful an impact on family structure as had been assumed.

By contrast, psychology has had a long history of concern for internal family dynamics; as Kagan points out, it has only recently begun to look outside the parent-child bond itself to explore the social network and historical circumstances that impinge on the child and help to account for the child's characteristics quite independent of direct parental influence.

In sociology, the family has been a longstanding scholarly focus as a central social institution in any society. The major shift in sociological perspectives on the family has been from broad macroscopic and historical analyses of the family in institutional terms, to a more fine-grained investigation of internal family roles and relations. One could characterize these shifts in perspective over the past few decades by noting that child psychologists have added a sociological and historical lens to their view of the family, whereas sociologists have added a social-psychological lens to theirs. As Kagan puts it in his summary essay below, psychologists have tended to look outward from the family to the social setting in which it is embedded, whereas sociologists have looked inward to internal family processes. Both developments, however, have been underway for more than a decade, and are therefore no longer an exceptional, but increasingly a modal perspective in these fields.

By contrast, we are only at the very beginning phase in 1978 of a closer articulation between the biological and social science perspectives on family behavior. I suspect that this coming together will be a far less smooth process than the articulation of history with psychology, social anthropology, and sociology. Social scientists have a long history of resistance to the incorporation of biological variables into their problem formulations. By 1978, there is also a great barrier to this articulation on the grounds of the sheer complexity of the biological sciences which a social scientist must master to attempt to bridge the gaps among the disciplines involved. This was brought home to me by the reaction of a new Ph.D. in sociology who read my essay; with considerable dismay, he said, "But I have just finished my studies. Now you are implying that I have to start all over again in an even more complicated field!"

There is a further hurdle ahead in the articulation of biological and sociological perspectives, not just in the area of family life but in social organization generally. The intellectual itch motivating the biologist centers far more on the desire to understand "what is" than "what could or should be," whereas large numbers of sociologists are as concerned for what can or should be as they are with what exists. Any suggestion that there are innate tendencies in the human animal beneath the surface of the social institutions he has developed is therefore seen by many sociologists as a brake or barrier to social change. Thus there are two major difficulties for the sociologist vis-à-vis the biological component of human social behavior: the complexity of the sciences involved, and the assumption—often erroneous—that any biological contribution to social behavior limits the potential for change in social organization.

It does not help matters when some biologists, extremely cautious about the solidity of a biological fact or theory in their own specialty, throw caution to the wind when they write about human social behavior. No sociologist would have the audacity to offer major interpretations of ant or bee social organization without intensive study of entymology and careful consultation with specialists in that field. But some biologists have shown precisely that audacity in moving from insect to human society, as witness many recent publications in sociobiology and the intellectual furor created in social science circles by Wilson's *Sociobiology*. Any expert in human kinship systems could raise several dozen objections to the sociobiologist's analysis on the sheer ground of ignorance and error in extrapolations from insect to human social organization. The sad part of this current controversy is that social scientists may rest content with defensively pointing out the errors of fact and assumption concerning human behavior committed by biologists in these early efforts at bridging the gap between the biological and social sciences, rather than seriously studying the biological evidence and doing their proper work of exploring whether and how the biological evidence might necessitate a reformulation of their own social science theory.

Because there is no area of human life in which the body is more intimately involved than the family, whether in the sex attraction and mating of adults, the conception, birth, and rearing of the young, or the physiological changes involved in growing up and growing old, it is my expectation that in the long run, family sociologists and developmental psychologists will have to reexamine their theories and revise them in a way that incorporates the new knowledge from the biological sciences. In so doing, I would predict an explosion of new insights on both sides of the issue, and not any shrinking of the jealously guarded turf of the social scientist.

It was already clear, when the three coeditors met in June 1977 to discuss the book edition of the *Daedalus* issue on *The Family*, that our task was a difficult one, in part because our background and perspectives are different, and in part on the mechanical grounds that we had a short summer in which to prepare the volume, with two of the three editors abroad for some or all of the summer months. We agreed to a rather unusual format in writing this epilogue, in which we would each write short sections in our own separate voices, and I would take the responsibility for writing an introduction and conclusion to the three separate sections. We could not envisage, at that brief meeting, exactly what the content of our separate-voice sections would be. Indeed,.what it required was a rereading in a new perspective, what we and our colleagues had written for the *Daedalus* issue, and then to distance ourselves from the entire enterprise and pull together some general observations about the new work on the family in the diverse fields represented in the collection of essays, and the likely developments in research on the family over the coming decade.

This has remained the plan for the epilogue. What follows now are the three voices, first that of Tamara Hareven, whose historical skills provide the most general perspective on the volume; then my own as a sociologist; and last, Jerome Kagan as child psychologist. My editorial voice will return to conclude the epilogue.

The Family and Non-Linear Historical Change

At a time when the family is still subject to a multitude of simplistic generalizations and stereotypes, these essays stress the diversity and complexity of family behavior. The family, the authors tell us, is affected by biological processes, psychological dynamics, cultural values, market conditions, population processes, institutions of industrial capitalism, churches, government planning agencies, and long-term historical change. The picture is further complicated by the fact that the family itself is not a static, homogeneous unit, but a complex organization of different age and sex configurations. Families contain husbands and wives, parents and children, brothers and sisters, grandparents and grandchildren, and all sorts of kin bound to each other by blood ties as well as a variety of social, emotional, and moral bonds. In certain societies, Wagatsuma and Whiting inform us, families encompass all dead as well as living members, over many generations, whereas in other societies, families are colonies of polygenous wives and their respective children.

The roles and status of each family member in relationship to other members, and in relation to the collective family unit at large, are defined differently in different cultural and historical contexts. Even individual and family moves are timed and synchronized differently. The family is not a static unit, but a process, involving varying relationships and configurations of family members which change over the course of the life span.

In view of all these diversities, one wonders how social scientists or policy planners, attempting to order and interpret social reality, can ever generalize, identify, and explain patterns of family behavior. Perhaps at this point in time, the wisest course would be to abandon a quest for uniformity in family behavior, and to explore diversity instead. One of the most refreshing aspects of this volume is precisely the emphasis on the diversity and complexity of family life. No author depicts the "universal" functions of the family, and no one writes of "the" American family, for the authors share an awareness of the diverse and complex range of family life and organization in the United States as well as abroad, in our own time as in times past.

In much sociological and historical writing, the simple, uniform model of the American nuclear family has not only been upheld as the ideal pattern but imposed on the interpretation of family life in the past, thus idealizing and oversimplifying patterns of historical change; it has inspired simplistic policy programs for day care, family assistance, and housing; and it has imposed a misleading, unrealistic example on modernizing societies in Africa. It is not surprising, therefore, that each essay, in its own way, voices a protest against oversimplification of family behavior. Rossi and Kagan tell us, respectively,

'hat the idealized model of the modern family is rendered diverse and complex
ɔy biological differences between fathers and mothers, and by psychological
dynamics among parents and children that in turn show important class and
ethnic variations. Hareven, Wrigley, Davis, and Wagatsuma counter the simplistic views of historical change implicit in modernization theory; Sawhill
protests the reduction of family behavior to simple economic exchange rules
in the household; and Woolsey, Blaydon, Stack and Downs protest the simplistic and uniform treatment of the family in welfare programs and urban
planning.

Beneath the crazy patchwork quilt of family patterns across cultures and
time periods, a few common threads run through and tie together the essays
in this volume: the focus on internal family interaction on the one hand, and
coping with external conditions and institutions on the other. How did families respond to changing social and economic conditions, to the large-scale as
well as the small-scale developments affecting their lives? How did they respond to such cataclysmic events as death, plagues and famine, migration,
wars, and depressions? How did families respond to the economic and social
changes which tore apart their traditional worlds, restructured their economy
and work patterns, reshaped the roles of their members, and redefined their
own positions in society? How, in the past, did families cope with dictates
and rules of behavior which were imposed on them by institutions such as
churches, welfare and housing agencies, schools, and bureaucratic governments? How, indeed, do contemporary families cope with these same large
external institutions?

Prevailing historical and sociological literature tends to concentrate on the
impact of institutions on the family, but most of the essays in this volume reverse the question, by redirecting attention to the family members themselves
and exploring the ways in which the family copes with social and economic
conditions. Despite the distance in time and location of their subjects, both
Hareven and Davis emphasize the extent to which families take charge of
their fate, plan their lives, and allocate their resources, in an effort to survive
or to secure their future and that of their children. In fact, the view of the
family in the historical essays of this volume, as an active agent rather than a
passive pawn, is found as well in the contemporary essays by Woolsey, and
by Blaydon and Stack on welfare families, families of working mothers, or
Kenyan families adjusting to African urban life. The nature of the struggle
and the style of coping has differed over time, but the basic pressures on the
family unit have not changed drastically. Some of the issues stressed in these
different essays are very similar: how to allocate resources within the family;
how to juggle multiple obligations as parents, as partners, and as children;
how to keep families together as functioning units despite the many external
threats and unsettling conditions they encountered. It is striking to note the
very similar ways in which families have coped with external pressures in very
different societies in very different time periods.

The most ubiquitous pattern shown in these essays is the use of kin as a
resource, a pattern found for seventeenth-century French peasants, nineteenth-
century American industrial workers, twentieth-century American welfare recipients, and Kenyan families caught in the process of urbanization. Before

the introduction of state welfare systems, kin were almost the only resource for family support and assistance. What is most surprising is that even in modern welfare states, three different authors conclude that kin-based support systems are present, effective, and in fact preferred by most families who need such support. Woolsey postulates child care by extended families as an alternative to day care centers; Blaydon and Stack claim that the families of the poor who are not reached by the welfare system rely on their kin more effectively than on welfare supports; and Whiting underscores the important social supports which kin provide to those Kenyans uprooted from polygenous families who are adapting to alien urban living conditions. Reliance on kin as a resource in coping with migration, economic insecurities, and life crises has been a recurring and continuous pattern. In many times and places, even work continues to be a collective family enterprise, despite the separation of the workplace from the home following the industrial revolution. Although it is understandable that kin were essential for survival and old age support prior to the rise of welfare institutions, it is surprising to find how extensively these patterns have survived in contemporary society.

The issue of family strategies is an integral part of the interdependence of family members. How did families allocate their resources, marshal the labor of their members, plan their future? What kind of tradeoffs did they make to achieve solvency, to buy a house, to save for the future, to secure higher status for their children, and to provide for old age? Sawhill warns us that the "new" household economists exaggerate the view of families plotting strategies and carefully calculating their economic services to each other, but some degree of purposeful planning and weighing of options seems clearly to be important characteristics of families past and present. On the other hand, Davis points out that family strategies in the past were not always clearly calculative: "strategies" did not always connote clearly formulated plans or carefully articulated deliberations. Even family limitation in preindustrial England, Wrigley tells us, was not an entirely "conscious" act by individual men and women, although it represented a form of planning nevertheless.

Whether one studies preindustrial England, early modern France, or nineteenth- and twentieth-century America, an important question is how families manage to discipline and marshall the efforts of their members collectively and to synchronize individual preferences with family priorities. Who plan the family's strategy, supervises their implementation and enforces discipline when members are remiss in family obligations? The tension between individual and collective family priorities is expressed dramatically in such issues of family timing as when to leave home, when and whom to marry, with whom to share a household, how to allocate responsibilities for parental support, and how to divide resources. In preindustrial rural societies such tensions were further heightened by the problems of land inheritance. Another source of tension is implicit in the fact that individuals are members of several families simultaneously—one's family of origin, one's spouse's family of origin, and one's family of procreation—with the clear potential for conflict of allegiance concerning which family takes priority at what point in time. If one's in-laws, parents, and children need assistance, who is most likely and least likely to be helped?

The problem of reconciling individual preferences with collective family needs takes different forms in different cultures. As Davis points out, seventeenth-century families planned for the future by invoking the past: avenging "ghosts" served important functions as reminders of unmet family obligations. In the nineteenth and twentieth centuries the ghosts disappeared, but strong familistic values embedded in the culture continued to haunt individuals and to remind them of their familial obligations, as did the grim necessities which made reciprocity among kin essential for survival.

Under historical conditions, the absence of state and institutional supports left the family as the only resource for assistance in daily routines as well as in critical life situations. Superficially, it would appear, therefore, that dependency of family members on each other was greater in the past than it is in the welfare state. This certainly holds true in the area of economic support and in the performance of a variety of health services for the ill and the aged. On the other hand, the fact that individuals still depend on their kin to the degree they do in contemporary society indicates both the continuity of traditions of kin support and the inadequacies of the public welfare system in meeting the many needs of family members.

In the areas of child care and the care of the sick and the elderly, the transfer of responsibilities from kin to public institutions is by no means complete. Nor should the fact that "welfare" families or working mothers are so resourceful in utilizing their kin be taken to mean that there is no need for the state to carry responsibility for family support and child care. We do not yet know what the social and psychological costs are to individuals who lend assistance to their kin in contemporary societies. The essays in this volume have emphasized the continuity of important functions of kin, but this emphasis should not be romanticized to assume that in contemporary society kin can take on the major functions of care and support rather than the state. The implication for public policy is to avoid any further breakdown of traditional family patterns without providing adequate substitutes, and to develop creative means by which kin support can be integrated with public support programs for families in need.

The essays also converge around the issue of social change in the structure of the family. Each society holds its own version of the history of the family, which is faintly shrouded in myth. In Western Europe and the United States, the myth has revolved around the existence of the great, extended and multigenerational family of the past. This myth about the family grew jointly with the ideal of the preindustrial community as a cohesive social organization based on extensive cooperation for both public and private good. Both the traditional family and the community were allegedly destroyed under the impact of industrialization. No one has done more than Peter Laslett and E. A. Wrigley and their colleagues to destroy this myth about preindustrial families in England. French, Swedish, and American scholars have done similar critiques for their own societies. Why this myth developed in the first place, and what the forces have been that have sustained it for more than a century in both popular belief and social science scholarship, is an important, as yet unanswered question.

Now that the myth is being disposed of by historical scholarship, and the impact of industrialization is placed in proper historical perspective, we are faced with a new set of questions. If industrialization did not cause the first major decline in fertility, and did not generate nuclear, two-generational households, as Wrigley so clearly tells us, the question is, did industrialization cause any significant changes in family behavior at all? If many of the important characteristics of "modern" family behavior preceded the industrial revolution, what then did cause the change in family structure and behavior? If it is the case that for centuries West European families have shown a basic nuclear form with periodic reliance on kin for assistance in life crises, whereas East European families have tended to show a more extended kin structure, then historical search for the answers to our questions must press far into the past indeed. On a more limited scale, the question also arises: if the process of industrialization did not cause the major changes attributed to it, did it leave any impact at all on family behavior?

Historians have not rejected significant changes in family behavior which are closely linked to industrialization and urbanization, namely changes in familial functions and values, as well as in the timing of family moves. Rather than viewing these changes as a continuous linear pattern encompassing the entire society, and moving inevitably to a more "modern" level, the most important contribution of historical research in this respect, has been to identify staggered, complex and fluctuating patterns of historical change.

Reacting against linear models of social change, particularly as exemplified in modernization theory, historians are now more hesitant to embark on grand explanations of social change. Most current historical research on the family is carried out on a synchronic level, examining family interaction with societal processes and institutions within specific community contexts. While such work has already contributed to the revisions of existing generalizations about the family, it will require the efforts of one or two generations of scholars to weld ongoing research into a more systematic pattern, ranging over historical time. At the moment, the contribution of historical knowledge to the overall understanding of social change and the family lies in three major areas: First, an understanding that changes in family behavior do not fit traditional periodization of historical change in Western society. Secondly, that changes in family behavior (as well as in many other aspects of society) do not follow a linear trend, as postulated in modernization theory. Third, that in the process of change, as well as in contemporary society, families are *active* agents in their interaction with social, economic and cultural forces, rather than merely being passive recipients of social change.   *Tamara K. Hareven*

Stability, Change, and Family Structure

I shall discuss three issues that are stimulated by the research on the family that has been conducted over the past few decades which in one way or another are reflected in the essays in this volume. The first question deals with the nature of the social changes which have occurred over the past few decades, in particular this past decade, and why the changes have stimulated a reexamination of social science theories concerning family life. The second is a brief examination of the toll taken by these social changes in the form of numerous indicators of social and economic stress in contemporary family life. Closely related to this are public-policy questions that flow from these indications of stress in the American family. The last issue concerns what I see as the major implications for my own discipline and for the understanding of contemporary family life, of historical research on families in the past.

Social Change and Theory

My first point is that the intellectual ferment in the social sciences dealing with family life has its roots in the fact that social change is impinging on the family roles and relationships we study in an unprecedented way, forcing us to realize that our theories need revision. In the decades in which social science theory about the family was developing, roughly from World War I through the 1950s, social change was largely a matter of technological and economic change, whereas the family seemed to have made a relatively stable adjustment to industrial urban society. Under such circumstances, it was congenial to hold theories stressing the long-lasting power of early family of origin experiences for adult personality and values. Parents were viewed as critical to and largely successful in the cross-generational transmission of norms, values, and personal goals to their children. Since the 1960s, however, social change has cut close to home and family, because it involved the two major variables intrinsic to the very organization of family life—age and sex.

The three major social movements of the decade—civil rights, feminism, and the antiwar movement—had particular appeal to the young: the civil rights movement to their idealistic concern for human justice, the feminist movement to the call for social equality, and the antiwar movement to the double concern of young people for personal survival and respect for the autonomy of another nation in a civil war. The combined impact of these movements was to question the legitimacy of authority, whether of government, school, parents, or men. Public opinion polls over the course of the decade showed a growing gap between young and old in the values and opinions they held on a wide range of issues. Interestingly, that gap has narrowed in recent years, perhaps reflecting the trickling up the age hierarchy of new attitudes, as older people were influenced by young people's values, and the expectable blurring of age differences took place as the younger cohort moved into the older age category. The implication of these political developments for social science theories concerning family life was the strong influence which historical events can have upon young people, not only in addition to but often in opposition to the values held by their parents. Parental influence as an explanatory variable for child behavior and values was clearly in need of reexamination.

The feminist movement has had even more serious impact upon family life, only now beginning to surface in the form of social indicators of personal stress and social problems. In the 1960s, when the feminist effort was largely concentrated on educational and job opportunities, the impact on the family was minor, compared to the impact it has begun to have in recent years as the issues shift to questions of equality in sex, marriage, home maintenance, and child rearing. Married women have always worked, either at home, on a paid job, or both; college education for women has long been accepted in American society. Pressure for more equitable roles for men and women in their sexual relationship, in marriage and parenthood, and in the maintenance of a household involves far more difficult issues in a young person's life. In addition, we are prepared through long years of schooling to embark on jobs very different from those held by our parents, but those years of education do little or nothing to change young people's anticipation of or skill in sexuality, marriage, or parenting, with the result that we tend to fall back on the models provided by our own parents, either unknowingly accepting them or unknowingly rejecting them, or we react with dismay when our efforts to translate a political ideology into the stuff of our private lives causes pain.

Let me give an example to show the way in which the same phenomenon was formulated in research more than a decade ago compared to the late 1970s. Twenty years ago, when social norms opposed the employment of women who had preschool-age children, it seemed theoretically reasonable to expect that such women had working mothers themselves, on the theory that these exceptional mothers of the older generation served as positive role models for their daughters that helped the latter withstand the negative reaction of friends and neighbors to their employment during the gender role traditionalism of the 1950s—a "like mother, like daughter" theoretical model. Today, researchers are far less likely to rely on such a parental role-model theory. Instead, they are likely to study the employed mother of a preschool child with variables such as her level of feminist awareness, the financial circumstances of the family, the marital happiness of the couple, and the accessibility of kin to care for her children in her absence. This shift in explanatory model stems from the realization, consciously or otherwise, that the younger generation of adults today are not simply living out the social scripts learned in their families of origin, but are forging decisions that are responsive to the social, economic, and political climate surrounding them as adults. One can expect, therefore, that behavioral science theories will change from an overemphasis on independent variables rooted in the biography of childhood to greater attention to contemporary political, economic, and ideological influences in adulthood.

There is a further interesting implication here of relevance to the relationship between history as a discipline and the social sciences: as the latter redefine themselves as historical fields and give up their old claim to universal truths, we can expect much greater interest and sympathy between historians and contemporary social-science scholars, to their mutual enrichment. Behavioral scientists are learning that to be 20 years old in 1978 means something very different from being a 20-year-old in 1878, and are beginning to suspect that such differences may even differentiate the 20-year-olds separated by no more than a decade rather than a century. Indeed, efforts to disentangle age from cohort effects—that is, how much of whatever differentiates a 20-year-old from a 40-year-old is due to the aging process and how much to a generational difference between them—is a current preoccupation of numerous developmental psychologists and sociologists who work in a life-course perspective.

Methodological purists in the social sciences may continue to reject this view of their fields as historical sciences, but the press of empirical evidence is bound in time to change this, as it becomes clear that empirical research may confirm a theory in one period of time and refute it in another. For example, it is quite possible that one could find a characteristic of a parent correlated with a characteristic of a child at a high level of say .60 in one era, but a replication years later might find the correlation has dropped to .10. The implication here is that theory building cannot be a cumulative process but must change with changes in the historical era. I believe it is for this reason that social science has such a poor track record in the prediction of future events: no theory can be a very powerful predictor if the same phenomena show a high interrelationship at one point in time and a low one in another.

An additional caution is that public policy based on the high explanatory power of a set of variables in 1978 could have the ground cut out from under that policy a decade hence. In the specific terms of currently fashionable social experiments, the painstaking and costly research effort to test such programs as income maintenance, housing vouchers, or child care for preschoolers may show significant treatment effects in the late 1970s and lead to public programs to extend that treatment to large numbers of people. A decade hence, however, the same treatment may have no effect, yet the program is likely to be perpetuated either because researchers have little interest in evaluating an established program and do not know that what worked a decade before is no longer working, or because any existing program is supported by bureaucratic inertia or an agency's defensive politics that might even prevent a research evaluation of its program.

The Human Toll of Social Change

Social change is probably always a painful process, inflicting a good deal of personal hurt and pain in the lives of individuals, and a good many indications of social stress when those lives are viewed in the aggregate. During the last five years, there has been a sharp rise in many demographic indicators of the stress attending change in age and sex roles in American society: the lowering of the age of sexual initiation is undoubtedly related to the increasing rate of illegitimacy and abortion among young adolescents; an increase in extramarital sex and the high levels of employment among married women are both relevant to the increase in the divorce rate and the dropping of the remarriage rate among divorced women. The rise in feminist consciousness now carries with it an airing of ambivalence toward having children and the desire to combine family and work roles, with the effect of an increase in childlessness or a postponement of childbearing, and a sharp drop in actual fertility rates and family size desires and expectations of young women. There is little doubt that the powerful combination of sexual and economic independence among women triggers marital stress, easier resort to divorce, and lowered willingness to embark on another marital career.

The combined effect of many of these changes can be seen in the unprecedented increase in recent years in the number of female-headed households with dependent-age children. Aid to the poor, in our era, increasingly translates to mean aid to women and their children, aid that covers a range from housing, retraining, employment, food stamps, child care, therapy, and very recently, innovations such as refuge centers for women and their children.

One should realize, I think, that no federal government program under the banner of "keeping the family together" can undo the complex set of changes that have triggered the sharp increase in women who alone carry the responsibility for the caring and support of children. Feminist thinking affects women of all ages and various stages of the family cycle, and the openness to accepting such thinking is far greater for women than for men. One may argue that in the long run men have as much to gain from gender role change as women, but in the short run there is no escaping the fact that women stand to gain more and men less. With all the good will in the world, it is still a very difficult thing for a young man and woman to act out even agreed-upon principles of equity in their private roles as spouses, parents, and homemakers, for they move in a larger world in which job obligations, the location and design of houses, and the support systems for child care and home maintenance are totally at odds with private principles of equity. The psychological price for individual men and women will be marital friction and divorce, and the social toll for the larger society will be the increase in the number of women and children whose incomes are so precarious that government supports are necessary to assure their health and sanity.

It is also important to realize that when women fall short of being able to provide for their families with an adequate income, this is rarely a shortcoming of the woman herself, but a reflection of the very basic inequality between the sexes in job access and pay, and the inadequate training in well-paying skills in the educational histories of the women involved. We have, in the United States, a phenomenon of "new poor" among women that has few historical precedents. This is a type of welfare family that rarely gets into the public press, for most people associate a welfare family with a lower-class black woman with many children and little opportunity for a job that would pay enough to feed, clothe, and house a family of five or six. The pay that women workers receive has been traditionally premised on the idea that women are at best periodic "secondary workers" in a household. This "new poor" phenomenon was brought home to me very dramatically in a questionnaire I have had in the field this summer. One question in that survey asked, "What is your present social class?" and a second, "What was the social class of the family you grew up in?" One woman crossed out several answers to the first question, and then wrote as follows:

> I find this an impossible question to answer. Financially I am clearly lower class, since I earn under $5,000 a year, despite the fact that I work full time and handle two part time jobs at home at night. But I don't feel like a lower class person: I grew up in an upper middle class family, and until a year ago when my husband walked out on me and the three kids, I lived on a $30,000 a year income.

The kind of rapid downward social mobility, the anguish of denying one's children and oneself what had come to be taken for granted in earlier years, the despair of trying to hold a family together on an impossibly low income, should be borne in mind as a profile that characterizes an increasing number of contemporary women, for whom all any public agency can do is to provide a cushion of financial aid to keep the family above the poverty level and to fund programs that provide local support groups that lend help to such families. These stress signals will persist until a new generation of women has the training and the experience to support themselves in an economy that no longer discriminates against women workers with low pay, low job security, and low opportunity for promotion, and until men are equally changed in the roles they are willing to play as partners with women in marriage, parenting, and homemaking. There is no way and no reason to urge that couples caught in the gender role changes of our time should "stay together" for the sake of the family, not only because value differences between the spouses can be irreconcilable without violating new and healthy demands for autonomy on the part of women, but because all we know from relevant research in this area suggests that psychologically children are more likely to suffer harm in an intact unhappy household than in a single-parent household. Once the basic legal and economic rights of women are assured, I doubt that social scientists will have much left to investigate concerning the negative effects of father absence on children.

Historical Research and Contemporary Social Science

It is a truism of our time to bemoan the overspecialization of the academic disciplines. Less often noted is the fact that such specialization extends to the internal organization of most disciplines themselves. It is perfectly possible for a sociologist to earn a degree in sociology and live out a career totally within the confines of one specialty area of the larger discipline: attending separate professional association meetings, reading exclusively in a few specialty journals, and publishing exclusively in those same journals. In many fields the very notion of an "expert" and the rewards for successful achievement are inseparable from the idea of the "superspecialist."

Against that background, this collection of essays is a refreshing stimulus to thinking in larger terms than our specialties encourage us to do, about the meaning of family in the totality of human experience in contemporary lives and in those of men and women who lived centuries ago. The overall impact of the volume encourages a dialogue concerning families in the past compared to the present, and families in the United States with those in other countries. I would like in this last section to discuss the impact of the new family history on my own perspective as a family sociologist.

The myth of the past: Family sociologists have had many cherished assumptions about families in the past dispelled by the findings that are emerging from contemporary research in family history. The image of the extended kin network in a rural society, a complex of three or more generations with ties to kin of quite distant collateral relatedness, is now refuted on such grounds as sheer demographic probability (few families could have had even three living generations in light of the average longevity in times past), and the effect of impartible inheritance rules which typically required the migration of children who would not inherit the land. In the American experience, our long history of settling a vast continent meant a continual history of breaks in intergenerational relations as young adults left parental households to settle western lands.

Indeed, it was the generational break between parents and children, experienced by millions of immigrants to American cities that misled several generations of sociologists concerning the nature of European kinship. They mistook the close ties of first-generation immigrants to distant kin (aunts, uncles, cousins) to represent kin relations in peasant communities in Europe, rather than adaptations to the stress of settling in an alien society by substituting less closely related kin for the parents and siblings they left in their country of origin. So, too, we were in error to assume that the extended-kin network at early stages of industrialization in English cities were typical of rural kinship patterns, rather than coping devices under unusual circumstances of great stress in the early industrial cities. It has been an important discovery to learn how prevalent the conjugal family is and in how many nations this family form predates industrialization, for this requires a revision in sociological theories about social and economic development in relation to family structure. Sociologists will be busy in the coming decade working through the implications for family theory of Wrigley's suggestion that modernization was not the linear process that industrialization seems to have been, for sociologists have largely equated the two processes.

Stability of family relations: A second error in historical assumptions among family theorists was the belief that families in the past were relatively stable units that embedded our ancestors in close kin ties throughout their lives, providing them with a stability of expectations for behavior structured on the grounds of age and sex. As Hareven notes, there was, if anything, more disruption in the lives of our ancestors than in our own: the death of a parent or a spouse was far more likely to be a common biographic experience in the past than today; with childbearing spread over the entire fertile period of the lifeline, parents as a group were far older than contemporary parents, but age segregation of roles was less typical in the past than in the twentieth century precisely because age differences in a sibling set were greater, with older siblings sharing parental responsibility for younger brothers and sisters, which blurred age status distinctions between parents and children. So too, women often had to take on the responsibility of a breadwinner lost through the death, illness, or unemployment of a husband. In fact, this shift to primary breadwinner may have been easier for women in the past than today, because when work is done in a family context the tasks of each spouse are readily observable and often shared by the other; and because household activity is more flexibly scheduled than factory work, time could be given to teaching and practicing the skills of the spouse.

Adaptability of the family: Whether one reads the new family history or contemporary essays on poor families in American inner cities, a general impression of great importance is the enormous adaptability of the family as a social institution, expanding and contracting not only in response to critical stages attending the life passage from birth to death, but to the fluctuations in political and economic circumstances of the time and place a family lives out its private history. The family is an institution that absorbs the human psychological cost of failures in government and economy: the greatest failure of government is surely the waging of war, the human cost of which in the death and physical disability of family members is absorbed by the family; and the greatest failure of the economy is surely unemployment, the human cost of which in damaged self-esteem and physical deprivation is similarly absorbed by the family.

In the institutional triad of government-economy-family, the flexibility and resilience of the family as an institution grows more difficult for modern social scientists to comprehend and to evaluate positively. Although government and business have gotten bigger and more stratified into complex hierarchical organizations, the family has become smaller, more egalitarian, more flexible in its expansion and contraction to meet the needs and desires of its members. Compared to government and business, the family is bound to be seen as an untidy, fragmented entity, difficult to assess, easy to find wanting.

Yet the small-scale flexible structure of the family may be its greatest strength, however difficult it is to formulate theoretical propositions about its structure. Fifty years ago, sociologists frequently bemoaned what they called a "cultural lag," arguing that the family, as the most conservative and traditional institution in society, lagged behind the state and the economy in accepting the rational scientific ethos appropriate to the organization of modern life. By the late 1970s, there are growing reasons for appreciating anew the resilience and perhaps the greater potential for adaptive change, of the flexible structure of the family compared to the self-serving and change-resistant bureaucracies of government and business.

The lesson for theory, research, and policy might be the importance of examining the strengths of the family instead of merely its weaknesses. Public agencies are accustomed to dealing largely with family "pathologies," and social scientists in the hire of such agencies tend to accept the assumption that families need to be restructured, helped, "done to," supplemented. Rarely do they investigate what it is that enables so many families to endure despite the battering their members receive at the hands of the more "rational" institutions of society. We are slow to learn that the rational organization of firms and factories may have irrational consequences for both individual workers and the larger society. At an even slower pace, we learn that structures like our contemporary family—untidy, unpredictable, seemingly irrational—have precisely the flexibility to adapt and to innovate that merits the label of "rational" adaptation to a world in flux.

The strength of the family: There is a further lesson in current family history research: one comes away from a reading of the way in which family units served as brokers with the early industrial employers in New England and New York a century ago, with admiration for the capacity of such families to endure, to work as communal units, to survive the strain to human health and energy of the early factory as a workplace. But I suspect that numerous families today actually perform much the same function for their members: families that absorb the economic burden of unemployed young adult children; parents who provide emotional and other help when grandchildren are born; families that expand to embrace nonkin through pseudokin networks that provide patterns of mutual help, as Stack shows among inner-city black families; female-headed families which men often desert when a woman is facing an unplanned pregnancy; and in these days of less inpatient and more outpatient care for physical and mental disorders, families who provide supplementary medical care for family members.

We might learn more of relevance to our desire to help families in trouble if we investigate families that fulfill these numerous functions very well, and to seek approximations to these successfully coping families in whatever programmatic efforts are designed to aid families in stress. It is quite possible that such programs would involve a minimum of elaborate and distant bureaucratic processing, and a maximum of direct aid to the immediate social setting within which a distressed family exists.

The great god of rationality: Because our social-science theories are themselves rational structures, there may be a tendency to assume that the behavior we study is itself rational. I find myself in considerable discomfort when reading of the economist's cost-benefit calculus applied to family decision making, that is, whether to have a child or not, or whether to get a divorce or not. Too often what can be measured is taken to exhaust what needs explanation. It is not clear that any metric can catch the emotional components in the meaning a child has to adults, with the result that such meanings are not likely to appear in the benefit or cost side of the economist's equation. In a secular age, our children or child-surrogates are our only hold or claim on the future. Few of us can hope to make lasting contributions that future generations will remember us for, so for most people living today, their children represent their one link to the future beyond their death. A significant function that the value of children has in people's lives could well be as a preventive to total hedonism and living for instant gratification.

There has been much written in recent years to the effect that family ties are broken with the launching of the child at the point of leaving for college or of taking on a first adult job, as there has been in dispelling the myth that postparental couples bemoan their empty-nest stage when in fact they show increased levels of personal gratification compared to the years when adolescent children shared the home. But it would be easy to misinterpret this profile to mean that children or parents have little emotional significance to each other beyond childhood. One suspects that most people who wish to share joyous news or to seek support to sustain tragedy, turn to their kin, and there is reason to suspect that the fact that a household is not physically shared tells us little of the vital emotional and social ties that continue to bind the generations.

The account which family historians have provided us with of family relations in the past, rich as they are in the details of kin support, family adaptability, and strength in the face of personal and social tragedy, are rarely matched by comparable accounts of contemporary family relations. Which prompts me to suspect that family sociology would be much enriched if it took up the substantive findings from the new family history and investigated contemporary families for the presence of comparable patterns. If in the past few decades family history has been enriched by taking up the tools and concepts of the behavioral sciences, in the decades ahead the tables may be turned, and the behavioral sciences may be enriched by taking up the substance of historical findings in studies of contemporary family life.   *Alice S. Rossi*

Social Context, Parental Practice, and the Child

Whenever citizens and intellectuals become preoccupied with the same topic, one immediately looks for the reasons for such shared concern. In the case of air pollution and armament control, the reasons are obviously rooted in individual and societal survival. It is less clear why the family has become of preeminent interest in and out of academe. The White House is planning a conference on the family; private philanthropies and governmental agencies have begun to allocate considerably more support for research on family dynamics and thoughtful essays on policy; the American Academy of Arts and Sciences has published a volume on the family; and economists, sociologists, anthropologists, and historians have joined a small cadre of psychologists in an attempt to untangle the relations between the home and society, on the one hand, and the qualities of family members and individual destinies, on the other.

It is likely that this effort is energized by the deep belief that childhood experiences in the home comprise the most important set of influences on adolescent and adult psychological profiles. This is an old idea in our society, although far from universal. John Bowlby's assertion that adult fragility can be traced to the uncertainties of early childhood is explicit both in Rousseau and the sermons of nineteenth-century clergy. Although some American parents and journalists have impulsively blamed current adolescent rebellion, delinquency, and drug usage on overly permissive parental practices during early childhood, even thoughtful citizens hold some version of this simple idea as part of their list of most cherished truths.

In trying to find the reasons for increased alienation, suicide, gang wars, illegitimacy, and declining scholastic aptitude test scores among the young, several explanatory candidates are available, including the structure and curriculum of our schools, social class inequities, and the content of the mass media. But even though acknowledging the potential relevance of each of these, there is a strong preference to assign primary causality to the family. More intense public emotion is generated over child neglect or the relocation of children from homes to day-care centers than over the size and quality of our schools, the plots of television or movie dramas, or the influence of friends. It is not that Americans believe these latter forces are irrelevant, but that they are sure the family is the most potent influence on the child.

Although that faith may well be justified, neither theory nor empirical data are firm enough to generate propositions that will explain how the family creates these unsettling outcomes. Until recently, most psychologists assumed that the heavy burden of explanatory power, let us say, with respect to IQ scores or school grades, lay with the material encounters between parent and child—the amount of play, encouragement, punishment, or even the number of mutual embraces that occurred each day. But unfortunately, no one has been able to find a set of parental practices that predicted IQ or grades in school as well as the social class of the child's family, a fact that implies the relevance of forces beyond child-rearing practices qua practices. Neither maternal behavior nor the child's psychological profile during the first two or three years of life is related in any serious way to future intellectual talent, when the effects of the child's social class are taken into account. Further, Diana Baumrind of the University of California at Berkeley has noted that the effect of authoritarian or permissive parental practices on the child's behavior must be qualified by taking into account many other factors, one of them being the child's sex.

There are typically two major responses to the limited empirical evidence on parental influence on the child. One is that most existing investigations of the effect of parental practices are insufficiently sensitive. If investigators had better methods of inquiry, this argument goes, they would have found that the material encounters between child and parent provided a commanding explanation of the child's characteristics and behavior. A second, more reasonable response is that the actual practices of the parent are less important than the interpretations that the child places on them, interpretations which are always colored by the youngster's perception of the parents as role models. The effect of a father's praise, detachment, criticism, or rejection will always depend on whether or not he is admired or respected by his children. Because there has been little careful study of the interaction between parental actions and the child's evaluation of parental character, one cannot yet claim that parental behaviors are unimportant.

Let us pose part of the dilemma in a context of a specific empirical fact. The education of a boy's father, at least among working and middle-class Caucasians in the United States, is as good a predictor of the son's occupational and educational attainment as the child's intellectual ability or personality profile during the first three to five years of life. Is this because the well-educated father behaves in a special way with his son, is a respected role model whom the son tries to emulate, or more simply because the family's affluence permits the child to attend schools whose peer composition and ethos make it likely that the boy will grow to value education and aspire to a professional or managerial vocation? Of course, we do not have to choose among these possibilities; perhaps all are operative. But if they are, we must be willing to acknowledge that factors other than particular parental behaviors must be given a prominent place in the equation that accounts for the child's profile in adulthood.

Finally, some might claim that the family influence is limited to a few very significant outcomes, like serious mental disorder or outstanding intellectual talent, whereas its contribution to more normative traits, although real, is far less critical than has been thought. Almost all one-year-olds protest when their parents leave them in an unfamiliar home, five-year-olds can infer cause and discriminate right from wrong, and fifteen-year-olds can detect inconsistencies in a set of personal beliefs, whether they are raised in an orphanage or a supportive family. But it is less common to find a Nobel laureate or Pulitzer Prize winner whose family did not value intellectual competence, or an adult schizophrenic whose family life was supportive and harmonious during his first decade—at least in the perception of the adult.

There is, moreover, an odd asymmetry in our statements about the effect of the family, for casual discussions of life histories more often describe the effects of the family on psychological failure and unhappiness than assert that a successful career or a happy marriage was the result of early parental practices. Negative outcomes are attributed to parental influence, whereas positive outcomes are attributed to individual effort, motivation, or chance. In short, parents are blamed when things go wrong, but rarely praised when they go well.

Recognition of these trends is leading some psychologists to select slightly different constructs to explain the relation between family dynamics and the child's development. The traditional paradigm during most of this century viewed the child as a surface to be shaped by parental manipulation, much as a sculptor forms a lovely statue from a piece of marble. The image contains two salient dimensions: the child is passively worked by the intelligent and loving actions of the parents, and there is a presumed veridicality between what is done by family members and some outcome in the child. The emergent view, which we owe in part to Piaget's emphasis on the constructive processes of the child's mind, is that many transformations occur in the course of parent-child interaction. The child is not simply a reservoir of skills and habits built up by parental handling: the child has unique characteristics present at birth, and develops complex and changing interpretations of the parents as he grows into puberty and adolescence; parents in turn are affected by the child's evolving response to them. Any particular talent, motive, or conflict that emerges in the child will reflect that complex interactive history of parent and child.

An interesting inference from the finding that the social network in which the family lives is as important as any specific parental practice for the child's development, is the likelihood that the parents' own experiences away from home—their response to the neighborhood, their jobs, or the larger political climate of the society at the time—will also be transmitted to the child. Troubling times may produce troubled parents; hence it is likely that one of the major inferences the child extracts from his immersion in the family is, to put it bluntly, sources of worry. Parents indirectly communicate to children what they should fear, be it parental disfavor, social prejudice, peer rejection, ill health, lack of money, exploitation, incompetence, or humiliation for violating social norms. These sources of uncertainty are probably established during the decade from the third to the thirteenth year and are likely to remain sturdy if the child does not have an opportunity to prove them incorrect directly, or to arrange his life so that he is protected from them.

Despite the considerably qualified conception of parental influence in recent developmental research, there are still many people who insist that if only we found the correct recipe for parental behavior, many of our social problems would be solved. The implication is that the excessive number of lower-class children who have difficulty mastering school subjects and who show asocial behavior patterns could be reduced considerably by altering parental practices. This belief tends to weaken cogent arguments that urge benevolent changes in neighborhoods, schools, and the economy. It is easier to place the blame on uneducated parents than to acknowledge the inadequacy of the social contexts in which these families live.

We note, finally, that there has been a shift in the focus of study among the disciplines working on the family. Anthropologists, historians, and sociologists, who initially ignored the microworld within the home and surrounding space, are now examining that environment more closely; whereas psychologists, who have traditionally put a magnifying glass to the family and counted every kiss and spank, are looking beyond the threshold of the home to the neighborhood and to the historical era in which the family acts. Two of our most eminent anthropologists, John and Beatrice Whiting, spent the last decade observing the behavior of children in Mexican barrios and Kenyan villages, noting the kinds of chores parents assign, convinced that important lessons are being taken from these simple experiences. By contrast, psychologists like William Kessen, Sheldon White, Robert Sears, and Michael Cole are turning to analyses of history, culture, and institutions to clarify developmental puzzles. To cite but one example, Michael Cole has been investigating the role of writing systems and amount of schooling on the Liberian child's cognitive development. These territorial invasions from different parts of the academy are necessary if we are to reduce the amount of dogma that surrounds propositions that tie intrafamilial events to the child's development and move us a bit closer to clarifying the many enigmas of psychological growth. With psychologists looking outward from the family, and historians, sociologists, and anthropologists looking inward to family interaction, we can look forward in the coming decade to a greatly expanded understanding of the impact of historical time, cultural setting, and parents themselves on the development of the child.   *Jerome Kagan*

Conclusion

It must be clear to anyone who has just read the preceding sections by the three coeditors that we were highly stimulated by the experience of putting together this volume of essays on the family. In the by now traditional mode followed by the American Academy of Arts and Sciences, the *Daedalus* editor, Stephen R. Graubard, first brought a few of us together two years ago, for a planning meeting on a possible issue on the family. At that meeting, a decision to go ahead was made on the basis of the conviction of the participants that such an issue was a good and timely idea, and a tentative list of topics and possible authors was worked out. During the year that followed, scholars were approached to write particular essays, and a conference was held in 1976 at which we spent two days in rigorous discussion of each other's papers. In revised form they were published in the spring 1977 issue of *Daedalus*.

In this concluding section of our epilogue, I shall deal with just two issues: a brief overview of what seemed to work well and what less well, in the collaborative work that lies behind this collection, and second, what is missing from our efforts now that we have the benefit of hindsight to assess our work and to look ahead to future efforts.

The coeditors can clearly speak for the other authors as well as themselves in reporting that we enjoyed and were stimulated by the *Daedalus* experience of working closely together at the academy conference and the months that followed when essays were in revision. We were a mixed group from many disciplines—history, economics, sociology, psychology, anthropology, and demography. But it now seems equally clear that an important reason for our association's being a fruitful one lies in the fact that most of us had some prior acquaintance with at least one other discipline beside our own, and in most cases, with several of the disciplines represented among us. The psychologists and sociologists who participated were familiar with at least some of the new work in family history; the historians were familiar with sociology, developmental psychology, and social anthropology; the anthropologists had had to grapple with issues of social and economic change in the societies they had studied and were well informed on earlier historical work on the impact of industrialization and sociological studies of immigrant assimilation in American history.

We were less successful in dealing with and making fruitful use of two important disciplines in any analysis of the family—biology and economics. There is no one among the authors of this collection whose primary training was in any of the biological sciences. As a consequence, my fellow authors could respond in only very general terms to my effort to bring a biological component to our analysis of family behavior, rather than in highly specific and informed terms that would have stimulated a rigorous debate and more extensive revision. In fact, I had to seek out that reaction from neuroendocrinologists whom I consulted before and after the *Daedalus* meeting. Some future collection of essays on the family could well be designed around a group of scholars from the biological and medical fields together with social scientists concerned with family life.

The case was different where economics is concerned: Isabel Sawhill, Anthony Downs, and Colin Blaydon ably represented the economist's perspective. The difficulty was that few of the rest of us had a sufficient knowledge of economic theory and research modes to contribute to any rigorous analysis of the economic aspect of family life. This was a serious lack, for economists have a great deal to contribute to our understanding of changes in the economy as they affect family life at various points in history, and under varying conditions in contemporary societies. Clearly any work focused on public policy and programs would have to rely on the cost and impact estimates of economists. But in this collection of essays, and in this epilogue, I sense a tendency either to neglect an economics perspective or to show a trace of disdain for the work that economists have done in the new household economics. I was guilty of such disdain in a paragraph of my own section of the epilogue, and both Hareven and I seem to have jumped much too readily on economist Sawhill's own criticism of the applicability of the economist's approach to childbearing and divorce decisions. There may be good reason to be critical of the economist's contribution to these particular issues in family life, but this in no sense means that there are not numerous areas of great importance to family study for which the primary skills called for are those possessed by economists. This would be the case in the area of household consumption patterns, goods production in the home, time utilization, the impact of credit reliance on family savings, to say nothing of any serious analysis of the relation between the family and the economy, either generally or in the specific terms of combinations of family and work roles carried by individual men and women. In retrospect, it was a loss not to have invited Isabel Sawhill to do an essay on the female-headed household in the United States, for her own work with Heather Ross, as represented in their *Time of Transition* monograph (Urban Institute, 1975), is an excellent example of what those of us in sociology and psychology stand to learn from economists who analyze household composition.

Indeed, an excellent candidate for some future collaborative volume is the topic of the Home or The Household in America, bringing together scholars from architecture, urban planning, economics, home economics, as well as those in psychology and sociology who have done either time-budget studies of family time utilization, or research on family interaction in the household itself. This microscopic ecology of the family home would seem to be an important research arena in which we have much to learn from a great mix of disciplines and professions. In our own conference, Anthony Downs' work on long-range trends in the location and quality of American homes had to stand largely by itself simply because few of us had the expertise or research experience to contribute any distinctive new dimension to Downs' analysis.

Another candidate for a future collaborative enterprise is the whole question of Work and Family, or The Family and the Economy, with a particular focus on gender differences and recent trends in the way in which men and women combine their responsibilities to each other, their children, and their jobs. Here, too, it would be imperative to have the contribution of economists as well as sociologists and psychologists. This is a topic on which there is already a good critical review of some central issues, Rosabeth Kanter's Russell Sage Foundation review monograph, *Work and Family in the United States: a Critical Review and Agenda for Research and Policy* (Russell Sage, 1977).

Yet another possible theme for the future, and one this volume hardly touches, is Our Bodies and Their Uses, covering the whole range from diet and eating habits and their changes over the past thirty years, food preparation and consumption, the impact of modern life on our sensory equipment all told, sexual patterns in and out of marriage, cultural taboos concerning body functions, the loss of privacy in the design of contemporary homes, etc.

Following up on Jerome Kagan's point about parents communicating their own sources of worry to their children, suggests yet another theme for the future: The Child and the Nonfamily World, an effort to locate the extent of the child's exposure to the external world of either a direct or mediated variety through the parent, and how the child responds to that world. That young children are showing the stamp of contemporary unease about even local environments is suggested by the findings from a recent Foundation for Child Development survey of 7- to 11-year-olds, that a quarter of the children reported being afraid that someone would hurt them when they were playing outside, two-thirds that someone bad might get into their house, and another two-thirds that their neighborhoods were not good places in which to grow up.

But one could go on to many other potential topics for future work relevant to the family—state-of-the-art review conferences, research agendas for individual scholars, and themes for other *Daedalus* issues in the family area. In the present collection, we have looked backward in time to earlier stages of family life as much as we have concentrated on our own time. My hope is that before long another planning conference will be proposed that narrows in to a particular theme in contemporary American family life, but that continues to rely on the disciplinary mix represented by the authors of the present volume both as a group and as individuals.

Notes on Contributors

PHILIPPE ARIÈS, born in 1914, in Blois, France, is the author of many works, among them *L'enfant et la vie familiale sous l'Ancien régime* (1960; translated into English in 1962 under the title *Centuries of Childhood*); *Western Attitudes Toward Death* (1974), and *Essais sur l'histoire de la mort en Occident du Moyen-Age à nos jours* (1975).

COLIN C. BLAYDON, born in 1940 in Newport News, Virginia, is associate professor of policy sciences and business administration at Duke University. He has directed special studies on human-resources programs pertaining to the financing of higher education, health manpower, pension and welfare reform, and health insurance. Two articles are forthcoming: "State Policies and Private Higher Education," and "Financing the Cities."

NATALIE ZEMON DAVIS, born in 1928 in Detroit, Michigan, is professor of history at the University of California at Berkeley. She is the author of *Society and Culture in Early Modern France* (1975).

ANTHONY DOWNS, born in 1930 in Evanston, Illinois, is chairman of the board of the Real Estate Research Corporation and the author of many publications on housing, racial relations, real estate markets, and urban economics and demography. His most recent books are *Opening Up the Suburbs* and *Federal Housing Subsidies: How Are They Working?* both published in 1973.

TAMARA K. HAREVEN, born in 1937 in Czernautz, Rumania, is professor of history at Clark University, director of the History of the Family Program, and editor of the *Journal of Family History*. She is the author of *Eleanor Roosevelt: An American Conscience* (1968), and *Anonymous Americans: Exploration in American Social History* (1971).

JEROME KAGAN, born in 1929 in Newark, New Jersey, is professor of human development at Harvard University. He is the author of *Birth to Maturity* (1962), *Change and Continuity in Infancy* (1971), *Understanding Children* (1971), and *Child Development and Personality* (4th ed., 1974).

ALICE S. ROSSI, born in 1922 in New York City, is professor of sociology at the University of Massachusetts at Amherst. She has published *The Feminist Papers* (1973–75), and has edited *Academic Women on the Move* (with Ann Calderwood), and *Essays on Sex Equality, John Stuart Mill and Harriet Taylor Mill* (1971).

ISABEL V. SAWHILL, born in 1937 in Washington, D.C., is director of the Program of Research on Women at the Urban Institute in Washington, D.C. She is the author (with Heather Ross) of *Time of Transition: The Growth of Families Headed by Women* (1975), and of several articles on women and the family.

CAROL B. STACK, born in 1940 in New York City, is associate professor at the Institute of Policy Sciences and the department of anthropology, Duke University. She is the author of *All Our Kin: Strategies for Survival in a Black Community* (1974), and of several articles.

HIROSHI WAGATSUMA, born in 1927 in Tokyo, is professor of anthropology at the University of California at Los Angeles. He is the author of many books and articles on psychological anthropology and social psychology in both English and Japanese, including (with George A. DeVos et al.), *Japan's Invisible Race* (1966), *Socialization for Achievement* (1973), and *The Heritage of Endurance* (forthcoming).

BEATRICE BLYTH WHITING, born in 1914 on Staten Island, is professor of education and anthropology at the Harvard Graduate School of Education. She is the author (with John Whiting) of *Children of Six Cultures: A Psycho-Cultural Analysis* (1975), and the editor of *Six Cultures: Studies of Child Rearing* (1963).

SUZANNE H. WOOLSEY, born in 1941 in San Francisco, is associate director of Human and Community Affairs, Office of Management and Budget, and the author of *Social Interaction Between Black and White Children: The Effects of Previous Desegregation and the Race of the Teacher* (1970).

E. ANTHONY WRIGLEY, born in 1931 in Manchester, England, is director of the SSRC Cambridge Group for the History of Population and Social Structure. He is the author of *Industrial Growth and Population Change* (1960); *Population and History* (1969), and the editor of several works.

Index